GCSE

Combined Science

Can't choose between Biology, Chemistry and Physics? Well, there's no need to pick a favourite — Combined Science includes them all. It's like the Neapolitan ice cream of GCSEs.

While we're on the ice theme, this CGP book makes it easy to stay cool throughout your revision. We've covered every inch of the course, from cells to compounds to radioactive contamination.

And don't forget the brilliant online extras. We've added step-by-step video solutions, brain-teasing quizzes, <u>and</u> a free Online Edition of the entire book. It's anything but vanilla.

Revision Guide
Foundation Level

Contents

You'll see **QR codes** throughout the book that you can scan with your smartphone.

A QR code next to a tip box question takes you to a **video** that talks you through solving the question. You can access **all** the videos by scanning this code here.

A QR code on a 'Revision Questions' page takes you to a **Retrieval Quiz** for that topic. You can access **all** the quizzes by scanning this code here.

You can also find the **full set of videos** at cgpbooks.co.uk/GCSEComb-EdexF/Videos and the **full set of quizzes** at cgpbooks.co.uk/GCSEComb-EdexF/Quiz

For useful information about **What to Expect in the Exams** and other exam tips head to cgpbooks.co.uk/GCSEComb-EdexF/Exams

Published by CGP

From original material by Richard Parsons

Editors: Ellen Burton, Emma Clayton, Josie Gilbert, Rob Hayman, Andy Hurst, Hannah Lawson, Duncan Lindsay, Jake McGuffie, Luke Molloy, Sarah Pattison, Charlotte Sheridan and George Wright.

Contributor: Paddy Gannon

ISBN: 978 1 78294 575 8

With thanks to Alice Dent for the copyright research.

Growth chart on page 21 reproduced with kind permission of the RCPCH/Harlow Printing.

Definition of health on page 39 reproduced from the WHO website, The Constitution of the World Health Organization https://www.who.int/about/governance/constitution. Accessed: 12th September 2022.

Hazard symbols on page 77 are public sector information published by the Health and Safety Executive and licensed under the Open Government Licence. http://www.nationalarchives.gov.uk/doc/open-government-licence/version/3/

CO_2 concentration data used to construct the graph on page 143 provided by The European Environment Agency.

Global temperature data used to construct the graph on page 143 provided by the NASA GISS.

Printed by Elanders Ltd, Newcastle upon Tyne.
Clipart from Corel®
Illustrations by: Sandy Gardner Artist, email sandy@sandygardner.co.uk

The Scientific Method

This section isn't about how to 'do' science — but it does show you the way most scientists work.

Science is All About Testing Hypotheses

Scientists make an observation.

1) Scientists <u>OBSERVE</u> (look at) something they don't understand, e.g. an illness.
2) They come up with a <u>possible explanation</u> for what they've observed.
3) This explanation is called a <u>HYPOTHESIS</u>.

Hundreds of years ago, we thought demons caused illness.

They test their hypothesis.

4) Next, they test whether the hypothesis is <u>right or not</u>.
5) They do this by making a <u>PREDICTION</u> — a statement based on the hypothesis that can be tested.
6) They then <u>TEST</u> this prediction by carrying out <u>experiments</u>.
7) If their prediction is <u>right</u>, this is <u>EVIDENCE</u> that their <u>hypothesis might be right</u> too.

Other scientists test the hypothesis too.

8) Other scientists <u>check</u> the evidence — for example, they check that the experiment was carried out in a <u>sensible</u> way. This is called <u>PEER-REVIEW</u>.
9) Scientists then <u>share their results</u>, e.g. in scientific papers.
10) Other scientists carry out <u>more experiments</u> to test the hypothesis.
11) Sometimes these scientists will find <u>more evidence</u> that the <u>hypothesis is RIGHT</u>.
12) Sometimes they'll find <u>evidence</u> that shows the <u>hypothesis is WRONG</u>.

Then we thought it was caused by 'bad blood' (and treated it with leeches).

The hypothesis is accepted or rejected.

13) If <u>all the evidence</u> that's been found <u>supports</u> the <u>hypothesis</u>, it becomes an <u>ACCEPTED THEORY</u> and goes into <u>textbooks</u> for people to learn.
14) If the <u>evidence</u> shows that the hypothesis is <u>wrong</u>, scientists must:
   - <u>Change the hypothesis</u>, OR
   - Come up with a <u>new hypothesis</u>.

Now we know that illnesses that can be spread between people are due to microorganisms.

Theories Can Involve Different Types of Models

1) A <u>model</u> is a <u>simple way</u> of <u>describing</u> or <u>showing</u> what's going on in <u>real life</u>.
2) Models can be used to <u>explain ideas</u> and <u>make predictions</u>. For example:
   - The <u>Bohr model</u> of an <u>atom</u> is a simple <u>picture</u> of what an atom looks like.
   - It can be used to explain <u>trends</u> in the <u>periodic table</u>. (See page 82 for more.)
3) All models have <u>limits</u> — a single model <u>can't explain</u> everything about an idea.

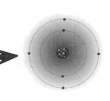

I'm off to the zoo to test my hippo-thesis...

You can see just how much testing has to be done before something gets accepted as a theory. If scientists aren't busy testing their own hypothesis, then they're busy testing someone else's. Or just playing with their models.

Communication & Issues Created by Science

Scientific developments can be great, but they can sometimes raise more questions than they answer...

It's Important to Tell People About Scientific Discoveries

1) Scientific discoveries can make a big difference to people's lives.
2) So scientists need to tell the world about their discoveries.
3) They might need to tell people to change their habits, e.g. stop smoking to protect against lung cancer.
4) They might also need to tell people about new technologies. For example:

> The discovery of molecules called fullerenes has led to a new technology that delivers medicine to body cells. Doctors and patients might need to be given information about this technology.

Scientific Evidence can be Presented in a Biased Way

1) Reports about scientific discoveries in the media (e.g. newspapers or television) can be misleading.
2) The data might be presented in a way that's not quite right — or it might be oversimplified.
3) This means that people may not properly understand what the scientists found out.
4) People who want to make a point can also sometimes present data in a biased way (in a way that's unfair or ignores one side of the argument). For example:

- A scientist may talk a lot about one particular relationship in the data (and not mention others).
- A newspaper article might describe data supporting an idea without giving any evidence against it.

Scientific Developments are Great, but they can Raise Issues

1) Scientific developments include new technologies and new advice.
2) These developments can create issues. For example:

> Economic (money) issues: Society can't always afford to do things scientists recommend, like spend money on green energy sources.

> Social (people) issues: Decisions based on scientific evidence affect people — e.g. should alcohol be banned (to prevent health problems)?

> Personal issues: Some decisions will affect individuals — e.g. people may be upset if a wind farm is built next to their house.

> Environmental issues: Human activity often affects the environment — e.g. some people think that genetically modified crops (see p.37) could cause environmental problems.

Science Can't Answer Every Question — Especially Ethical Ones

1) At the moment scientists don't agree on some things — like what the universe is made of.
2) This is because there isn't enough data to support the scientists' hypotheses.
3) But eventually, we probably will be able to answer these questions once and for all.
4) Experiments can't tell us whether something is ethically right or wrong. For example, whether it's right for people to use new drugs to help them do better in exams.
5) The best we can do is make a decision that most people are more or less happy to live by.

THE GAZETTE
BRAIN-BOOSTING DRUGS MAKE A MOCKERY OF EXAMS

THE POST
GENIUS PILLS TO BECOME THE NEW COFFEE

Tea to milk or milk to tea? — Totally unanswerable by science...

Science can't tell you whether or not you should do something. That's for you and society to decide. But there are tons of questions science might be able to answer, like where life came from and where my superhero socks are.

Risk

By reading this page you are agreeing to the risk of a paper cut...

Nothing is Completely Risk-Free

1) A hazard is something that could cause harm.

2) All hazards have a risk attached to them — this is the chance that the hazard will cause harm.

3) New technology can bring new risks. For example, new nanoparticles are being used in suncream. Scientists are unsure whether they might harm the cells in our bodies. These risks need to be considered alongside the benefits of the technology, e.g. better sun protection.

4) To make a decision about activities that involve hazards, we need to think about:
   • the chance of the hazard causing harm,
   • how bad the outcome (consequences) would be if it did.

People Make Their Own Decisions About Risk

1) Not all risks have the same consequences. For example, if you chop veg with a sharp knife you risk cutting your finger, but if you go scuba-diving you risk death.

2) Most people are happier to accept a risk if the consequences don't last long and aren't serious.

3) People tend to think familiar activities are low-risk. They tend to think unfamiliar activities are high-risk. But this isn't always true. For example:

   • Cycling on roads is often high-risk. But it's a familiar activity, so many people are happy to do it.
   • Air travel is actually pretty safe, but a lot of people think it is high-risk.

4) The best way to estimate the size of a risk is to look at data. E.g. you could estimate the risk of a driver crashing by recording how many people in a group of 100 000 drivers crashed their cars over a year.

Investigations Can Have Hazards

1) Hazards from science experiments include things like:

microorganisms (e.g. bacteria)

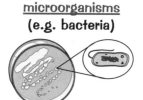

chemicals

electricity

fire

2) When you plan an investigation you need to make sure that it's safe.

3) You should identify all the hazards that you might come across.

4) Then you should think of ways of reducing the risks. For example:

   • If you're working with sulfuric acid, always wear gloves and safety goggles. This will reduce the risk of the acid burning your skin and eyes.
   • If you're using a Bunsen burner, stand it on a heat proof mat. ➡ This will reduce the risk of starting a fire.

There's more on safety in experiments on page 212.

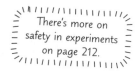

Not revising — an unacceptable exam hazard...

The world is a dangerous place. You need to look out for hazards and find ways to reduce their risks.

Working Scientifically

Designing Investigations

Dig out your lab coat and dust down your safety goggles... It's investigation time.
Investigations include lab experiments and studies done in the real world.

Investigations Produce Evidence to Support or Disprove a Hypothesis

1) Scientists observe things and come up with hypotheses to explain them (see p.1).
You need to be able to do the same. For example:

> Observation: People have big feet and spots. Hypothesis: Having big feet causes spots.

2) To find out if your hypothesis is right, you need to do an investigation to gather evidence.

3) To do this, you need to use your hypothesis to make a prediction — something you think will happen
that you can test. E.g. people who have bigger feet will have more spots.

4) Investigations are used to see if there are patterns or relationships between two variables (see below).

To Make an Investigation a Fair Test You Have to Control the Variables

1) In a lab experiment you usually change one thing (a variable) and measure how it affects another thing
(another variable).

> EXAMPLE: you might change the temperature of an enzyme-controlled
> reaction and measure how it affects the rate of reaction.

2) Everything else that could affect the results needs to stay the same.
Then you know that the thing you're changing is the only thing that's affecting the results.

> EXAMPLE continued: you need to keep the pH the same. If you don't, you won't know if any
> change in the rate of reaction is caused by the change in temperature, or the change in pH.

3) The variable that you CHANGE is called the INDEPENDENT variable.

4) The variable you MEASURE is called the DEPENDENT variable.

5) The variables that you KEEP THE SAME are called CONTROL variables.

6) Because you can't always control all the variables,
you often need to use a CONTROL EXPERIMENT.

> EXAMPLE continued:
> Independent = temperature
> Dependent = rate of reaction
> Control = pH, concentration
> of enzyme used, etc.

7) This is an experiment that's kept under the same conditions as the rest of the investigation, but doesn't
have anything done to it. This is so that you can see what happens when you don't change anything.

Evidence Needs to be Repeatable, Reproducible and Valid

1) REPEATABLE means that if the same person does the experiment again, they'll get similar results.
To check your results are repeatable, repeat the readings at least three times.
Then check the repeat results are all similar.

2) REPRODUCIBLE means that if someone else does the experiment, the results will still be similar.
To make sure your results are reproducible, get another person to do the experiment too.

3) VALID results come from experiments that were designed to be a fair test.
They're also repeatable and reproducible.

> If data is repeatable and
> reproducible, it's reliable and
> scientists are more likely to trust it.

This is no high street survey — it's a designer investigation...

You need to be able to plan your own investigations. You should also be able to look at someone else's plan and
decide whether or not it needs improving. Those examiners are pretty demanding.

Collecting Data

Ah ha — now it's time to get your hands mucky and <u>collect some data</u>.

The Bigger the Sample Size the Better

1) Sample size is <u>how many things you test</u> in an investigation, e.g. 500 people or 20 types of metal.

2) The <u>bigger</u> the sample size the <u>better</u> — to <u>reduce</u> the chance of any <u>weird results</u>.

3) But scientists have to be <u>sensible</u> when choosing how big their sample should be.
E.g. if you were studying how lifestyle affects weight it'd be great to study everyone in the UK
(a huge sample), but it'd take ages and cost loads. So the sample size should be <u>big</u>, but not <u>too big</u>.

Your Data Should be Accurate and Precise

1) <u>ACCURATE</u> results are results that are <u>really close</u> to the <u>true answer</u>.

2) The accuracy of your results usually depends on your <u>method</u>.
You need to make sure you're measuring the <u>right thing</u>.

3) You also need to make sure you <u>don't miss anything</u> that
should be included in the measurements. For example:

> If you're measuring the <u>volume of gas</u> released by
> a reaction, make sure you <u>collect all the gas</u>.

Repeat	Data set 1	Data set 2
1	12	11
2	14	17
3	13	14
Mean	13	14

Data set 1 is more precise
than data set 2 — the results are all
close to the mean (not spread out).

4) <u>PRECISE</u> results are ones where the data is <u>all really close</u> to the <u>mean</u> (average) of your repeated results.

Your Equipment has to be Right for the Job

1) The <u>measuring equipment</u> you use has to be able to <u>accurately</u> measure the
chemicals you're using. E.g. if you need to measure out 11 cm³ of a liquid,
use a <u>measuring cylinder</u> that can measure to 1 cm³ — not 5 or 10 cm³.

2) You also need to <u>set up the equipment properly</u>. For example, make sure
your <u>mass balance</u> is set to <u>zero</u> before you start weighing things.

You Need to Look out for Errors and Anomalous Results

1) The results of your experiment will always <u>vary a bit</u> because of <u>RANDOM ERRORS</u> —
for example, mistakes you might make while <u>measuring</u>.

2) You can <u>reduce</u> the effect of random errors by taking <u>repeat readings</u> and finding the <u>mean</u>.
This will make your results <u>more precise</u>.

3) If a measurement is wrong by the <u>same amount every time</u>, it's called a <u>SYSTEMATIC ERROR</u>.
For example:

> If you measure from the <u>very end</u> of your <u>ruler</u> instead of from the
> <u>0 cm mark</u> every time, <u>all</u> your measurements would be a bit <u>small</u>.

Always measure from here...

...not here.

4) If you know you've made a systematic error, you might be able to <u>correct it</u>.
For example, by adding a bit on to all your measurements.

5) Sometimes you get a result that <u>doesn't fit in</u> with the rest. This is called an <u>ANOMALOUS RESULT</u>.

6) You should try to <u>work out what happened</u>. If you do (e.g. you find out that you measured
something wrong) you can <u>ignore</u> it when processing your results (see next page).

The bigger the better — what's true for cakes is true for samples...

Make sure you take lots of care when collecting data — there's plenty to watch out for, as you can see.

Processing and Presenting Data

Processing your data means doing <u>calculations</u> with it so it's <u>more useful</u>. Then you get to draw pretty graphs...

Data Needs to be Organised

1) <u>Tables</u> are useful for <u>organising data</u>.
2) When you draw a table <u>use a ruler</u>.
3) Make sure <u>each column</u> has a <u>heading</u> (including the <u>units</u>).

Test tube	Repeat 1 (cm³)	Repeat 2 (cm³)
A	28	37
B	47	51

You Might Have to Find the Mean and the Range

1) When you've done repeats of an experiment you should always calculate the <u>mean</u> (a type of average).
2) You might also need to calculate the <u>range</u> (how spread out the data is).

EXAMPLE The results of an experiment to find the volume of gas produced in a reaction are shown in the table below. Calculate the mean volume and the range.

Volume of gas produced (cm³)		
Repeat 1	Repeat 2	Repeat 3
28	37	32

1) To calculate the <u>mean</u>, <u>add together</u> all the data values. Then <u>divide</u> by the <u>total number</u> of values in the sample.

$(28 + 37 + 32) \div 3$
$= 32$ cm³

2) To calculate the <u>range</u>, <u>subtract</u> the <u>smallest</u> number from the <u>largest</u> number.

$37 - 28 = 9$ cm³

3) To find the <u>median</u>, put all your data in <u>order</u> from smallest to largest. The median is the <u>middle value</u>.
4) The number that appears <u>most often</u> is the <u>mode</u>.
5) When calculating any of these values, always <u>ignore</u> any <u>anomalous results</u>.

If you have an even number of values, the median is halfway between the middle two values.

Round to the Lowest Number of Significant Figures

1) The <u>first significant figure</u> of a number is the first digit that's <u>not zero</u>.
2) The second and third significant figures come <u>straight after</u> (even if they're zeros).
3) In <u>any</u> calculation, you should round the answer to the <u>lowest number of significant figures</u> (s.f.) given.
4) If your calculation has more than one step, <u>only</u> round the <u>final</u> answer.

1st significant figure
0.0307
2nd 3rd

EXAMPLE The mass of a solid is 0.24 g and its volume is 0.715 cm³. Calculate the density of the solid.

Density = 0.24 g ÷ 0.715 cm³ = 0.33566... = 0.34 g/cm³ (2 s.f.) — Final answer should be rounded to 2 s.f.
2 s.f.   3 s.f.

Bar Charts can be Used to Show Different Types of Data

<u>Bar charts</u> can be used to display:
1) Data that comes in <u>clear categories</u>, e.g. blood group, types of metal.
2) Data that can have <u>any value</u> in a range, e.g. length, volume, temperature.
There are some <u>golden rules</u> you need to follow for <u>drawing</u> bar charts:

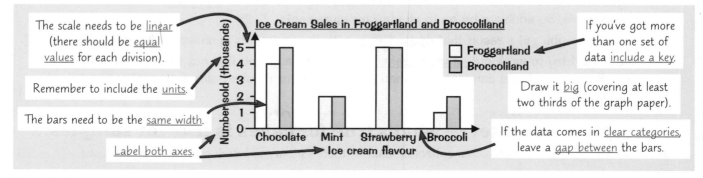

The scale needs to be <u>linear</u> (there should be <u>equal values</u> for each division).

Remember to include the <u>units</u>.

The bars need to be the <u>same width</u>.

Label both axes.

Ice Cream Sales in Froggartland and Broccoliland

Number sold (thousands)

Chocolate   Mint   Strawberry   Broccoli
Ice cream flavour

☐ Froggartland
■ Broccoliland

If you've got more than one set of data <u>include a key</u>.

Draw it <u>big</u> (covering at least two thirds of the graph paper).

If the data comes in <u>clear categories</u>, leave a <u>gap between</u> the bars.

Working Scientifically

Graphs can be Used to Plot Continuous Data

If both variables can have any value <u>within a range</u> (e.g. length, volume) use a <u>graph</u> to display the data.

Here are the rules for plotting points on a graph:

Use the biggest data values you've got to draw a <u>sensible scale</u> on your axes.

The <u>dependent</u> variable goes on the <u>y-axis</u> (the <u>vertical</u> one).

The <u>independent</u> variable goes on the <u>x-axis</u> (the <u>horizontal</u> one).

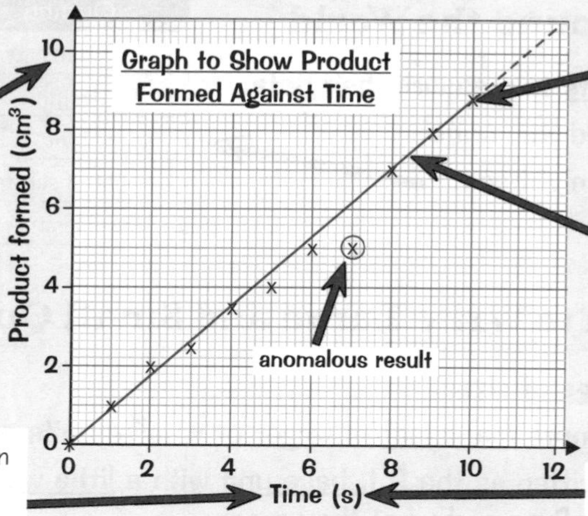

Graph to Show Product Formed Against Time

Product formed (cm³) vs Time (s)

anomalous result

To plot points, use a sharp pencil and make <u>neat little crosses</u> (don't do blobs).

nice clear mark / smudged unclear marks

To draw a <u>line</u> (or <u>curve</u>) of <u>best fit</u>, draw a line <u>through</u>, or as <u>near</u> to, as <u>many points as possible</u>. Ignore any <u>anomalous results</u>. <u>Don't</u> join the crosses up.

Draw it <u>big</u> (covering at least two thirds of the graph paper).

Remember to include the <u>units</u>.

You Can Calculate the Rate of a Reaction from the Gradient of a Graph

1) This is the <u>formula</u> you need to calculate the <u>gradient</u> (slope) of a graph:
2) You can use it to work out the <u>rate of a reaction</u> (how <u>quickly</u> the reaction happens).

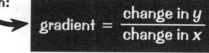

$$\text{gradient} = \frac{\text{change in } y}{\text{change in } x}$$

EXAMPLE

The graph shows the volume of gas produced in a reaction against time. Calculate the rate of reaction.

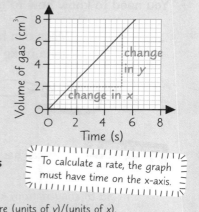

Volume of gas (cm³) vs Time (s)

change in y

change in x

To calculate a rate, the graph must have time on the x-axis.

1) To calculate the <u>gradient</u>, pick <u>two points</u> on the line that are easy to read. They should also be a <u>good distance</u> apart.
2) Draw a line <u>down</u> from one of the points. Then draw a line <u>across</u> from the other, to make a <u>triangle</u>.
3) The line drawn <u>down the side</u> of the triangle is the <u>change in y</u>. The line <u>across the bottom</u> is the <u>change in x</u>.
4) Read points <u>off the graph</u> to work out the change in y and the change in x:

Change in y = 6.8 − 2.0 = **4.8 cm³**   Change in x = 5.2 − 1.6 = **3.6 s**

5) Then put these numbers in the formula above to find the rate of the reaction:

$$\text{Rate = gradient} = \frac{\text{change in } y}{\text{change in } x} = \frac{4.8 \text{ cm}^3}{3.6 \text{ s}} = 1.3 \text{ cm}^3\text{/s}$$

The units are (units of y)/(units of x). cm³/s can also be written as cm³ s⁻¹.

Graphs Show the Relationship Between Two Variables

1) You can get <u>three</u> types of <u>correlation</u> (relationship) between variables:
2) A correlation <u>doesn't mean</u> the change in one variable is <u>causing</u> the change in the other (see page 9).

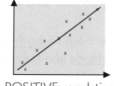

<u>POSITIVE</u> correlation: as one variable <u>increases</u> the other <u>increases</u>.

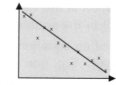

<u>INVERSE</u> (negative) correlation: as one variable <u>increases</u> the other <u>decreases</u>.

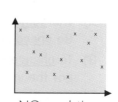

<u>NO</u> correlation: <u>no relationship</u> between the two variables.

I love eating apples — I call it core elation...

Science is all about finding relationships between things. And I don't mean that chemists gather together in corners to discuss whether or not Devini and Sebastian might be a couple... though they probably do that too.

Working Scientifically

Units

Graphs and maths skills are all very well, but the numbers don't mean much if you can't get the <u>units</u> right.

S.I. Units Are Used All Round the World

1) All scientists use the same <u>units</u> to measure their data.
2) These are <u>standard units</u>, called S.I. units.
3) Here are some S.I. units you might see:

Quantity	S.I. Base Unit
mass	kilogram, kg
length	metre, m
time	second, s
amount of substance	mole, mol
temperature	kelvin, K

Different Units Help you to Write Large and Small Quantities

Kilogram is an exception. It's an S.I. unit with the prefix already on it.

1) Quantities come in a huge <u>range</u> of sizes.
2) To make the size of numbers more <u>manageable</u>, larger or smaller units are used.
3) Larger and smaller units are written as the <u>S.I. base unit</u> with a <u>little word</u> in <u>front</u> (a prefix).
   Here are some <u>examples</u> of <u>prefixes</u> and what they mean:

prefix	mega (M)	kilo (k)	deci (d)	centi (c)	milli (m)	micro (μ)
how it compares to the base unit	1 000 000 times bigger	1000 times bigger	10 times smaller	100 times smaller	1000 times smaller	1 000 000 times smaller

E.g. 1 <u>kilo</u>metre is <u>1000</u> metres.   E.g. there are <u>1000</u> <u>milli</u>metres in 1 metre.

You Need to be Able to Convert Between Units

You need to know how to <u>convert</u> (change) one unit into another. Here are some useful conversions:

DIVIDE to go from a <u>smaller unit</u> to a <u>bigger unit</u>.

Mass can have units of kg and g.

$$kg \underset{\div 1000}{\overset{\times 1000}{\rightleftarrows}} g$$

Energy can have units of kJ and J.

$$kJ \underset{\div 1000}{\overset{\times 1000}{\rightleftarrows}} J$$

Length can have lots of units, including m, mm, and μm.

$$m \underset{\div 1000}{\overset{\times 1000}{\rightleftarrows}} mm \underset{\div 1000}{\overset{\times 1000}{\rightleftarrows}} \mu m$$

MULTIPLY to go from a <u>bigger unit</u> to a <u>smaller unit</u>.

EXAMPLE   A car has travelled 0.015 kilometres. How many metres has it travelled?

1) 1 km = 1000 m.
2) So to convert from km (a bigger unit) to m (a smaller unit) you need to <u>multiply</u> by 1000.

0.015 km × 1000 = 15 m

Make sure the values you put into an equation or formula have the right units.

You Can Rearrange Equations

1) Equations show <u>relationships</u> between <u>variables</u>. For example, speed = $\dfrac{distance}{time}$.
2) The <u>subject</u> of an equation is the variable <u>by itself</u> on one side of the equals sign.
   So <u>speed</u> is the <u>subject</u> in the equation above.
3) To <u>change</u> the <u>subject</u> of an equation do the same thing to <u>both sides</u> of the equation until you've got the subject you <u>want</u>. E.g. you can make <u>distance</u> the subject of the equation above:

1) <u>Multiply</u> both sides by <u>time</u>:   speed = $\dfrac{distance}{time}$ 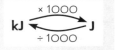 speed × time = $\dfrac{distance \times time}{time}$

2) Time is now on the top <u>and</u> the bottom of the fraction, so it cancels out: speed × time = $\dfrac{distance \times \cancel{time}}{\cancel{time}}$

3) This leaves <u>distance</u> by itself. So it's the <u>subject</u>:   speed × time = distance

I wasn't sure I liked units, but now I'm converted...

If you're moving from a smaller unit to a larger unit (e.g. g to kg) the number should get smaller, and vice versa.

Drawing Conclusions

Congratulations — you've made it to the <u>final step</u> of an investigation — <u>drawing conclusions</u>.

You Can Only Conclude What the Data Shows and NO MORE

1) To come to a conclusion, <u>look at your data</u> and <u>say what pattern you see</u>.

<u>EXAMPLE</u>: The table on the right shows the heights of pea plant seedlings grown for three weeks with different fertilisers.

Fertiliser	Mean growth / mm
A	13.5
B	19.5
No fertiliser	5.5

<u>CONCLUSION</u>: <u>Pea plant</u> seedlings grow taller over a <u>three week</u> period with fertiliser B than with fertiliser A.

2) It's important that the conclusion <u>matches the data</u> it's based on — it <u>shouldn't go any further</u>.

<u>EXAMPLE continued</u>: You can't conclude that <u>any other type of plant</u> would grow taller with fertiliser B than with fertiliser A — the results could be totally different.

3) You also need to be able to <u>use your results</u> to <u>justify your conclusion</u> (i.e. back it up).

<u>EXAMPLE continued</u>: The pea plants grew 6 mm more on average with fertiliser B than with fertiliser A.

4) When writing a conclusion you need to say whether or not the data <u>supports</u> the <u>original hypothesis</u>:

<u>EXAMPLE continued</u>: The hypothesis might have been that adding different types of fertiliser would affect the growth of pea plants by different amounts. If so, the data <u>supports</u> the hypothesis.

Correlation DOES NOT Mean Cause

1) If two things are <u>correlated</u>, there's a <u>relationship</u> between them — see page 7.
2) But a correlation <u>doesn't always</u> mean that a change in one variable is <u>causing</u> the change in the other.
3) There are <u>three possible reasons</u> for a correlation:

① CHANCE

There is <u>no scientific reason</u> for the correlation — it just happened <u>by chance</u>.
Other scientists <u>wouldn't</u> get a correlation if they carried out the same investigation.

② LINKED BY A 3rd VARIABLE

There's <u>another factor</u> involved.

E.g. there's a correlation between water temperature and shark attacks.
They're linked by a <u>third variable</u> — the number of people swimming (more people swim when the water's hotter, which means you get more shark attacks).

③ CAUSE

Sometimes a change in one variable does <u>cause</u> a change in the other. You can only conclude this when you've <u>controlled all the variables</u> that could be affecting the result.

I conclude that this page is a bit dull...

In the exams you could be given a conclusion and asked whether some data supports it — so make sure you understand how far conclusions can go. And remember, correlation does not mean cause.

Uncertainties and Evaluations

Hurrah! The end of another investigation. Well, now you have to work out all the things you did <u>wrong</u>.

Uncertainty is the Amount of Error Your Measurements Might Have

1) Measurements you make will have some <u>uncertainty</u> in them (i.e. they won't be completely perfect).

2) This can be due to <u>random errors</u> (see page 5). It can also be due to <u>limits</u> in what your <u>measuring equipment</u> can measure.

3) This means that the <u>mean</u> of your results will have some uncertainty to it.

4) You can <u>calculate</u> the uncertainty of a <u>mean result</u> using this equation: ➡

5) The <u>less precise</u> your results are, the <u>higher</u> the uncertainty will be.

6) Uncertainties are shown using the '±' symbol.

> The range is the largest value minus the smallest value (p.6).

$$\text{uncertainty} = \frac{\text{range}}{2}$$

EXAMPLE The table below shows the results of an experiment to find the speed of a trolley. Calculate the uncertainty of the mean.

Repeat	1	2	3	mean
Speed (m/s)	2.02	1.98	2.00	2.00

1) First work out the range:
   Range = 2.02 − 1.98
   = 0.04 m/s

2) Use the range to find the uncertainty:
Uncertainty = range ÷ 2 = 0.04 ÷ 2 = 0.02 m/s   So, uncertainty of the mean = 2.00 ± 0.02 m/s

---

Evaluations — Describe How it Could be Improved

> I'd value this E somewhere in the region of 250-300k

In an evaluation you look back over the whole investigation.

1) You should comment on the <u>method</u> — was it <u>valid</u>? Did you control all the other variables to make it a <u>fair test</u>?

2) Comment on the <u>quality</u> of the <u>results</u> — was there <u>enough evidence</u> to reach a valid <u>conclusion</u>? Were the results <u>repeatable</u>, <u>reproducible</u>, <u>accurate</u> and <u>precise</u>?

3) Were there any <u>anomalous</u> results? If there were <u>none</u> then <u>say so</u>. If there were any, try to <u>explain</u> them — were they caused by <u>errors</u> in measurement?

4) You should comment on the level of <u>uncertainty</u> in your results too.

5) Thinking about these things lets you say how <u>confident</u> you are that your conclusion is <u>right</u>.

6) Then you can suggest any <u>changes</u> to the <u>method</u> that would <u>improve</u> the quality of the results, so you could have <u>more confidence</u> in your conclusion.

7) For example, taking measurements at <u>narrower intervals</u> could give you a <u>more accurate result</u>. E.g.

   • Say you do an experiment to find the <u>temperature</u> at which an enzyme <u>works best</u>.

   • You take measurements at <u>30 °C</u>, <u>40 °C</u> and <u>50 °C</u>. The results show that the enzyme works best at <u>40 °C</u>.

   • To get a more accurate result, you could <u>repeat</u> the experiment and take <u>more measurements around 40 °C</u>. You might then find that the enzyme actually works best at <u>42 °C</u>.

8) You could also make more <u>predictions</u> based on your conclusion. You could then carry out <u>further experiments</u> to test the new predictions.

Evaluation — next time, I'll make sure I don't burn the lab down...

So there you have it — Working Scientifically. Make sure you know this stuff like the back of your hand. It's not just in the lab that you'll need to know how to work scientifically. You can be asked about it in the exams as well.

Cells

Cells are the <u>building blocks</u> of <u>every organism on the planet</u>.
You need to know about the <u>features</u> of a few <u>different types</u> of cells.

Cells Can be Eukaryotic or Prokaryotic

1) <u>All living things</u> are made of <u>cells</u>.
2) <u>Eukaryotic</u> cells are <u>complex</u>. All <u>animal</u> and <u>plant</u> cells are eukaryotic.
3) <u>Prokaryotic</u> cells are <u>smaller</u> and <u>simpler</u>. <u>Bacteria</u> are prokaryotic cells.

Plant and Animal Cells Have Similarities and Differences

The different parts of a cell are called <u>sub-cellular structures</u>.
Most <u>animal</u> cells have these sub-cellular structures:

Sub-cellular structures are also known as organelles.

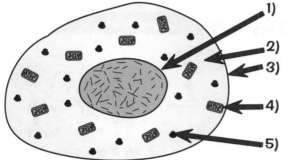

1) <u>Nucleus</u> — contains <u>DNA</u> (see p.27). DNA <u>controls</u> what the cell <u>does</u>. It is stored in structures called <u>chromosomes</u>.
2) <u>Cytoplasm</u> — where most <u>chemical reactions</u> happen.
3) <u>Cell membrane</u> — holds the cell together and controls what goes <u>in</u> and <u>out</u>.
4) <u>Mitochondria</u> — where most <u>respiration</u> happens (see page 63). Respiration <u>releases energy</u> for the cell.
5) <u>Ribosomes</u> — join <u>amino acids</u> together to make <u>proteins</u>.

Plant cells usually have <u>all the bits</u> that <u>animal</u> cells have. They also have:

1) A <u>cell wall</u> made of <u>cellulose</u>. It <u>supports</u> the cell and strengthens it.
2) <u>Chloroplasts</u> — where <u>photosynthesis</u> happens. Photosynthesis makes food for the plant (see page 47).
3) A <u>large vacuole</u> — stores <u>cell sap</u> (a solution of sugar and salts).

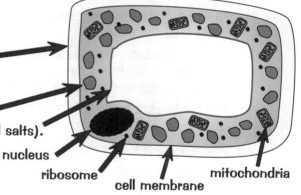

nucleus
ribosome
cell membrane
mitochondria

Bacterial Cells DON'T Have a Nucleus

<u>Bacterial cells</u> have these <u>sub-cellular structures</u>:

1) <u>Chromosomal DNA</u> — <u>one</u> long circular strand of DNA. This <u>controls</u> what the cell does.
2) <u>Ribosomes</u>
3) <u>Cell membrane</u>
4) <u>Plasmid DNA</u> — small loops of <u>extra DNA</u>.

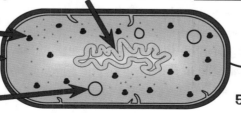

5) <u>Flagellum</u> — a long, hair-like structure that helps the cell <u>move</u>.

Cell structures — become a property developer...

On this page are typical cells with all the typical bits you need to know. Make sure you learn them all.

Q1   What is the function of ribosomes?   [1 mark]

Specialised Cells

The previous page shows the structure of some <u>typical cells</u>.
However, most cells are <u>specialised</u> for a particular function, so their <u>structure</u> can vary...

Different Cells Have Different Functions

1) <u>Multicellular organisms</u> contain lots of different <u>types</u> of cells (i.e. cells with different <u>structures</u>).
2) Cells with a structure that makes them <u>adapted</u> (suited) to their function are called <u>specialised cells</u>.

Egg Cells and Sperm Cells Are Specialised for Reproduction

1) In <u>sexual reproduction</u>, an <u>egg cell</u> and a <u>sperm cell</u> combine (see p.26).
2) This creates a <u>fertilised egg</u>, which then develops into an <u>embryo</u>.
3) The <u>egg</u> cell's function is to <u>carry the female DNA</u> and <u>feed</u> the developing embryo.
4) The <u>sperm</u> cell's function is to <u>carry the male DNA</u> to the egg.

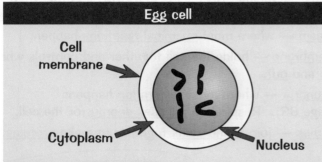

Egg cell

1) An egg cell contains <u>nutrients</u> in its <u>cytoplasm</u>. These <u>feed</u> the embryo.
2) After <u>fertilisation</u>, the <u>cell membrane</u> changes <u>structure</u>. This stops <u>more</u> sperm getting <u>in</u> — so only <u>one</u> sperm can fertilise the egg.
3) It has a <u>haploid nucleus</u> (see below).

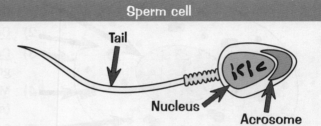

Sperm cell

1) A sperm cell has a <u>tail</u>, so it can <u>swim</u> to the egg.
2) It has lots of <u>mitochondria</u>. These release the <u>energy</u> the sperm needs to <u>swim</u>.
3) It has an <u>acrosome</u> — this stores <u>enzymes</u> that <u>digest</u> through the <u>membrane</u> of the egg cell.
4) It has a <u>haploid nucleus</u> (see below).

Chromosomes are coiled up lengths of DNA — see p.27 for more.

- 'Haploid' means that the cells only have <u>half</u> the number of <u>chromosomes</u> found in a <u>normal</u> body cell.
- So when an egg and sperm nucleus <u>combine</u>, the <u>embryo</u> has the <u>full number</u> of <u>chromosomes</u>.

Ciliated Epithelial Cells Are Specialised for Moving Materials

1) Epithelial cells <u>line the surfaces</u> of organs.
2) Some of them have <u>cilia</u> on the <u>top surface</u> of the cell.
3) Cilia are tiny <u>hair-like</u> structures. They can <u>move substances</u> by beating them <u>along the surface</u> of the tissue.
4) For example, ciliated epithelial cells in the <u>lining of the airways</u> help to move <u>mucus</u> up to the <u>throat</u> so it can be <u>swallowed</u>.

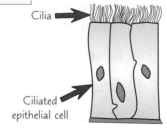

Cilia

Ciliated epithelial cell

Everyone knows eggs are specialised — fried, boiled, scrambled...

Nearly every cell in your body is specialised to carry out some kind of function. The ones on this page are the examples you need to learn for your exams. Right, now have a go at this question to see what you remember.

Q1   a)   What is the function of sperm cells?   [1 mark]
          b)   Give two ways in which sperm cells are adapted for swimming.   [2 marks]

Microscopy

Without <u>microscopes</u> we would never have discovered cells. We can even use them to look <u>inside</u> cells.

Cells are Studied Using Microscopes

1) Microscopes use <u>lenses</u> to <u>magnify</u> things (make them look <u>bigger</u>).
2) <u>Light microscopes</u> can be used to look at cells.
   They let us see <u>some sub-cellular structures</u>, e.g. <u>chloroplasts</u> and the <u>nucleus</u>.
3) <u>Electron microscopes</u> were invented <u>after</u> light microscopes.
4) Electron microscopes can make specimens look <u>bigger</u> and show <u>more detail</u> than light microscopes.
5) Electron microscopes have given us a <u>better understanding</u> of what sub-cellular structures do.

There's more on sub-cellular structures on page 11.

This is How to View a Specimen Using a Light Microscope   PRACTICAL

Preparing your specimen

1) Take a <u>thin slice</u> of your specimen (the thing you're looking at).
2) Take a clean <u>slide</u> and use a <u>pipette</u> to put one <u>drop of water</u> in the middle of it.
3) Then use <u>tweezers</u> to place your specimen on the slide.
4) You might need to add a drop of <u>stain</u> to make your specimen <u>easier to see</u>.
5) Carefully lower a <u>cover slip</u> onto the slide using a <u>mounted needle</u>.
   Try not to trap any <u>bubbles</u> under the cover slip.

Cover slip
Specimen
Slide

Viewing your specimen

1) <u>Clip</u> the slide onto the <u>stage</u>.
2) Select the <u>objective lens</u> with the <u>lowest</u> magnification.
3) Use the <u>coarse adjustment knob</u> to move the stage <u>up</u> to <u>just underneath</u> the objective lens.
4) <u>Look</u> down the <u>eyepiece</u>, then move the stage <u>down</u> until the specimen is <u>nearly in focus</u>.
5) <u>Move</u> the <u>fine adjustment knob</u>, until you get a <u>clear image</u>.
6) If you want to make the image bigger, use an objective lens with a <u>higher magnification</u> (and <u>refocus</u>).

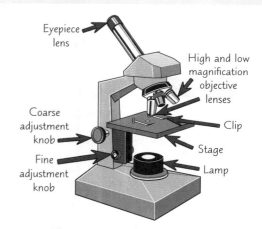

Eyepiece lens
High and low magnification objective lenses
Coarse adjustment knob
Fine adjustment knob
Clip
Stage
Lamp

This is How to Do a Scientific Drawing of a Specimen   PRACTICAL

1) Use a <u>sharp</u> pencil to draw <u>smooth</u> <u>outlines</u> of the <u>main features</u>.
2) <u>Label</u> the <u>features</u> with <u>straight lines</u>.
   Make sure the lines <u>don't cross over</u> each other.
3) Don't do any <u>colouring</u> or <u>shading</u>.
4) The drawing should take up <u>at least half</u> the space available.
5) Include the <u>magnification</u> used and a <u>scale</u>.

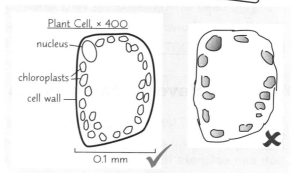

Plant Cell, × 400
nucleus
chloroplasts
cell wall
0.1 mm

I take my microscope everywhere — good job it's a light one...

There's lots of important stuff here about how you use a light microscope to view specimens — so get learning.

Q1   A student wants to look at a thin piece of onion skin under a light microscope.
      Describe the steps she could take to prepare the skin for viewing.   [3 marks]

 **PRACTICAL**

More Microscopy

Sometimes you need to do a bit of <u>maths</u> with microscope images. It's time to get your <u>numbers head on</u>...

Magnification is How Many Times Bigger the Image is

1) You can work out the <u>total magnification</u> of an image under a microscope using this formula:

total magnification = eyepiece lens magnification × objective lens magnification

> **EXAMPLE**
> What's the total magnification of an image viewed with an eyepiece lens magnification of × 10 and an objective lens magnification of × 40?
> total magnification = 10 × 40 = × 400

2) You can also work out the magnification of an image if you <u>don't know</u> what <u>lenses</u> were used.

3) You need to be able to <u>measure the image</u>, and you also need to know the <u>real size</u> of the specimen.

4) This is the <u>formula</u> you need:

$$\text{magnification} = \frac{\text{image size}}{\text{real size}}$$

Both measurements should have the same units (see below).

> **EXAMPLE**
> The width of a specimen is 0.02 mm. The width of its image under a microscope is 8 mm. What magnification was used to view the specimen?
> magnification = 8 mm ÷ 0.02 mm = × 400

5) You can find the <u>image size</u> or the <u>real size</u> of an object, using the <u>formula triangle</u> below.

6) <u>Cover</u> the thing you want to find. The parts you can <u>see</u> are the formula you need to use.

> **EXAMPLE**
> The width of a specimen's image underneath a microscope is 3 mm. The magnification is × 100. What is the real width of the specimen?
>
> Cover up '<u>real size</u>' on the formula triangle.
> This leaves the formula: image size ÷ magnification
> So, the real width = 3 mm ÷ 100 = 0.03 mm

What are you looking at?

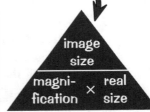
image size
magnification × real size

You Might Need to Convert Units

1) <u>Millimetres</u> (mm), <u>micrometres</u> (µm) and <u>nanometres</u> (nm) are <u>units</u> used when measuring very small objects, e.g. cells.

2) This diagram shows you how to <u>convert between these units</u>.

3) E.g. to write <u>0.007 mm</u> in µm, you <u>times it</u> by 1000 to get <u>7 µm</u>.

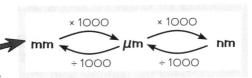
× 1000   × 1000
mm   µm   nm
÷ 1000   ÷ 1000

If You Don't Have the Information to Calculate a Size, Estimate it

1) To estimate size, you can <u>make comparisons</u> with things that you <u>do</u> know the size of.

2) E.g. if you know a cell is <u>10 µm</u> wide and the nucleus looks about <u>half the width</u> of the cell, you can estimate the width of the nucleus to be <u>5 µm</u>.

Mi-cros-copy — when my twin gets annoyed...

You can put standard form numbers into your scientific calculator using the 'EXP' or the '×10ˣ' button. For example, enter 2.67×10^{15} by pressing 2.67 then 'EXP' or '×10ˣ', then 15. Easy.

Q1   A cheek cell is viewed under a microscope with × 40 magnification. The image of the cell is 2.4 mm wide. Calculate the real width of the cheek cell. Give your answer in µm.   [2 marks]

Q1 Video Solution

Enzymes

Chemical reactions are what make you work. And enzymes are what make them work.

Enzymes Are Catalysts Produced by Living Things

1) Enzymes are biological catalysts.
2) This means they speed up chemical reactions in living organisms.
3) A substrate is a molecule that gets changed in a chemical reaction.
4) Every enzyme has an active site — the part where it joins on to its substrate to catalyse the reaction.
5) Enzymes are substrate specific — this means that they usually only work with one substrate.
6) This is because, for the enzyme to work, the substrate has to fit into the active site.

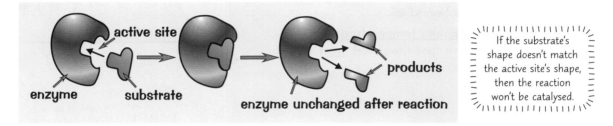

active site

enzyme   substrate   products   enzyme unchanged after reaction

If the substrate's shape doesn't match the active site's shape, then the reaction won't be catalysed.

Enzymes Catalyse Breakdown and Synthesis Reactions

1) Proteins, lipids and some carbohydrates are big molecules.
2) Organisms often need to break down big molecules into smaller ones — e.g. during digestion.
3) Organisms also need to synthesise (make) big molecules from small molecules — e.g. to make new cells.
4) Enzymes catalyse breakdown and synthesis reactions.

- Enzymes called carbohydrases break carbohydrates into simple sugars.
- E.g. amylase is a type of carbohydrase. It breaks down starch.
- Different enzymes are used to join simple sugars together to make bigger carbohydrates.

Starch → Amylase → Sugars

- Proteases break down proteins into amino acids.
- Other enzymes make proteins from amino acids.

Proteins → Proteases → Amino acids

- Lipases break down lipids into glycerol and fatty acids.
- Again, other enzymes are involved in making lipids.

Lipid → Lipases → Glycerol & fatty acids

What do you call an acid that's eaten all the pies...

There's lots more on enzymes coming up, so make sure you really understand how they work before you move on.

Q1   Name the molecules that result from the breakdown of: a) carbohydrates, b) proteins.   [2 marks]

Factors Affecting Enzyme Activity

Lots of things can <u>affect</u> how well enzymes can do their job. Here are a <u>few examples</u> that you need to know.

Temperature Affects Enzyme Shape and Activity

1) A <u>higher</u> temperature <u>increases</u> the rate of an enzyme-catalysed reaction at first.

2) But if it gets <u>too hot</u>, some of the <u>bonds</u> holding the enzyme together <u>break</u>.

3) This changes the <u>shape</u> of the enzyme's <u>active site</u>, so the substrate <u>won't fit</u> any more.

4) If this happens, the enzyme is said to be <u>denatured</u>. It can't catalyse the reaction at all.

5) All enzymes have an <u>optimum temperature</u> — this is the temperature that they work <u>best</u> at.

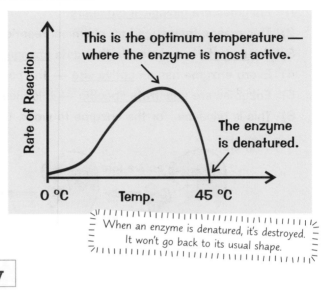

This is the optimum temperature — where the enzyme is most active.

The enzyme is denatured.

When an enzyme is denatured, it's destroyed. It won't go back to its usual shape.

pH Also Affects Enzyme Shape and Activity

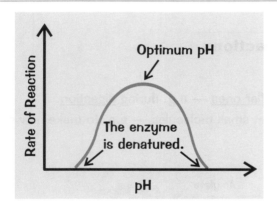

Optimum pH

The enzyme is denatured.

1) If pH is <u>too high</u> or <u>too low</u>, it affects the <u>bonds</u> holding the active site together.

2) This changes the <u>shape</u> of the <u>active site</u> and <u>denatures</u> the enzyme.

3) All enzymes have an <u>optimum pH</u> that they work best at.

4) The optimum pH is often <u>neutral pH 7</u>, but <u>not always</u>.

5) E.g. <u>pepsin</u> is an enzyme in the <u>stomach</u>. It works best at <u>pH 2</u>.

Substrate Concentration Also Affects the Rate of Reaction

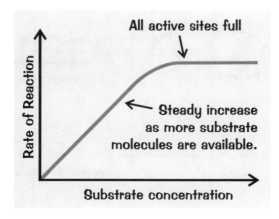

All active sites full

Steady increase as more substrate molecules are available.

1) The higher the <u>substrate concentration</u>, the <u>faster the reaction</u>.

2) This is because it's more likely that the enzyme will <u>meet up</u> and <u>react</u> with a substrate molecule.

3) This is only true <u>up to a point</u> though.

4) After that, there are <u>so many</u> substrate molecules that all the <u>active sites</u> on the enzymes are <u>full</u>.

5) At this point, adding more substrate molecules makes <u>no difference</u>.

If only enzymes could speed up revision...

Make sure you use the special terms like 'active site' and 'denatured' — the examiners will love it.

Q1   Explain why enzymes denature if the pH is too high.   [2 marks]

More on Enzyme Activity PRACTICAL

You'll soon know how to investigate the effect of pH on the rate of enzyme activity... I bet you're thrilled.

Here's How You Can Investigate How pH Affects Enzyme Activity

1) The enzyme amylase catalyses the breakdown of starch to sugar.
2) You can detect starch using iodine solution — if starch is present, the iodine solution will change from browny-orange to blue-black.

1) Put a drop of iodine solution into every well of a spotting tile.
2) Set up a water bath at 35 °C.
   (You could use a Bunsen burner and a beaker of water, or an electric water bath.)
3) Add some amylase solution and a buffer solution with a pH of 5 to a boiling tube.
4) Put the boiling tube in the water bath and wait for five minutes.
5) Add some starch solution to the boiling tube, mix, and start a stop clock.
6) Every ten seconds, take a sample from the boiling tube using a dropping pipette.
7) Put a drop of the sample into a well on the spotting tile.
8) When the iodine solution stays browny-orange, all the starch in the sample has been broken down. Record how long this takes.

This is an example of continuous sampling.

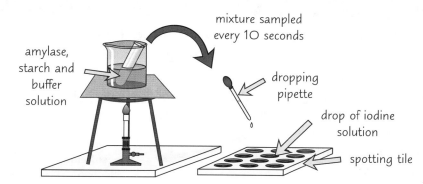

amylase, starch and buffer solution

mixture sampled every 10 seconds

dropping pipette

drop of iodine solution

spotting tile

9) Repeat the experiment with buffer solutions of different pH values.
10) As the pH changes, the time it takes for the starch to be broken down should also change.
11) Remember to control any variables each time you repeat the experiment. This will make it a fair test. For example, the concentration and volume of the amylase solution should always be the same.

Here's How to Calculate the Rate of Reaction

1) It's often useful to calculate the rate of reaction after an experiment.
2) Rate is a measure of how much something changes over time.
3) For the experiment above, you can calculate the rate of reaction using this formula:

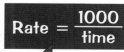

$$\text{Rate} = \frac{1000}{\text{time}}$$

EXAMPLE

At pH 6, the time taken for amylase to break down all of the starch in a solution was 50 seconds. Find the rate of this reaction.

rate of reaction = 1000 ÷ time   1000 ÷ 50 = 20 s^{-1}

You could also use the formula 1/t but 1000/time will give you a bigger number that's easier to plot on a graph.

At this rate, you'll be sick of enzymes...

You could easily change this experiment to investigate how factors like temperature affect the rate of an enzyme-controlled reaction. But remember, only change the thing you're testing and nothing else.

Q1 Video Solution

Q1   Calculate the rate of a reaction that finished in 2.5 minutes.
     Give your answer in s^{-1}.

[2 mark]

Diffusion, Osmosis and Active Transport

Substances can move in and out of cells by <u>diffusion</u>, <u>osmosis</u> and <u>active transport</u>...

Diffusion — Don't be Put Off by the Fancy Word

1) <u>Diffusion</u> is the <u>movement</u> of particles from where there are <u>lots</u> of them to where there are <u>fewer</u> of them. Here's the fancy <u>definition</u>:

> <u>DIFFUSION</u> is the <u>spreading out</u> of <u>particles</u> from an area of <u>higher concentration</u> to an area of <u>lower concentration</u>.

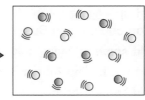

2) This diagram shows what's happening when the smell of perfume <u>diffuses</u> through the <u>air</u> in a room:

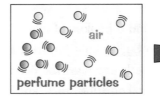

perfume particles diffused in the air

Osmosis Involves Water Molecules

> <u>OSMOSIS</u> is the movement of <u>water molecules</u> across a <u>partially permeable membrane</u> from a <u>less concentrated</u> solution to a <u>more concentrated</u> solution.

1) A <u>partially permeable</u> membrane is a membrane with very <u>small holes</u> in it.

2) <u>Small molecules</u> can pass through the holes, but <u>bigger</u> molecules <u>can't</u>.

3) Water molecules pass <u>both ways</u> through a membrane during osmosis.

Cell membranes are partially permeable membranes.

4) But the <u>overall movement</u> of <u>water molecules</u> is from the <u>less concentrated</u> solution (where there are lots of water molecules) to the <u>more concentrated</u> solution (where there are fewer water molecules).

5) This means the more concentrated solution gets <u>more dilute</u>.

6) The water acts like it's trying to "<u>even up</u>" the concentration on either side of the membrane.

The sucrose is a solute — a molecule dissolved in the water.

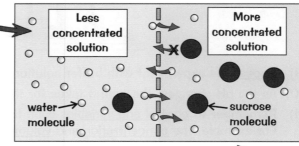

Less concentrated solution

More concentrated solution

water molecule

sucrose molecule

Overall movement of water molecules

Active Transport Works The Opposite Way to Diffusion

> <u>ACTIVE TRANSPORT</u> is the <u>movement of particles</u> across a membrane from an area of <u>lower concentration</u> to an area of <u>higher concentration</u>. It uses <u>energy</u>.

1) Active transport moves particles in the <u>opposite direction</u> to <u>diffusion</u>.

2) Scientists say that active transport moves particles <u>against</u> a <u>concentration gradient</u>.

3) This requires <u>energy</u> (unlike diffusion). The energy is released by <u>respiration</u> (see p.63).

Revision by diffusion — you wish...

Hopefully there'll have been a net movement of information from this page into your brain...

Q1   A sodium ion moves from inside a nerve cell, where there is a low sodium ion concentration, to outside the cell, where the concentration is higher. Name the process by which the ion is moving across the membrane.

[1 mark]

Q1 Video Solution

Investigating Osmosis PRACTICAL

For all you non-believers — here's an <u>experiment</u> you can do to see <u>osmosis in action</u>.

You Can Do an Experiment to Investigate Osmosis

1) Start by preparing <u>sucrose solutions</u> of different concentrations.

2) Next, use a cork borer to cut a <u>potato</u> into <u>cylinders</u> of the <u>same length</u> and <u>width</u>.

3) Divide the cylinders into <u>groups of three</u> and use a <u>mass balance</u> to measure the <u>mass</u> of each <u>group</u>.

4) Place <u>one group</u> in each solution.

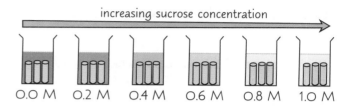

'M' is a unit of concentration. The beaker labelled 0.0 M is pure water. It doesn't have any sucrose in it, so the concentration is zero.

increasing sucrose concentration

0.0 M   0.2 M   0.4 M   0.6 M   0.8 M   1.0 M

5) <u>Leave</u> the cylinders in the solution for <u>at least 40 minutes</u>.

6) <u>Remove</u> the cylinders and pat dry <u>gently</u> with a paper towel.

7) <u>Weigh</u> each <u>group</u> again and record your results.

8) The <u>only</u> thing that you should <u>change</u> in this experiment is the <u>concentration</u> of the <u>sucrose solution</u>. Everything else (e.g. the volume of the solution) must be kept the <u>same</u> or your results <u>won't be valid</u>.

You Need to Find the Change in Mass of Your Cylinders

1) Once you've got your results, <u>calculate</u> the <u>percentage change in mass</u> for each group of cylinders.

2) Use this formula to find the percentage change in mass:

$$\text{Percentage change} = \frac{\text{final mass} - \text{starting mass}}{\text{starting mass}} \times 100$$

Calculating percentage change allows you to compare cylinders that didn't have the same starting mass.

EXAMPLE

A group of cylinders weighed 13.2 g at the start of the experiment. At the end they weighed 15.1 g. Calculate the percentage change in mass.

$$\text{percentage change} = \frac{15.1 - 13.2}{13.2} \times 100 = 14.4\%$$

The positive result tells you the potato cylinders gained mass. If the answer was negative then the potato cylinders lost mass.

3) In solutions with <u>high</u> sucrose concentrations, the cylinders should <u>lose mass</u>. This is because water moves <u>out</u> of them by osmosis.

4) In solutions with <u>low</u> sucrose concentrations, the cylinders should <u>gain mass</u>. This is because water moves <u>into</u> them by osmosis.

5) If the cylinders <u>don't change mass</u>, then the concentration of the <u>sucrose solution</u> is <u>the same</u> as the concentration of the fluid <u>inside the cylinders</u>.

So that's how they make skinny fries...

This experiment used sucrose as a solute, but you could do it with different solutes (e.g. salt).

Q1   Explain what will happen to the mass of a piece of potato added to a concentrated salt solution.

Q1 Video Solution

[2 marks]

Mitosis

In order to survive and grow, our cells have got to be able to <u>divide</u>. And that means our DNA as well...

Chromosomes Contain Genetic Information

1) The <u>nucleus</u> of a cell contains <u>chromosomes</u>.
2) Chromosomes are <u>coiled up</u> lengths of <u>DNA molecules</u> (see p.27 for more on DNA).
3) <u>Body cells</u> normally have <u>two copies</u> of each <u>chromosome</u> — this makes them '<u>diploid</u>' cells.
4) One copy of each chromosome comes from the organism's <u>mother</u>, and one comes from its <u>father</u>.

two copies of each chromosome

nucleus

The Cell Cycle Makes New Cells for Growth and Repair

1) <u>Cells</u> in <u>multicellular</u> organisms <u>divide</u> to produce new cells during a process called the <u>cell cycle</u>.
2) The stage of the cell cycle when the cell divides is called <u>mitosis</u>.
3) <u>Mitosis</u> is used for <u>growth</u> and to <u>replace damaged cells</u>.
4) Some organisms also use mitosis to <u>reproduce</u> — this is called <u>asexual reproduction</u>.

You Need to Know What Happens in the Main Stages of the Cell Cycle

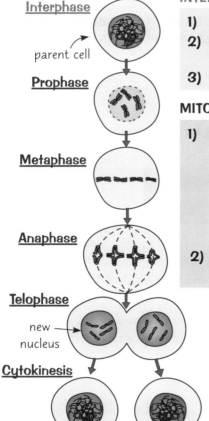

Interphase
parent cell
Prophase
Metaphase
Anaphase
Telophase
new nucleus
Cytokinesis
daughter cells

Interphase

The Cell Cycle

Mitosis and Cytokinesis

INTERPHASE

1) During <u>interphase</u>, the DNA is all spread out in <u>long strings</u>.
2) Before mitosis, the cell makes a <u>copy</u> of its <u>DNA</u>. The DNA forms <u>X-shaped</u> chromosomes.
3) The cell also <u>copies</u> some of its <u>subcellular structures</u>.

MITOSIS and CYTOKINESIS

1) <u>Mitosis</u> is divided into <u>four stages</u>:

① PROPHASE — The <u>membrane</u> around the <u>nucleus breaks down</u>.
② METAPHASE — The chromosomes <u>line up</u> at the <u>centre</u> of the cell.
③ ANAPHASE — Each chromosome is <u>split in half</u>. Each half is <u>exactly the same</u> as the other. The two halves are pulled to <u>opposite ends</u> of the cell.
④ TELOPHASE — <u>Membranes</u> form around each new set of chromosomes.

2) <u>Cytokinesis</u> is when the <u>cytoplasm</u> and <u>cell membrane</u> divide. This forms <u>two separate cells</u>, called <u>daughter cells</u>.

The Daughter Cells are Genetically Identical

1) <u>Both</u> daughter cells are <u>identical</u> to the <u>parent cell</u> and to <u>each other</u>.
2) Each daughter cell is <u>diploid</u> (has two copies of each chromosome).
3) The <u>daughter cells</u> can also divide by mitosis. The <u>total</u> number of cells present <u>doubles</u> with each <u>division</u>.

1 division   2 divisions   3 divisions

Mitosis — not to be confused with my toe zits. I need a doctor...

Mitosis can seem tricky at first. But don't worry — just go through it slowly, one step at a time.

Q1   A student looks at cells in the tip of a plant root under a microscope.
       She counts 11 cells that are undergoing mitosis and 62 cells that are not.
       a) Calculate the percentage of cells that are undergoing mitosis.   [1 mark]
       b) Suggest how the student can tell whether a cell is undergoing mitosis or not.   [1 mark]

Q1 Video Solution

Cell Division and Growth

Growth — it happens to us all. You need to know the <u>processes</u> involved in both <u>animal</u> and <u>plant</u> growth.

Growth Involves Cell Division, Elongation and Differentiation

1) <u>Growth</u> is an <u>increase</u> in <u>size</u> or <u>mass</u>.
2) <u>All growth</u> in <u>animals</u> happens by <u>CELL DIVISION</u>.
   <u>Cell division</u> happens by <u>mitosis</u> (see previous page).
3) <u>Plants</u> grow by <u>cell division</u> and <u>CELL ELONGATION</u>.
4) <u>Cell elongation</u> is when a plant cell <u>expands</u>, making the cell <u>bigger</u>.
5) <u>Development</u> in animals and plants happens by <u>CELL DIFFERENTIATION</u>.
6) <u>Cell differentiation</u> is how a cell <u>changes</u> to become <u>specialised</u> for its <u>job</u>.

See page 12 for more on specialised cells.

Cancer is a Case of Uncontrolled Cell Division

1) An organism's <u>DNA</u> controls how quickly cells divide by mitosis.
2) <u>Changes</u> in a cell's DNA may lead to <u>uncontrolled cell division</u>.
3) This can result in a <u>mass of abnormal cells</u> called a <u>tumour</u>.
4) If the tumour <u>spreads</u> into surrounding tissue it is called <u>cancer</u>.

A random change in DNA is called a mutation — see page 31.

Percentile Charts are Used to Monitor Growth

1) <u>Growth charts</u> are used to check that babies and children are growing <u>normally</u>.
2) For example, this is a growth chart for <u>weight</u>.
3) A baby's weight would be <u>recorded regularly</u> and the measurements <u>plotted</u> on the <u>chart</u>.
4) The <u>purple lines</u> mark different '<u>percentiles</u>'. These are used to check how the baby's weight <u>compares</u> to the weight of <u>other babies</u> of the <u>same age</u>.
5) For example, the <u>red lines</u> on this chart show that a <u>three-month-old</u> who weighs <u>7 kg</u> is in the <u>75th percentile</u>.
6) This means that roughly <u>75%</u> of three-month-olds are <u>lighter</u> and <u>25%</u> are <u>heavier</u>.
7) A doctor may be <u>concerned</u> about a baby's growth if:
   - it doesn't stay <u>roughly</u> within the <u>same percentiles</u> as it grows,
   - its size is <u>above</u> the <u>top percentile line</u> or <u>below</u> the <u>bottom percentile</u> line.

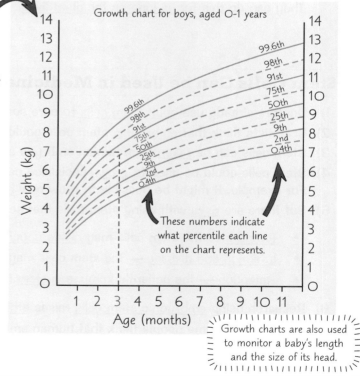

Growth chart for boys, aged 0-1 years

These numbers indicate what percentile each line on the chart represents.

Growth charts are also used to monitor a baby's length and the size of its head.

I'm growing rather sick of this section...

Growth is pretty important. Without it, you wouldn't be able to reach anything on the top shelf.

Q1   Amol is 4 months old and weighs 6 kg. Benjamin is 7 months old and weighs 5 kg.
       Using the percentile chart above, suggest whether a doctor might be concerned about
       the growth of either of these babies. Explain your answer.

Q1 Video Solution

[2 marks]

Stem Cells

Your body is made up of all sorts of <u>weird and wonderful cells</u>. This page tells you where they all <u>came from</u>...

Stem Cells can Differentiate into Different Types of Cells

1) Cells <u>differentiate</u> (change) to become <u>specialised cells</u>.
2) <u>Undifferentiated</u> cells are called <u>stem cells</u>.
3) Stem cells found in early <u>animal embryos</u> are called <u>embryonic stem cells</u>.
4) Embryonic stem cells can produce <u>any kind</u> of specialised cell at all.
5) They are important in the <u>growth</u> and <u>development</u> of organisms.
6) <u>Adults</u> also have stem cells, but they're only found in <u>certain places</u>, like <u>bone marrow</u> (a tissue inside bones).
7) Adult stem cells can <u>only</u> produce <u>certain types</u> of specialised cell.
8) In animals, adult stem cells are used to <u>replace damaged cells</u>, e.g. to make new skin cells.

An embryo develops from a fertilised egg cell. Eventually it can become a full organism.

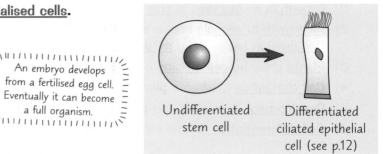

Undifferentiated stem cell → Differentiated ciliated epithelial cell (see p.12)

Meristems Contain Plant Stem Cells

1) <u>Plants</u> have tissues called <u>meristems</u>.
2) Meristems are found in the areas of a plant that are <u>growing</u>, e.g. the tips of the <u>roots and shoots</u>.
3) Meristems produce <u>stem cells</u> that are able to divide and form <u>any cell type</u> in the plant. They can do this <u>for as long as the plant lives</u>.

meristems

Stem Cells Can be Used in Medicine

1) Doctors already use <u>adult stem cells</u> to cure some <u>diseases</u>.
2) Scientists think that <u>embryonic</u> stem cells could be really useful in <u>medicine</u> too.
3) Stem cells can be <u>taken</u> from human embryos and made to <u>differentiate</u> into <u>specialised cells</u>.
4) Stem cells could be used to <u>grow</u> specialised cells to replace <u>damaged</u> tissue in a patient. For example, it might be possible to grow new <u>heart muscle cells</u> to help someone with <u>heart disease</u>.
5) But there are <u>risks</u> with using stem cells that scientists need to learn more about. For example:

- <u>Tumours</u> — the stem cells may <u>divide uncontrollably</u> in the patient and form a <u>tumour</u> (see p.21).
- <u>Infection and disease</u> — the stem cells may contain a <u>virus</u> which could be <u>passed on</u> to the patient.
- <u>Rejection</u> — the patient's <u>immune system</u> (see p.41) may <u>reject</u> (try to <u>fight off</u>) the stem cells.

6) Research using <u>embryonic stem cells</u> raises <u>ethical issues</u>.
7) For example, some people think that human embryos <u>shouldn't</u> be used as each is a <u>potential human life</u>.
8) Others think that <u>curing patients</u> who are <u>suffering</u> is <u>more important</u> than the potential life of embryos.

A merry stem.

Cheery cells, those merry-stems...

Turns out stem cells are pretty clever. Now, let's see if you're specialised to answer this question...

Q1   Give one potential benefit of human stem cells in medicine.   [1 mark]

The Nervous System

The <u>nervous system</u> is what lets you <u>react</u> to what goes on around you, so you'd find life tough without it.

The CNS Coordinates a Response

1) The nervous system is made up of <u>neurones</u> (nerve cells) which go to <u>all parts</u> of the body.

2) The body has lots of <u>sensory receptors</u> — groups of <u>cells</u> that can detect a <u>change in your environment</u> (a <u>stimulus</u>). Different receptors detect <u>different stimuli</u>. E.g. receptors in your <u>eyes</u> detect <u>light</u>.

3) When a <u>stimulus</u> is detected by <u>receptors</u>, the information is <u>converted</u> to a <u>nervous (electrical) impulse</u>.

4) This nervous impulse is sent along <u>sensory neurones</u> to the <u>CNS</u> (the brain and spinal cord).

5) Impulses travel through the CNS along <u>relay neurones</u>.

6) The CNS sends impulses along a <u>motor neurone</u> to an <u>effector</u> (<u>muscle</u> or <u>gland</u>).

7) The effector then <u>responds</u> — e.g. a <u>muscle</u> may <u>contract</u> or a <u>gland</u> may <u>secrete a hormone</u> (see p.52).

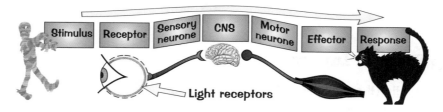

Light receptors

Neurones Transmit Information Rapidly as Electrical Impulses

1) All neurones have a <u>cell body</u>, <u>dendrites</u> or <u>dendrons</u>, and an <u>axon</u>.

2) <u>Dendrites</u> and <u>dendrons</u> are extensions that carry nervous impulses <u>towards</u> the cell body.

3) <u>Axons</u> are extensions that carry nervous impulses <u>away</u> from the cell body.

4) Some axons are surrounded by a <u>myelin sheath</u> (a fatty material). This <u>speeds up</u> the electrical impulse.

5) You need to know the <u>structure</u> and <u>function</u> of <u>sensory</u>, <u>motor</u> and <u>relay</u> neurones.

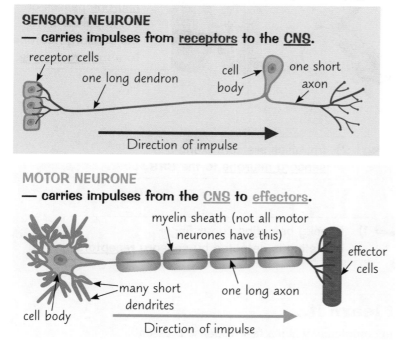

SENSORY NEURONE
— carries impulses from <u>receptors</u> to the <u>CNS</u>.

receptor cells
one long dendron
cell body
one short axon
Direction of impulse

MOTOR NEURONE
— carries impulses from the <u>CNS</u> to <u>effectors</u>.

myelin sheath (not all motor neurones have this)
effector cells
many short dendrites
one long axon
cell body
Direction of impulse

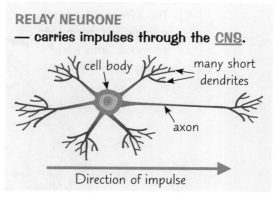

RELAY NEURONE
— carries impulses through the <u>CNS</u>.

cell body
many short dendrites
axon
Direction of impulse

Sensory and relay neurones can also have a myelin sheath.

Don't let the thought of exams play on your nerves...

Make sure you understand how the different parts of the nervous system work together to coordinate a response.

Q1   Describe the structure of a sensory neurone.

[2 marks]

Synapses and Reflexes

Information is passed between neurones <u>really quickly</u>, especially when there's a <u>reflex</u> involved...

Synapses **Connect Neurones**

1) A <u>synapse</u> is where two neurones <u>join together</u>.
2) When an electrical impulse reaches a synapse, chemicals called <u>neurotransmitters</u> move across the <u>gap</u>.
3) The neurotransmitters then set off a <u>new electrical impulse</u> in the <u>next</u> neurone.

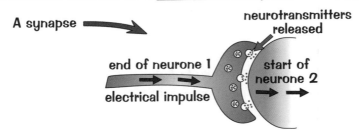

Reflexes Help Prevent Injury

1) <u>Reflexes</u> are <u>automatic</u> (they happen without you <u>thinking</u>).
   This makes them <u>quicker</u> than normal responses.
2) Reflexes help to stop you <u>injuring yourself</u>, e.g. you <u>quickly</u> move your hand if you touch something <u>hot</u>.
3) The passage of information in a reflex (from receptor to effector) is called a <u>reflex arc</u>.
4) The neurones in reflex arcs go through the <u>spinal cord</u> or through an <u>unconscious part of the brain</u> (part of the brain not involved in thinking).
5) Here's an example of how a reflex arc would work if you were <u>stung by a bee</u>:

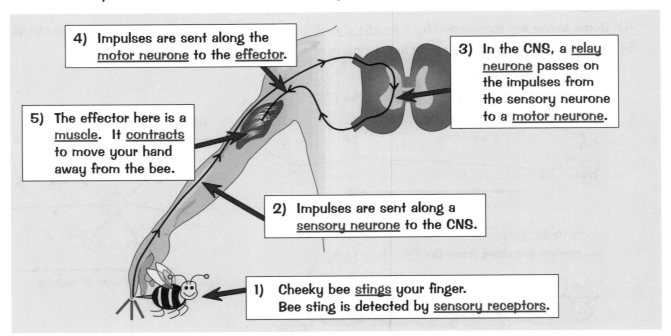

4) Impulses are sent along the <u>motor neurone</u> to the <u>effector</u>.

3) In the CNS, a <u>relay neurone</u> passes on the impulses from the sensory neurone to a <u>motor neurone</u>.

5) The effector here is a <u>muscle</u>. It <u>contracts</u> to move your hand away from the bee.

2) Impulses are sent along a <u>sensory neurone</u> to the CNS.

1) Cheeky bee <u>stings</u> your finger. Bee sting is detected by <u>sensory receptors</u>.

Don't get all twitchy — just learn it...

Q2 Video Solution

Reflexes bypass conscious parts of your brain completely when a fast response is essential.
If you had to stop and think first, you'd end up a lot more sore (or worse).

Q1   What is a reflex action?   [1 mark]

Q2   A chef touches a hot pan. A reflex reaction causes him to immediately move his hand away.
      a) State the effector in this reflex reaction.   [1 mark]
      b) Describe the pathway of the reflex from stimulus to effector.   [4 marks]

Revision Questions for Sections 1 and 2

Here's your chance to check you've learnt all the stuff from Section 1, as well as the stuff from Section 2. Enjoy.

For even more practice, try the Retrieval Quizzes for Sections 1 and 2 — just scan these QR codes!

- Try these questions and <u>tick off each one</u> when you <u>get it right</u>.
- When you're <u>completely happy</u> with a sub-topic, tick it off.

Cells and Specialised Cells (p.11-12) ☑

1) What is the function of the cell membrane?
2) Give three structures found in plant cells but not in animal cells.
3) Name one structure that's found in an animal cell but not in a bacterial cell.
4) What is the function of an egg cell?
5) What does the term 'haploid' mean?
6) What are cilia? What do they do?

Microscopy (p.13-14) ☐

7) What do microscopes do?
8) Give an advantage of electron microscopes over light microscopes.
9) What is the formula for finding the magnification of an object using its image size and real size?
10) Describe how you would convert a measurement from mm to μm.

Enzymes (p.15-17) ☑

11) What part of an enzyme makes it specific to a particular substrate?
12) Which two molecules are produced when lipids are broken down?
13) Explain how temperature affects enzyme activity.
14) A student is investigating how pH affects amylase activity.
    a) What could he do to measure how quickly amylase breaks down starch?
    b) What type of solution could he use to change the pH of the reaction mixture?

Diffusion, Osmosis and Active Transport (p.18-19) ☐

15) Define the term diffusion.
16) When investigating osmosis using potato cylinders in sucrose solution, why might the mass of a potato cylinder increase?

Mitosis, Growth and Stem Cells (p.20-22) ☑

17) Give three uses of mitosis in organisms.
18) Name the four stages of mitosis.
19) What happens during cytokinesis?
20) What major illness can result from uncontrolled cell division?
21) What does it mean if a baby's weight is in the 75th percentile of a growth chart?
22) What is a stem cell?
23) What are meristems? Where are they found?
24) Give one potential risk of using stem cells in medicine.

The Nervous System (p.23-24) ☐

25) Draw and label a motor neurone.
26) What is a synapse?
27) Why are reflexes faster than normal responses?

Sexual Reproduction and Meiosis

Ever wondered how <u>sperm</u> and <u>egg cells</u> are made? Well today's your lucky day.

Sexual Reproduction Involves Gametes

1) <u>Gametes</u> are 'sex cells'. In <u>animals</u> they're <u>sperm</u> and <u>egg</u> cells.

2) During <u>sexual reproduction</u>, an egg and a sperm cell <u>combine</u>.

3) This forms a <u>new cell</u> called a <u>zygote</u>.

4) <u>Gametes</u> only have <u>one copy</u> of each <u>chromosome</u> — this makes them '<u>haploid</u>' cells.

5) Zygotes have <u>two copies</u> of each <u>chromosome</u> — this makes them '<u>diploid</u>' cells.

Flowering plants also have gametes, e.g. pollen contains male gametes.

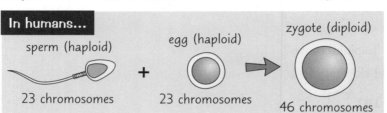

In humans...

sperm (haploid)   +   egg (haploid)   →   zygote (diploid)

23 chromosomes   23 chromosomes   46 chromosomes

6) <u>Two matching copies</u> of a chromosome make a <u>chromosome pair</u>.
So <u>humans</u> have <u>46 chromosomes</u> in <u>23 pairs</u>.

Gametes are Produced by Meiosis

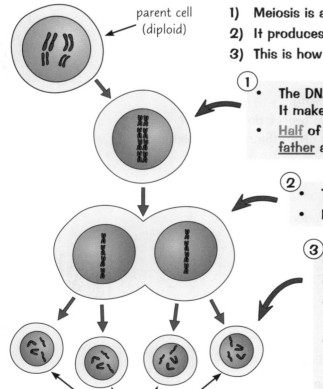

parent cell (diploid)

gametes (haploid)

1) Meiosis is a type of <u>cell division</u>.

2) It produces <u>four gametes</u> from each parent cell.

3) This is how it happens:

① • The DNA in the parent cell is <u>copied</u>.
It makes <u>X-shaped chromosomes</u>.

• <u>Half</u> of the chromosomes have come from the organism's <u>father</u> and half have come from the organism's <u>mother</u>.

② • The cell <u>divides</u>.

• Each new cell gets <u>half</u> of the chromosomes.

③ • Each cell divides <u>again</u>.

• The <u>X-shaped chromosomes</u> are <u>pulled apart</u>.

• You end up with <u>four</u> new <u>daughter cells</u>.
These are the <u>gametes</u>.

• Each gamete is:

  • <u>haploid</u> (has only <u>one copy</u> of each chromosome),

  • <u>genetically different</u> (each has a <u>different mix</u> of the <u>mother's</u> and <u>father's</u> chromosomes).

Now that I have your undivided attention...

Remember — in humans, meiosis only occurs in the reproductive organs.

Q1   Human body cells contain 46 chromosomes each. The graph on the right shows how the mass of DNA per cell changed as some cells divided by meiosis in a human ovary. How many chromosomes were present in each cell when they reached stage 6?   [1 mark]

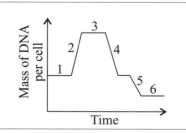

DNA

Reproduction is all about <u>passing on your DNA</u> to the next generation. Time to find out what DNA <u>actually is</u>...

DNA is Made Up of Nucleotides

1) DNA strands are <u>polymers</u>. This means they're made up of lots of <u>repeating units</u> joined together.

2) Each 'unit' is called a <u>nucleotide</u>.

3) Each nucleotide is made of a <u>sugar</u>, a <u>phosphate group</u> and <u>one 'base'</u>.

4) One of <u>four</u> different <u>bases</u> joins to each <u>sugar</u>. The bases are: <u>A</u> (adenine), <u>T</u> (thymine), <u>C</u> (cytosine) and <u>G</u> (guanine).

5) A DNA molecule has <u>two strands coiled together</u>. They make a <u>double helix</u> (a double stranded spiral).

6) Each base <u>links</u> to a base on the opposite strand.

7) A pairs up with T, and C pairs up with G:

This is called <u>complementary base pairing</u>.

8) The complementary base pairs are joined together by <u>weak hydrogen bonds</u>.

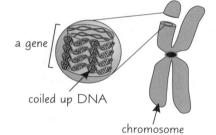

Part of a DNA strand

phosphate — sugar — base — nucleotide

Part of a DNA double helix

strands

base on one strand is joined to a base on the other strand — bases

DNA is Stored as Chromosomes

1) <u>Chromosomes</u> are <u>long</u>, <u>coiled up</u> molecules of <u>DNA</u>.

2) A <u>gene</u> is a <u>section</u> of DNA on a chromosome.

3) Each gene codes for a <u>particular protein</u>.

4) The <u>order</u> of bases in the gene decides <u>what</u> protein is made.

5) An organism's <u>genome</u> is <u>all</u> of its DNA.

a gene — coiled up DNA — chromosome

You Need to Know How to Extract (Remove) DNA From Fruit Cells

Here's how you do it using strawberries:

1) Put some <u>detergent</u> (e.g. washing up liquid) and <u>salt</u> in a beaker.

2) <u>Mash</u> up some <u>strawberries</u> and add them to the <u>beaker</u>.

3) <u>Mix</u> the contents of the beaker well.
   - The <u>detergent</u> will <u>break down</u> the <u>cell membranes</u> to release the DNA.
   - The <u>salt</u> will make the <u>DNA stick together</u>.

4) <u>Filter</u> the mixture to remove the <u>insoluble</u> parts (the parts that <u>won't dissolve</u> — e.g. big bits of cell).

5) Gently add some <u>ice-cold alcohol</u> (ethanol) to the filtered mixture.

6) The DNA will start to come <u>out of solution</u>.

7) It will appear as a <u>stringy white precipitate</u> (a solid).

8) The white precipitate can be carefully fished out with a <u>glass rod</u>.

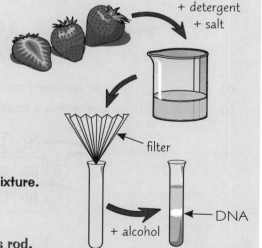

+ detergent + salt

filter

+ alcohol — DNA

My band has a great rhythm section — it has paired basses...

The way that DNA bases pair up together is really important. Make sure you know which base goes with which.

Q1   Why is it useful to use salt when extracting DNA from fruit cells?   [1 mark]

Genetic Diagrams

Genetic diagrams help to predict how characteristics will be passed on from parents to offspring (children).

Different Genes Control Different Characteristics

1) Some characteristics are controlled by a single gene.
2) However, most characteristics are controlled by several genes.

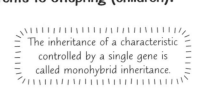

The inheritance of a characteristic controlled by a single gene is called monohybrid inheritance.

All Genes Exist in Different Versions Called Alleles

1) You have two alleles of every gene in your body — one on each chromosome in a pair.
2) If the two alleles are the same, then the organism is homozygous.
3) If the two alleles are different, then the organism is heterozygous.
4) Some alleles are dominant (these are shown with a capital letter on genetic diagrams, e.g. 'C').
   Some alleles are recessive (these are shown by a small letter on genetic diagrams, e.g. 'c').
5) For an organism to show a recessive characteristic, both its alleles must be recessive (e.g. cc).
   But to show a dominant characteristic, only one allele needs to be dominant (e.g. either CC or Cc).
6) The mix of alleles you have is called your genotype.
7) Your alleles determine your characteristics. The characteristics you have is called your phenotype.

Genetic Diagrams Can Show How Characteristics are Inherited

You can use genetic diagrams to show how characteristics are inherited (passed from parents to offspring). For example:

1) An allele that causes hamsters to have superpowers is recessive ("b").
2) Normal hamsters don't have superpowers due to a dominant allele ("B").
3) Two homozygous hamsters (BB and bb) are crossed (bred together).
   A genetic diagram shows what could happen:

A hamster with the genotype BB or Bb will be normal. A hamster with the genotype bb will have superpowers.

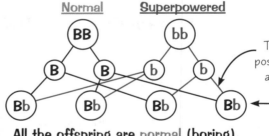

Parents' phenotypes: Normal Superpowered
Parents' genotypes: BB bb

Gametes' genotypes: B B b b
(each gamete just has one allele)

The lines show all the possible ways the parents' alleles could combine.

Offspring's genotypes: Bb Bb Bb Bb

Each offspring must have one allele from each of its parents.

Offspring's phenotypes: All the offspring are normal (boring).

4) A Punnett square is another type of genetic diagram.
5) This Punnett square shows a cross between two heterozygous hamsters (Bb and Bb):

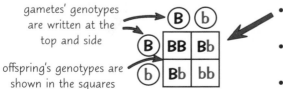

gametes' genotypes are written at the top and side

offspring's genotypes are shown in the squares

	B	b
B	BB	Bb
b	Bb	bb

- There's a 3 in 4 (75%) chance that offspring will be normal.
- There's a 1 in 4 (25%) chance that offspring will have superpowers.
- This gives a 3 normal : 1 superpowers ratio (3:1).

Your meanotype determines how nice you are to your sibling...

Remember, genetic diagrams only tell you probabilities. They don't say what will definitely happen.

Q1 Round peas are caused by the dominant allele, R. The allele for wrinkly peas, r, is recessive.
Using a Punnett square, predict the ratio of plants with round peas to plants with wrinkly peas for a cross between a heterozygous pea plant and a pea plant that is homozygous recessive. [3 marks]

Q1 Video Solution

More Genetic Diagrams

Here's <u>another</u> page of funny diagrams with squares, circles and lines going everywhere.

A Genetic Diagram Can Show Why Males and Females are Created

1) There are <u>23 pairs</u> of chromosomes in every human body cell (see page 26).

2) The <u>23rd pair</u> is labelled <u>XX</u> or <u>XY</u>.

3) They're the two chromosomes that decide your sex (whether you're <u>male</u> or <u>female</u>).

4) Males have an <u>X</u> and a <u>Y</u> chromosome (XY).

5) Females have <u>two X chromosomes</u> (XX).

6) Whether a baby is <u>male</u> or <u>female</u> depends on whether the <u>sperm</u> that <u>fertilises</u> the mother's egg carries an <u>X</u> or a <u>Y</u> chromosome.

7) Here's a <u>genetic diagram</u> to show the chance of having a male or a female child:

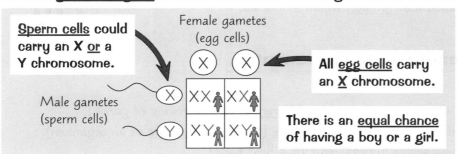

<u>Sperm cells</u> could carry an **X** <u>or</u> a **Y** chromosome.

Female gametes (egg cells)

All <u>egg cells</u> carry an <u>X</u> chromosome.

Male gametes (sperm cells)

There is an <u>equal chance</u> of having a boy or a girl.

The genetic diagram to show how X and Y chromosomes are inherited is similar to a genetic diagram for alleles (on the previous page). It just shows chromosomes rather than different alleles.

Family Pedigrees Can Also Show Genetic Inheritance

1) A <u>family tree</u> can show how <u>genetic disorders</u> are inherited.

2) Here's an example using <u>cystic fibrosis</u> — a genetic disorder of the cell membranes.

Genetic disorders are health conditions. They are often caused by inheriting faulty alleles.

   1) The allele which causes cystic fibrosis is a <u>recessive allele</u>, 'f'.

   2) People with <u>two copies</u> of the 'f' allele (genotype 'ff') will have the disorder.

   3) People with only <u>one copy</u> of the recessive allele (genotype '<u>Ff</u>') <u>won't</u> have the disorder — they're known as <u>carriers</u>.

   4) Below is a <u>family pedigree</u> for a family that includes <u>carriers</u> of <u>cystic fibrosis</u>.

   5) The <u>horizontal lines</u> (—) <u>link parents</u>. The <u>vertical lines</u> (|) link <u>parents</u> to their <u>children</u>.

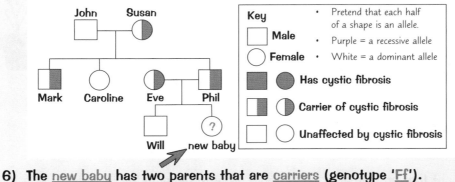

John   Susan

Mark   Caroline   Eve   Phil

Will   new baby

Key
- Pretend that each half of a shape is an allele.
- Purple = a recessive allele
- White = a dominant allele

☐ Male
○ Female

⬛ ⬤ Has cystic fibrosis

◧ ◖ Carrier of cystic fibrosis

☐ ○ Unaffected by cystic fibrosis

unaffected by cystic fibrosis

F   f

F   FF   Ff

f   Ff   ff

carrier of cystic fibrosis

has cystic fibrosis

6) The <u>new baby</u> has two parents that are <u>carriers</u> (genotype '<u>Ff</u>').

7) So, the new baby has a <u>1 in 4 chance</u> of having <u>cystic fibrosis</u>.

Have you got the Y-factor...

That family pedigree makes a nice change from all those other genetic diagrams...

Q1   Cystic fibrosis is caused by a recessive allele, f. The dominant allele is F. The family pedigree on the right shows the inheritance of cystic fibrosis. What is Tamsin's genotype? Use the key above to help you.   [1 mark]

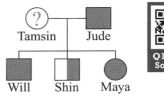

Tamsin   Jude

Will   Shin   Maya

Q1 Video Solution

Variation

There's been a lot of talk about genes in this section. When it comes to variation in organisms though, the environment is also really important. So make sure you don't forget about it.

Organisms of the Same Species Have Differences

1) Different species look... well... different — my dog definitely doesn't look like a daisy.

2) But even organisms of the same species usually look slightly different. E.g.

- All dogs are the same species.
- But different breeds of dog look different from each other.
- For example, a Dalmatian looks quite different to a Pug.

3) These differences are called the variation within a species.

Variation Can be Genetic or Environmental

GENETIC VARIATION

1) Genetic variation within a species is caused by different alleles (versions of genes).

2) Different alleles can lead to differences in phenotype (the characteristics of an organism).

3) Mutations can lead to new alleles in organisms (see next page).

4) Sexual reproduction can also lead to genetic variation in a species. This is because offspring end up with a mix of their mother and father's genes.

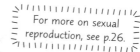
For more on sexual reproduction, see p.26.

5) There tends to be a lot of genetic variation within a population of a species. This is mostly due to mutations .

ENVIRONMENTAL VARIATION

1) Variation within a species is also caused by the environment (the conditions in which organisms live).

2) For example:

A plant grown on a sunny windowsill could grow luscious and green.

The same plant grown in darkness would grow tall and spindly with yellow leaves.

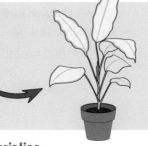

3) These environmental variations in phenotype are also called acquired characteristics.

BOTH

1) Most variation in phenotype is caused by a mixture of genes and the environment.

2) For example:

- The maximum height that an animal or plant could grow to depends on its genes.
- But whether it actually grows that tall depends on its environment (e.g. how much food it gets).

Environmental variation — pretty much sums up British weather...

So, the variation that you see around you is usually caused by a mixture of genes and the environment.
In fact, it's often really tricky to decide which factor is more important.

Q1   Why does sexual reproduction cause genetic variation in a population?   [1 mark]

Section 3 — Genetics

Mutations and The Human Genome Project

Scientists <u>love</u> finding out more about our <u>DNA</u> and all our <u>different alleles</u>. The <u>Human Genome Project</u> got scientists very excited. Some people even called it "more exciting than the first moon landing"...

Genetic Mutations Create Alleles

1) <u>Mutations</u> are changes to the <u>order of bases</u> within DNA.

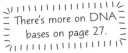
There's more on DNA bases on page 27.

2) When mutations happen within a <u>gene</u> they create an <u>allele</u> (a <u>different version</u> of the gene).

3) <u>Most</u> mutations don't have <u>any effect</u> on the <u>phenotype</u> of an organism.

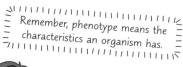
Remember, phenotype means the characteristics an organism has.

4) But <u>some</u> mutations do alter an individual's characteristics <u>slightly</u>. E.g. a mutation might give a hamster <u>long hair</u> instead of <u>short hair</u>.

5) Very <u>rarely</u>, a single mutation will have a <u>big effect</u> on phenotype.

Scientists Found the Position of Over 20 000 Human Genes

1) Thousands of scientists from all over the world worked together on the <u>Human Genome Project</u>.

2) The big idea was to find <u>every single</u> human gene.

3) The project was <u>completed</u> in <u>2003</u>.

4) Now scientists are trying to figure out <u>what</u> all the genes <u>do</u>.

5) This may have many <u>medical</u> benefits. For example:

- It may make it easier to <u>predict</u> and <u>prevent</u> diseases in a person.
- This is because <u>certain genes</u> may make a disease <u>more likely</u> in an individual.

- Genes that cause <u>genetic disorders</u> can be <u>identified</u> in a person.
- A person can then start <u>treatment</u> for the disease at an early stage.

- People with <u>particular genes</u> may <u>react differently</u> to different <u>drugs</u>.
- If a doctor knew what <u>genes</u> a <u>patient</u> had, they'd be able to choose the <u>best drug</u> to suit that <u>individual patient</u>.
- Scientists may also be able to <u>develop better drugs</u> for people with particular genes.

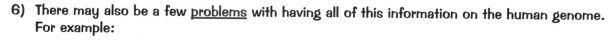

6) There may also be a few <u>problems</u> with having all of this information on the human genome. For example:

- If someone knew that they were <u>more likely</u> to get a disease, it may cause them <u>stress</u>.
- People with <u>genetic problems</u> could come under <u>pressure</u> not to have children.
- It may be <u>harder</u> for people with genetic problems to get <u>jobs</u>.

DNA lipstick is part of my genetic make-up...

The Human Genome Project has resulted in some pretty useful discoveries, but there's still loads of work to do.

Q1   What is meant by a mutation?

[1 mark]

Natural Selection and Evidence for Evolution

Evolution is the <u>slow and continuous change</u> of organisms from one generation to the next.
<u>Charles Darwin</u> came up with the theory of <u>natural selection</u> to explain how <u>evolution</u> happens.

Natural Selection is Sometimes Called "Survival of the Fittest"

1) <u>Selection pressures</u> are things that affect an organism's chance of <u>surviving</u> and <u>reproducing</u>.
2) <u>Predators</u>, <u>competition for resources</u> (e.g. food) and <u>disease</u> are all <u>selection pressures</u>.
3) Individuals in a population show <u>variation</u> in their <u>characteristics</u> because of <u>differences</u> in their <u>genes</u>.
4) Some individuals will have <u>characteristics</u> that make them <u>better adapted</u> to the <u>selection pressures</u> in their environments.
5) These individuals are <u>more likely</u> to <u>survive</u> and <u>reproduce</u> than other individuals in the population.
6) This means that their adaptations are more likely to be <u>passed on</u> to the <u>next generation</u>.
7) The <u>adaptations</u> become more <u>common</u> in the population over time.

Adaptations are characteristics that help an organism survive or reproduce.

You Need to Learn this Example:

1) <u>Antibiotics</u> are drugs that kill <u>bacteria</u>.
2) Bacteria can become <u>resistant to</u> an antibiotic. This means they're <u>not killed</u> by it.
3) Antibiotic resistance <u>spreads</u> through <u>natural selection</u>:

- Bacteria show <u>variation</u> in their characteristics.
  This means that <u>most</u> bacteria <u>won't be resistant</u> to an antibiotic, but <u>a few will</u>.
- A person who is being <u>treated with antibiotics</u> might have <u>resistant bacteria</u> inside them.
- The resistant bacteria are more likely to <u>survive</u> and <u>reproduce</u> than the non-resistant bacteria.
- This leads to antibiotic resistance being <u>passed on</u> to lots of <u>offspring</u>.
- So, antibiotic resistance becomes <u>more common</u> in a population of bacteria <u>over time</u>.

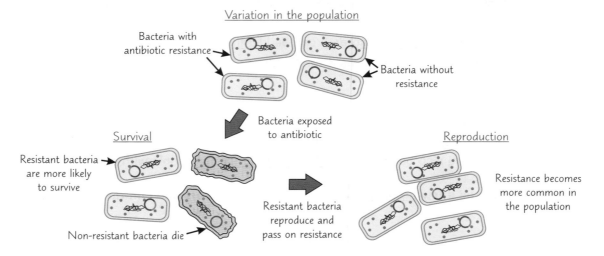

Variation in the population

Bacteria with antibiotic resistance

Bacteria without resistance

Bacteria exposed to antibiotic

Survival

Resistant bacteria are more likely to survive

Non-resistant bacteria die

Resistant bacteria reproduce and pass on resistance

Reproduction

Resistance becomes more common in the population

The Spread of Antibiotic Resistance Provides Evidence for Evolution

1) <u>Antibiotics</u> are a <u>selection pressure</u> for bacteria.
2) <u>Antibiotic resistance</u> is an <u>adaptation</u> to this selection pressure. It's become <u>more common</u> over time.

Natural Selection — sounds like vegan chocolates...

So the evidence for evolution is right under our feet. But you've got to know what you're looking for.

Q1   The sugary nectar in some orchid flowers is found at the end of a long tube behind the flower.
There are moth species with long tongues that can reach the nectar.
Explain how natural selection could have led to the moths developing long tongues.   [4 marks]

Q1 Video Solution

Fossil Evidence for Human Evolution

So, you're about to find out why your great, great, great (plus a lot more greats) grandad would have been a lot better at Go Ape than you...

Fossils Give Us Clues About What Human Ancestors Were Like...

1) A fossil is any trace of an animal or plant that lived a very long time ago.
2) About 6 million years ago, there was a species of ape that doesn't exist today.
3) This ape was an ancestor of both humans and chimps.
4) Fossils have been found that show how humans might have evolved from this ancestor. These fossils are of more recent human ancestors.
5) The more recent human ancestors have characteristics that are in between apes and humans.
6) Here are some examples that you need to know...

> An ancestor is a relative that lived a long time before you, e.g. your grandad's grandad.

'Ardi' is a 4.4 Million Year Old Human Ancestor

Ardi is a fossil from Ethiopia. She is 4.4 million years old.

Ardi's features are a mixture of those found in humans and in apes:

1) The structure of her feet suggests she climbed trees. For example, she had an ape-like big toe to grasp branches.
2) She also had long arms and short legs (more like an ape than a human).
3) Her brain size was about the same as a chimpanzee's.
4) But the structure of her legs suggests that she walked upright like a human.

'Lucy' is Around 3.2 Million Years Old

Lucy is also a fossil from Ethiopia. She is 3.2 million years old.

Lucy also has a mixture of human and ape features, but she is more human-like than Ardi.

1) Lucy's feet were more suitable for walking than climbing.
2) She had no ape-like big toe.
3) The size of her arms and legs was between what you find in apes and humans.
4) Her brain was slightly larger than Ardi's. But it was still similar in size to a chimp's brain.
5) The structure of Lucy's leg bones and feet suggest she was better at walking upright than Ardi.

Leakey and His Team Found 1.6 Million Year Old Fossils

Scientist Richard Leakey and his team discovered fossils of human ancestors in Kenya.

1) One of their finds was Turkana Boy.
2) Turkana Boy is 1.6 million years old.
3) He had a mixture of human and ape-like features, but was more human-like than Lucy.
4) He had short arms and long legs. This is more like a human than an ape.
5) His brain size was much larger than Lucy's. It's similar to a human brain size.
6) The structure of his legs and feet suggest he was even better at walking upright than Lucy.

Section 4 — Natural Selection and Genetic Modification

Fossil Evidence for Human Evolution

Fossils Can be Put on a Timeline to Show Human Evolution

By putting fossils in order of <u>how old</u> they are, you can see how organisms have <u>evolved</u> (changed) <u>over time</u>.
Ardi, Lucy and Turkana Boy have all been put on a <u>timeline</u> here, to show how <u>humans</u> have <u>evolved</u>:

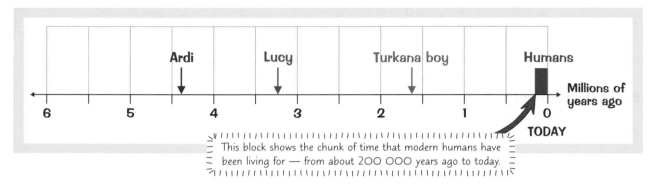

This block shows the chunk of time that modern humans have been living for — from about 200 000 years ago to today.

Stone Tools Also Provide Evidence For Human Evolution

1) <u>More recent</u> human ancestors (from about 2.5 million years ago) started using <u>stone tools</u>.
2) These stone tools gradually became more <u>complex</u>.
3) This shows that their <u>brains</u> must have been getting <u>larger</u>.

You need to think harder to do more complex tasks. So to make more complex tools, our ancestors needed bigger brains that could think better.

Time	Tools
2.5-1.5 million years ago	<u>Simple</u> stone tools called pebble tools. These were made by hitting rocks together to make sharp flakes. These could be used to scrape meat from bones or crack bones open.
2-0.3 million years ago	Rocks were <u>shaped</u> to make more complex tools, such as simple hand-axes. These could be used to hunt, dig, chop and scrape meat from bones.
300 000-200 000 years ago	Even <u>more complex</u> tools. Evidence of flint tools, <u>pointed tools</u> and wooden spears. *Flint is a type of hard rock.*
200 000 years ago-present	<u>Flint tools</u> widely used. <u>Pointed tools</u> including fish hooks, needles and arrowheads.

4) When an ancient <u>stone tool</u> or a <u>fossil</u> is found, there are several ways to work out <u>how old it is</u>:

1) By looking at the <u>features</u> of the tools or fossils.
   E.g. <u>simpler</u> tools are likely to be <u>older</u> than more <u>complex</u> tools.
2) By studying the <u>rock layers</u> they are found in.
   - <u>Older</u> rock layers are normally found <u>below</u> younger layers.
   - So tools or fossils in <u>deeper layers</u> are usually <u>older</u>.

. Dating stone tools or fossils isn't always very accurate, e.g. rock layers can move over time.

Dating fossils — I might have better luck with them...

'Ardi', 'Lucy' and the fossils discovered by Richard Leakey are all key findings in the study of human evolution.
Make sure you learn the key features of these fossils, including their ages, for your exam.

Q1   State one method that can be used to find the age of an ancient stone tool.   [1 mark]

Classification

People really seem to like putting things into groups — biologists certainly do anyway...

Classification is Organising Living Organisms into Groups

1) In the past, organisms were classified according to characteristics you can see (like number of legs).

2) The more similar two organisms appeared, the more closely related they were thought to be.

3) These characteristics were used to classify organisms in the five kingdom classification system.

4) In this system, living things are divided into five groups called kingdoms. These are:

- Animals — fish, mammals, reptiles, etc.
- Plants — grasses, trees, etc.
- Fungi — mushrooms and toadstools, yeasts, all that mouldy stuff on your loaf of bread (yuck).
- Prokaryotes — all single-celled organisms without a nucleus.
- Protists — eukaryotic single-celled organisms, e.g. algae.

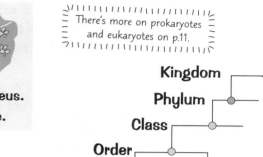

There's more on prokaryotes and eukaryotes on p.11.

5) The kingdoms are then split into smaller and smaller groups.

6) These groups are phylum, class, order, family, genus and species.

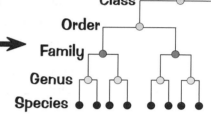

Kingdom
Phylum
Class
Order
Family
Genus
Species

Classification Systems Change Over Time

1) Because of developments in technology, our understanding of things like genetics has increased.

2) For example, we can now work out the sequence of DNA bases in different organisms' genes.

3) The more similar the base sequence of a gene in different organisms, the more closely related they are.

4) This sort of genetic analysis showed that members of the Prokaryote kingdom were LESS closely related than first thought.

5) This led to the development of the three domain classification system.

There's more on DNA on page 27.

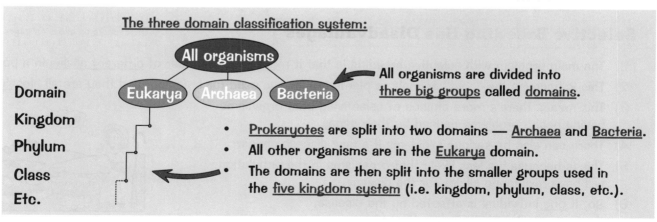

The three domain classification system:

All organisms

Domain — Eukarya Archaea Bacteria

All organisms are divided into three big groups called domains.

Kingdom
Phylum
Class
Etc.

- Prokaryotes are split into two domains — Archaea and Bacteria.
- All other organisms are in the Eukarya domain.
- The domains are then split into the smaller groups used in the five kingdom system (i.e. kingdom, phylum, class, etc.).

Why did the Bacterium break up with the Archaean?

...they didn't have much in common. Biologists have the best jokes. It's strange to think that Archaea and Bacteria, which look really similar, are actually more different than we are to a mushroom.

Q1   What are the names of the three domains in the three domain classification system?   [3 marks]

Selective Breeding

'Selective breeding' sounds like it could be a tricky topic, but it's actually dead simple.

Selective Breeding is Very Simple

1) Selective breeding is when humans choose which plants or animals are going to breed.
2) Organisms are selectively bred to develop features that are useful or attractive. For example:

- Animals that produce more meat or milk.
- Crops with disease resistance.
- Dogs with a good, gentle personality.
- Plants that produce bigger fruit.

This is the basic process involved in selective breeding:
1) From your existing stock, select the ones which have the feature you're after.
2) Breed them with each other.
3) Select the best of the offspring, and breed them together.
4) Continue this process over several generations. Eventually, all offspring will have the feature you want.

This is how we ended up with crops we can eat from plants that were once wild.
It's also how we got farm animals and pets from wild animals.

Here's an Example:

A farmer might want her cattle to produce more meat:

- Genetic variation means some cattle will have better characteristics for producing meat than others, e.g. a larger size.
- The farmer could select the largest cows and bulls and breed them together.
- She could then select the largest offspring and breed them together.
- After several generations, she would get cows with a very high meat yield.

Selective breeding isn't just useful in agriculture. It's used in all sorts of ways — for example, in medical research.

Selective Breeding Has Disadvantages

There's more on alleles on page 28.

1) The main problem with selective breeding is that it reduces the number of different alleles in a population.
2) This is because the "best" animals or plants are always used for breeding, and they are all closely related.
3) This means there's more chance of selectively bred organisms having health problems caused by their genes.
4) There can also be serious problems if a new disease appears.
5) This is because it's less likely that organisms in the population will have resistance alleles for the disease.
6) So, if one individual is affected by the disease, the rest are also likely to be affected.

I use the same genes all the time too — they flatter my hips...

Different breeds of dog came from selective breeding. For example, somebody thought 'I really like this small, yappy wolf — I'll breed it with this other one'. After thousands of generations, we got poodles.

Q1   Explain how you could selectively breed for floppy ears in rabbits.   [4 marks]

Q1 Video Solution

Section 4 — Natural Selection and Genetic Modification

Genetic Engineering

As well as <u>selective breeding</u>, humans can also use <u>genetic engineering</u> to control an organism's features.

Genetic Engineering Involves Changing an Organism's Genome

1) <u>Genetic engineering</u> is used to give organisms <u>new</u> and <u>useful characteristics</u>.
2) It involves <u>cutting a gene</u> out of one organism's genome and <u>putting it into</u> another organism's genome.
3) Organisms that have had a new gene <u>inserted</u> are called <u>genetically modified</u> (GM) organisms.

Remember, an organism's genome is all of its DNA (see p.27).

Genetic Engineering is Useful in Agriculture and Medicine

For example, in <u>agriculture</u> (farming):

1) <u>Crops</u> can be genetically engineered to be <u>resistant to herbicides</u> (chemicals that kill plants).
2) This means that farmers can <u>spray</u> their crops to <u>kill weeds</u>, <u>without</u> affecting the crop itself.
3) This can <u>increase crop yield</u> (the amount of food produced).

Remember, 'resistant to' means 'not killed by'.

In <u>medicine</u>:

1) <u>Bacteria</u> can be genetically engineered to produce <u>human insulin</u>.
2) The bacteria can be grown in <u>large numbers</u>.
3) They can then be used to produce insulin for people with <u>diabetes</u> (see p.56).

But There are Some Concerns About Genetic Engineering

There are <u>concerns</u> about using genetic engineering in <u>animals</u>:

1) It can be hard to <u>predict</u> how changing an animal's genome will affect the animal.
2) Many genetically modified embryos <u>don't survive</u>.
3) Some genetically modified <u>animals</u> also suffer from <u>health problems</u> later in life.

There are also <u>concerns</u> about growing <u>genetically modified crops</u>:

1) <u>Genes</u> used in genetic engineering may get out into the <u>environment</u>. E.g. a herbicide resistance gene may be picked up by <u>weeds</u>, creating a new '<u>superweed</u>' that can't be killed.
2) Some people are worried that GM crops might have a <u>negative effect</u> on <u>food chains</u> or <u>human health</u>.

I say it's great.

If only there was a gene to make revision easier...

Genetically modified (GM) organisms could be very useful. But we don't yet know what all the consequences of using them might be — so make sure you know the arguments for and against them.

Q1   Explain one benefit of being able to genetically engineer herbicide-resistant crops.   [2 marks]

Revision Questions for Sections 3 and 4

A double whammy here — just make sure you can answer
the Section 3 bits before moving on to Section 4.

- Try these questions and <u>tick off each one</u> when you <u>get it right</u>.
- When you're <u>completely happy</u> with a sub-topic, tick it off.

For even more practice, try the Retrieval Quizzes for Sections 3 and 4 — just scan these QR codes!

Sexual Reproduction, Meiosis and DNA (p.26-27) ☐

1) Name the gametes in humans.
2) What does it mean if a cell is haploid?
3) How many daughter cells are produced when a cell divides by meiosis?
4) What is meant by the term 'double helix'?
5) What word is used to describe all of an organism's DNA?
6) When extracting DNA from fruit, why do you mix the fruit with detergent?

Genetic Diagrams (p.28-29) ☑

7) What does it mean if an organism is homozygous for a gene?
8) On a genetic diagram, what are capital letters used for?
9) A person has **XX** chromosomes. What is their sex — male or female?
10) How are carriers shown on a family pedigree?

Variation, Mutations and The Human Genome Project (p.30-31) ☐

11) What is the main cause of genetic variation within a species?
12) What is an acquired characteristic?
13) True or False? Most mutations cause major changes to an organism's phenotype.
14) Give one possible medical benefit of the Human Genome Project.

Natural Selection and Evolution (p.32-34) ☑

15) Describe how organisms evolve by the process of natural selection.
16) How do antibiotic-resistant bacteria provide evidence for evolution?
17) Which fossil is older — "Ardi" or "Lucy"?
18) What age were the fossil discoveries of Richard Leakey?
19) Why do stone tools provide evidence that the brains of human ancestors increased in size over time?

Classification (p.35) ☑

20) Write down all the differences you can think of between the five kingdom classification system and the three domain classification system.
21) Why were prokaryotes split into two different domains?

Selective Breeding and Genetic Engineering (p.36-37) ☑

22) What is selective breeding?
23) Describe the basic process involved in selective breeding.
24) Why does selective breeding make harmful genetic defects more likely?
25) Give one use of genetic engineering in medicine.
26) Give two concerns over genetically modifying animals.

Health and Disease

If you're hoping I'll ease you gently into this new section, no such luck. Straight on to the <u>baddies</u> of biology.

You Need to Know How 'Health' is Defined

1) The <u>World Health Organisation</u> (the <u>WHO</u>) says that:

> "Health is a state of <u>complete physical</u>, <u>mental</u> and <u>social well-being</u>,
> and not merely the absence of disease or infirmity".

Infirmity means weakness or frailness, usually due to old age.

2) This means that even if someone <u>doesn't have any diseases</u>, they might still be <u>unhealthy</u>.
For example, they could have <u>mental health</u> issues.

Diseases Can be Communicable or Non-Communicable

1) <u>Communicable diseases</u> are diseases that can be spread <u>between</u> individuals. See the table below.
2) <u>Non-communicable diseases</u> can't be spread between individuals.
They include things like <u>cancer</u> and <u>heart disease</u>. There's more on these on page 44.
3) If you are affected by <u>one</u> disease, it could make you <u>more susceptible</u> to others.
4) This is because your body may become <u>weakened</u> by the disease,
so it's less able to fight off others.

Being susceptible to a disease, means that you have an increased chance of getting it.

Communicable Diseases are Caused by Pathogens

1) <u>Pathogens</u> are <u>organisms</u> that cause <u>communicable diseases</u>.
2) Pathogens include <u>viruses</u>, <u>bacteria</u>, <u>fungi</u> and <u>protists</u>.
3) You need to know about these <u>communicable diseases</u>:

Protists are single-celled eukaryotes.

Disease	Pathogen	Symptoms/Effects	How it spreads	How to reduce/prevent spread
Cholera 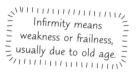	A <u>bacterium</u>.	Diarrhoea.	Via <u>water</u> sources that contain the pathogen.	Make sure that people have <u>clean water supplies</u>.
Tuberculosis	A <u>bacterium</u>.	Coughing and <u>lung damage</u>.	Through the <u>air</u> when infected individuals cough or sneeze.	Infected people should: • <u>avoid crowded public areas</u>, • <u>practise good hygiene</u>, • <u>sleep alone</u>.
Malaria	A <u>protist</u>.	Damage to <u>red blood cells</u> and the <u>liver</u>.	<u>Mosquitoes</u> act as animal <u>vectors</u> (carriers) — they pass on the <u>protist</u> to humans.	Use <u>mosquito nets</u> and <u>insect repellent</u>. These stop mosquitoes from <u>biting</u> people.
Chalara ash dieback	A <u>fungus</u> that infects ash trees.	<u>Leaf loss</u> and <u>bark lesions</u> (wounds).	Carried through the <u>air</u> by the <u>wind</u>.	<u>Remove infected ash trees</u> and <u>replant</u> with different species.

Coughs and sneezes spread diseases...

Yuck, lots of nasties out there that can cause disease. Plants need to be worried too, as you can see.

Q1   Give one way to reduce the spread of cholera.

[1 mark]

STIs

I hope you're not too squeamish... this page is about diseases that can be spread between people during <u>sex</u>.

STIs are Sexually Transmitted Infections

1) <u>STIs</u> are infections that are spread through <u>sexual contact</u>.

2) Sexual contact includes <u>sexual intercourse</u>.

HIV is a Sexually Transmitted Virus

1) Viruses <u>aren't cells</u>.

2) This means that they have to <u>infect living cells</u> in order to <u>reproduce</u>.

3) HIV is the <u>Human Immunodeficiency Virus</u>.

4) It infects and kills <u>white blood cells</u>.

5) White blood cells are part of the body's <u>immune system</u> (see p.41). They help the body to <u>fight disease</u>.

HIV

white blood cell

HIV Eventually Leads to AIDS

1) AIDS is a condition where the <u>immune system</u> becomes <u>very weak</u> and eventually <u>stops working</u>.

2) This means the person is much <u>more likely</u> to get <u>other</u> communicable diseases.

HIV is Spread via Infected Bodily Fluids

1) These <u>bodily fluids</u> include blood, semen and vaginal fluids.

2) One of the main ways to prevent the spread of HIV is to use a <u>condom</u> when having sex.

3) <u>Drug users</u> should also avoid <u>sharing needles</u>.

4) <u>Medication</u> can <u>reduce the risk</u> of an infected individual passing the virus on to others.

5) This means that <u>screening</u> (testing people for HIV) and <u>proper treatment</u> are also important.

Chlamydia is a Sexually Transmitted Bacterial Infection

1) *Chlamydia* are a kind of <u>bacteria</u>. They cause a disease with the same name.

2) The disease Chlamydia doesn't always cause <u>symptoms</u>.
However, it can result in <u>infertility</u>.

Infertility means that a person can't have children.

There are Ways to Reduce the Spread of Chlamydia

The <u>spread</u> of Chlamydia can be <u>reduced</u> by:

• wearing a <u>condom</u> when having sex,

• <u>screening</u> individuals so they can be <u>treated</u> for the infection,

• <u>avoiding sexual contact</u>.

Some STIs, including Chlamydia, are spread by genital contact, not just sexual intercourse.

STIs are no joke...

Condoms are a cheap and effective way of reducing the spread of HIV and Chlamydia, as well as many other STIs. They can also be used to prevent pregnancy (see page 54). Neat.

Q1   What is meant by the term 'STI'?   [1 mark]

Q2   Give two ways of reducing the spread of HIV.   [2 marks]

Fighting Disease

The human body has some pretty neat features when it comes to <u>fighting disease</u>.

Physical and Chemical Barriers Stop Pathogens Entering the Body

PHYSICAL BARRIERS

1) The SKIN

1) Skin <u>stops pathogens</u> getting <u>inside</u> you.
2) If it gets <u>damaged</u>, your blood forms <u>sticky clots</u>. These <u>seal cuts</u> and <u>keep pathogens out</u>.

2) MUCUS and CILIA

1) The <u>airways</u> are lined with <u>mucus</u> and <u>cilia</u>.
2) The mucus catches <u>dust</u> and <u>pathogens</u> before they reach the lungs.
3) The cilia <u>push</u> the <u>gunk-filled mucus</u> up to the <u>back of the throat</u>, where it can be <u>swallowed</u>.

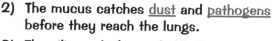

Mucus in your nose is called snot.
Cilia are hair-like structures.

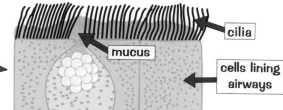

cilia

mucus

cells lining airways

CHEMICAL BARRIERS

1) The EYES

1) The <u>eyes</u> produce a chemical called <u>lysozyme</u>.
2) This <u>kills bacteria</u> on the <u>surface</u> of the eye.

2) The STOMACH

1) The <u>stomach</u> produces <u>hydrochloric acid</u>.
2) This <u>kills</u> most pathogens that are swallowed.

Your Immune System Can Attack Pathogens

1) If pathogens do make it into your body, your <u>immune system</u> kicks in to <u>destroy</u> them.
2) The most important part of your immune system is the <u>white blood cells</u>.
3) <u>Lymphocytes</u> are a type of white blood cell.
4) They are involved in the <u>specific immune response</u> — this is the immune response to a <u>specific pathogen</u>.
5) Here's how it works:

> 1) Every pathogen has <u>unique molecules</u> on its surface called <u>antigens</u>.
> 2) When your lymphocytes come across an antigen on a <u>pathogen</u>, they start to make <u>antibodies</u>.
> 3) Antibodies <u>bind</u> (lock on) to the new <u>pathogen</u>.
> 4) This means the pathogen can be <u>found</u> and <u>destroyed</u> by other white blood cells.
> 5) The antibodies are <u>specific</u> to that pathogen — they won't lock on to any <u>other</u> pathogens.
> 6) Lots of <u>antibodies</u> are then made <u>quickly</u>. They flow all round the body to find all similar <u>pathogens</u>.

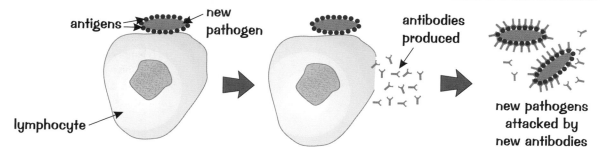

antigens — new pathogen

antibodies produced

lymphocyte

new pathogens attacked by new antibodies

Fight disease — blow your nose with boxing gloves...

The barriers at the top of the page are non-specific. This means they work against different types of pathogens.

Q1   What are lymphocytes?

[1 mark]

Section 5 — Health, Disease and the Development of Medicines

Memory Lymphocytes and Immunisation

Forgive and forget, they always say. Fortunately for us, though, our <u>immune system</u> tends to hold grudges...

Memory Lymphocytes **Make You Immune**

1) When the body is fighting off a new pathogen, it makes <u>antibodies</u> (see previous page).

2) It also makes cells called <u>memory lymphocytes</u>.

3) Memory lymphocytes stay in the body for a <u>long time</u>. They '<u>remember</u>' a <u>specific</u> antigen.

4) If the <u>same pathogen</u> enters the body again, the memory lymphocytes will <u>recognise</u> its <u>antigens</u>.
The memory lymphocytes will then make <u>antibodies</u> against the pathogen.

5) Memory lymphocytes make a person <u>immune</u> to a pathogen.
This means their immune system can <u>respond quickly</u> to a <u>second</u> infection.

6) The <u>secondary response</u> often <u>gets rid</u> of the pathogen
<u>before</u> you begin to show any symptoms.

> A 'secondary response' means it's not the body's first time at fighting the pathogen.

Immunisation **Can Stop You Getting Infections**

1) You can be <u>immunised</u> against some diseases, e.g. measles.

2) <u>Immunisation</u> usually involves injecting <u>dead</u> or <u>inactive</u> pathogens into the body.
Dead or inactive pathogens don't cause you <u>any harm</u>.

3) The pathogens have antigens, so your body makes <u>antibodies</u> to help destroy them.

4) Your body also makes <u>memory lymphocytes</u>.

5) If <u>living pathogens</u> of the same type get into the body, the <u>memory lymphocytes</u>
will quickly make antibodies to help destroy them.

6) This means that you're <u>less likely</u> to get the disease. Cool.

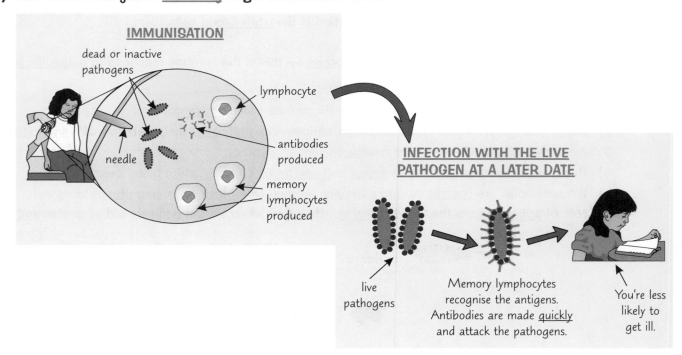

IMMUNISATION

dead or inactive pathogens

lymphocyte

needle

antibodies produced

memory lymphocytes produced

INFECTION WITH THE LIVE PATHOGEN AT A LATER DATE

live pathogens

Memory lymphocytes recognise the antigens. Antibodies are made <u>quickly</u> and attack the pathogens.

You're less likely to get ill.

Take that, you evil antigen...

Make sure you know how immunisation works, including the role of memory lymphocytes.

Q1   Basia is immunised against flu and Cassian isn't. They are both exposed to a flu virus.
Cassian falls ill whereas Basia doesn't. Explain why.   [2 marks]

Q1 Video Solution

Antibiotics and Other Medicines

New medicines are constantly being <u>developed</u>. This little page tells you all about how that happens.

Antibiotics Are Used to Treat Bacterial Infections

1) <u>Antibiotics</u> are drugs that <u>kill bacteria</u>.
2) They work by <u>inhibiting</u> (stopping) <u>processes</u> in <u>bacterial cells</u>.
   For example, they stop <u>cell walls</u> from being built.
3) They <u>don't</u> inhibit processes in cells of the <u>host organism</u> (the organism taking the antibiotic).
4) So antibiotics <u>kill</u> bacterial cells, but <u>not</u> the host cells.
5) Antibiotics <u>don't destroy viruses</u> (e.g. <u>flu</u> or <u>cold</u> viruses).

There Are Several Stages in the Development of New Drugs

1) First a drug has to be <u>discovered</u>. E.g. by finding <u>molecules</u> that could be used to <u>fight</u> a certain <u>disease</u>.
2) Once a possible drug has been <u>discovered</u>, it needs to be <u>developed</u>.
3) This involves <u>preclinical</u> and <u>clinical testing</u>.

Preclinical testing:

1) Drugs are <u>first</u> tested on <u>human cells and tissues</u> in the lab.
2) Next the drug is tested on <u>live animals</u>. This is to <u>find out</u>:
   - if the drug <u>works</u>,
   - how <u>toxic</u> (<u>harmful</u>) it is,
   - the <u>dose</u> at which it <u>works best</u>.

Clinical testing:

1) If the drug <u>passes</u> the tests on animals then it's tested on <u>human volunteers</u> in a <u>clinical trial</u>.
2) First, the drug is tested on <u>healthy volunteers</u>. This is to make sure that it doesn't have any <u>harmful side effects</u> when the body is working <u>normally</u>.
3) If these results are <u>good</u>, the drugs can be tested on people with the <u>illness</u>.
4) To test how well the drug works, patients are put into <u>two groups</u>...

> Group 1 is given the <u>new drug</u>.

> Group 2 is given a <u>placebo</u> (a substance that's like the drug being tested but doesn't do anything).

5) The doctor <u>compares</u> the two groups of patients to see if the <u>drug</u> makes a <u>real difference</u>.
6) Clinical trials are <u>blind</u> — the patient <u>doesn't know</u> whether they're getting the drug or the placebo.
7) In fact, they're often <u>double-blind</u> — neither the <u>patient nor the doctor</u> knows who's taken the drug and who's taken the placebo until all the results have been gathered.
8) This is so the doctors <u>studying</u> the results aren't <u>influenced</u> by their knowledge.

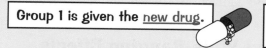
After clinical testing, the results need to be looked at by a medical agency (a group of medical experts). The agency decides whether or not the drug can be used to treat patients.

It was SO funny when my auntie married Mr Biotic...

Testing, retesting and then...yep, more testing. You'd know all about that anyway, it's just like being in school...

Q1   Explain how a double-blind trial would be carried out.   [2 marks]

Non-Communicable Diseases

Non-communicable diseases <u>aren't caused by pathogens</u>. Instead, there are <u>risk factors</u> associated with them.

Lifestyle Factors May Increase the Risk of a Non-Communicable Disease

1) Some people are more <u>at risk</u> than others of developing <u>certain diseases</u>.

2) Anything that <u>increases</u> a person's <u>chance</u> of getting a disease is called a <u>risk factor</u>.

3) Risk factors for a disease can be things a person <u>can't change</u>, e.g. their age.

4) But they can also be <u>lifestyle factors</u>, which a person <u>can change</u>. For example:

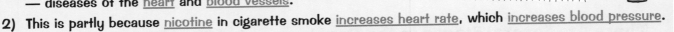

See page 46 for more on cardiovascular disease and how it is caused.

Smoking

1) Smoking is a <u>big risk factor</u> for <u>cardiovascular disease</u> — diseases of the <u>heart</u> and <u>blood vessels</u>.

2) This is partly because <u>nicotine</u> in cigarette smoke <u>increases heart rate</u>, which <u>increases blood pressure</u>.

3) <u>High blood pressure</u> can damage the <u>heart</u> and <u>blood vessels</u> and cause <u>disease</u>.

Diet and Exercise

1) A diet with <u>too many</u> or <u>too few nutrients</u> can lead to a condition called <u>malnutrition</u>. Malnutrition can cause many different <u>health problems</u>.

2) Having a diet <u>high</u> in <u>fat</u> and <u>sugar</u> is a risk factor for <u>obesity</u>. So is not getting enough <u>exercise</u>.

Alcohol

1) Drinking too much <u>alcohol</u> increases the risk of <u>liver disease</u>, e.g. <u>cirrhosis</u> (scarring of the liver).

2) This is because the liver <u>breaks down</u> alcohol, and some of the products can <u>damage liver tissue</u>.

Non-Communicable Diseases Have Many Risk Factors

1) Many <u>non-communicable</u> diseases are caused by <u>several different</u> risk factors <u>interacting</u> (working together).

2) For example, the risk of developing cardiovascular disease can be <u>increased</u> by all of <u>these factors</u>:

<u>smoking</u>   too much <u>alcohol</u>   <u>not enough exercise</u>   a diet <u>high</u> in saturated <u>fat</u>   being <u>obese</u>

3) Other diseases caused by several risk factors include <u>cancer</u>, <u>liver diseases</u>, <u>lung diseases</u> and <u>obesity</u>.

Non-Communicable Diseases Can Have Wide-Ranging Effects

Non-communicable diseases can have effects at <u>local</u>, <u>national</u> and <u>global</u> levels. For example:

1) <u>LOCAL</u> — in areas where there are high levels of <u>smoking</u>, there's likely to be a lot of <u>cardiovascular disease</u>. This can put <u>pressure</u> on <u>local hospitals</u>.

2) <u>NATIONAL</u> — people with non-communicable diseases may not be able to <u>work</u>. If there are lots of people in a country who can't work, it can <u>affect</u> the amount of <u>money</u> in the country. It also <u>costs</u> a lot of <u>money</u> to <u>treat people</u> who have non-communicable diseases.

3) <u>GLOBAL</u> — non-communicable diseases are <u>very common</u> and affect people all over the world. For example, <u>cardiovascular disease</u> is the <u>number one</u> cause of death <u>worldwide</u>.

Best put down that cake and go for a run...

You may be given data about risk factors in the exam — see p.9 for how you can draw conclusions using data.

Q1   Give one example of a lifestyle factor that increases the risk of cardiovascular disease.   [1 mark]

Measures of Obesity

People come in all sorts of <u>shapes</u> and <u>sizes</u> — this page tells you how doctors <u>work out</u> if a person is <u>obese</u>.

A Body Mass Index Helps to Show If You're Under- or Overweight

1) The <u>Body Mass Index</u> (<u>BMI</u>) is used as a guide to help decide whether someone is <u>underweight</u>, of <u>healthy weight</u>, <u>overweight</u> or <u>obese</u>.

2) It's calculated from their <u>height</u> and <u>mass</u>. This is the formula:

$$BMI = \frac{mass\ (kg)}{(height\ (m))^2}$$

3) This table shows how different BMI values are <u>classified</u>. The ranges used depend on the person's ethnicity.

	Underweight	Healthy Weight	Overweight	Obese
People of white heritage	BMI of below 18.5	BMI of 18.5 - 24.9	BMI of 25 - 29.9	BMI of 30 or over
People in black, Asian or certain other minority ethnic groups	BMI of below 18.5	BMI of 18.5 - 22.9	BMI of 23 - 27.4	BMI of 27.5 or over

People in black, Asian or certain other minority ethnic groups are at a higher risk of obesity-related health problems at a lower BMI.

EXAMPLE
Calculate the BMI of a person of white heritage who has a mass of 63.0 kg and is 1.70 m tall. Is this person overweight?

1) Put the numbers you've been given into the formula. You need to square the number for height.

$$BMI = \frac{mass\ (kg)}{(height\ (m))^2} = \frac{63.0}{(1.70^2)}$$

2) Round your answer to the same number of significant figures that were used in the question (see p.6).

$$= 21.799... = 21.8\ kg\ m^{-2}$$

3) Find where the BMI you have calculated lies in the table above. Read the weight description.

This person is not overweight — their BMI lies between 18.5 and 24.9 (the healthy weight range).

A Waist-to-Hip Ratio Can Also Be Used

$$waist\text{-}to\text{-}hip\ ratio = \frac{waist\ circumference}{hip\ circumference}$$

Make sure both are in the same units (e.g. in cm)

The <u>circumference</u> of a person's waist or hips is the distance right round their body at that point.

EXAMPLE
A woman has a waist measurement of 29 cm and a hip measurement of 36 cm. Find her waist-to-hip ratio.

$$waist\text{-}to\text{-}hip\ ratio = \frac{waist\ circumference\ (cm)}{hip\ circumference\ (cm)} \begin{array}{l} = 29 \div 36 \\ = 0.81 \end{array}$$

1) <u>Abdominal obesity</u> is when you have too much weight around your tummy.

2) A <u>man</u> with a waist-to-hip ratio <u>above 1.0</u> has abdominal obesity.

3) A <u>woman</u> with a ratio <u>above 0.85</u> has abdominal obesity.

4) A person with abdominal obesity has a <u>bigger risk</u> of developing <u>health problems</u> — for example, <u>type 2 diabetes</u> (see p.56).

Body Mass Index? My cat uses a 'Chonk Chart'...

Seriously though, obesity is a major health issue. BMI and waist-to-hip ratios might not be perfect but they do provide a good guide for helping people know when it's time to lose weight.

Q1 Video Solution

Q1 A person of Asian ethnicity has a mass of 76.0 kg and has a height of 1.62 m.
   a) Calculate the person's BMI. [1 mark]
   b) Use the table above to find the weight description of the person. [1 mark]

Treatments for Cardiovascular Disease

Cardiovascular disease is a big, big problem in the UK. The good news is there are lots of ways to treat it.

Cardiovascular Disease Affects Your Heart and Blood Vessels

1) Cardiovascular disease (CVD) is any disease to do with your heart and blood vessels.
2) Too much cholesterol (a fatty substance) in the blood can cause fatty deposits to build up in arteries (a type of blood vessel).
3) This reduces blood flow.
4) Blood vessels can become damaged, e.g. by high blood pressure.
5) The damage can cause blood clots to form.
6) These can block blood flow completely.
7) If blood flow to the heart muscles is blocked, it can cause a heart attack.
8) If blood flow to the brain is blocked, it can cause a stroke.

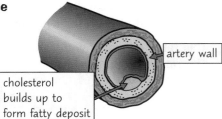

cholesterol builds up to form fatty deposit

artery wall

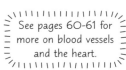

See pages 60-61 for more on blood vessels and the heart.

Lifestyle Changes Can be Used to Treat CVD

1) People with CVD may be encouraged to eat a healthy, balanced diet. The diet should be low in saturated fat.
2) They may also be encouraged to: → • exercise regularly • lose weight if necessary • stop smoking
3) Lifestyle changes are often recommended before other forms of treatment. This is because they don't really have any downsides.

Some Drugs Can Reduce the Risk of a Heart Attack or Stroke

1) Some people may need to take medicines to treat CVD for the rest of their lives.
2) Here are some examples:

- Statins — reduce the amount of cholesterol in the bloodstream.
- Anticoagulants — make blood clots less likely to form.
- Antihypertensives — reduce blood pressure.

3) All of these medicines can have negative side effects, e.g. antihypertensives can cause fainting.

Surgery is Sometimes Needed to Repair Damage

1) Here are some examples of things surgeons can do to treat CVD:

- Put in stents — these are tubes that are inserted inside arteries. Stents keep arteries open. This lets blood flow to the heart muscles.
- Coronary bypass surgery — a healthy blood vessel is put into the heart. This lets blood flow around a blocked artery.
- A heart transplant — the whole heart is replaced with a donor heart (a heart from another person).

2) Surgery is risky. For example, there's a risk the person could get an infection or lose a lot of blood.

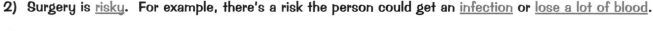

Look after yerselves me hearties...

Make sure you're aware of the drawbacks of each treatment for cardiovascular disease, as well as the advantages.

Q1   Why might surgery be the last thing a doctor wants to recommend to a patient with CVD?   [2 marks]

Section 5 — Health, Disease and the Development of Medicines

Photosynthesis

Photosynthesis is one the most important reactions on Earth. Here's a whole page on it...

Plants and Algae Make Their Own Food by Photosynthesis

1) During photosynthesis, energy from the Sun is used to make glucose (a type of sugar).

2) Some of the glucose is used to make larger molecules that the plants or algae need to grow. These molecules make up the organism's biomass. Biomass means 'the mass of living material'.

3) When an animal eats a plant, the energy in the plant's biomass is passed on to the animal. When this animal is eaten by other animals, energy gets passed up the food chain.

4) So, plants and algae are really important — they produce food for nearly all life on Earth.

5) This is the equation for photosynthesis:

carbon dioxide + water $\xrightarrow{\text{LIGHT}}$ glucose + oxygen

Photosynthesis happens inside chloroplasts (see p.11). These contain chlorophyll, which absorbs light.

6) Photosynthesis is an endothermic reaction — this means that energy is taken in during the reaction.

7) These three things can all affect the rate of photosynthesis:

- Light intensity — photosynthesis gets faster as light intensity (the strength of light) increases.
- Carbon dioxide — photosynthesis gets faster as carbon dioxide concentration increases.
- Temperature — photosynthesis gets faster as temperature increases, but only up to a certain temperature. If it gets too hot, photosynthesis slows down and can stop all together.

8) These factors are known as limiting factors — they can stop photosynthesis from happening any faster.

Light Intensity Can Affect the Rate of Photosynthesis

PRACTICAL

Pondweed can be used to investigate the rate of photosynthesis. Here's how:

1) The apparatus is set up as shown in the diagram.

2) A light is placed at a set distance from the pondweed.

3) The oxygen (O_2) produced in photosynthesis collects in the gas syringe.

4) The volume of O_2 produced in a set time is measured.

5) The whole experiment is repeated with the light at different distances from the pondweed. The further away the light, the lower the intensity of light reaching the pondweed.

6) The rate of oxygen production at each distance is then calculated.

7) For this experiment, any variables that could affect the results should be controlled. E.g.:

- Temperature — You can use a water bath to control this.
- Carbon dioxide concentration — you can control this by adding a set amount of sodium hydrogencarbonate to a set volume of water (in the flask). Sodium hydrogencarbonate releases carbon dioxide.

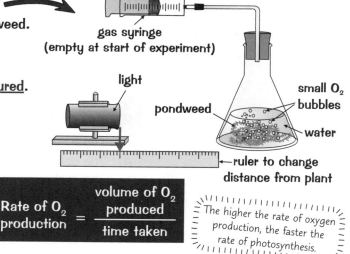

gas syringe
(empty at start of experiment)

light

pondweed

small O_2 bubbles

water

ruler to change distance from plant

$$\text{Rate of } O_2 \text{ production} = \frac{\text{volume of } O_2 \text{ produced}}{\text{time taken}}$$

The higher the rate of oxygen production, the faster the rate of photosynthesis.

You can also investigate the rate of photosynthesis with algal balls instead of pondweed. These are little balls of jelly which contain algae.

I'm working on sunshine — woah oh...

You could also measure how much oxygen is produced by counting the bubbles (but it's a less accurate method).

Q1   State three limiting factors of photosynthesis.

[3 marks]

Transport in Plants

Plants need to move stuff around <u>inside them</u>. Flowering plants have <u>two types</u> of <u>transport tube</u> — <u>xylem</u> and <u>phloem</u>. Both types of tube go to <u>every part</u> of the plant, but they are totally <u>separate</u>.

Root Hairs Take In Minerals and Water

1) The cells on the <u>surface</u> of <u>plant roots</u> grow into "<u>hairs</u>". These <u>stick out</u> into the soil.
2) Each branch of a root has <u>millions</u> of these hairs.
3) This gives the plant a <u>large surface area</u> for absorbing <u>water</u> and <u>mineral ions</u> from the soil.
4) Mineral ions are absorbed by <u>active transport</u> (see p.18).
5) Water is absorbed by <u>osmosis</u> (see p.18).

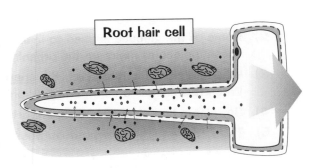

Root hair cell

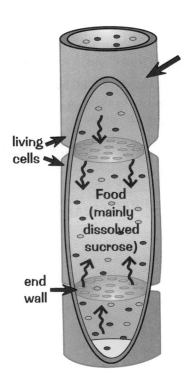

living cells

Food (mainly dissolved sucrose)

end wall

Phloem Tubes Transport Food

1) Phloem tubes are made of <u>living cells</u>.
2) There are <u>end walls</u> between the cells.
3) These end walls have small <u>holes</u> to allow stuff to <u>flow through</u>.
4) Plants make <u>food substances</u> in their <u>leaves</u>.
5) Phloem tubes transport these <u>food substances</u> (mainly <u>sucrose</u>) around the plant.
6) This process is called <u>translocation</u>.
7) Translocation uses <u>energy</u> from respiration (see p.63).

Sucrose is a type of sugar.

Xylem Tubes Take Water UP

1) Xylem tubes are made of <u>dead cells</u>.
2) There is a <u>hole</u> down the middle of the dead cells.
3) There are <u>no</u> end walls between the cells.
4) The cells contain a material called <u>lignin</u>. This makes them <u>stronger</u>.
5) Xylem tubes carry <u>water</u> and <u>mineral ions</u> from the <u>roots</u> to the <u>stem</u> and <u>leaves</u>.
6) The movement of water <u>from</u> the <u>roots</u>, <u>through</u> the <u>xylem</u> and <u>out</u> of the <u>leaves</u> is called the <u>transpiration stream</u> (see next page).

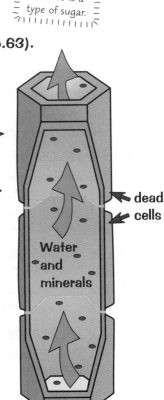

dead cells

Water and minerals

Don't let revision stress you out — just go with the phloem...

Phloem tubes transport substances in any direction around a plant. Xylem tubes only transport things upwards.

Q1   Describe the structure of phloem tubes. [3 marks]

Transpiration and Stomata

Make sure you understand all about <u>root hairs</u> and <u>xylem tubes</u> from the previous page.
The <u>transpiration stream</u> joins up the roots, xylem and leaves. Read on for more...

Transpiration is the Loss of Water from the Plant

1) Transpiration is caused by the <u>evaporation</u> and <u>diffusion</u> of water from a plant's surface (mainly the leaves).

2) Here's how it happens:

Evaporation is when water turns from a liquid into a gas. See page 18 for more on diffusion.

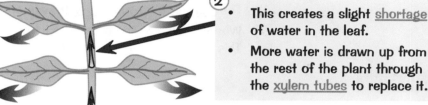

① Water <u>evaporates</u> from the leaves and <u>diffuses</u> into the air.

② • This creates a slight <u>shortage</u> of water in the leaf.
   • More water is drawn up from the rest of the plant through the <u>xylem tubes</u> to replace it.

③ This in turn means more water is drawn up from the <u>roots</u>.

3) So there's a constant <u>stream of water</u> through the plant. This is called the <u>transpiration stream</u>.

4) The transpiration stream carries <u>mineral ions</u> that are dissolved in the water along with it.

Stomata are Involved in Transpiration

1) Stomata are <u>tiny pores</u> (holes) on the surface of a plant.

2) They're mostly found on the <u>lower surface</u> of <u>leaves</u>.

3) Stomata can <u>open</u> and <u>close</u>.

4) When they are open, <u>carbon dioxide</u> and <u>oxygen</u> can <u>diffuse</u> in and out of a leaf. <u>Water vapour</u> can also diffuse <u>out</u> of the leaf during <u>transpiration</u>.

Remember, plants need to take in carbon dioxide for photosynthesis.

5) This is how stomata open and close:

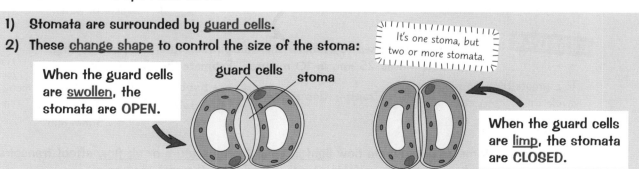

1) Stomata are surrounded by <u>guard cells</u>.
2) These <u>change shape</u> to control the size of the stoma:

It's one stoma, but two or more stomata.

When the guard cells are <u>swollen</u>, the stomata are OPEN.

guard cells   stoma

When the guard cells are <u>limp</u>, the stomata are CLOSED.

I say stomaaarta, you say stomaaayta...

Remember, stomata are the little holes between guard cells, not the guard cells themselves. When the stomata are open, water vapour can escape from the leaf. This gets the whole transpiration stream moving.

Q1   Describe how stomata allow transpiration to happen.   [1 mark]

Transpiration Rate

This page is about the factors that affect transpiration <u>rate</u> (the <u>speed</u> of transpiration). During transpiration, water is taken up by a plant — so a faster rate of <u>transpiration</u> means a faster rate of <u>water uptake</u>.

Transpiration Rate is Affected by These Factors:

LIGHT INTENSITY

1) The <u>brighter</u> the light, the <u>faster</u> transpiration happens.
2) <u>Stomata close</u> as it gets darker. This is because photosynthesis can't happen in the dark, so stomata don't need to be open to let <u>carbon dioxide</u> in.
3) When the stomata are <u>closed</u>, very little water can <u>escape</u>.

TEMPERATURE

1) The <u>warmer</u> it is, the <u>faster</u> transpiration happens.
2) When it's warm, the water particles in the leaf have <u>more energy</u>. This means they move out of the stomata <u>more quickly</u>.

AIR FLOW

1) The <u>more windy</u> it is, the <u>faster</u> transpiration happens.
2) <u>Fast</u> moving air means that water vapour around the leaf is <u>swept away</u>.
3) This means there's a <u>higher concentration</u> of water vapour <u>inside</u> the leaf compared to <u>outside</u>. So water vapour moves <u>out</u> of the leaf quickly by <u>diffusion</u> (see p.18).

You Can Estimate Transpiration Rate

1) A <u>potometer</u> is a special piece of equipment.
2) You can use a <u>potometer</u> to <u>estimate transpiration rate</u>.
3) Here's what you do:

- Set up the equipment as in the diagram.
- Record the <u>starting position</u> of the <u>air bubble</u>.
- Start a <u>stopwatch</u>.
- As the plant takes up water, the air bubble gets <u>sucked</u> along the tube.
- Record <u>how far</u> the air bubble moves in a <u>set time</u>.
- Then you can <u>estimate</u> the <u>transpiration rate</u>.

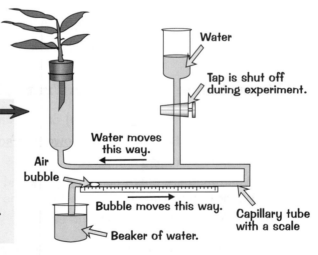

Water

Tap is shut off during experiment.

Water moves this way.

Air bubble

Bubble moves this way.

Capillary tube with a scale

Beaker of water.

EXAMPLE

A potometer was used to estimate the transpiration rate of a plant cutting. The bubble moved 25 mm in 10 minutes. Estimate the transpiration rate.

To estimate the <u>transpiration rate</u>, divide the <u>distance</u> the bubble moved by the <u>time taken</u>.

$$\text{Transpiration rate} = \frac{\text{distance bubble moved}}{\text{time taken}} = \frac{25 \text{ mm}}{10 \text{ min}}$$
$$= 2.5 \text{ mm min}^{-1}$$

mm min^{-1} means the same as mm/min.

4) You can use a potometer to estimate how <u>light intensity</u>, <u>temperature</u> or <u>air flow</u> affect transpiration rate. Just remember to <u>only change one variable at a time</u> and keep the rest <u>the same</u>.

So, blowing on a plant makes it thirsty...?

Sunny, warm and windy — the perfect conditions for transpiration and for hanging out your washing.

Q1 A student is using a potometer to estimate the transpiration rate of a plant cutting.
    a) The bubble moved 48 mm in 20 minutes. Estimate the transpiration rate.   [1 mark]
    b) Explain how light intensity affects the rate of transpiration through a plant.   [3 marks]

Q1 Video Solution

51

Revision Questions for Sections 5 and 6

Well there you go. Some nasty stuff on <u>diseases</u>,
followed by some lovely(ish) stuff on <u>plants</u>.

- Try these questions and <u>tick off each one</u> when you <u>get it right</u>.
- When you're <u>completely happy</u> with a sub-topic, tick it off.

For even more practice, try the Retrieval Quizzes for Sections 5 and 6 — just scan these QR codes!

Health, Disease and STIs (p.39-40)

1) Explain why being healthy doesn't just mean not being sick.
2) What is a 'non-communicable' disease?
3) How can the spread of malaria be prevented?
4) How can the spread of Chlamydia be reduced?
5) What is AIDS?

Fighting Disease (p.41-42)

6) Give two types of chemical barriers that prevent pathogens from infecting humans.
7) What is an antigen?
8) What does a lymphocyte do when it recognises a pathogen?
9) How does immunisation prepare the immune system against infection by a particular pathogen?

Antibiotics and Other Medicines (p.43)

10) Which type of pathogen can antibiotics be used to kill?
11) What is a placebo?

Non-Communicable Diseases (p.44-46)

12) Describe how smoking can increase the risk of cardiovascular diseases.
13) Give a risk factor related to lifestyle for the development of liver disease.
14) Write the equation for finding the body mass index of an individual.
15) Give three examples of lifestyle changes that can help to prevent cardiovascular disease.

Photosynthesis (p.47)

16) Name the sugar produced in photosynthesis.
17) What does 'biomass' mean?
18) Write out the equation for photosynthesis.
19) Why is photosynthesis described as an endothermic reaction?
20) What does it mean if something is a 'limiting factor' of photosynthesis?
21) Describe how you could investigate the effect of light intensity on the rate of photosynthesis.

Transport in Plants, Stomata and Transpiration (p.48-50)

22) Name two things that root hair cells take in from the soil.
23) What happens in translocation?
24) Describe the structure of xylem tubes.
25) Describe the movement of water in the transpiration stream.
26) What are stomata?
27) Give three factors that affect the rate of transpiration.
28) Describe how you could use a potometer to estimate the rate of transpiration.

Section 6 — Plant Structures and Their Functions

Hormones

As well as nervous impulses (see page 23), hormones are another way of communicating across the body.

Hormones Are Chemical Messengers Sent in the Blood

1) Hormones are chemicals released by glands.

2) These glands are called endocrine glands. They make up your endocrine system.

3) Hormones are carried in the blood to other parts of the body.

4) They only affect particular cells in particular organs (called target organs).

5) These are the endocrine glands you need to know:

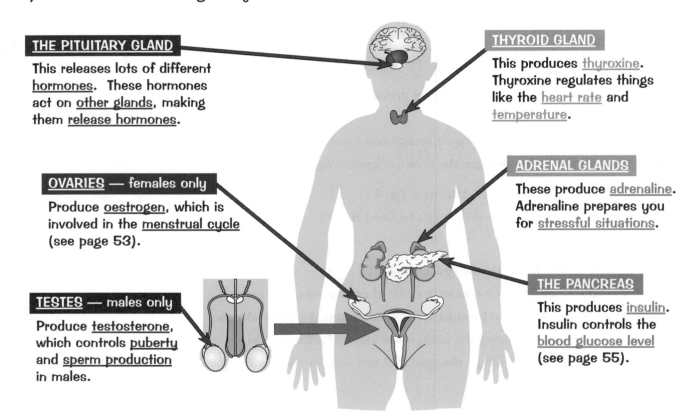

THE PITUITARY GLAND
This releases lots of different hormones. These hormones act on other glands, making them release hormones.

OVARIES — females only
Produce oestrogen, which is involved in the menstrual cycle (see page 53).

TESTES — males only
Produce testosterone, which controls puberty and sperm production in males.

THYROID GLAND
This produces thyroxine. Thyroxine regulates things like the heart rate and temperature.

ADRENAL GLANDS
These produce adrenaline. Adrenaline prepares you for stressful situations.

THE PANCREAS
This produces insulin. Insulin controls the blood glucose level (see page 55).

Hormones and Neurones Have Differences

NEURONES:

Very FAST action.
Act for a very SHORT TIME.
Act on a very PRECISE AREA.

HORMONES:

SLOWER action.
Act for a LONG TIME.
Act in a more GENERAL way.

Nerves, hormones — no wonder revision makes me tense...

Hormones control many different organs and cells in the body. They tend to control things that aren't immediately life-threatening (so things like sexual development, blood glucose level, etc.).

Q1   Name the endocrine glands that only males have.   [1 mark]

The Menstrual Cycle

The menstrual cycle is the <u>monthly</u> release of an <u>egg</u> from a woman's <u>ovaries</u>.
It's also the <u>build-up</u> and <u>breakdown</u> of the protective lining in the <u>uterus</u> (womb).

The Menstrual Cycle Has Four Stages

<u>Stage 1</u> — Day 1 is when <u>menstruation</u> (bleeding) <u>starts</u>. The lining of the uterus breaks down and is released.

<u>Stage 2</u> — The <u>uterus lining</u> is <u>built up</u> from day 4 to day 14.
It becomes a thick spongy layer full of blood vessels. It's now ready for a fertilised egg to implant there.

<u>Stage 3</u> — An <u>egg develops</u> and is <u>released</u> from the ovary at about day 14. This is <u>ovulation</u>.

<u>Stage 4</u> — The <u>lining</u> is then <u>maintained</u> (kept thick) until day 28.

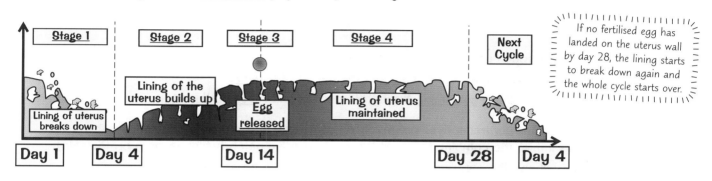

If no fertilised egg has landed on the uterus wall by day 28, the lining starts to break down again and the whole cycle starts over.

The Menstrual Cycle is Controlled by Hormones

Oestrogen

1) Released by the <u>ovaries</u>.
2) Causes the lining of the uterus to <u>thicken</u> and <u>grow</u>.
3) A <u>high level</u> stimulates the release of a hormone which causes <u>ovulation</u>.

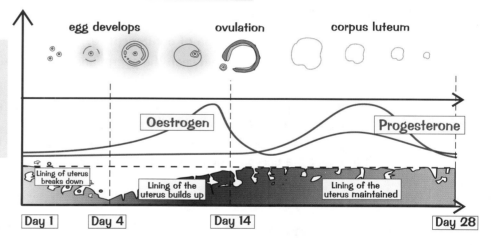

Progesterone

1) Released by the <u>corpus luteum</u> after ovulation.
2) <u>Maintains</u> the lining of the uterus.

After ovulation, the structure that the egg developed in is called a <u>corpus luteum</u>.

3) <u>Prevents</u> the release of hormones which cause egg development and ovulation.
4) When the level of progesterone <u>falls</u> (and there's a low oestrogen level) the uterus lining <u>breaks down</u>.
5) If a fertilised egg implants in the uterus, then the level of <u>progesterone</u> will <u>stay high</u>.
6) This <u>maintains</u> the lining of the uterus during pregnancy.

Remember, oestrogen is said EEEstrogen...

...a bit like <u>Easter</u> — which is when you get <u>eggs</u>. And <u>oestrogen</u> helps to stimulate the <u>release</u> of eggs. Ta-dah!
That might help you remember at least one of these pesky hormones.

Q1   Describe the role of progesterone in the menstrual cycle.   [2 marks]

Contraception

Hormones can be used to stop women from becoming pregnant.

Contraceptives are Things That Prevent Pregnancy

Women Can Take Hormones to Prevent Pregnancy

1) The hormones that control the menstrual cycle (see p.53) can be used in contraceptives. For example:

- Oestrogen helps to stimulate the release of eggs.
- But if oestrogen levels are kept high for a long time, egg development stops.
- So oestrogen can be used to stop an egg being released.

- Progesterone can be used to reduce fertility in several ways.
- For example, it makes the mucus in the cervix very thick.
- This stops sperm swimming through the cervix and reaching the egg.

The cervix is the opening to the uterus.

2) Some hormonal contraceptives contain both oestrogen and progesterone — for example, the combined pill and the contraceptive patch (which is worn on the skin).

3) The mini-pill and the contraceptive injection only contain progesterone.

The combined pill and the mini-pill are both oral contraceptives — that means that they're taken through the mouth.

Barrier Methods Can Also be Used to Prevent Pregnancy

1) Barrier methods are another type of contraceptive.

2) Barrier methods put a barrier between the sperm and egg so they don't meet. For example:

- Condoms — male condoms are worn over the penis during sexual intercourse. Female condoms are worn inside the vagina.
- Diaphragms — these are flexible, dome-shaped devices that cover the cervix. They are inserted before sex.

Diaphragms must be used with a spermicide — a chemical that kills sperm.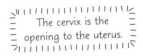

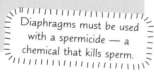

I've got this barrier thing sorted...

Hormonal and Barrier Contraceptive Methods Have Pros and Cons

1) When they're used correctly, hormonal methods are usually better at preventing pregnancy than barrier methods.

2) Also, when using hormonal methods, a couple don't have to think about contraception each time they have sex (as they would if they relied on barrier methods).

3) But hormonal methods can have unpleasant side-effects, like headaches and mood changes.

4) Hormonal methods don't protect against sexually transmitted infections (STIs) — condoms are the only form of contraception that do this.

Pills, patches and barriers — I think we've got things covered...

In the exam, you could be given data about hormonal and barrier contraceptive methods. You could then be asked to compare the two. Make sure you read the data carefully and refer to it in your answer.

Q1 Explain one reason why someone may decide to use a barrier method of contraception instead of a hormonal method of contraception.

[2 marks]

Homeostasis — Control of Blood Glucose

Homeostasis means keeping the right conditions inside your body, so that everything works properly. Ace.

Homeostasis is Maintaining a Constant Internal Environment

1) Conditions in your body need to be kept steady.
2) For example, the amount of glucose in your blood shouldn't get too high or too low (see below).
3) Conditions need to be kept steady because your cells need the right conditions in order to work properly.
4) For example, they need the right conditions for enzyme action (see p.16).
5) To keep conditions steady, your body needs to respond to:

- Changes that happen outside it (external changes).
  For example, if it gets hotter or colder.
- Changes that happen inside it (internal changes).
  For example, if the blood glucose concentration rises.

6) It can be dangerous for your health if conditions vary too much from normal levels.

Jane wished she'd responded to external changes sooner.

Insulin Helps to Control Blood Glucose Concentration

1) Eating carbohydrates puts glucose into the blood.
2) Glucose is removed from the blood by cells (which use it for energy).
3) When you exercise, a lot more glucose is removed from the blood.
4) Changes in blood glucose are monitored and controlled by the pancreas.
5) If blood glucose concentration gets too high, the pancreas releases the hormone insulin.
6) Insulin converts glucose into glycogen.
7) Glycogen is stored in the liver and muscle cells.
8) So insulin removes glucose from the blood.

Carbohydrates are broken down into simple sugars such as glucose during digestion — see page 15.

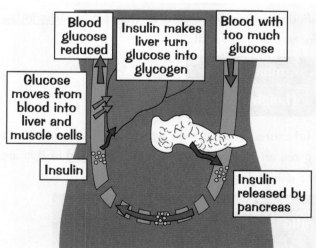

My sister's not coming out today — she's got homeo-stay-sis...

Homeostasis is really important for keeping processes in your body working.
Make sure you can explain how blood glucose concentration is regulated by insulin.

Q1 The graph shows the changes in concentration of glucose and insulin in a person's blood over time, after they ate a meal.
Which curve represents insulin?
Explain your answer. [2 marks]

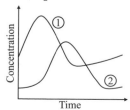

Diabetes

You need to know how <u>insulin</u> affects <u>blood glucose concentration</u> before trying to understand diabetes.
Flick back to page 55 if you're not sure.

Type 1 Diabetes — The Pancreas Stops Making Insulin

Remember, insulin reduces blood glucose level.

1) <u>Type 1 diabetes</u> is a condition where the <u>pancreas stops making insulin.</u>
2) This means that the person's blood glucose can <u>rise</u> to a level that can <u>kill them</u>.
3) A person with type 1 diabetes needs <u>insulin therapy</u> — this usually means <u>injecting insulin</u>.
4) The <u>amount of insulin</u> that needs to be injected depends on the person's <u>diet</u> and how <u>active</u> they are.

Type 2 Diabetes is When a Person is Resistant to Insulin

1) A person can get type 2 diabetes if their body cells become <u>resistant to insulin</u>.
   This means that their cells <u>don't respond</u> properly to the hormone.
2) A person can also have type 2 diabetes if their <u>pancreas doesn't produce enough insulin</u>.
3) In both cases, the blood glucose level <u>rises</u>.
4) Type 2 diabetes can be <u>controlled</u> by:

   - eating a <u>healthy diet</u>
   - getting regular <u>exercise</u>
   - <u>losing weight</u> if needed

5) Some people with type 2 diabetes also have <u>medication</u> or <u>insulin injections</u>.

Being Obese Makes You More Likely to Get Type 2 Diabetes

1) There is a <u>correlation</u> (see p.7) between <u>obesity</u> and <u>type 2 diabetes</u> —
   this means that obese people are <u>more likely</u> to develop type 2 diabetes.
2) People can be classified as <u>obese</u> by looking at their <u>body mass index</u> (<u>BMI</u>).
3) This is the formula for working out BMI:

$$BMI = \frac{mass\ (kg)}{(height\ (m))^2}$$

There's more on calculating BMI and waist-to-hip ratios on page 45.

4) People with a lot of fat stored around their <u>waists</u> are also more likely to develop type 2 diabetes.
5) A waist-to-hip ratio gives an idea of how much fat is <u>stored</u> in this area.
6) This is the formula for calculating it:

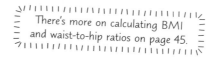

$$Waist\text{-}to\text{-}hip\ ratio = \frac{waist\ circumference\ (cm)}{hip\ circumference\ (cm)}$$

7) <u>Males</u> with a waist-to-hip ratio <u>bigger than 1.0</u> and <u>females</u> with a ratio
   <u>bigger than 0.85</u> are more likely to develop diabetes.

And people used to think the pancreas was just a cushion... (true)

Remember that obesity is a big risk factor for developing <u>type 2</u> diabetes — not type 1 diabetes.

Q1   Describe the cause of type 1 diabetes.   [1 mark]

Exchange of Materials

All organisms need to do a little bit of give and take to survive...

Organisms Exchange Substances with their Environment

Organisms need to take in substances from the environment. They also need to get rid of waste products. For example, they...

TAKE IN:

* oxygen
* water
* food
* mineral ions

GET RID OF:

* carbon dioxide (a waste product of aerobic respiration)
* urea (a waste product of protein breakdown in animals)

Oxygen and carbon dioxide move between cells and the environment by diffusion. Water moves by osmosis.

There's more on diffusion and osmosis on page 18.

You Can Calculate an Organism's Surface Area to Volume Ratio

1) A ratio shows how big one value is compared to another.

2) So, a surface area to volume ratio shows how big a shape's surface is compared to its volume.

3) Here's one way of calculating an organism's surface area to volume ratio:

* A 2 cm × 4 cm × 4 cm block can be used to estimate the surface area to volume ratio of this hippo.
* The area of a square or rectangle is found by the equation: LENGTH × WIDTH.
  * The top and bottom surfaces of the block have a length of 4 cm and a width of 4 cm.
  * There are four sides to the block. They each have a length of 4 cm and a height of 2 cm.
  * So the hippo's total surface area is:
    $(4 \times 4) \times 2$ (top and bottom surfaces)
    $+ (4 \times 2) \times 4$ (four sides)
    $= 64$ cm^2.

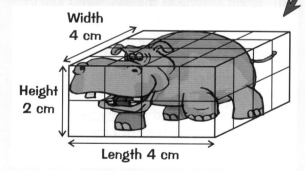

Width
4 cm

Height
2 cm

Length 4 cm

* The volume of a block is found by the equation: LENGTH × WIDTH × HEIGHT.
  So the hippo's volume is $4 \times 4 \times 2 = 32$ cm^3.

The surface area to volume ratio (SA : V) of the hippo can be written as 64 : 32.
To get the ratio so that volume is equal to one, divide both sides of the ratio by the volume.
So the SA : V of the hippo is 2 : 1.

4) The larger the organism, the smaller its surface area is compared to its volume.

   Example: SA : V of hippo = 2 : 1   SA : V of mouse = 6 : 1

   The mouse has a larger surface area compared to its volume.

Simplifying ratios so that the volume is equal to one, means that you can easily compare the surface area to volume ratios of different organisms.

5) The smaller its surface area compared to its volume, the harder it is for an organism to exchange substances with its environment.

Not that I'm endorsing putting animals in boxes...

Have a go at this question to make sure you understand how to calculate surface area to volume ratios.

Q1   A bacterial cell can be represented by a 2 μm × 2 μm × 1 μm block.
      Calculate the cell's surface area to volume ratio.   [3 marks]

Q1 Video Solution

Specialised Exchange Surfaces — the Alveoli

The alveoli are a specialised exchange surface found in the lungs of mammals.
You're about to find out why we need them. So take a deep breath and dive in...

Multicellular Organisms Need Exchange Surfaces

There's more on surface area to volume ratios on the previous page.

1) Single celled organisms have a large surface area compared to their volume.
2) So, they can exchange all the substances they need across their surface (the cell membrane).
3) Multicellular organisms (such as animals) have a smaller surface area compared to their volume.
4) They can't normally exchange enough substances across their outside surface alone.
5) Instead, multicellular organisms have specialised exchange surfaces — for example, the alveoli.
6) Multicellular organisms also have a mass transport system to move substances between exchange surfaces and the rest of the body. In animals, this is the circulatory system (see pages 59-61).

Gas Exchange in Mammals Happens in the Alveoli

1) Oxygen (O_2) and carbon dioxide (CO_2) are exchanged in the lungs in mammals.
2) The lungs contain millions of little air sacs called alveoli. Here's how gas exchange happens in the alveoli:

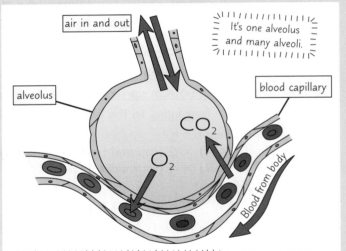

air in and out

It's one alveolus and many alveoli.

alveolus

blood capillary

CO_2

O_2

Blood from body

1) The alveoli fill up with air from the environment when a mammal breathes in.
2) This air has lots of oxygen but very little carbon dioxide.
3) The alveoli are surrounded by lots of capillaries (see p.60), which carry blood.
4) Blood arriving at the alveoli has lots of carbon dioxide and not much oxygen.
5) The oxygen diffuses from the air into the blood.
6) The carbon dioxide diffuses from the blood into the air.
7) The carbon dioxide is released when the air is breathed out.

Remember, diffusion of a substance is from where the substance is more concentrated to where it is less concentrated (see p.18).

The Alveoli are Adapted for Gas Exchange

If something is adapted for a job, its features help it to carry out that job.

The alveoli are specialised for the diffusion of O_2 and CO_2. They have:
- A moist (slightly wet) lining for dissolving gases.
- A good blood supply.
- Very thin walls (so gases don't have far to diffuse).

They also give the lungs a really big surface area to volume ratio.
This maximises the rate of diffusion.

Al Veoli — the Italian gas man...

Without gas exchange surfaces like the alveoli, multicellular organisms wouldn't be able to absorb oxygen quickly enough to supply all of their cells. Have a go at this question and see what you've learnt.

Q1 Give one way in which the alveoli are adapted for gas exchange. [1 mark]

Section 8 — Exchange and Transport in Animals

Circulatory System — Blood

One of the jobs of blood is to act as a huge <u>transport</u> system. There are four main things in blood...

Red Blood Cells Carry Oxygen

1) The job of red blood cells is to <u>carry oxygen</u> from the lungs to all the cells in the body.
2) Their shape gives them a <u>large surface area</u> for <u>absorbing oxygen</u>.
3) They contain a red substance called <u>haemoglobin</u>.
4) Haemoglobin is the stuff that allows red blood cells to <u>carry oxygen</u>.
5) Red blood cells <u>don't</u> have a <u>nucleus</u> — this leaves more space for carrying oxygen.

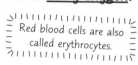
Red blood cells are also called erythrocytes.

White Blood Cells Defend Against Infection

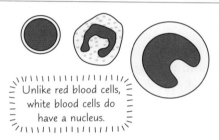

Unlike red blood cells, white blood cells do have a nucleus.

1) White blood cells are part of your <u>immune system</u> — see page 41.
2) <u>Lymphocytes</u> are white blood cells that produce <u>antibodies</u> against microorganisms.
3) <u>Phagocytes</u> are white blood cells that can change shape to gobble up unwelcome <u>microorganisms</u>.

Platelets Help Blood Clot

1) These are <u>small fragments</u> of <u>cells</u>. They have <u>no nucleus</u>.
2) They help the blood to <u>clot</u> (clump together) at a wound.
3) This <u>stops</u> all your <u>blood pouring out</u> of cuts.
4) It also stops any <u>microorganisms</u> from <u>getting in</u>.

Plasma is the Liquid That Carries Everything in Blood

This is a pale straw-coloured liquid. It <u>carries just about everything</u> in the blood, including:

1) <u>Red</u> and <u>white blood cells</u> and <u>platelets</u>.
2) Nutrients like <u>glucose</u> and <u>amino acids</u>.
3) Waste products like <u>carbon dioxide</u> and <u>urea</u> (see p.57).
4) <u>Hormones</u>.
5) <u>Antibodies</u> produced by the white blood cells.

Platelets — ideal for small dinners...

Every single drop of blood contains millions of red blood cells — all of them perfectly designed for carrying plenty of oxygen to where it's needed. Right now, that's your brain, so you can get on with learning this page.

Q1 Describe the purpose of platelets in blood. [1 mark]

Q2 Explain two ways in which red blood cells are adapted to carry oxygen. [2 marks]

Circulatory System — Blood Vessels

As well as blood, your circulatory system is made up of all the <u>tubes</u> that carry blood.
These are the <u>blood vessels</u>. There are <u>three</u> different types...

Arteries Carry Blood Under Pressure

1) This is an <u>artery</u>.
2) The walls are <u>thick</u>.
   The hole in the middle (the <u>lumen</u>) is <u>small</u>.
3) Arteries carry blood <u>away from</u> the heart.
4) Artery walls are <u>strong</u> and <u>elastic</u>.
5) This is because the heart pumps blood out at <u>high pressure</u>.
6) The walls have thick layers of <u>muscle</u> to make them <u>strong</u>.
   They also have <u>elastic fibres</u> to allow them to <u>stretch</u>.

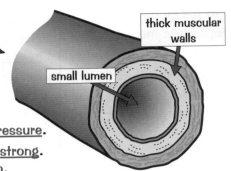

thick muscular walls

small lumen

Capillaries are Really Small

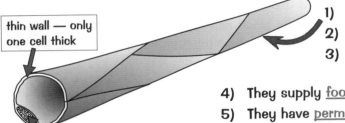

thin wall — only one cell thick

nucleus of cell

1) Arteries branch into <u>capillaries</u>.
2) Capillaries are really <u>tiny</u> — too small to see.
3) They can squeeze into the gaps between cells and carry blood <u>really close</u> to <u>every cell</u> in the body.
4) They supply <u>food</u> and <u>oxygen</u>, and take away <u>waste</u> like CO_2.
5) They have <u>permeable walls</u>, so substances can <u>diffuse in</u> and <u>out</u>.
6) Their walls are usually <u>only one cell thick</u>, so substances can diffuse in and out <u>quickly</u> (because they only have a <u>small distance</u> to cross).

Veins Take Blood Back to the Heart

1) Capillaries <u>join up</u> to form <u>veins</u>.
2) The walls of veins are <u>thinner</u> than artery walls.
3) This is because veins carry blood at <u>low pressure</u>.
4) Veins have a <u>bigger lumen</u> than arteries.
5) This helps the blood to <u>flow</u>, even though the pressure is <u>low</u>.
6) Veins also have <u>valves</u>.
7) These help to stop the blood flowing <u>backwards</u>.

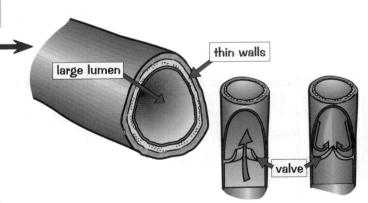

large lumen

thin walls

valve

Learn this page — don't struggle in vein...

Here's an interesting fact for you — your body contains about 60 000 miles of blood vessels.
That's about six times the distance from London to Sydney in Australia. It's hard to imagine all of that inside you.

Q1   Why are capillary walls only one cell thick? [1 mark]

Q2   Explain how veins are adapted to carry blood back to the heart. [2 marks]

Circulatory System — The Heart

The heart basically just <u>pushes</u> the blood around — it's kind of a bully...

Mammals Have a Double Circulatory System

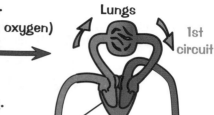

Blue = deoxygenated blood.
Red = oxygenated blood.

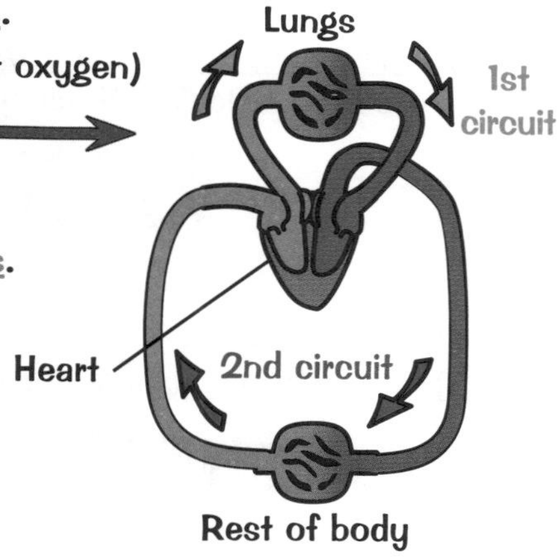

1) This means that the heart pumps blood around the body in <u>two circuits</u>.
2) In the <u>first</u> circuit, the heart pumps <u>deoxygenated blood</u> (blood without oxygen) to the <u>lungs</u>. The blood picks up <u>oxygen</u> in the lungs.
3) <u>Oxygenated blood</u> (blood with oxygen) then returns to the heart.
4) In the <u>second circuit</u>, the heart pumps <u>oxygenated blood</u> around all the <u>other organs</u> of the body. This delivers oxygen to the <u>body cells</u>.
5) <u>Deoxygenated blood</u> then returns to the heart.
6) <u>Fish</u> have a <u>single circulatory system</u>.
7) The fish's heart pumps blood to the <u>gills</u> to pick up <u>oxygen</u>, and then round the rest of the <u>body</u> in <u>one circuit</u>.

The Heart Pumps Blood Through the Blood Vessels

1) A mammal's heart has <u>four chambers</u> and <u>four major blood vessels</u>.
2) This diagram shows how <u>oxygenated blood</u> and <u>deoxygenated blood</u> flow through the chambers and vessels of the heart:

A fish's heart only has two chambers.

Right Side   **Left Side**

This is the right and left side of the person whose heart it is.

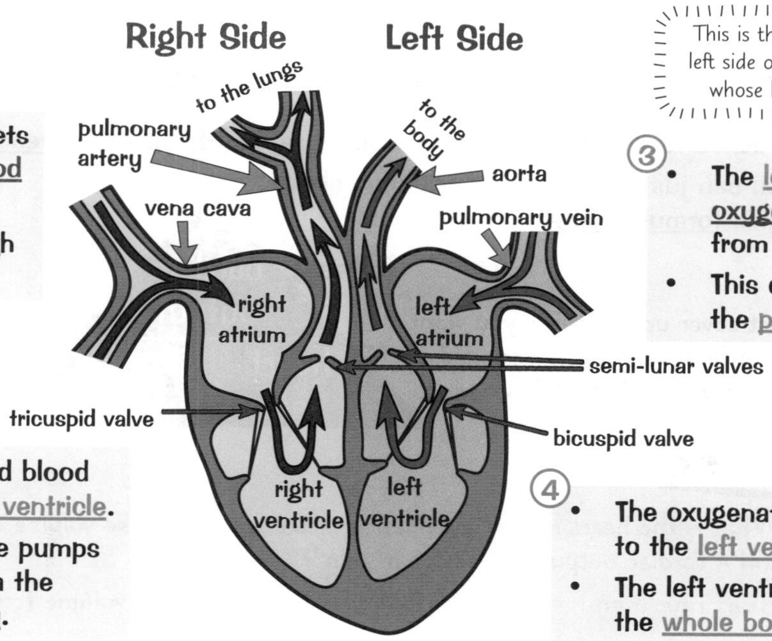

pulmonary artery

to the lungs

to the body

aorta

vena cava

pulmonary vein

right atrium

left atrium

semi-lunar valves

tricuspid valve

bicuspid valve

right ventricle   left ventricle

① • The <u>right atrium</u> gets <u>deoxygenated blood</u> from the <u>body</u>.
• This comes through the <u>vena cava</u>.

② • The deoxygenated blood goes to the <u>right ventricle</u>.
• The right ventricle pumps it to the <u>lungs</u> via the <u>pulmonary artery</u>.

③ • The <u>left atrium</u> gets <u>oxygenated blood</u> from the <u>lungs</u>.
• This comes through the <u>pulmonary vein</u>.

④ • The oxygenated blood then goes to the <u>left ventricle</u>.
• The left ventricle pumps it round the <u>whole body</u> via the <u>aorta</u>.

Features of the heart

1) The <u>left</u> ventricle has a much <u>thicker wall</u> than the <u>right</u> ventricle. It needs more <u>muscle</u> because it has to pump blood around the <u>whole body</u>, not just to the <u>lungs</u>.
2) The heart has <u>valves</u>. These prevent the <u>backflow</u> of blood in the heart.

Are you pumped after this page? I know I am...

Make sure you learn the diagram of the heart and all its labels. It won't be fun, but it'll help you in the exam.

Q1   Describe how deoxygenated blood gets from the vena cava to the lungs.   [3 marks]

Heart Rate Calculations

Exercise and the boy/girl next door are both guaranteed to increase your heart rate. But stop thinking about your next door neighbour for now — there's a whole page of heart rate calculations to look at first.

You Can Calculate How Much Blood is Pumped Every Minute

1) Cardiac output is the total volume of blood pumped by a ventricle every minute. You can calculate it using this equation:

$$\text{cardiac output} = \text{heart rate} \times \text{stroke volume}$$

in cm^3 min^{-1} in beats per minute   in cm^3

cm^3 min^{-1} means cm^3 per minute. It can also be written as cm^3/min.

2) The heart rate is the number of beats per minute (bpm).

3) The stroke volume is the volume of blood pumped by one ventricle each time it contracts.

EXAMPLE

A person has an average heart rate of 65 bpm and a stroke volume of 60 cm^3. Calculate their cardiac output.

cardiac output (cm^3 min^{-1}) = heart rate (bpm) × stroke volume (cm^3)

= 65 × 60

= 3900 cm^3 min^{-1}

You Can Also Find the Stroke Volume or Heart Rate

1) You might be asked to find stroke volume or heart rate in the exam, instead of cardiac output.

2) To do this, you can just rearrange the equation above. You can use this formula triangle to help you:

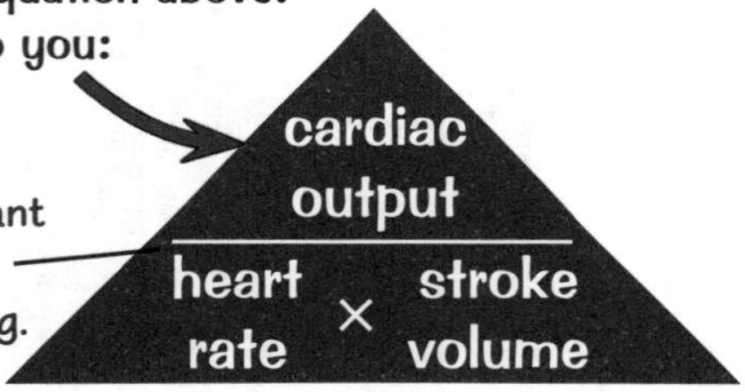

Just cover up the thing you want to find with your finger and write down what's left showing.

$$\frac{\text{cardiac output}}{\text{heart rate} \times \text{stroke volume}}$$

Greta has excellent stroke volume — as you can see.

EXAMPLE

What is the heart rate of a person with an average stroke volume of 72 cm^3 and a cardiac output of 5420 cm^3 min^{-1}?

Heart rate (bpm) = cardiac output (cm^3 min^{-1}) ÷ stroke volume (cm^3)

= 5420 ÷ 72

= 75 bpm

If these equations don't get your heart racing, what will...?

Make sure you learn what's meant by cardiac output, heart rate and stroke volume. And if you know the formula triangle here you'll be fully prepared for any heart rate calculation that you might get in the exam.

Q2 Video Solution

Q1   Calculate the cardiac output of a person with a heart rate of 80 bpm and a stroke volume of 75 cm^3.   [2 marks]

Q2   Calculate the stroke volume for a heart rate of 67 bpm and a cardiac output of 4221 cm^3 min^{-1}.   [2 marks]

Respiration

You need <u>energy</u> to keep your body going. Energy comes from <u>food</u>, and it's <u>released</u> by <u>respiration</u>.

Cellular Respiration Releases Energy

1) Respiration is <u>NOT</u> breathing in and breathing out, as you might think.
2) Respiration is the process of <u>releasing energy</u> from <u>glucose</u>. It's a <u>chemical reaction</u>.
3) It happens in <u>every cell</u> of <u>all</u> living organisms — and it happens <u>all the time</u>.
4) Respiration is an <u>exothermic reaction</u> — it <u>releases energy</u>.
5) Some of this energy is released as <u>heat</u>. Some is used in <u>metabolic reactions</u> — such as making larger molecules from smaller ones (e.g. proteins from amino acids).
6) There are <u>two types</u> of respiration, <u>aerobic</u> and <u>anaerobic</u>.

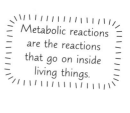
Metabolic reactions are the reactions that go on inside living things.

Aerobic Respiration Needs Plenty of Oxygen

1) <u>Aerobic</u> just means "<u>with oxygen</u>".
2) So, <u>aerobic respiration</u> is respiration with oxygen.
3) This type of respiration goes on <u>all the time</u> in <u>plants</u> and <u>animals</u>.
4) Here's the equation:

$$\text{glucose} + \text{oxygen} \longrightarrow \text{carbon dioxide} + \text{water}$$

Anaerobic Respiration Doesn't Use Oxygen At All

1) <u>An</u>aerobic just means "<u>without</u> oxygen".
2) So <u>anaerobic respiration</u> happens without oxygen.
3) It releases much <u>less energy</u> than aerobic respiration — but it's still <u>useful</u>.
4) During <u>hard exercise</u>, your muscles can't get <u>enough oxygen</u> to only respire aerobically.
5) So they start to respire <u>anaerobically</u> too.
6) This is the word equation for anaerobic respiration in <u>animals</u>:

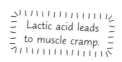

Finish

$$\text{glucose} \longrightarrow \text{lactic acid}$$

Lactic acid leads to muscle cramp.

Anaerobic Respiration in Plants is Slightly Different

1) <u>Plants</u> can respire <u>without oxygen</u> too, but they produce <u>ethanol</u> (alcohol) and CO_2 <u>instead</u> of lactic acid.
2) This is <u>the word equation</u> for anaerobic respiration in <u>plants</u>:

$$\text{glucose} \longrightarrow \text{ethanol} + \text{carbon dioxide}$$

Fungi such as yeast also do anaerobic respiration like this.

I reckon aerobics classes should be called anaerobics instead...

Remember, anaerobic respiration has different products to aerobic respiration. It also transfers much less energy, and happens without oxygen. They're both exothermic though — don't forget that.

Q1 Video Solution

Q1   A scientist measured the concentration of lactic acid in her blood after walking for 5 minutes. She also measured the concentration of lactic acid in her blood after running for 5 minutes. Suggest why the concentration of lactic acid in her blood was higher after running than after walking.   [3 marks]

 # Investigating Respiration

You need to know how to <u>investigate</u> the <u>rate of respiration</u>. Time to get hands on with some little critters...

You Can Measure the Rate of Respiration Using a Respirometer

In <u>aerobic respiration</u>, organisms <u>use up oxygen</u> from the air (see previous page).
- By measuring <u>how much oxygen</u> organisms use in a <u>given time</u>, you can calculate their <u>rate of respiration</u>.
- Here's an experiment which uses <u>woodlice</u>, a <u>water bath</u> and a <u>respirometer</u>.
- It allows you to measure the effect of <u>temperature</u> on the <u>rate of respiration</u> of the woodlice.

1) Set up the <u>respirometer</u> as shown in the diagram.

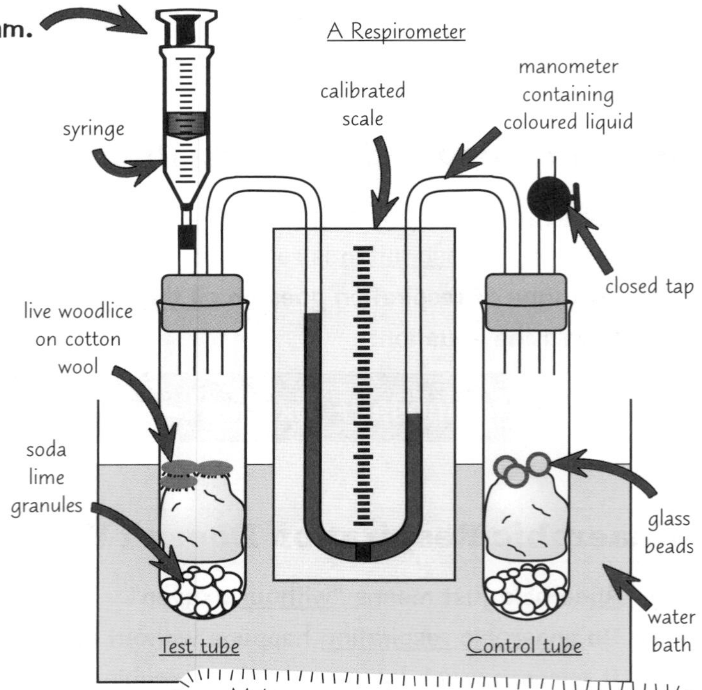

2) The <u>glass beads</u> are there to act as a <u>control</u>. (There's more on controls on page 4.)

3) Use the <u>syringe</u> to set the <u>coloured liquid</u> to a <u>known level</u>.

4) Set a <u>water bath</u> to <u>15 °C</u>. <u>Leave</u> the respirometer in the water bath for a set period of time.

5) The woodlice will <u>use up oxygen</u> during respiration. The <u>carbon dioxide</u> they release will be <u>absorbed</u> by the <u>soda lime granules</u>.

6) So there'll be a <u>decrease</u> in the <u>volume</u> of the air in the <u>tube</u> containing the <u>woodlice</u>.

7) This decrease in volume will cause the <u>coloured liquid</u> in the manometer to move <u>towards</u> the <u>test tube</u> containing the <u>woodlice</u>.

A Respirometer

syringe

calibrated scale

manometer containing coloured liquid

closed tap

live woodlice on cotton wool

soda lime granules

glass beads

water bath

<u>Test tube</u>

<u>Control tube</u>

Make sure you wear safety goggles and gloves when handling the test tubes containing soda lime. Don't touch or let the woodlice touch the soda lime.

8) <u>Subtract</u> the reading of the liquid level at the <u>start</u> of the experiment from its level at the <u>end</u>. This will give you the <u>distance moved</u> by the liquid during the experiment.

9) You can then use this value to calculate the <u>volume of oxygen taken in</u> by the woodlice <u>in a minute</u>. This gives you the <u>rate of respiration</u> in, e.g. cm^3 min^{-1}.

10) <u>Repeat</u> steps 1-9 with the water bath set at <u>different temperatures</u>, e.g. <u>20 °C</u> and <u>25 °C</u>. This lets you see how <u>temperature</u> affects the rate of respiration.

Make sure that you treat any live animals in this experiment <u>ethically</u>. For example, it's important not to <u>leave</u> the woodlice in the respirometer for <u>too long</u>, or they may <u>run out</u> of oxygen and <u>die</u>.

There's more on the ethical treatment of organisms in experiments on page 212.

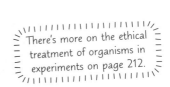

My rate of respiration has increased after all that...

Controls are mega important in experiments — they check that the thing you're observing is what's affecting the results and nothing else. So you should make sure everything else is kept exactly the same.

Q1   A student is carrying out an experiment to measure the effect of temperature on the rate of respiration in germinating beans. What could she use to keep the beans at different temperatures?   [1 mark]

Revision Questions for Sections 7 and 8

Right, time to test yourself on all the many processes
in animals that you've covered in Sections 7 and 8.

For even more practice, try the
Retrieval Quizzes for Sections 7
and 8 — just scan these QR codes!

- Try these questions and tick off each one when you get it right.
- When you're completely happy with a sub-topic, tick it off.

Hormones (p.52) ☑

1) What is a hormone?

2) How do hormones travel to their target organs?

3) What is an endocrine gland?

4) Name the gland where each of the following hormones is produced:
   a) oestrogen, b) testosterone, c) adrenaline.

The Menstrual Cycle and Contraception (p.53-54) ☐

5) Describe two effects of oestrogen in the menstrual cycle.

6) Which hormone is secreted by a corpus luteum?

7) Explain one way in which progesterone in contraceptives prevents pregnancy.

8) Give one advantage of hormonal contraceptives over barrier contraceptives.

Homeostasis and Diabetes (p.55-56) ☑

9) What does the body need to do in order to maintain a constant internal environment?

10) Why is maintaining a constant internal environment important?

11) What causes an increase in blood glucose concentration?

12) Which organ produces insulin?

13) What causes type 2 diabetes?

14) Give one factor which makes a person more likely to develop type 2 diabetes.

Exchange of Materials (p.57-58) ☐

15) Name three substances that animals have to take in from their environment.

16) Why do multicellular organisms need specialised exchange surfaces?

17) Name the specialised gas exchange surface in the lungs.

The Circulatory System (p.59-62) ☑

18) Describe the job of red blood cells.

19) What is haemoglobin?

20) What are phagocytes?

21) List four different substances that are carried in the plasma.

22) Do arteries carry blood away from or towards the heart?

23) Why do veins have valves?

24) Name the blood vessel that carries blood into the right atrium of the heart.

25) What is the equation for cardiac output?

26) What is meant by the term stroke volume?

Respiration (p.63-64) ☐

27) Is respiration exothermic or endothermic? Explain your answer.

28) Write down the equation for anaerobic respiration in animals.

29) Why is soda lime used in a respirometer when investigating the rate of respiration in woodlice?

Section 8 — Exchange and Transport in Animals

Ecosystems and Interdependence

This page is all about the <u>relationships</u> between living things. And sadly I don't mean romantic relationships...

Here are Some Words You Need to Learn Before You Start

1) <u>Individual</u> — A <u>single</u> organism.

2) <u>Species</u> — A <u>group</u> of <u>similar organisms</u> that can <u>reproduce</u> to give offspring that can also reproduce.

3) <u>Habitat</u> — The <u>place</u> where an organism <u>lives</u>, e.g. a rocky shore or a field.

4) <u>Population</u> — All the organisms of <u>one species</u> in a <u>habitat</u>.

5) <u>Community</u> — All the organisms of <u>different species</u> living in a <u>habitat</u>.

6) <u>Ecosystem</u> — A community of <u>organisms</u>, along with all the <u>non-living</u> conditions (see next page) in the area where they live.

Ecosystems are Organised into Different Levels

1) These are the <u>levels</u> of organisation in an ecosystem:

Individual ⟶ Population ⟶ Community ⟶ Ecosystem

2) The <u>smallest</u> level is an <u>individual organism</u>.

3) Individual organisms make up a <u>population</u>. Several populations make up a <u>community</u>.

4) The <u>biggest</u> level is the <u>ecosystem</u>.

Organisms in a Community Are Interdependent

1) Organisms <u>depend</u> on each other for things like <u>food</u> and <u>shelter</u>.

2) This is called <u>interdependence</u>. It means <u>all</u> organisms have <u>relationships</u> with other organisms.

3) <u>Mutualism</u> is one type of relationship between two organisms.

4) In mutualism, <u>both</u> organisms <u>benefit</u> from the relationship. For example:

- <u>Bees</u> and <u>flowering plants</u> have a <u>mutualistic relationship</u>.
- When bees visit <u>flowers</u> to get nectar, <u>pollen</u> is transferred to their bodies.
- The bees then <u>spread</u> the pollen to <u>other plants</u> when they land on their flowers.
- This transfer of pollen between flowers allows flowering plants to <u>reproduce</u>.
- So, the bees get <u>food</u> and the plants get <u>help reproducing</u>.

5) <u>Parasitism</u> is another type of relationship between organisms.

6) <u>Parasites</u> live on or in a <u>host species</u>.

7) Parasites take what they need to survive, but the host <u>doesn't</u> benefit. For example:

- <u>Fleas</u> are <u>parasites</u> of <u>animals</u> such as <u>dogs</u>.
- Fleas feed on their host's blood, but the host doesn't benefit at all.

8) Interdependence means that a <u>change</u> in the population of <u>one species</u> can <u>affect</u> <u>other species</u> in the same community. There's more on this on the next page.

Everybody needs good neighbours...

Lots of words to learn on this page — but if you do learn them, it'll make your life much easier in the exam.

Q1   What is meant by the term 'community'?   [1 mark]

Q2   What is a mutualistic relationship between two organisms?   [1 mark]

Factors Affecting Ecosystems

Let me stop you right there. If you haven't learnt all the words at the top of page 66, go back and do it now.

Communities are Affected by Abiotic and Biotic Factors

1) Abiotic factors are non-living factors, e.g. temperature.
2) Biotic factors are related to living things, e.g. predation (predators eating prey).
3) Both abiotic and biotic factors affect population size — they can make a population bigger or smaller.
4) They also affect the distribution of populations (where organisms live).

Abiotic Factors Include...

LIGHT INTENSITY

1) As trees grow they make the ground below more shaded.
2) This might stop grass growing underneath the trees because grass needs lots of light.
3) But mosses and fungi might grow there instead — they grow well in shade.

AMOUNT OF WATER

1) Daisies grow best in soils that are slightly wet.
2) If the soil becomes too wet or too dry, the population of daisies will decrease in size.

TEMPERATURE

1) If a cold country gets warmer, organisms that prefer warmer temperatures might move there.
2) But organisms that prefer the cold might be forced out.

LEVELS OF POLLUTANTS

1) Sulfur dioxide is an air pollutant.
2) A type of organism called a lichen can't survive if the concentration of sulfur dioxide is too high.

Pollutants are chemicals that damage the environment.

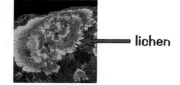 lichen

Biotic Factors Include...

Competition
1) Red and grey squirrels live in the same habitat and eat the same food.
2) The population size of red squirrels is decreasing in some areas.
3) This is partly because of competition with grey squirrels for food and shelter.

Predation
1) Foxes are predators. Rabbits are their prey.
2) If the number of foxes decreases, then the number of rabbits will increase.
3) This is because fewer rabbits will be eaten by the foxes.
4) And if the number of foxes increases, then the number of rabbits will decrease.
5) This is because more rabbits will be eaten by the foxes.

Revision — an abiotic factor causing stress in my community...

Organisms like everything to be just right — temperature, light, food... I'd never get away with being that fussy.

Q1 Give two abiotic factors that could affect a community. [2 marks]

Investigating Ecosystems

Studying <u>ecosystems</u> allows you to <u>rummage around</u> in bushes and get your hands <u>dirty</u>. It's proper fun.

Use a Quadrat to Study The Population Size of Small Organisms

1) Place a <u>quadrat</u> on the <u>ground</u> in your sample area.
   Quadrats need to be placed <u>at random</u> so that you get a <u>sample</u> which shows the general features of the whole area.

2) <u>Count</u> all the organisms you're interested in <u>within</u> the quadrat.

3) <u>Repeat</u> steps 1 and 2 lots of times.

4) <u>Work out</u> the <u>mean</u> number of organisms per quadrat.

5) <u>Divide</u> the <u>area</u> of the <u>habitat</u> by the <u>quadrat size</u>.

6) <u>Multiply</u> this figure by the <u>mean number</u> of organisms per quadrat.

A quadrat (square frame):

$$\text{Mean} = \frac{\text{total number of organisms}}{\text{number of quadrats}}$$

> **EXAMPLE**
>
> Students used quadrats, each with an area of 0.5 m², to randomly sample daisies in a field. They found a mean of 10 daisies per quadrat. The field's area was 800 m². Estimate the population of daisies in the field.
>
> 1) Divide the area of the habitat by the quadrat size. $800 \div 0.5 = 1600$
>
> 2) Multiply this by the mean number of organisms per quadrat. $1600 \times 10 = 16\ 000$ daisies in the field

Use Belt Transects to Study Distribution Along a Gradient   PRACTICAL

1) Sometimes <u>abiotic factors</u> will <u>change across a habitat</u>.

2) This change is known as a <u>gradient</u>.

3) You can use <u>quadrats</u> to help find out how organisms (like plants) are <u>distributed along a gradient</u>.

4) For example, how a species becomes <u>more</u> or <u>less common</u> as you move from an area of <u>shade</u> to an area of <u>full sun</u>.

5) The quadrats are laid out along a <u>line</u>, making a <u>belt transect</u>. Here's what you do:

> 1) <u>Mark a line</u> in the area you want to study.
>
> 2) Place <u>quadrats</u> next to each other along the line.
>
> 3) <u>Count</u> the organisms you're interested in within each quadrat.
>
> 4) <u>Record</u> the <u>abiotic factor</u> you're interested in within each quadrat. E.g. use a <u>light meter</u> to measure <u>light intensity</u>.
>
> 5) <u>Repeat</u> steps 1-4 several times.
>
> 6) Work out the <u>mean</u> number of organisms for <u>each quadrat</u> along the transect.
>
> 7) Plot a graph of your results. This will help you to see if the <u>changing abiotic factor</u> is <u>correlated</u> (see page 7) with a change in the <u>distribution</u> of the species you're studying.

tape measure

Make sure you can correctly identify the organisms you're investigating. If necessary, use books or information from the internet to help you.

quadrat 1

Drat, drat, and double drat — my favourite use of quadrats...

Unless you're doing a transect, it's key that you put your quadrat down in a random place.

Q1   A 1200 m² field was randomly sampled for buttercups using a quadrat with an area of 0.25 m².
A mean of 0.75 buttercups were found per quadrat.
Estimate the total population of buttercups.

[2 marks]

Q1 Video Solution

Section 9 — Ecosystems and Material Cycles

Human Impacts on Biodiversity

Humans have a big effect on ecosystems. That effect can be <u>good</u> or it can be <u>very, very bad</u>...

Human Activities Affect Biodiversity

1) <u>Biodiversity</u> is the <u>variety of living organisms</u> in an <u>ecosystem</u>.
2) If the number of species in an area <u>decreases</u>, biodiversity will also <u>decrease</u>.
3) If the number of species in an area <u>increases</u>, so will <u>biodiversity</u>.
4) <u>Humans</u> often affect biodiversity.
5) Sometimes we have a <u>positive</u> effect on biodiversity (see bottom of next page).
6) But we often have a <u>negative</u> effect. Here are some examples:

Eutrophication Can Reduce Biodiversity

1) <u>Nitrates</u> are put onto fields as <u>fertilisers</u> (see p.73).
2) If <u>too much fertiliser</u> is put on and it <u>rains</u>, nitrates can get into rivers and lakes.
3) This can cause <u>eutrophication</u> — an <u>excess of nutrients</u> in water.
4) Eutrophication can cause the <u>death</u> of many species in the water.
5) This <u>reduces</u> the <u>biodiversity</u> of the water.
6) Here's what happens:

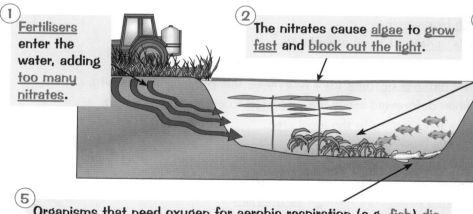

① <u>Fertilisers</u> enter the water, adding <u>too many nitrates</u>.

② The nitrates cause <u>algae</u> to <u>grow fast</u> and <u>block out the light</u>.

③ Plants don't get enough <u>light</u> to <u>photosynthesise</u>. They <u>start to die</u> and <u>decompose</u> (break down).

④ <u>Microorganisms</u> that feed on decomposing plants have more food. So they <u>increase</u> in <u>number</u> and <u>use up</u> <u>oxygen</u> in the water.

⑤ Organisms that need oxygen for aerobic respiration (e.g. <u>fish</u>) <u>die</u>.

Fish Farms Can Also Reduce Biodiversity

1) <u>Fish</u> can be farmed in <u>big nets</u> in <u>lakes</u> or the <u>sea</u>.
2) This can <u>reduce biodiversity</u> in the water around the nets. Here's how:

- <u>Fish food</u> and <u>fish poo</u> from the farm can <u>get out</u> into the water around the nets. This can cause <u>eutrophication</u> (see above).
- <u>Parasites</u> (see page 66) can infect fish in the fish farm. These parasites can <u>get out</u> of the farm and <u>infect wild animals</u>, sometimes <u>killing</u> them.
- <u>Predators</u> (e.g. sea lions) are attracted to the nets. They can become <u>trapped</u> in the nets and <u>die</u>.
- If farmed fish <u>escape</u> into the wild, they can cause <u>problems</u> for wild species. For example, they might eat a lot of food, so there's not enough left for the wild species.

A fish farm is an area where fish are kept and bred so that we can eat them.

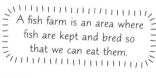

Section 9 — Ecosystems and Material Cycles

Human Impacts on Biodiversity

Non-Indigenous Species Can Reduce Biodiversity

1) <u>Non-indigenous</u> species are species that <u>aren't naturally found</u> in an area.

2) They can be brought into an area <u>on purpose</u> (e.g. for food or hunting) or <u>accidentally</u>.

3) The introduction of a non-indigenous species may cause <u>problems</u> for species that already live in the area.

4) For example:

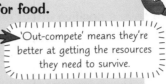

- <u>Signal crayfish</u> were brought to <u>rivers</u> in the <u>UK</u> for food.
- However, they <u>out-compete</u> UK crayfish.
- They carry a <u>disease</u> that <u>kills</u> UK crayfish.
- They <u>eat</u> other UK river species.
- So the introduction of signal crayfish <u>reduced biodiversity</u> in UK rivers.

'Out-compete' means they're better at getting the resources they need to survive.

Humans Can Also Maintain or Increase Biodiversity

Maintaining biodiversity has <u>benefits</u> on a <u>local</u> and <u>global scale</u>.

Reforestation Can Increase Biodiversity in Deforested Areas

1) <u>Forests</u> have a <u>high biodiversity</u>.

2) They contain a <u>wide variety</u> of trees and plants.

3) The trees and plants provide <u>food</u> and <u>shelter</u> for lots of different <u>animals</u>.

4) <u>Deforestation</u> is the <u>removal of trees</u> from forests — this <u>reduces</u> biodiversity.

5) <u>Reforestation</u> is when deforested areas are <u>replanted</u> to create a new forest.

6) This helps to <u>restore</u> biodiversity to the <u>local area</u>. It also increases <u>global</u> biodiversity.

7) Reforestation doesn't just benefit <u>wildlife</u> — it helps <u>humans</u> too.

8) For example, reforestation can <u>create jobs</u> for local people. It can also bring <u>money</u> to an area through <u>ecotourism</u> (environmentally-friendly tourism).

Conservation Schemes Protect At-Risk Species

1) Conservation schemes can help to <u>protect biodiversity</u> by preventing species from dying out.

2) Conservation methods include:

- <u>Protecting</u> a species' <u>natural habitat</u> so that individuals have a place to live.
- <u>Protecting</u> species in <u>safe areas</u> outside of their natural habitat (e.g. animals can be protected in <u>zoos</u>).
- <u>Breeding</u> organisms in safe areas to increase their population size.

If a reforested area is cut down again, is that redeforestation...

Once a species is gone it's gone forever, so it's really important to maintain biodiversity while we can.

Q1 Suggest two ways in which introducing a non-indigenous species could reduce the biodiversity of an area.

[2 marks]

The Carbon Cycle

All the <u>nutrients</u> in our environment are constantly being <u>recycled</u> — there's a nice balance between what <u>goes in</u> and what <u>goes out</u> again.

Materials are Constantly Recycled in an Ecosystem

There's more on ecosystems on page 66.

1) <u>Living things</u> need materials such as <u>carbon</u>, <u>water</u> and <u>nitrogen</u> to <u>survive</u>.

2) But there <u>isn't</u> an <u>endless supply</u> of these materials — so they're <u>recycled</u> through an ecosystem.

3) As materials are recycled, they pass through the <u>biotic</u> (living) parts of the ecosystem — these include <u>animals</u>, <u>plants</u> and <u>microorganisms</u>.

4) Materials are also recycled through the <u>abiotic</u> (non-living) parts of the ecosystem — for example, the <u>air</u> and <u>soil</u>.

The Carbon Cycle Shows How Carbon is Recycled

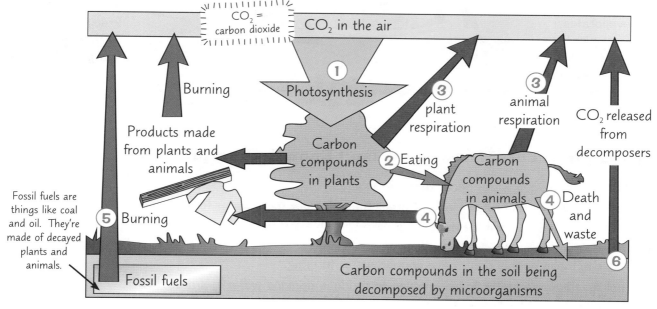

1) <u>Plants</u> take in <u>CO_2</u> from the air during <u>photosynthesis</u>. They use the carbon in CO_2 to make carbon compounds, e.g. <u>carbohydrates</u>.

2) <u>Eating</u> passes the carbon compounds in plants along to <u>animals</u> in the <u>food chain</u>.

3) Both plant and animal <u>respiration</u> releases <u>CO_2</u> back into the <u>air</u>.

4) Plants and animals eventually <u>die</u>, or are killed and turned into <u>useful products</u>.

5) <u>Burning</u> plant and animal products (and fossil fuels) releases <u>CO_2</u> back into the air.

6) <u>Decomposers</u> (microorganisms such as bacteria and fungi) break down <u>animal waste</u> and <u>dead organisms</u>. As they break down the material, decomposers <u>release CO_2</u> back into the air through <u>respiration</u>.

The Carbon Cycle — a great gift for any bike enthusiast...

The <u>biotic</u> parts of the ecosystem shown in the big diagram above are the horse, tree and microorganisms in the soil. The <u>abiotic</u> parts include the air and the soil. Make sure you don't mix the two terms up.

Q1   Describe the role of microorganisms in the carbon cycle.

[3 marks]

The Water Cycle

Next time you get <u>soaked</u> on your way to school and moan about the <u>rain</u>, think back to this page.
Rain is a really important part of the <u>water cycle</u>, and it's the water cycle that keeps us all <u>alive</u>.

The Water Cycle Means Water is Constantly Recycled

1) All living things need <u>water</u> to survive.

2) The <u>water cycle</u> constantly <u>recycles</u> water so that we <u>don't run out</u> of it.

3) This is the <u>water cycle</u>:

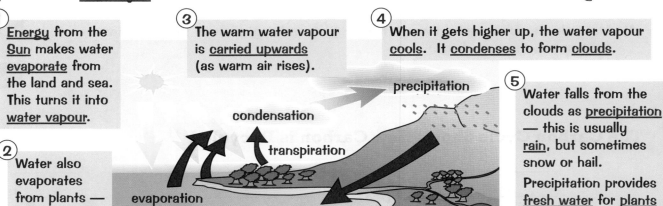

① <u>Energy</u> from the <u>Sun</u> makes water <u>evaporate</u> from the land and sea. This turns it into <u>water vapour</u>.

② Water also evaporates from plants — this is called <u>transpiration</u> (see p.49).

③ The warm water vapour is <u>carried upwards</u> (as warm air rises).

④ When it gets higher up, the water vapour <u>cools</u>. It <u>condenses</u> to form <u>clouds</u>.

⑤ Water falls from the clouds as <u>precipitation</u> — this is usually <u>rain</u>, but sometimes snow or hail.
Precipitation provides <u>fresh water</u> for <u>plants</u> and <u>animals</u> on land.

⑥ Water then <u>drains</u> into the <u>sea</u> and the whole process starts again.

condensation

transpiration

evaporation

precipitation

A Drought Occurs When There Isn't Enough Precipitation

1) We can't drink <u>sea water</u> because it's too <u>salty</u>.

2) So we need <u>rain</u> and other kinds of <u>precipitation</u> to get <u>fresh water</u> for drinking.

3) Water that can be used for drinking is called <u>potable water</u>.

4) If there's <u>not enough rain</u>, it can lead to a <u>drought</u>.
This can mean people don't have enough water to <u>drink</u>.

5) Luckily, there are <u>methods</u> we can use to <u>produce drinking water</u> in a drought.

6) One of these methods is called <u>desalination</u>.

Desalination Can Be Used to Produce Potable Water From Salt Water

1) Desalination <u>removes salts</u> from salt water (e.g. sea water).

2) One really <u>simple</u> method of desalination is <u>distillation</u>.

3) This is where salt water is <u>boiled</u> in a large enclosed vessel, so that the water <u>evaporates</u>.

4) The steam <u>rises</u> to the top of the vessel, but the salts stay at the <u>bottom</u>.

5) The steam then travels down a pipe from the top of the vessel and <u>condenses</u> back into <u>pure water</u>.

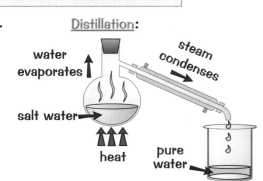

<u>Distillation</u>:

water evaporates
steam condenses
salt water
heat
pure water

Come on out, it's only a little water cycle, it won't hurt you...

Make sure you really understand the water cycle and how desalination works before you turn over.

Q1   Explain how water from the sea can eventually fall as rain.   [4 marks]

Q1 Video Solution

The Nitrogen Cycle

<u>Nitrogen</u> is <u>recycled</u> in the <u>nitrogen cycle</u>. (No surprises there then). There are lots of <u>bacteria</u> involved...

There are Four Types of Bacteria in the Nitrogen Cycle

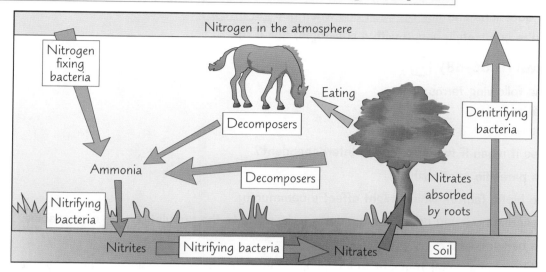

1) **NITROGEN-FIXING BACTERIA** take <u>nitrogen gas</u> from the air and turn it into <u>ammonia</u>.
2) **NITRIFYING BACTERIA** turn ammonia into <u>nitrites</u> and then into <u>nitrates</u>. Nitrates can be taken up by <u>plants</u>.
3) Plants use the nitrogen in nitrates to make <u>proteins</u>.
4) <u>Animals</u> take in nitrogen when they <u>eat plants</u> (and each other).
5) Bacteria working as **DECOMPOSERS** break down <u>dead plants</u> and <u>animals</u> (and animal waste). This releases more <u>ammonia</u>.
6) **DENITRIFYING BACTERIA** turn nitrates back into <u>nitrogen gas</u>. This <u>doesn't help</u> organisms at all. Boo.

Plants and animals can't use the nitrogen gas in the air.

Farmers Can Increase the Amount of Nitrates in the Soil

1) When crops are <u>harvested</u>, the nitrogen in them isn't <u>recycled back</u> into the soil when they <u>die</u>.
2) Over time, the amount of <u>nitrogen</u> in the soil <u>decreases</u>, so crops <u>can't grow</u> as well.
3) Increasing the amount of <u>nitrates</u> in the soil can help crops to <u>grow better</u>.
4) Here are <u>two methods</u> that farmers can use to increase the amount of nitrates in the soil:

CROP ROTATION
1) This is when <u>different crops</u> are grown in the <u>same field</u> each year in a <u>cycle</u>.
2) One of the crops in the cycle is usually a <u>nitrogen-fixing crop</u>, e.g. peas or beans.
3) A nitrogen-fixing crop has <u>nitrogen-fixing bacteria</u> in its <u>roots</u>. The bacteria help to put <u>nitrates</u> back into the soil.

FERTILISERS
1) <u>Animal manure</u> or <u>compost</u> can be spread on fields.
2) When these <u>decompose</u>, nitrogen gets put back into the soil.
3) <u>Artificial fertilisers</u> containing <u>nitrates</u> can also be used. However, these can be <u>expensive</u>.

It's the cyyyycle, the cyycle of liiiiife...

Bacteria do a lot of the hard work in the nitrogen cycle. Make sure you learn the four types that play an important role: nitrogen-fixing, nitrifying, decomposers and denitrifying — then that's it for cycles.

Q1   Describe how the nitrogen compounds in dead leaves are turned into nitrates in the soil. [3 marks]

Q1 Video Solution

Revision Questions for Section 9

Well, that was a bit of a mucky section if you ask me. All that <u>fieldwork</u>, <u>farming</u> and <u>bacteria</u> — I feel like I need a hot bath now to freshen up a bit. Anyway, there's no lying around in the bath for you...

For even more practice, try the Retrieval Quiz for Section 9 — just scan this QR code!

Section 9 Quiz

- Try these questions and <u>tick off each one</u> when you <u>get it right</u>.
- When you're <u>completely happy</u> with a sub-topic, tick it off.

Ecosystems (p.66-68) ☑

1) Define the following terms:
   a) population,
   b) ecosystem.
2) What does it mean if two species are interdependent?
3) What is a parasitic relationship?
4) State two biotic factors which might affect a community.
5) Briefly describe how you could use quadrats to investigate the population size of a species.
6) What is a belt transect?
7) How could you use a belt transect to investigate the distribution of a species along a gradient?

Biodiversity (p.69-70) ☐

8) What is meant by the term 'eutrophication'?
9) Describe one way in which fish farms can reduce biodiversity.
10) What is a non-indigenous species?
11) Explain why forested areas often have a high biodiversity.
12) Give three examples of conservation schemes.

The Carbon, Water and Nitrogen Cycles (p.71-73) ☑

13) Name the process that removes carbon from the air in the carbon cycle.
14) Name two processes that put carbon back into the air in the carbon cycle.
15) Produce a labelled diagram of the water cycle.
16) Why do you need to be able to produce potable water in a drought?
17) What does desalination mean?
18) Describe a common method of desalination.
19) Describe the role of nitrogen-fixing bacteria in the nitrogen cycle.
20) Why aren't denitrifying bacteria helpful in the nitrogen cycle?
21) What is crop rotation?
22) Why is crop rotation beneficial to farmers?

Chemical Equations

If you're going to get anywhere in chemistry you need to know about <u>chemical equations</u>.
These are just a simple way of showing what happens when different chemicals <u>react</u> with each other.

Chemical Changes are Shown Using Chemical Equations

1) One way to show a chemical reaction is to write a <u>word equation</u>.

2) Here's an example:

   1) <u>Methane</u> burns in <u>oxygen</u> giving <u>carbon dioxide</u> and <u>water</u>:

      methane + oxygen $\rightarrow$ carbon dioxide + water

   2) The chemicals on the <u>left-hand side</u> of the equation are called the <u>reactants</u> (because they react with each other).

   3) The chemicals on the <u>right-hand side</u> are called the <u>products</u> (because they've been produced from the reactants).

I have no idea what I'm doing.

Symbol Equations Show the Atoms on Both Sides

1) Chemical <u>reactions</u> can be shown by <u>symbol equations</u>.

2) They just show the <u>symbols</u> or <u>formulas</u> of the <u>reactants</u> and <u>products</u>.

   <u>Word</u> equation: magnesium + oxygen $\rightarrow$ magnesium oxide

   <u>Symbol</u> equation: $2Mg + O_2 \rightarrow 2MgO$

3) Symbol equations should have the <u>same number</u> of <u>atoms</u> of each element on <u>each side</u> of the equation. See the next page for more.

You Need to Learn the Formulas of Some Simple Compounds and Ions

1) It's a good idea to <u>learn</u> the chemical formulas of these common molecules.

- Water — H_2O
- Ammonia — NH_3
- Carbon dioxide — CO_2
- Hydrogen — H_2
- Chlorine — Cl_2
- Oxygen — O_2

2) You also need to remember the formulas of <u>some ions</u>.

3) For <u>single atoms</u>, you can use the periodic table to work out what <u>charges</u> their ions will form (see page 83).

Ions are charged particles (see page 83).

4) For ions made up of groups of atoms, it's not so simple. You just have to <u>learn</u> these ones.

- Ammonium — NH_4^+
- Hydroxide — OH^-
- Nitrate — NO_3^-
- Carbonate — CO_3^{2-}
- Sulfate — SO_4^{2-}

5) Ions with names ending in <u>-ate</u> are negative ions containing <u>oxygen</u> and at least <u>one other element</u>.

6) Ions with names ending in <u>-ide</u> are negative ions containing <u>only one element</u> (except hydroxide ions).

ReVISe$_2$ — it's the formula for success...

You can't always write out a symbol equation straight from the word equation for a reaction — you might have to balance the equation. You'll learn how to do just that on the next page, but first make sure you know the basics.

Q1   Carbon dioxide is the only substance formed in a reaction between carbon and oxygen. State the word equation of this reaction.

         [1 mark]

Balancing Equations

This page shows you how to <u>balance</u> symbol equations. And it's time to meet <u>state symbols</u>. Get ready...

Symbol Equations Need to be Balanced

1) There must be the <u>same</u> number of atoms of <u>each element</u> on <u>both sides</u> of the equation. For example:

$$H_2SO_4 + NaOH \rightarrow Na_2SO_4 + H_2O$$

2) In this equation, the numbers of some atoms <u>don't match up</u> on both sides.

	H	S	O	Na
Left side	3	1	5	1
Right side	2	1	5	2

3) You <u>can't change formulas</u> like NaOH to Na_2OH. You can only put numbers <u>in front</u> of the formulas where needed. Here's what you should do:

- Find an element that <u>doesn't balance</u>. <u>Write in a number</u> to try and sort it out.
- This might mean that <u>another element</u> becomes unbalanced.
- So, write in <u>another number</u> to balance that element.
- Carry on doing this, until <u>all of the elements</u> are balanced in the equation.

$E=mc^2$

4) Here's one way you could balance the above equation:

EXAMPLE   There aren't enough <u>Na atoms</u> on the LHS (Left-Hand Side) of the equation.

1) The only thing you can do about that is make it <u>2NaOH</u> instead of just NaOH:

$$H_2SO_4 + 2NaOH \rightarrow Na_2SO_4 + H_2O$$

2) Now there <u>aren't enough</u> O atoms or H atoms on the RHS (Right-Hand Side). To balance that you could try putting a <u>2</u> in front of the <u>H₂O</u> on the RHS:

$$H_2SO_4 + 2NaOH \rightarrow Na_2SO_4 + 2H_2O$$

	H	S	O	Na
Left side	4	1	6	2
Right side	2	1	5	2

	H	S	O	Na
Left side	4	1	6	2
Right side	4	1	6	2

3) And suddenly there it is — <u>everything balances</u>.

State Symbols Tell You the State of a Substance in an Equation

1) Symbol equations can also include <u>state symbols</u> next to each substance.

2) State symbols are written in <u>brackets after</u> the element.

3) They tell you what <u>physical state</u> (see page 96) the reactants and products are in:

(s) — solid   (l) — liquid   (g) — gas   (aq) — aqueous

'Aqueous' means 'dissolved in water'.

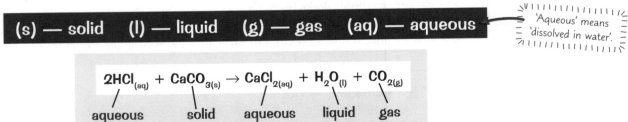

$$2HCl_{(aq)} + CaCO_{3(s)} \rightarrow CaCl_{2(aq)} + H_2O_{(l)} + CO_{2(g)}$$

aqueous   solid   aqueous   liquid   gas

I'm in a Texan percussion band — we're the State Cymbals...

Balancing equations is all about practice. Once you have a few goes you'll see it's not that scary. Read the green box above on how to balance equations, then follow each step to answer this question.

Q2 Video Solution

Q1   Balance the equation: $Fe + Cl_2 \rightarrow FeCl_3$ [1 mark]

Q2   Hydrogen and oxygen molecules are formed in a reaction where water splits apart. For this reaction: a) State the word equation.   b) Give a balanced symbol equation.   [3 marks]

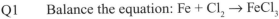

Hazards and Risk

Chemistry's a risky business. You need to be able to <u>identify</u> any <u>hazards</u> or <u>risk</u> in experiments that you do.

You Need to Learn the Common Hazard Symbols

1) A <u>hazard</u> is anything that could cause <u>harm</u> or <u>damage</u>.
2) A <u>risk</u> for a hazard is how likely it is that someone (or something) will be <u>harmed</u> by it.
3) Containers for chemicals often have <u>symbols</u> on them. These show what the <u>dangers</u> of the chemical are.
4) Here's what some of these symbols <u>mean</u> and examples of ways that you can <u>protect yourself</u>:

Oxidising
<u>Provides oxygen</u> which allows other materials to <u>burn more fiercely</u>.
<u>Protection</u>: Keep them away from <u>flammable</u> materials.

Highly Flammable
<u>Catches fire</u> easily.
<u>Protection</u>: Keep them away from flames.

Environmental Hazard
<u>Harmful</u> to <u>plants or animals</u> and to the <u>environment</u>.
<u>Protection</u>: Get rid of them carefully (don't pour them down the sink).

Harmful
Can cause irritation, <u>reddening</u> or <u>blistering of the skin</u>.
<u>Protection</u>: Wear gloves, goggles and a lab coat.

Toxic
<u>Can cause death</u> e.g. if it's swallowed, breathed in or absorbed through skin.
<u>Protection</u>: Wear gloves, goggles and a lab coat. For gases, use a fume cupboard.

Corrosive
<u>Destroys materials</u>, so could damage eyes and skin.
<u>Protection</u>: Wear gloves, a lab coat and goggles.

Experiments Involve Risks and Hazards

Err... Doug, it's meant to be a <u>risk</u> assessment

1) When you <u>plan</u> an experiment, you need to <u>identify all the hazards</u>.
2) You also need to work out the risk of each hazard.
3) Then you need to think of ways to <u>reduce</u> these risks.
4) This is called a <u>risk assessment</u>. For example:

Here's part of a risk assessment for an experiment that uses <u>sodium hydroxide</u> solution.

- Sodium hydroxide is <u>harmful</u> at low concentrations.
- If it gets on the <u>skin</u> it might cause <u>blistering</u> or <u>reddening</u>.
- At high concentrations, it's <u>corrosive</u>. That means that it's much <u>more dangerous</u> if it touches your skin or eyes.
- To <u>reduce the risks</u> you should try to use <u>low concentrations</u> of the sodium hydroxide.
- You should also <u>wear gloves</u>, a <u>lab coat</u> and <u>goggles</u> when handling the sodium hydroxide.

I always carry out a risk assessment on my cuppa — safe-tea first...

With all those dangerous chemicals, knowing this page just might save you from a nasty accident.

Q1 A student is using a flammable chemical in an experiment.
Give one way in which the student could minimise the risk in this experiment. [1 mark]

The History of the Atom

Atoms are pretty tiny. But what exactly are they like? Scientists have been trying to work it out for years...

The Theory of Atomic Structure Has Changed

Atoms are tiny particles. They make up everything in the universe...

1) At the start of the 1800s, John Dalton described atoms as solid spheres.
2) He said that different spheres made up the different elements.
3) But then it was shown that atoms weren't solid spheres.
4) Atoms were found to have even smaller, negatively charged particles. These are electrons.
5) This new theory for the structure of the atom was called the 'plum pudding model'.
6) In this model, negatively charged electrons are stuck in a positively charged 'pudding'.
7) The positive charge was thought to be spread out through the 'pudding' of the atom.

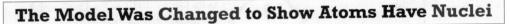

electrons

positively charged 'pudding'

delicious pudding

The Model Was Changed to Show Atoms Have Nuclei

1) Experiments showed that the positive charge couldn't be spread out through the atom.
2) It was found instead that atoms have a small, positively charged nucleus. The nucleus is in the centre of the atom.
3) It was also found that most of the mass of the atom is in the nucleus.
4) Scientists suggested that the nucleus is surrounded by a cloud of negatively charged electrons.

Electron Shells Were Discovered

1) Instead of electrons being in a cloud around the nucleus, a new model was developed.
2) In this model, all the electrons are found in shells and not anywhere in between.
3) This model was supported by many experiments and observations.

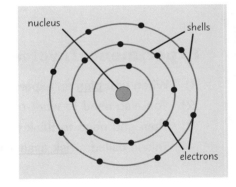

nucleus

shells

electrons

Later Experiments Found Protons and Neutrons

1) More experiments by scientists showed that the nucleus can be divided into smaller particles. Each particle has the same positive charge. These particles were named protons.
2) Experiments showed that the nucleus also contained neutral particles — neutrons.
3) This led to a model of the atom which was pretty close to the one we have today (see next page).

Weather in the atom — not as cloudy as expected...

This is a great example of how science works. Scientists working together to find evidence. Lovely.

Q1 Describe two ways in which the discovery of the nucleus changed the 'plum pudding' model of the atom.

[2 marks]

The Atom

All substances are made of <u>atoms</u>. They're really <u>tiny</u> — too small to see, even with a microscope.

Atoms Contain Protons, Neutrons and Electrons

The atom is made up of three <u>subatomic particles</u> — protons, neutrons and electrons.

1) <u>Protons</u> are <u>heavy</u> and <u>positively charged</u>.
2) <u>Neutrons</u> are <u>heavy</u> and <u>neutral</u>.
3) <u>Electrons</u> have <u>hardly any mass</u> and are <u>negatively charged</u>.

Particle	Relative mass	Relative charge
Proton	1	+1
Neutron	1	0
Electron	0.0005	−1

Relative mass measures mass on a scale where the mass of a proton or neutron is 1.

Protons and neutrons are still teeny tiny — they're just heavy compared to electrons.

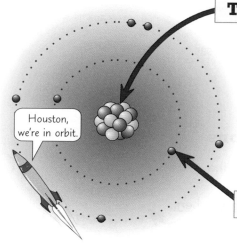

Houston, we're in orbit.

The Nucleus

1) It's in the <u>middle</u> of the atom.
2) It contains <u>protons</u> and <u>neutrons</u>.
3) It has a <u>positive charge</u> because of the protons.
4) Almost the <u>whole mass</u> of the atom is found in the <u>nucleus</u>.
5) Compared to the overall size of the atom, the nucleus is <u>tiny</u>.

The Electrons

Electron shells are also called energy levels.

1) Electrons move <u>around</u> the nucleus in electron <u>shells</u>.
2) They're <u>negatively charged</u>.
3) They're <u>tiny</u>, but the shells they're in cover <u>a lot of space</u>.
4) The <u>size</u> of the shells determines the size of the atom.
5) Atoms have a radius of about 10^{-10} m.
6) Electrons have a <u>tiny</u> mass (so small that it's sometimes given as zero).

In an Atom the Number of Protons Equals the Number of Electrons

1) Atoms are <u>neutral</u> — they have <u>no charge</u> overall (unlike ions).
2) This is because they have the <u>same number</u> of <u>protons</u> as <u>electrons</u>.
3) The <u>charge</u> on the electrons is the <u>same size</u> as the charge on the <u>protons</u>.
4) But electrons are negative and protons are positive — so the charges <u>cancel out</u>.

An ion is an atom or group of atoms that has lost or gained electrons — see page 83 for more.

Don't trust atoms — they make up everything...

Make sure you've learnt the relative masses and charges of protons, neutrons and electrons. It'll be really useful when you learn about the mass and atomic number of an atom on the next page.

Q1 Explain why atoms have no overall charge.

[1 mark]

Atomic Number, Mass Number and Isotopes

Here are a few more things that you need to know about <u>atoms</u>. Oh, and here come <u>isotopes</u> to confuse things.

Atomic Number and Mass Number Describe an Atom

1) The <u>nuclear symbol</u> of an atom tells you its <u>atomic number</u> and <u>mass number</u>.

2) The <u>atomic number</u> tells you how many <u>protons</u> an atom has. Every atom of an element has the <u>same number of protons</u>.

3) The atomic number is <u>unique</u> to an element — this means that different elements have <u>different</u> numbers of protons.

4) For a <u>neutral</u> atom, the number of protons is the same as the number of electrons.

5) So, the number of electrons is the same as the <u>atomic number</u>.

6) The <u>mass number</u> is the <u>total number</u> of <u>protons and neutrons</u> in the atom.

7) To work out the number of <u>neutrons</u> in an atom, take away the <u>atomic number</u> from the <u>mass number</u>.

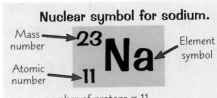

Nuclear symbol for sodium.

Mass number → $^{23}_{11}$Na ← Element symbol

Atomic number →

- number of protons = 11
- number of electrons = 11
- number of neutrons = 23 − 11 = 12

Sometimes the mass number and atomic number are written the other way around to what's on the diagram here. Just remember the bigger one is the mass number.

Isotopes are the Same Except for Extra Neutrons

1) <u>Isotopes</u> are different forms of the same element. They have the <u>same number</u> of <u>protons</u> but a <u>different number</u> of <u>neutrons</u>.

2) So isotopes have the <u>same atomic number</u> but <u>different mass numbers</u>.

3) For example, <u>carbon-12</u> and <u>carbon-13</u> are both isotopes of carbon.

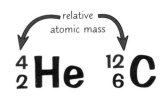

Carbon-12	Carbon-13
$^{12}_{6}$C	$^{13}_{6}$C
6 PROTONS	6 PROTONS
6 ELECTRONS	6 ELECTRONS
6 NEUTRONS	7 NEUTRONS

Relative Atomic Mass Takes Isotopes Into Account

1) In the periodic table (see next page), the elements all have <u>two</u> numbers next to them. The <u>bigger one</u> is the <u>relative atomic mass</u> (A_r) of the element.

> The <u>relative atomic mass</u> of an element is the <u>average mass</u> of <u>one atom</u> of the element, compared to $\frac{1}{12}$ of the <u>mass</u> of <u>one atom</u> of <u>carbon-12</u>.

relative atomic mass

$^{4}_{2}$He $\quad$ $^{12}_{6}$C

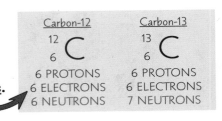

2) If an element only has <u>one isotope</u>, its A_r will be the same as its <u>mass number</u>.

3) If an element has <u>more than one</u> isotope, its A_r will be the <u>average</u> of the <u>mass numbers</u> of <u>the different isotopes</u>. It takes into account <u>how much</u> there is of each isotope, so it might not be a whole number. For example:

- Chlorine has two isotopes, <u>chlorine-35</u> and <u>chlorine-37</u>.
- There's <u>quite a lot</u> of chlorine-35 and <u>not so much</u> chlorine-37.
- So chlorine's A_r works out as <u>35.5</u>.

It's elemental my dear Watson...

Atoms, elements and isotopes — make sure you know what they are and the differences between them.

Q1   An atom of gallium has an atomic number of 31 and a mass number of 70. Give the number of electrons, protons and neutrons in the atom.
$\qquad$ [3 marks]

Q1 Video Solution

The Periodic Table

Early chemists tried to find <u>patterns</u> in the <u>properties</u> of elements. They also <u>organised</u> them into a neat table.

Dmitri Mendeleev Made the First Proper Periodic Table

1) One of the first periodic tables was made by a scientist called <u>Mendeleev</u>.

2) He took the elements that had been <u>found</u> at the time and placed them in order of <u>atomic mass</u>.

3) He then arranged the elements into <u>groups</u> based on how they (and their compounds) <u>behaved</u>.

4) There were a few elements that seemed to be in the <u>wrong groups</u>.

5) In some cases this was because the <u>atomic mass</u> he had was <u>wrong</u> (due to <u>isotopes</u>).

6) But some elements didn't quite fit the pattern. Wherever this happened, he <u>switched</u> the order of the elements to keep those with the same properties in the same columns.

7) He also had to leave some <u>gaps</u> (shown by the *s in the table above) to keep elements with <u>similar properties</u> together.

8) These gaps showed where elements that <u>hadn't been discovered</u> yet would <u>go</u>.

9) He <u>predicted</u> the properties of <u>missing elements</u> using the properties of other elements.

Mendeleev's Table of the Elements

```
H
Li Be                              B  C  N  O  F
Na Mg                              Al Si P  S  Cl
K  Ca *  Ti V  Cr Mn Fe Co Ni Cu Zn *  *  As Se Br
Rb Sr Y  Zr Nb Mo *  Ru Rh Pd Ag Cd In Sn Sb Te I
Cs Ba *  *  Ta W  *  Os Ir Pt Au Hg Tl Pb Bi
```

The missing elements have been found and fit the patterns Mendeleev predicted. This supports his ideas.

This is How the Periodic Table Looks Today

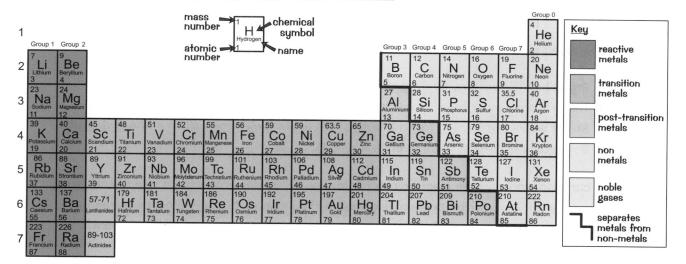

1) The <u>modern</u> periodic table puts elements in order of increasing <u>atomic number</u> instead of <u>mass number</u>.

2) The periodic table is laid out so elements with <u>similar chemical properties</u> form <u>columns</u> called <u>groups</u>.

3) An element's group number is the same as the <u>number of electrons</u> it has in its <u>outer shell</u>. E.g. <u>Group 1</u> elements have <u>1</u> outer shell electron, <u>Group 7</u> elements have <u>7</u>, etc. But <u>Group 0</u> elements have <u>full</u> outer shells of <u>8</u> electrons (or 2 in the case of helium).

4) The rows are called <u>periods</u>. An element's period number tells you how many <u>shells</u> of electrons it has.

Why did Dmitri's granddaughter inherit his antique table..?

...because he Men-de-leev it. You can use the periodic table to predict how reactions will occur. How neat is that?

Q1 Based on its position in the periodic table, would you expect the chemical properties of potassium to be more similar to those of sodium or calcium? Explain your answer. [2 marks]

Electronic Configurations

The <u>electronic configuration</u> of an atom is how electrons are <u>organised</u> into the different <u>shells</u> of the atom.

You Need to Know How to Work Out Electronic Configurations

1) If you know <u>how many</u> electrons an atom has, you can work out how its electrons are <u>arranged</u> (its <u>electronic configuration</u>).

2) You just need to follow these <u>rules</u>:

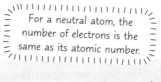

For a neutral atom, the number of electrons is the same as its atomic number.

- Electrons always occupy <u>shells</u> (sometimes called <u>energy levels</u>).
- The <u>lowest</u> energy levels are <u>always filled first</u>.
- Only <u>a certain number</u> of electrons are allowed in each shell:

1st shell	2nd shell	3rd shell
<u>2</u> electrons	<u>8</u> electrons	<u>8</u> electrons

- Electronic configurations can be shown as diagrams like this:
- ... or as numbers like this: 2.8.1

Number of electrons in <u>1st shell</u>.
Number of electrons in <u>2nd shell</u>.
Number of electrons in <u>3rd shell</u>.

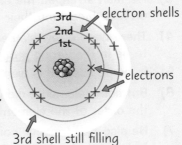

3rd — electron shells
2nd
1st
electrons
3rd shell still filling

3) Make sure you can <u>work out</u> the electronic configuration of the <u>first 20 elements</u> in the periodic table.

4) Here are some examples:

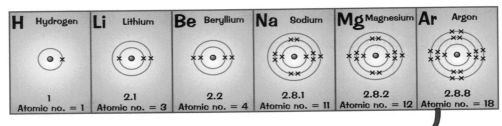

H Hydrogen	**Li** Lithium	**Be** Beryllium	**Na** Sodium	**Mg** Magnesium	**Ar** Argon
1 Atomic no. = 1	2.1 Atomic no. = 3	2.2 Atomic no. = 4	2.8.1 Atomic no. = 11	2.8.2 Atomic no. = 12	2.8.8 Atomic no. = 18

1) Argon has 18 protons, so it <u>must</u> have 18 electrons.
2) The first shell must have <u>2</u> electrons and the second shell must have <u>8</u>.
3) So far we've got <u>10 electrons</u> (2 + 8). The other <u>8 electrons</u> all fit in the <u>3rd shell</u>.
4) So argon's electronic configuration is <u>2.8.8</u>.

5) You can also work out the electronic configuration of an element from its <u>period</u> and <u>group</u>.
6) The <u>number of shells</u> which contain electrons is the same as the <u>period</u> of the element.
7) The <u>group number</u> tells you <u>how many electrons</u> occupy the <u>outer shell</u> of the element.

1) Sodium is in <u>period 3</u>, so it has <u>3</u> shells occupied.
2) The first two shells must be full (2.8).
3) It's in <u>Group 1</u>, so it has <u>1</u> electron in its outer shell.
4) So its electronic configuration is <u>2.8.1</u>.

The electronic configuration of the fifth element is a bit boron...

Electronic configurations may seem a bit complicated but once you learn the rules, it's a piece of cake.

Q1   Give the electronic configuration of aluminium (atomic number = 13).   [1 mark]

Q2   In which group and period of the periodic table would you expect to find the element with the electronic configuration 2.8.8.2?   [2 marks]

Q1 Video Solution

Ions

Some atoms are keen on getting rid of some of their electrons. Others want more. That's life. And ions...

Simple Ions Form When Atoms Lose or Gain Electrons

1) Ions are charged particles. They can be single atoms (e.g. Na^+) or groups of atoms (e.g. NO_3^-).
2) Atoms lose or gain electrons to form ions with a full outer shell. This is a "stable electronic structure".
3) Negative ions (anions) form when atoms gain electrons — they have more electrons than protons.
   Positive ions (cations) form when atoms lose electrons — they have more protons than electrons.
4) The number of electrons lost or gained is the same as the charge on the ion.

- F^- has a single negative charge, so it must have one more electron than protons.
  F has an atomic number of 9, so has 9 protons. So F^- must have $9 + 1 = 10$ electrons.

- Fe^{2+} has a 2+ charge, so it must have two more protons than electrons.
  Fe has an atomic number of 26, so has 26 protons. So Fe^{2+} must have $26 - 2 = 24$ electrons.

Groups 1 & 2 and 6 & 7 are the Most Likely to Form Ions

1) The elements in Groups 1, 2, 6 and 7 form ions very easily.
2) Group 1 and 2 elements are metals. They lose electrons to form positive ions.
3) Group 6 and 7 elements are non-metals. They gain electrons to form negative ions.
4) Elements in the same group all have the same number of outer electrons.
5) So they have to lose or gain the same number to get a full outer shell.
6) And this means that they form ions with the same charges:

- Group 1 elements form 1+ ions. Group 2 elements form 2+ ions.
- Group 6 elements form 2– ions. Group 7 elements form 1– ions.

You Can Work Out the Formula of an Ionic Compound

1) Ionic compounds (see page 85) are made up of positively charged parts and negatively charged parts.
2) The overall charge of any ionic compound is zero.
3) So, all the negative charges in the compound balance all the positive charges.
4) You can use the charges on the ions to work out the formula for the ionic compound.

EXAMPLE   What is the chemical formula of the ionic compound calcium nitrate?

1) Write out the formulas of the calcium and nitrate ions. Ca^{2+}, NO_3^-

2) The overall charge on the formula must be zero, so work out the ratio of Ca : NO_3 that gives an overall neutral charge.

To balance the 2+ charge on Ca^{2+}, you need two NO_3^- ions: $(+2) + (2 \times -1) = 0$.
The formula is $Ca(NO_3)_2$
The brackets show you need two of the whole nitrate ion.

Calcium nitrate isn't sarcastic, it's just an ironic compound...

Don't forget about ions made up of groups of atoms, like the ones on page 75. You can't use the periodic table to work out the charges on these, like you can with simple ions. You just need to learn them.

Q1   What is the formula of the ionic compound, lithium oxide?   [1 mark]

Q1 Video Solution

Section 10 — Key Concepts in Chemistry

Ionic Bonding

Time to find out how particles bond together to form compounds (bet you can't wait). First up, it's <u>ionic bonds</u>.

Ionic Bonding — Transfer of Electrons

The name's Bond.
Ionic Bond.

1) When <u>metals</u> and <u>non-metals</u> react together, the <u>metal atoms lose</u> electrons to form <u>positive ions</u> (cations) and the <u>non-metal atoms gain these electrons</u> to form <u>negative ions</u> (anions).

2) These oppositely charged ions are <u>strongly attracted</u> to one another by <u>electrostatic forces</u>.

3) This attraction is called an <u>ionic bond</u>.

Dot and Cross Diagrams Can Show How Ionic Compounds are Formed

1) <u>Dot and cross diagrams</u> show the <u>arrangement</u> of electrons in an atom or ion.

2) Each electron is represented by a <u>dot</u> or a <u>cross</u> (but don't get confused, they're really <u>all the same</u>).

3) These diagrams can show which <u>atom</u> the electrons in an <u>ion</u> originally came from.

Sodium Chloride (NaCl)

1) The <u>sodium</u> atom gives up its outer electron. It forms an <u>Na+</u> ion.

2) The <u>chlorine</u> atom picks up the electron. It forms a <u>Cl−</u> (<u>chloride</u>) ion.

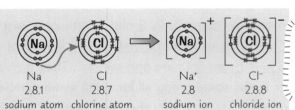

Here, the dots are the Na electrons and the crosses are the Cl electrons.

Here, we've only shown the outer shell of electrons for each atom on the dot and cross diagram — it makes it much simpler to see what's going on.

Magnesium Oxide (MgO)

1) The <u>magnesium</u> atom gives up its <u>two</u> outer electrons. It forms an <u>Mg²⁺</u> ion.

2) The <u>oxygen</u> atom picks up the electrons. It forms an <u>O²⁻</u> (<u>oxide</u>) ion.

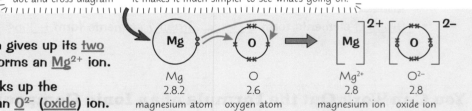

Remember, you can work out how many electrons an atom will gain or lose from its group number.

Magnesium Chloride (MgCl₂)

1) The <u>magnesium</u> atom gives up its <u>two</u> outer electrons. It forms an <u>Mg²⁺</u> ion.

2) The two <u>chlorine</u> atoms pick up <u>one electron each</u>. They form <u>two Cl⁻</u> (<u>chloride</u>) ions.

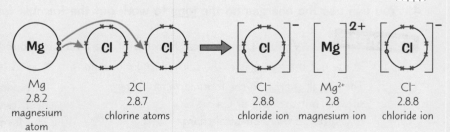

Any old ion, any old ion — any, any, any old ion...

You need to be able to describe how ionic compounds are formed using both words and dot and cross diagrams. It gets easier with practice, so here are some questions to get you started.

Q2 Video Solution

Q1 What is a cation? [1 mark]

Q2 Draw a dot and cross diagram to show how potassium (a Group 1 metal) and bromine (a Group 7 non-metal) form potassium bromide (KBr). [3 marks]

Ionic Compounds

Ionic compounds don't really look like the diagrams on the previous page — <u>lots</u> of ions are in <u>each one</u>.

Ionic Compounds Have a Regular Lattice Structure

1) <u>Ionic compounds</u> always have <u>giant ionic lattice</u> structures (see the diagrams of NaCl below).
2) The ions form a <u>repeating pattern</u>.
3) There are very strong <u>electrostatic forces of attraction</u> between <u>oppositely charged</u> ions. These are <u>ionic bonds</u>.

    1) A single crystal of <u>sodium chloride</u> (salt) is <u>one giant ionic lattice</u>.
    2) The <u>Na$^+$</u> and <u>Cl$^-$</u> ions are held together in a regular lattice.
    3) Throughout the lattice, the <u>Na$^+$</u> and <u>Cl$^-$</u> ions alternate.

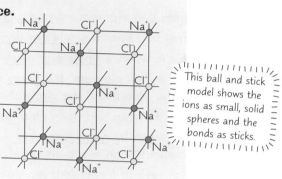

This 3D model shows the ions as solid spheres that are touching.

= Cl$^-$
= Na$^+$

This ball and stick model shows the ions as small, solid spheres and the bonds as sticks.

Ionic Compounds All Have Similar Properties

1) Ionic compounds have <u>high melting</u> and <u>boiling points</u>. This is because it takes lots of energy to break the <u>strong attraction</u> between the ions.
2) Many ionic compounds can <u>dissolve</u> in water.
3) Solid ionic compounds <u>don't</u> conduct electricity. This is because the ions <u>can't move</u>.
4) When the ions are <u>free to move</u>, they can carry an <u>electric charge</u>. This happens when the compound <u>melts</u>, or when it <u>dissolves</u> in water.

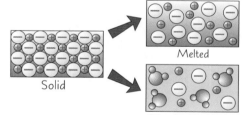

Solid

Melted

Dissolved in Water

There are Different Types of Models We Can Use

Displayed formulae and dot and cross diagrams are examples of 2D (2 dimensional) models. Ball and stick models are 3D.

1) We use <u>models</u> to give an idea of what substances look like.
2) For example, <u>displayed formulas</u> are a kind of model.
3) These are <u>simple</u>. They show all of the <u>atoms</u> in a substance and how they are <u>connected</u>.
4) But they don't show the <u>shape</u> of the substance. Also, they don't show the <u>sizes</u> of the atoms.
5) E.g. this is the displayed formula for <u>methane</u> (CH$_4$).

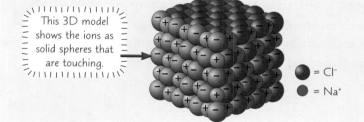

6) <u>Dot and cross diagrams</u> can show <u>where the electrons</u> in the bonds or ions in a substance <u>came from</u>. But they <u>don't</u> show the <u>size</u> of the atoms or ions or how they're <u>arranged</u>.
7) <u>Ball and stick models</u> (like the one for sodium chloride, above) show how the atoms in a substance are <u>connected</u>. But they show <u>big gaps</u> between the atoms, which aren't actually there.

What's a chemist's favourite game? Dots and crosses...

Make sure you know the properties of ionic compounds inside out and back to front. They may crop up in the exams.

Q1   Explain why ionic compounds have high melting points.

                 [1 mark]

Covalent Bonding

These molecules might be <u>simple</u>, but you've still got to know about them. I know, the world is a cruel place.

Learn These Examples of Simple Molecular Substances

1) A <u>covalent bond</u> is formed when two atoms share a <u>pair of electrons</u>. They can cause <u>molecules</u> to form.
2) Atoms form covalent bonds to get a <u>full outer shell</u> of electrons.
3) <u>Simple molecular substances</u> are made up of molecules containing a <u>few atoms</u> joined by <u>covalent bonds</u>.
4) You can draw <u>dot and cross diagrams</u> for simple molecular substances. Only the electrons in the <u>outer shell</u> are shown. Electrons shown in the <u>overlap</u> between two circles are <u>shared</u>. For example:

- Hydrogen atoms need <u>one more electron</u> for a <u>full outer shell</u>.
- They can form a <u>single covalent bond</u> with another hydrogen atom to get this.
- This is when a <u>single pair of electrons</u> is shared between the two atoms.
- E.g. in this diagram, the <u>cross</u> shows an electron that comes from one of the atoms and the <u>circle</u> shows an electron that comes from the other.
- The atoms in hydrogen chloride, methane and water also form single covalent bonds:
- There can be <u>more than one</u> covalent bond in a compound.
- E.g. carbon forms <u>four</u> covalent bonds in methane and oxygen forms <u>two</u> covalent bonds in water.

Hydrogen, H_2

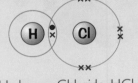
Hydrogen Chloride, HCl

Water, H_2O

Methane, CH_4

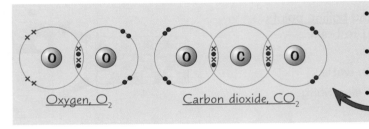
Oxygen, O_2 Carbon dioxide, CO_2

- Sometimes <u>two pairs of electrons</u> are shared between atoms in a molecule.
- This is called a <u>double covalent bond</u>.
- Both atoms gain <u>two</u> extra electrons.
- E.g. oxygen and carbon dioxide both have double covalent bonds.

5) Simple molecules are <u>tiny</u> — they're not much bigger than single atoms.

These dot and cross diagrams only show the electrons in the <u>outer shell</u> of each atom.

Properties of Simple Molecular Substances

1) In simple molecular substances, the covalent bonds between the atoms are <u>very strong</u>.
2) The molecules are also attracted <u>to each other</u>.
3) The forces of attraction <u>between molecules</u> are called <u>intermolecular forces</u>. They are <u>very weak</u>.
4) When simple molecules melt or boil, the <u>weak intermolecular forces</u> break. The <u>strong covalent bonds</u> don't get broken.
5) It's <u>easy</u> to <u>break</u> the intermolecular forces. So the melting and boiling points are <u>very low</u>.
6) Most molecular substances are <u>gases or liquids</u> at room temperature.
7) Molecular compounds <u>don't conduct electricity</u>. This is because they don't have <u>electrons</u> or <u>ions</u> that can <u>move</u> through the substance.
8) Some simple molecules <u>are soluble</u> in water and some <u>aren't</u>.

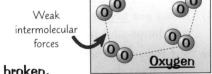
Weak intermolecular forces
<u>Oxygen</u>

May the intermolecular force be with you...

Remember, it's just the weak forces between molecules that are broken when a simple molecular substance melts.

Q1   Explain why oxygen, O_2, is a gas at room temperature.   [2 marks]

Giant Covalent Structures

Even more <u>covalent structures</u> for you to feast your eyes on... These ones are <u>bigger</u>, so they're better right?

Most Giant Covalent Structures Have Certain Properties

1) In giant covalent structures, <u>all</u> the atoms are <u>bonded</u> to <u>each other</u> by <u>strong</u> covalent bonds.

2) They have <u>very high</u> melting and boiling points.
This is because <u>lots of energy</u> is needed to break the covalent bonds.

3) They generally <u>don't</u> have charged particles that are free to move. ◄— Apart from graphite and graphene.
This means that they <u>can't conduct electricity</u>.

4) They <u>aren't</u> soluble in water.

5) The following examples are both <u>giant covalent structures</u> made up of carbon atoms.

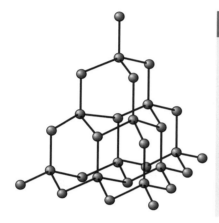

DIAMOND

- Diamond is made up of carbon atoms that each form <u>four covalent bonds</u>.
- This makes diamond <u>really hard</u>.
- So it's used to <u>strengthen cutting tools</u> (e.g. saw teeth and drill bits).
- The <u>strong covalent bonds</u> take lots of energy to break. So diamond has a <u>high melting point</u>.
- <u>All</u> the outer electrons of the carbon atoms are in <u>covalent bonds</u>, so <u>aren't free</u> to move.
- This means it <u>doesn't conduct electricity</u>.

The diagrams here only show part of the structure of diamond and graphite.

GRAPHITE

- In graphite, each carbon atom only forms <u>three covalent bonds</u>. This makes <u>sheets</u> of <u>carbon atoms</u> arranged in <u>hexagons</u>.
- There <u>aren't</u> any covalent bonds <u>between</u> the layers of sheets. So the layers are only held together <u>weakly</u>.
- The weak attraction between the layers means that they're free to <u>move</u> over each other. This makes graphite <u>soft</u> and <u>slippery</u>.
- Because it's so soft, graphite's used as a <u>lubricating material</u>.
- Graphite's got a <u>high melting point</u>. This is because the covalent bonds in the layers need <u>loads of energy</u> to break.
- Each carbon atom has <u>one</u> electron that's <u>free</u> to move. So graphite <u>conducts electricity</u> and is often used to make electrodes (see p.110).

Graphite — or as I call it, a boxing match for bar charts...

Make sure you know why each of these giant covalent structures has the properties that it has. You should also be able to describe why these properties make them useful for certain functions.

Q1   Describe the structure and bonding of graphite.   [4 marks]

Q1 Video Solution

Section 10 — Key Concepts in Chemistry

Polymers and Fullerenes

Here we go, more covalent compounds. And they're all carbon-based again too. Fun fun fun.

Polymers Are Made of Covalently Bonded Carbon Chains

1) Polymers are molecules that contain long chains of covalently bonded carbon atoms.

2) A famous example is poly(ethene).

- This is known as the repeat unit.
- The n shows that there's loads of these units joined, one after another.

3) Polymers are formed when lots of small molecules called monomers join together.

Fullerenes Are Also Formed from Carbon

1) Fullerenes are molecules of carbon. They are shaped like closed tubes or hollow balls.

2) They can be made of carbon atoms in hexagons, pentagons (rings of five) or heptagons (rings of seven).

3) They can be used to 'cage' other molecules.
   This could be used to deliver a drug directly to cells in the body.

4) Fullerenes have a huge surface area.
   This could be used to make good catalysts.

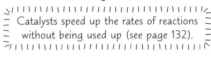
Catalysts speed up the rates of reactions without being used up (see page 132).

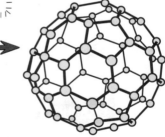

- This is an example of a fullerene with a molecular formula of C_{60}.
- It is a hollow sphere made up of 20 hexagons and 12 pentagons.
- This means that it can be used to cage other molecules.
- It's a stable molecule that forms soft brownish-black crystals.

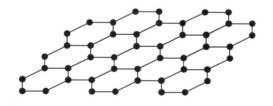

- Graphene is one layer of graphite (see previous page).
- It's a sheet of carbon atoms joined together in hexagons.
- The sheet is just one atom thick.
- Each carbon atom is covalently bonded to three other carbon atoms. These covalent bonds make it very strong.
- Each carbon atom has one other electron that's free to move. The free electrons mean it can conduct electricity.

No fullerene around, this stuff won't learn itself...

You need to know how the bonding of the carbon atoms in fullerenes gives them their properties. Like diamond and graphite on the previous page, fullerenes are only made of carbon. One element — loads of structures.

Q1   What is meant by a polymer?   [1 mark]

Q2   Describe the structure of graphene.   [3 marks]

Metallic Bonding

Ever wondered what makes <u>metals</u> tick? Well, either way, this is the page for you.

Metallic Bonding Involves Free Electrons

1) <u>Metals</u> have a <u>giant structure</u>.
2) They are made up of metal atoms arranged in <u>regular layers</u>.
3) The electrons in the <u>outer shell</u> of the metal atoms are free to move around between the layers of metal ions (they are <u>delocalised</u>).
4) The electrons are <u>shared</u> across the whole metal.
5) There are strong forces of <u>electrostatic attraction</u> between the <u>positive metal ions</u> and the <u>negative electrons</u>.
6) This is called <u>metallic bonding</u>. Metallic bonding is very <u>strong</u>.

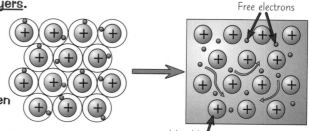
Free electrons

Metal ions

Metals Have Certain Physical Properties

1) Most substances with metallic bonds have very <u>high</u> melting and boiling points. This is because <u>lots of energy</u> is needed to <u>break</u> the <u>strong metallic bonds</u>.
2) Metals are <u>shiny solids</u> at room temperature.
3) They also <u>can't dissolve</u> in water.
4) Metals are <u>more dense</u> than non-metals.
5) Metals are <u>malleable</u>. This means that they can be <u>hammered</u> or <u>rolled</u> into <u>different shapes</u>. This is because the <u>layers</u> of atoms can easily <u>slide over</u> each other.
6) The <u>free electrons</u> mean that metals can <u>conduct electricity</u>. This is because the electrons can <u>carry a charge</u> through the material.

Metals and Non-Metals Have Different Physical Properties

1) All metals have <u>metallic bonding</u>. They're found on the <u>left</u> or towards the <u>bottom</u> of the periodic table.
2) Non-metals <u>don't</u> have metallic bonding. They're found on the <u>right</u> or towards the <u>top</u> of the periodic table.
3) Non-metals have <u>different physical properties</u> to metals.
4) Non-metals usually have <u>low boiling points</u>. They <u>don't</u> generally <u>conduct electricity</u>.
5) Metals and non-metals also have <u>different chemical properties</u>.
6) Non-metals usually have <u>more than half</u> of their outer shell filled. This means that they <u>gain electrons</u> to fill their outer shells.
7) Metals usually have <u>less than half</u> of their outer shell filled. This means that they <u>lose electrons</u> to fill their outer shells.

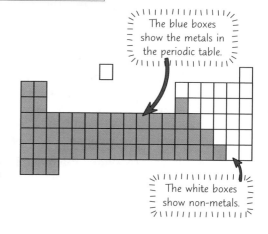
The blue boxes show the metals in the periodic table.

The white boxes show non-metals.

I saw a metal on the bus once — he was the conductor...

There's a lot to remember on this page. It might help to write out a list of the properties of metals here. Then see if you can remember why metals have each of those properties. Here's a question to get you started.

Q1   Copper is a metal. Explain why copper can conduct electricity.

[1 mark]

Conservation of Mass

Being a diva, I prefer the conservation of sass. <u>Conservation of mass</u> is more useful in science exams though.

In a Chemical Reaction, Mass Stays the Same

1) During a chemical reaction <u>no atoms are destroyed</u> and <u>no atoms are made</u>.
Instead the atoms in the reactants are <u>rearranged</u> to make the products of the reaction.

2) This means there are the <u>same number and types of atoms</u> on each side of a reaction equation.
So the total mass of the reactants <u>is the same as</u> the total mass of the products.
This is the <u>law of conservation of mass</u>.

3) If a reaction happens in a system where nothing can get in or out
(a <u>closed system</u>), the <u>mass</u> of the system <u>won't change</u>.

4) A good way of showing this is to do a <u>precipitation</u> reaction.

A precipitation reaction happens when two solutions react and an insoluble solid, called a precipitate, forms in the solution.

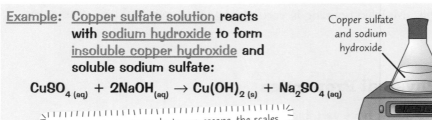

Example: <u>Copper sulfate solution</u> reacts with <u>sodium hydroxide</u> to form <u>insoluble copper hydroxide</u> and soluble sodium sulfate:

Copper sulfate and sodium hydroxide

A cloudy mixture of insoluble copper hydroxide precipitate in sodium sulfate solution

$$CuSO_{4\,(aq)} + 2NaOH_{(aq)} \rightarrow Cu(OH)_{2\,(s)} + Na_2SO_{4\,(aq)}$$

As no reactants or products can escape, the scales will read the same throughout the experiment.

Sometimes, the Mass Seems to Change

In a <u>non-enclosed system</u> (where substances can go in or out), the mass <u>inside</u> the reaction container may show a <u>change</u> during a reaction. But the <u>total</u> mass doesn't actually change. E.g.

Increase in mass

1) This can happen if one of the <u>reactants</u> is a <u>gas</u> that's found in the air and the <u>products</u> are <u>solid</u>, <u>liquid</u> or <u>in solution</u>.

2) <u>Before</u> the reaction, this gas is <u>not held</u> in the reaction container.
That means its mass won't be <u>measured</u>.

3) When the gas <u>reacts</u>, it forms a <u>product</u> that's held <u>inside</u> the reaction container.

4) So the total mass of the stuff <u>inside</u> the reaction container <u>goes up</u>. For example:

$$metal_{(s)} + oxygen_{(g)} \rightarrow metal\ oxide_{(s)}$$

- In this reaction, the mass inside the container <u>goes up</u>.

- The mass of the metal oxide produced <u>is the same as</u> the total mass of the <u>metal</u> and the <u>oxygen</u> that reacted from the air.

Decrease in mass

1) This can happen if one of the <u>products</u> is a <u>gas</u> and the <u>reactants</u> are <u>solids</u>, <u>liquids</u> or <u>in solution</u>.

2) <u>Before</u> the reaction, the reactants are held in the reaction container.

3) The gas can <u>escape</u> from the reaction container as it's formed. It's no longer held in the container, so you <u>can't</u> measure its <u>mass</u>.

4) So the total mass of the stuff <u>inside</u> the reaction container <u>goes down</u>. For example:

$$metal\ carbonate_{(s)} \rightarrow metal\ oxide_{(s)} + carbon\ dioxide_{(g)}$$

- In this reaction, the mass of the container <u>goes down</u> because the carbon dioxide escapes as it forms.

- The mass of the <u>metal oxide</u> and <u>carbon dioxide</u> formed is the same as the mass of the metal carbonate.

There's more on why gases escape unsealed containers on p.96.

Conservation of mass — protecting mass for future generations...

Never, ever forget that, in a reaction, the total mass of reactants is the same as the total mass of products.

Q1 The following reaction occurs in an unsealed container: $2Cu_{(s)} + O_{2(g)} \rightarrow 2CuO_{(s)}$
Predict how the mass of the reaction container will change over the reaction.
Explain your answer.
[3 marks]

Q1 Video Solution

Relative Masses

Time for some <u>maths</u>. "But this is <u>chemistry</u>, not maths," I hear you cry. "Tough cookies," I reply.

Here's How to Calculate Relative Formula Masses of Compounds

The <u>relative formula mass</u>, M_r, of a compound is the relative atomic masses (A_r) of all the atoms in its formula <u>added together</u>.

Look back at page 80 for more about relative atomic masses.

EXAMPLE   a)   **Find the relative formula mass of magnesium chloride, MgCl₂.**

1) Use the <u>periodic table</u> to find the <u>relative atomic masses</u> of magnesium and chlorine.

$$A_r(Mg) = 24 \qquad A_r(Cl) = 35.5$$

2) Add up the relative atomic masses of all the atoms in the formula to get the <u>relative formula mass</u>.

$$M_r(MgCl_2) = 24 + (2 \times 35.5) = 24 + 71 = 95$$
$$M_r \text{ of } MgCl_2 = 95$$

b)   **Find the relative formula mass of calcium hydroxide, Ca(OH)₂.**

1) Use the <u>periodic table</u> to find the <u>relative atomic masses</u> of calcium, oxygen and hydrogen.

$$A_r(Ca) = 40 \quad A_r(O) = 16 \quad A_r(H) = 1$$

2) Add up the relative atomic masses of all the atoms in the formula to get the <u>relative formula mass</u>.
The <u>small number 2</u> after the bracket in the formula Ca(OH)₂ means that <u>there's two of everything inside the brackets</u>.

$$M_r(Ca(OH)_2) = 40 + [(16 + 1) \times 2]$$
$$= 40 + 34 = 74$$
$$M_r \text{ of } Ca(OH)_2 = 74$$

You can Calculate the Amount of Product Using a Balanced Equation

If you know the <u>balanced chemical equation</u> for a reaction and the <u>mass of one substance</u> in the reaction, you can figure out the masses of the rest of the substances. Here's how:

1) <u>Work out relative formula masses</u> (M_r) of the substances you're interested in.

2) For the substance that you know the mass of, work out the <u>relative amount</u> of it in the reaction. To do this, you have to <u>divide its mass</u> by its <u>relative formula mass</u>.

3) Use the balanced equation to work out the <u>relative amount</u> of the <u>other</u> substance.

4) Then <u>multiply</u> the <u>relative amount</u> of the substance you don't know the mass of by its <u>relative formula mass</u>, to give the <u>mass</u> of the substance in the reaction.

Make sure you have a balanced equation for your reaction before you start these steps.

EXAMPLE   Calculate the mass of zinc oxide, ZnO, formed when 195 g of zinc is burned in air.
The balanced equation for this reaction is: $2Zn + O_2 \rightarrow 2ZnO$

1) Calculate the <u>relative formula masses</u> of the reactants and products you're interested in.

Zn: 65   O₂: 16 + 16 = 32   ZnO: 65 + 16 = 81

2) <u>Calculate the relative amount</u> of zinc in 195 g:

Relative amount = mass ÷ M_r = 195 ÷ 65 = 3

3) Look at the <u>ratio</u> of the reactants in the equation:

The ratio of Zn to ZnO in the equation is 2:2 or, more simply, 1:1. This means that 1 particle of zinc will react to form 1 particle of zinc oxide. So the relative amount of ZnO will be 3.

4) <u>Calculate the mass</u> of zinc oxide.

mass = relative amount × M_r = 3 × 81 = **243 g**

This page is a relative masterpiece...

Relative formula mass comes up a lot in chemistry. Make sure you can calculate it by doing loads of practice questions. Use the periodic table on page 236 to find the A_r values you need.

Q1   Calculate the relative formula mass of ethanol, C_2H_5OH.

[1 mark]

Q1 Video Solution

Empirical Formulas and Percentage Mass

You can find the <u>empirical formula</u> of a compound, and the <u>percentage mass</u> of an element in a compound.

The Empirical Formula is the Simplest Ratio of Atoms

1) The <u>empirical formula</u> tells you the <u>smallest whole number ratio</u> of atoms in a compound.
2) Here's how to work it out, using the <u>molecular formula</u> for a compound:

EXAMPLE   Find the empirical formula of glucose, $C_6H_{12}O_6$.

The numbers in the <u>molecular formula</u> of <u>glucose</u> are <u>6</u>, <u>12</u> and <u>6</u>.
To find the empirical formula, divide them by the <u>largest number</u> that goes into 6, 12 and 6 <u>exactly</u> — that's <u>6</u>.

C: 6 ÷ 6 = 1
H: 12 ÷ 6 = 2
O: 6 ÷ 6 = 1

The empirical formula of glucose is CH_2O.

Empirical Formulas can be Calculated from Masses

1) You can work out the <u>empirical formula</u> of a compound from the masses of the elements it contains.

EXAMPLE   A sample of a hydrocarbon contains 36 g of carbon and 6 g of hydrogen. Work out the empirical formula of the hydrocarbon.

1) Divide the mass of each element in the hydrocarbon by its <u>relative atomic mass</u>. This is to find the <u>relative amount</u> of each element.

$A_r(C) = 12$ C = 36 ÷ 12 = 3
$A_r(H) = 1$ H = 6 ÷ 1 = 6

2) Write the relative amount of each element as a ratio.

Ratio C:H = 3:6.

3) Work out the <u>smallest whole number ratio</u> between the C and H atoms by dividing by the smallest number (here it's 3).

C: 3 ÷ 3 = 1   H: 6 ÷ 3 = 2
So, the ratio C:H = 1:2.

4) Use this ratio to write the empirical formula.

The empirical formula must be CH_2.

2) You can also work out the empirical formula of a compound from its <u>percentage composition</u>. The percentage composition is the <u>percentage by mass</u> of each element in a compound.

3) The method for doing this is the <u>same</u> as the one above but in step 1) you divide the <u>percentage of each element</u> by its relative atomic mass.
E.g. if carbon makes up <u>48%</u> of a compound's mass, then you <u>divide 48 by 12</u> (the A_r of carbon).

You Can Calculate the Percentage Mass of an Element in a Compound

To work out the <u>percentage mass</u> of an element in a compound, you need to use this <u>formula</u>:

$$\text{Percentage mass of an element in a compound} = \frac{A_r \times \text{number of atoms of that element}}{M_r \text{ of the compound}} \times 100$$

EXAMPLE   Find the percentage mass of sodium (Na) in sodium bromide (NaBr).

1) Look up the <u>relative atomic masses</u> of all the elements in the compound on the periodic table.

A_r of Na = 23 A_r of Br = 80

2) Add up the relative atomic masses of all the atoms in the compound to find the <u>relative formula mass</u>.

M_r of NaBr = 23 + 80 = 103

3) Use the formula to calculate the percentage mass.

$$\text{Percentage mass of sodium} = \frac{A_r \times \text{number of atoms of that element}}{M_r \text{ of the compound}} \times 100$$
$$= \frac{23 \times 1}{103} \times 100 = 22\%$$

How do you compare hedgehogs? Use an emprickle formula...

Don't get confused between empirical and molecular formulas. It could make a big difference.

Q1   A sample of an oxide of nitrogen contains 28 g of nitrogen and 64 g of oxygen. What is the empirical formula of the nitrogen oxide?   [2 marks]

Q1 Video Solution

Finding Empirical Formulas by Experiments

If you're still not sure about <u>empirical formulas</u>, go over the previous page again.
This page looks at how you can use an <u>experiment</u> to find the empirical formula of a compound.

You can Use Experiments to Find Empirical Formulas

1) Here's an <u>experiment</u> you could use to find the empirical formula of a metal oxide, e.g. magnesium oxide.

2) First of all you have to work out the <u>change in mass</u> that happens when you react <u>pure magnesium</u> in oxygen to get <u>magnesium oxide</u>.

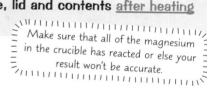

crucible containing magnesium ribbon

lid

gauze

tripod

HEAT

1) <u>Weigh</u> an empty crucible and its lid.
2) Add some clean <u>magnesium ribbon</u> to the crucible.
3) <u>Weigh</u> the crucible, lid and <u>magnesium ribbon</u>.
4) The <u>mass of magnesium</u> you're using is the second reading minus the first reading for the mass of the crucible and lid.
5) Put the lid on the crucible to <u>stop</u> any bits of solid from <u>escaping</u>. You should leave a <u>small gap</u> to allow <u>oxygen</u> to get into the crucible.
6) Heat the crucible strongly until <u>all</u> the magnesium ribbon has turned <u>white</u>. The magnesium ribbon has now reacted to form <u>magnesium oxide</u>.
7) Allow the crucible to <u>cool</u>.
8) <u>Weigh</u> the crucible with the lid and its contents.
9) The mass of the <u>magnesium oxide</u> equals the mass of the crucible, lid and contents <u>after heating</u> <u>minus</u> the mass of the crucible and lid <u>before heating</u>.

Make sure that all of the magnesium in the crucible has reacted or else your result won't be accurate.

3) Then you can use the information from this experiment to figure out the <u>empirical formula</u> of the magnesium oxide. Here's how:

EXAMPLE

A student heats 1.08 g of magnesium ribbon in a crucible so it completely reacts to form magnesium oxide. The total mass of magnesium oxide formed was 1.80 g. Calculate the empirical formula of magnesium oxide.

1) The extra mass in the magnesium oxide must have come from oxygen. So the <u>mass of oxygen</u> that reacted is the same as the mass of magnesium oxide <u>minus</u> the mass of magnesium.

mass of O = 1.80 − 1.08 = 0.72 g

2) Work out the <u>relative amount</u> of <u>magnesium</u> and <u>oxygen atoms</u> involved in the reaction by dividing the <u>mass</u> of each one by their own <u>relative atomic mass</u> (A_r).

relative amount of Mg = 1.08 ÷ 24 = 0.045   relative amount of O = 0.72 ÷ 16 = 0.045

3) Work out the <u>lowest whole number ratio</u> between Mg and O by dividing the relative amount of both by the <u>smallest number</u>.

Mg = 0.045 ÷ 0.045 = 1   O = 0.045 ÷ 0.045 = 1

This shows that the ratio between O and Mg in the formula is 1:1, so the empirical formula of the magnesium oxide must be MgO.

The empirical strikes back...

You may be given experimental results and asked to find the empirical formula of the compound formed. So read through the example thoroughly and make sure you can follow what's going on.

Q1   A crucible and its lid weighs 21 g. Magnesium is placed inside the crucible. It now weighs 23.2 g. The crucible is then heated strongly until the magnesium has all reacted to form magnesium oxide. Its final mass is 25 g. How much more does the magnesium oxide weigh than the magnesium?   [2 marks]

Concentration

A little bit more <u>maths</u> to get through. Then we're all done with this section. Phew. Keeping paying attention, though, there's a <u>formula</u> you need to know on this page. And a handy way of <u>remembering it</u>.

Concentration is a Measure of How Crowded Things Are

1) The <u>concentration</u> of a solution is <u>how much</u> dissolved solid there is in it.

2) The <u>more solid</u> that's dissolved in a set volume of solution, the <u>more concentrated</u> the solution.

3) Concentration can be measured in <u>grams per decimetre cubed</u> ($g\ dm^{-3}$).
1 gram of stuff dissolved in $1\ dm^3$ of solution has a concentration of <u>$1\ g\ dm^{-3}$</u>.

$1\ dm^3$
$= 1$ litre
$= 1000\ cm^3$

4) Here's the formula for finding <u>concentration</u> from the <u>mass of solid dissolved</u>:

$$\text{concentration} = \text{mass of solid} \div \text{volume of solution}$$

> **EXAMPLE**
>
> 14 g of sodium carbonate is dissolved in $2\ dm^3$ of water. What is its concentration in $g\ dm^{-3}$?
>
> concentration = mass ÷ volume of solution
> $= 14 \div 2 = 7\ g\ dm^{-3}$

> **EXAMPLE**
>
> 25 g of copper sulfate is dissolved in $500\ cm^3$ of water. What's the concentration in $g\ dm^{-3}$?
>
> 1) Make sure the values are in the <u>right units</u>. The mass is already in g, but you need to convert the volume to dm^3.
>
> $1000\ cm^3 = 1\ dm^3$, so
> $500\ cm^3 = (500 \div 1000)\ dm^3 = 0.5\ dm^3$
>
> 2) Now just substitute the values into the formula:
>
> concentration $= 25 \div 0.5 = 50\ g\ dm^{-3}$

5) You can rearrange the equation above to find the <u>mass of the solid</u> or the <u>volume of the solution</u>.

6) This handy triangle shows how you can do this.

7) Just <u>cover</u> the part of the triangle that you want to <u>find</u>. <u>Whatever's left</u> is the equation you need to use.

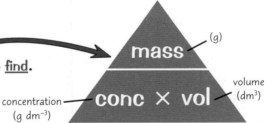

mass (g)

concentration (g dm⁻³) — conc × vol — volume (dm³)

> **EXAMPLE**
>
> A solution of sodium chloride has a volume of $0.30\ dm^3$ and a concentration of $12\ g\ dm^{-3}$. What mass of sodium chloride is in the solution?
>
> 1) You want to find the mass. So cover up 'mass' in the formula triangle. This leaves 'concentration × volume'.
>
> 2) Use the equation to calculate the mass.
>
> mass = concentration × volume
> mass $= 12 \times 0.30 = 3.6\ g$

Concentration = mass of revision ÷ hours of good daytime TV...

Try writing out the equations for finding the concentration and volume of a solution, so that you know you can use the formula triangle on this page. Then have a go at this question to check that you really get it.

Q1   Calculate the concentration, in $g\ dm^{-3}$, of a solution
that contains 0.60 g of salt in $15\ cm^3$ of solvent.   [2 marks]

Q1 Video Solution

Revision Questions for Section 10

Phew. That's <u>Section 10</u> over already. And I always say,
Section 10 is always, well sometimes, the hardest...

For even more practice, try the
Retrieval Quiz for Section 10 —
just scan this QR code!

Section 10
Quiz

* Try these questions and <u>tick off each one</u> when you <u>get it right</u>.
* When you're <u>completely happy</u> with a sub-topic, tick it off.

Chemical Equations, Risks and Hazards (p.75-77) ☑

1) What are the chemicals on the left-hand side of a chemical equation called?
2) Write out the formulas for the following compounds: a) ammonia   b) carbon dioxide
3) Write out the four state symbols used in chemical equations, and state what each one means.
4) Sketch the following hazard symbols: a) toxic,   b) harmful.

Atoms, Isotopes and Electronic Configurations (p.78-82) ☐

5) Describe the main features of the plum pudding model of the atom.
6) Name the three subatomic particles found in an atom.
7) What does the mass number tell you about an atom?
8) Explain how you would find the number of neutrons in an atom using its atomic and mass numbers.
9) State what isotopes are.
10) Describe how Dmitri Mendeleev organised his version of the periodic table.
11) What does the group number of an element in the periodic table tell you about its electronic structure?
12) What can you say about the number of electron shells in elements in the same period?
13) How many electrons can fit into the first electron shell?

Types of Bonding and Structures (p.83-89) ☐

14) What charge will the ion of a Group 6 element have?
15) What is an ionic bond?
16) Draw a dot and cross diagram to show how magnesium chloride forms.
17) Why can't solid ionic compounds conduct electricity?
18) Give one limitation of using a ball and stick model to represent a molecule.
19) Draw a dot and cross diagram to show the bonding in a molecule of water.
20) Do simple molecular substances have high or low boiling points? Explain your answer.
21) How many covalent bonds does each carbon atom form in: a) diamond,   b) graphite?
22) Briefly describe what a fullerene is.
23) Give three physical properties of metals.

Conservation of Mass and Calculations (p.90-94) ☐

24) Why might the mass of an unsealed system increase during a chemical reaction?
25) Give a definition for the relative formula mass of a compound.
26) What is the empirical formula of a compound?
27) Outline an experiment you could use to work out the empirical formula of magnesium oxide.
28) What equation links the concentration of a solution with its volume and the mass of solute used?

States of Matter

All stuff is made of <u>particles</u> (molecules, ions or atoms). These can be in a <u>solid</u>, <u>liquid</u> or a <u>gas state</u>.

States of Matter Depend on the Forces Between Particles

1) There are <u>three states of matter</u> that you need to know about — <u>solids</u>, <u>liquids</u> and <u>gases</u>.

2) The <u>properties</u> of each state depend on how <u>strong</u> the <u>forces</u> between the particles are.

3) You need to be able to <u>describe</u> the three different states.
To do this, think of each particle as a <u>tiny sphere</u>.

Solids

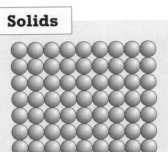

1) There are <u>strong forces</u> of attraction between particles.
This holds them in <u>fixed positions</u> in a regular <u>arrangement</u>.

2) The particles <u>can't move</u> around. They can only <u>vibrate</u> a bit.
This means that solids have a <u>definite shape</u> and <u>volume</u>.

3) The particles in a solid <u>don't</u> have much <u>energy</u>.

4) The <u>hotter</u> the solid gets, the <u>more</u> the particles vibrate.
This causes solids to <u>expand</u> (get bigger) when heated.

It's all a matter of force...

Liquids

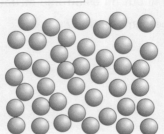

1) There is <u>some</u> attraction between the particles.
They're <u>free</u> to <u>move</u> past each other, but they tend to <u>stick together</u>.

2) Liquids <u>don't</u> have a <u>definite shape</u>. They will flow to fill the
bottom of a container. But they do keep the <u>same volume</u>.

3) Particles have <u>more energy</u> in the <u>liquid state</u> than in the <u>solid state</u>.
They have <u>less</u> energy than in the <u>gas state</u>.

4) The particles are moving <u>all the time</u>. The <u>hotter</u> the liquid gets, the
<u>faster</u> they move. This causes liquids to <u>expand</u> slightly when heated.

Gases

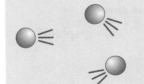

1) There is almost <u>no</u> attraction between the particles. They're <u>free</u> to <u>move</u>.
They travel in <u>straight lines</u> and sometimes <u>bump</u> into each other.

2) Gases <u>don't</u> keep a definite <u>shape</u> or <u>volume</u>.
They always <u>fill</u> any container.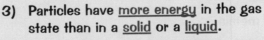

This means a gas will escape from a container if it isn't air-tight.

3) Particles have <u>more energy</u> in the gas
state than in a <u>solid</u> or a <u>liquid</u>.

4) When particles bounce off the walls of a container they create <u>pressure</u>.

5) The particles are always moving <u>randomly</u>.
The <u>hotter</u> the gas gets, the <u>faster</u> they move.
Gases either <u>expand</u> when heated, or their <u>pressure increases</u>.

Don't ignore gases — they matter too...

Time to get to the bottom of the matter with all these states of matter. Try your hand at these questions...

Q1   Put solids, liquids and gases in order of the strength of the forces
of attraction between their particles. Start with the weakest.   [1 mark]

Q2   Describe the movement of the particles in a gas.   [2 marks]

Changes of State

By <u>adding</u> or <u>taking away energy</u> from a substance, you can <u>change</u> it from one <u>state</u> to another.

Heating or Cooling a Substance can Change its State

1) When a substance changes from one state of matter to another, it's a <u>physical change</u>.

2) <u>Heating</u> and <u>cooling</u> substances will cause them to <u>change state</u>. Here's how:

3 At a certain temperature, the particles have <u>enough energy</u> to <u>break</u> free from their positions. This is called <u>melting</u>. The solid turns into a <u>liquid</u>.

2 This makes the particles <u>vibrate more</u>. The forces between the particles are weakened. This makes the solid <u>expand</u>.

1 When a <u>solid</u> is <u>heated</u>, its particles <u>gain</u> more <u>energy</u>.

4 When a liquid is <u>heated</u> the particles get even <u>more energy</u>.

5 This energy makes the particles <u>move faster</u>. This <u>weakens</u> and <u>breaks</u> the <u>forces</u> holding the liquid together.

6 At a certain temperature, the <u>forces</u> between the particles break. The liquid turns into a <u>gas</u>. This is called <u>evaporating</u>.

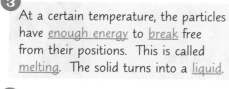

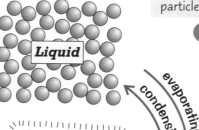

melting / freezing

evaporating / condensing

The red arrows show heat being added. The blue arrows show heat being given out.

Liquid

Solid

Gas

subliming

If you cool a gas then the opposite will happen. First it will condense to form a liquid. Then it will freeze to form a solid.

Atoms are Rearranged During Chemical Reactions

1) <u>Chemical changes</u> happen during <u>chemical reactions</u>.

2) In chemical reactions, <u>chemical bonds</u> between atoms break and the atoms <u>change places</u>.

3) The atoms in the substances you <u>start off</u> with (the <u>reactants</u>) are rearranged to form <u>different substances</u> (the <u>products</u>).

4) Chemical changes are <u>more difficult to undo</u> than <u>physical changes</u>.

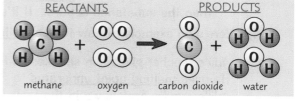

REACTANTS   PRODUCTS

methane   oxygen   carbon dioxide   water

Making Predictions about Substances from their Properties

You might be asked to <u>use data</u> to work out what <u>state</u> substances will be in under <u>certain conditions</u>.

EXAMPLE
A substance has a melting point of 801 °C and a boiling point of 1413 °C.
Predict the state of this substance at 1000 °C.

1) The substance is a solid <u>below 801 °C</u>. It's a gas <u>above 1413 °C</u>. It's a liquid <u>between these temperatures</u>.

2) <u>1000 °C</u> is between 801 °C and 1413 °C, so... **The substance is a liquid at 1000 °C.**

I felt like changing state, so I moved from Texas to Michigan...

Predicting the state of something at a certain temperature isn't too tricky. Best get some practice in anyway...

Q1   Ethanol melts at −114 °C and boils at 78 °C. Predict the state that ethanol is in at:
       a) −150 °C   b) 0 °C   c) 25 °C   d) 100 °C   [4 marks]

Q1 Video Solution

Purity

Be careful how you use the word 'pure' in your exam. 'Purity' has a very specific meaning in chemistry.

Pure Substances Contain Only One Thing

1) In normal life, the word 'pure' can be used to mean 'clean' or 'natural'.

2) In chemistry, a pure substance is one that's made up of just one element or compound.

3) If there's more than one compound or element in the substance then it's not pure. It's a mixture.

4) For example, fresh air might be thought of as nice and 'pure', but it's chemically impure. It's a mixture of gases, including nitrogen and oxygen.

5) Lots of mixtures are really useful — for example, metal alloys. But sometimes chemists need a pure sample of a substance.

Having impure thoughts again, Henry?

You Can Test For Purity Using Melting Points

1) Every pure substance has a sharp melting point and boiling point. This means that it will only melt or boil at a single temperature. For example, pure ice melts at 0 °C, and pure water boils at 100 °C.

2) If a substance is a mixture (chemically impure) then it will melt bit by bit over a range of temperatures.

3) If you know the melting point for a pure substance, you can test if a sample of that substance is pure. Here's how you do it:

- Measure the melting point of the sample using melting point apparatus.

- This apparatus lets you heat up a small sample of a solid very slowly. So you can find the exact temperature that it melts at.

- If the melting point is the same as the expected melting point, then the substance is pure. If it's different, then it's a mixture.

If you don't have melting point apparatus, you could use an oil bath and a thermometer instead — but it's harder to control the temperature.

4) Here's an example of how to use melting point data to find out if a substance is pure or not:

Adil's teacher gives him samples of four powdered solids, labelled A, B, C and D.
He uses melting point apparatus to find the melting point of each one.
Adil's results are shown in the table below.

Solid	A	B	C	D
Melting point (°C)	82	72-79	101	63

Which of the four solids, A, B, C or D, is a mixture?

Answer: B (B must be a mixture, because it melted over a range of temperatures.)

If in doubt, heat it up until it melts — that's my motto...

It can be important to know if a substance is pure or not. E.g. you often need to use pure substances in experiments.

Q1   Rachel buys a carton of juice labelled '100% pure orange juice'.
Explain whether or not the word 'pure' on this label means it's chemically pure.   [2 marks]

Q2   Fatima is going to use melting point apparatus to test the melting point of a sample of pure benzoic acid.
She says "I expect the sample to melt over a range of temperatures."
Do you agree with Fatima? Explain your answer.   [1 mark]

Distillation

Distillation separates mixtures that are <u>liquid</u>. You need to know about <u>simple</u> and <u>fractional</u> distillation.

Simple Distillation Separates Out Solutions

Sea water is a <u>solution</u> of salt in water. Here's how to use simple distillation to get <u>pure water</u> from <u>seawater</u>:

1) Pour your sample of seawater into the <u>distillation flask</u>.

2) Set up the <u>apparatus</u> as shown in the diagram.

3) Connect the bottom end of the <u>condenser</u> to a cold tap. Run <u>cold water</u> through the condenser to keep it cool.

4) <u>Heat</u> the distillation flask slowly. The water will <u>evaporate</u> before the salt. This is because it has a <u>lower boiling point</u>.

5) The water <u>vapour</u> goes into the condenser. It cools and <u>condenses</u> (turns back into a liquid).

6) It then flows into the beaker where it is <u>collected</u>.

7) Once <u>all</u> the water has evaporated, the <u>salt</u> will be left.

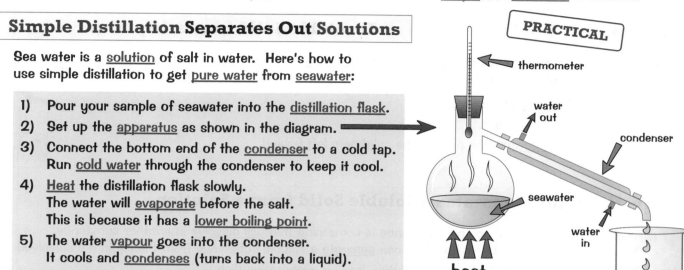

Simple distillation can only be used to separate things with <u>very different</u> boiling points.

Fractional Distillation is Used to Separate a Mixture of Liquids

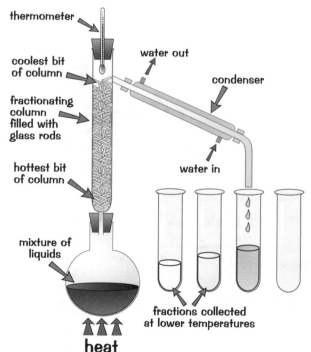

Fractional distillation can be used to separate a <u>mixture of liquids</u> with <u>similar boiling points</u>.

1) Put your <u>mixture</u> in a flask. Attach a <u>fractionating column</u> and condenser above the flask as shown.

2) <u>Heat</u> the flask slowly.

3) The liquid with the <u>lowest</u> boiling point will evaporate <u>first</u>. It will reach the <u>top</u> of the column when the <u>temperature</u> on the thermometer reaches its <u>boiling point</u>.

4) Then it will <u>condense</u> and run down the condenser.

5) The column is <u>cooler</u> nearer the <u>top</u>. So if liquids with <u>higher</u> boiling points evaporate, they will <u>condense</u> before they reach the top and run back down into the flask.

6) When the first liquid has been collected, <u>increase the temperature</u> until the <u>next one</u> evaporates.

The different liquids separated using this method are called 'fractions'.

Fractionating — sounds a bit too much like maths to me...

The method for fractional distillation shown here is a bit like the process used to separate crude oil. You can find out a bit more about the separation of crude oil on page 136.

Q1 Propan-1-ol, methanol and ethanol have boiling points of 97 °C, 65 °C and 78 °C respectively. A student uses fractional distillation to separate a mixture of these compounds. State which liquid will be collected in the second fraction and explain why. [2 marks]

Filtration and Crystallisation

For a mixture of a <u>solid and a liquid</u>, the method used to <u>separate</u> them depends on how <u>soluble</u> the solid is.

Filtration is Used to Separate an Insoluble Solid from a Liquid

An <u>insoluble</u> substance is something that <u>doesn't dissolve</u> in another substance. E.g. <u>sand</u> is insoluble in water. To filter an <u>insoluble solid</u> from a liquid <u>mixture</u>:

Filter paper folded into a cone shape.

The solid is left in the filter paper.

1) Put some <u>filter paper</u> into a <u>funnel</u>.
2) <u>Pour</u> your mixture into it.
3) The liquid <u>runs through</u> the paper. The solid gets <u>left behind</u>.

Crystallisation Separates a Soluble Solid from a Solution

evaporating dish

A soluble substance is something that <u>will dissolve</u> in another substance. Here's how you can <u>separate</u> a soluble substance from the liquid it's dissolved in:

1) Pour the solution into an <u>evaporating dish</u>.
2) Gently <u>heat</u> the solution. The water will start to <u>evaporate</u>.
3) Once crystals start to form, <u>stop heating</u> it.
4) Leave the solution to <u>cool</u>.
5) <u>Filter</u> the crystals out of the solution, and leave them in a warm place to <u>dry</u>.

Choose the Right Purification Method

1) Methods for <u>separating substances</u> can be used to separate a <u>pure substance</u> out of a <u>mixture</u>.
2) You might have to <u>pick</u> a method to separate a mixture.
3) The best method to use will depend on the <u>properties</u> of the <u>substances</u> in the mixture.

Example:
A <u>mixture</u> contains two substances, **X** and **Y**.
- <u>Substance X</u> is a <u>liquid</u> at room temperature.
- <u>Substance Y</u> is a <u>solid</u> at room temperature. It <u>dissolves completely</u> in substance **X**.

a) Suggest a <u>method</u> you could use to get a pure sample of <u>substance X</u> from the mixture.

Answer: <u>Simple distillation</u>. Fractional distillation isn't needed as there's only <u>one liquid</u> in the solution. ←

You know that you need to use some kind of distillation because you want to get a <u>liquid</u> from a <u>solution</u>.

b) Suggest a method you could use to get a pure sample of <u>substance Y</u>.

Answer: Crystallisation. (Crystallisation is used to get a <u>soluble solid</u> out of a solution.)
You could try and distil all of substance X off so that only substance Y is left behind. But there might be a <u>small amount</u> of substance X left. Crystallisation is a better way of getting a <u>pure sample</u> of a solid from a solution.

Its mum calls it Philliptration...

If one method isn't enough to get a pure sample of a substance from a mixture you can use a few different methods. For example, filtration and then crystallisation. Now, to test your understanding, try this question.

Q1   You are given a solution that has been made by dissolving copper sulfate crystals in water.
Describe how you could use crystallisation to separate copper sulfate from the solution.   [4 marks]

Chromatography

Here we go, another method for separating a mixture. Chromatography has a fancy name, but it's not too bad.

Chromatography Separates Soluble Substances

1) Chromatography is a method used to separate a mixture of soluble substances and identify them.

2) The type of chromatography you need to know about is paper chromatography.

3) Here's how you can set it up:

- Draw a line near the bottom of a sheet of filter paper using a pencil. This is the baseline.
- Put a spot of the mixture to be separated on the line.
- Pour a small amount of solvent (e.g. water or ethanol) into a beaker.
- Place the bottom of the paper into the solvent (make sure the baseline isn't in the solvent).
- Put a watch glass on the top of the beaker to stop the solvent from evaporating away.
- The solvent will start to move up the paper.
- When the chemicals in the mixture dissolve in the solvent, they will move up the paper too.

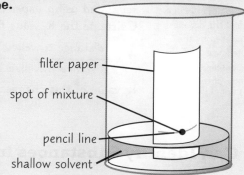

filter paper
spot of mixture
pencil line
shallow solvent

4) In paper chromatography, the paper is called the 'stationary phase'. The molecules of the mixture can't move when they're in the stationary phase.

5) The solvent is called the 'mobile phase'. The molecules can move when they're dissolved in the solvent.

6) Substances dissolved in the solvent are called solutes.

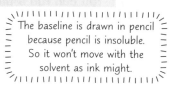

The baseline is drawn in pencil because pencil is insoluble. So it won't move with the solvent as ink might.

The Different Parts of the Mixture Form Spots

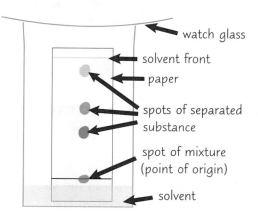

watch glass
solvent front
paper
spots of separated substance
spot of mixture (point of origin)
solvent

1) During chromatography, the different substances (solutes) in the mixture move up the paper at different speeds.

2) This separates the different substances. They will form spots at different places on the paper.

3) Remove the paper from the beaker before the solvent reaches the top.

4) Mark the distance the solvent has moved (the solvent front) in pencil.

5) If some of the substances in the mixture don't dissolve in the mobile phase they'll stay as a spot on the baseline. To separate them, you could try using a different solvent.

All hairdressers have to master Combatography...

Like a solvent working its way up some filter paper, let this chromatography stuff work its way into your brain...

Q1   In paper chromatography, what is the stationary phase?   [1 mark]

Q2   A mixture of two chemicals, A and B, is separated using paper chromatography.
Explain why the chemicals form two separate spots on the paper.   [1 mark]

PRACTICAL Interpreting Chromatograms

So, what use is chromatography, apart from making a pretty pattern of spots? Let's find out...

You can Calculate the R_f Value for Each Chemical

1) In paper chromatography, the piece of paper that you end up with is called a chromatogram.
2) The spots on a chromatogram will have R_f values.
3) You can find R_f values using this formula:

$$R_f = \frac{\text{distance travelled by solute}}{\text{distance travelled by solvent}}$$

EXAMPLE

To find the distance travelled by the solute, measure from the baseline to the centre of the spot.

The diagram on the right shows the position of a single spot after a mixture was separated using paper chromatography.
Calculate the R_f value for the spot.

$$R_f = \frac{\text{distance travelled by solute}}{\text{distance travelled by solvent}}$$

R_f value of this chemical = 3 ÷ 10 = 0.3

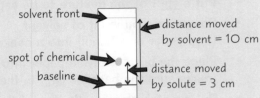

solvent front
distance moved by solvent = 10 cm
spot of chemical
baseline
distance moved by solute = 3 cm

You Can Identify Substances in Mixtures Using Chromatography

1) You can run a pure sample of a substance (a reference) next to the mixture you are analysing.
2) If the R_f value of the reference matches one of the spots in the mixture, the substance could be in the mixture. For example:

A pure substance will only produce one spot, as it can't be separated.

The mixture contains two different substances.

The mixture has been run next to pure samples of three different substances.

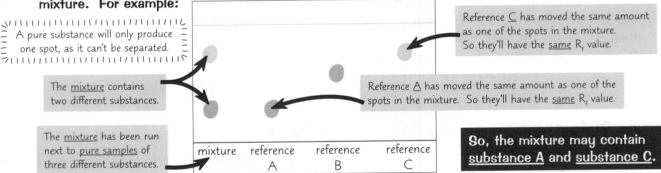

mixture   reference A   reference B   reference C

Reference C has moved the same amount as one of the spots in the mixture. So they'll have the same R_f value.

Reference A has moved the same amount as one of the spots in the mixture. So they'll have the same R_f value.

So, the mixture may contain substance A and substance C.

3) If the R_f values match in one solvent, you can check to see if the chemicals are the same by repeating with a different solvent. If they match again, there's a greater chance that they're the same.

You Can Use a Couple of Different Methods to Analyse a Mixture

1) Ink is a mixture of different dyes dissolved in a solvent.
2) You can use simple distillation and chromatography to analyse (study) an ink:

  1) Use simple distillation (see page 99) to find the boiling point of the solvent in the ink.
      To do this, read the temperature on the thermometer when the solvent is evaporating.
  2) The boiling point can help you work out what the solvent is.
      E.g. if the boiling point is 100 °C the solvent is probably water.
  3) Take a new sample of ink and separate it by paper chromatography. You can then see how many substances are in the ink and use reference substances and R_f values to work out what they are.

J'aime la chromatographie... hmm, I need an interpreter...

You could be asked to work out R_f values in the exams, so make sure you know the formula.

Q1 A spot on a chromatogram moved 6.3 cm from the baseline.
    The solvent front moved 8.4 cm. Calculate the R_f value.   [1 mark]

Q1 Video Solution

Water Treatment

Water, water, everywhere... well, there is if you live in a submarine.

There are Different Sources of Water in the UK

A source of water is somewhere or something that water can be taken from.

The water that we use can come from three different sources:

1) Surface water comes from lakes, rivers and reservoirs.
2) Ground water comes from rocks that trap water underground.
3) Waste water comes from water that's been produced as a waste in a human process. For example, from some industrial processes.

Water is Purified for Drinking

1) The water that comes out of your taps has been purified.
2) This is so that it is safe to drink (potable).
3) Purification happens in three stages:

- Filtration — a wire mesh stops large bits going through, e.g. twigs. Then gravel and sand beds filter out any other solid bits.
- Sedimentation — chemicals are added which make smaller particles clump together and settle at the bottom.
- Chlorination — chlorine gas is bubbled through the water. This kills harmful bacteria and other microbes.

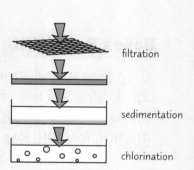

filtration

sedimentation

chlorination

You Can Get Potable Water by Distilling Sea Water

1) In some very dry countries, sea water is distilled to produce drinking water.
2) Distillation needs a lot of energy. This makes it very expensive.

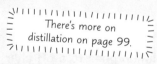

There's more on distillation on page 99.

Water Used in Chemical Experiments must be Pure

1) Most water, including the water from the tap, has ions in it.
2) If this water is used in a chemical reaction, the ions in it can affect the reaction.
3) Deionised water has had the ions that are in normal tap water removed.
4) If you're doing an experiment that involves mixing or dissolving something in water, use deionised water.
5) Using normal water could give your experiment a false result.

If water from the ground is ground water, is rain sky water?

Ahhh... Every glass of tap water tastes all the sweeter for knowing what it's gone through to get to me...

Q1 Describe the steps used to treat waste water to make it potable. [3 marks]

Q1 Video Solution

Q2 A student plans to make a solution to use in an experiment by dissolving pure, solid sodium iodide in water. Suggest why the student should **not** use tap water. State what he should use instead. [2 marks]

Acids and Bases

Acids and bases are substances with different pH values.
Testing the pH of a solution means using an indicator — and that means pretty colours...

Acids Have a pH Less Than 7

1) The pH scale is a measure of how acidic or alkaline a solution is.
2) A neutral substance has pH 7.
3) An acid is a substance with a pH of less than 7.
4) All acids can ionise (or dissociate) in water.
   They split up to produce H^+ ions and another ion.
   For example:

   $$HCl \rightarrow H^+ + Cl^-$$
   $$HNO_3 \rightarrow H^+ + NO_3^-$$

   HCl and HNO_3 don't produce hydrogen ions until they meet water.

Bases React With Acids

ouch

1) A base is a substance that reacts with an acid to produce a salt and water.
2) An alkali is a base that is soluble in water.
3) All alkalis have a pH of more than 7.
4) They form OH^- ions (hydroxide ions) in water.

Indicators Change Colour Depending on pH

1) An indicator is a dye that changes colour depending on whether it's above or below a certain pH.
2) Here's how to use them:

   • Add a few drops to the solution you're testing.
   • Compare the colour the solution goes to a pH chart for that indicator.
     For example, here's the pH chart for Universal indicator.

   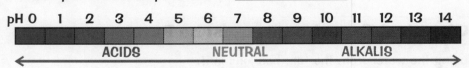

   pH 0 1 2 3 4 5 6 7 8 9 10 11 12 13 14
   ← ACIDS   NEUTRAL   ALKALIS →

3) There are different types of indicator.
4) Some indicators that you need to know about are:

   • litmus — is red in acidic solutions, purple in neutral solutions and blue in alkaline solutions.
   • methyl orange — is red in acidic solutions and yellow in neutral and alkaline solutions.
   • phenolphthalein — is colourless in acidic or neutral solutions and pink in alkaline solutions.

This page should have all bases covered...

pHew, you got to the end of the page, so here's an interesting fact — your skin is slightly acidic (pH 5.5).
Make sure you understand what acids and bases are. The rest of this section has lots of reactions involving them.

Q1   The pH of a solution is 2. Is the solution acidic or alkaline?   [1 mark]

Neutralisation Reactions

Acids and bases react with each other to give <u>neutral products</u>. This is called a <u>neutralisation reaction</u>.

Acids and Bases Neutralise Each Other

1) The reaction between an acid and a base is called <u>neutralisation</u>.
2) It produces a <u>salt</u> and <u>water</u>.
3) This example shows a reaction between an <u>acid</u> and an <u>alkali</u> (a soluble base).

$$HCl + NaOH \rightarrow NaCl + H_2O$$
$$\text{acid} \quad\quad \text{base} \quad\quad \text{salt} \quad\quad \text{water}$$

4) The <u>H^+ ions</u> from the acid and the <u>OH^- ions</u> from the alkali react with each other.
5) This forms the <u>water</u> in the equation above. You can write this reaction like so:

$$H^+_{(aq)} + OH^-_{(aq)} \rightarrow H_2O_{(l)}$$

6) In a neutralisation reaction, the <u>products</u> are <u>neutral</u>. They have a <u>pH of 7</u>.
7) At pH 7, the concentration of hydrogen ions is <u>the same as</u> the concentration of hydroxide ions.

You Need to be Able to Investigate a Neutralisation Reaction | PRACTICAL

1) Calcium oxide is a <u>base</u>. It reacts with <u>dilute hydrochloric acid</u> in a <u>neutralisation</u> reaction.
2) Here's how you could investigate this reaction:

1) Measure 150 cm³ of <u>dilute hydrochloric acid</u> into a conical flask.
    Use a <u>pipette</u> or a <u>measuring cylinder</u> to do this (see page 208).

2) Measure out <u>0.5 g</u> of calcium oxide using a <u>mass balance</u>.

3) Add the calcium oxide to the hydrochloric acid.

4) Wait for <u>all</u> of the base to <u>react</u>.

5) Then <u>record the pH</u> of the solution.
    Use a <u>pH probe</u> (see page 209)
    or <u>Universal</u> indicator paper.

6) <u>Repeat</u> steps 2 to 5 until <u>all</u>
    the acid has reacted. (This will be
    when there is <u>unreacted</u> calcium oxide
    sitting at the bottom of the flask.)

7) <u>Plot a graph</u> to see how pH changes
    with the mass of base added.
    It should look a bit like this.

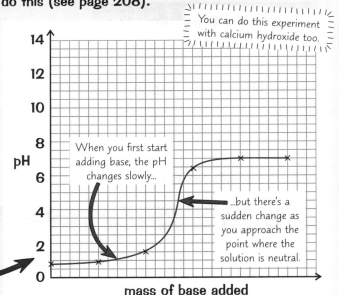

You can do this experiment
with calcium hydroxide too.

When you first start adding base, the pH changes slowly...

...but there's a sudden change as you approach the point where the solution is neutral.

mass of base added

Neutralise... That thing that vets do, right?

Remember to be very careful when working with acids and alkalis — they can be harmful or even corrosive.
Also remember to take lots of readings in this experiment, otherwise your curve might not look right.

Q1   Explain how water is produced in a neutralisation reaction.   [2 marks]

Q1 Video Solution

Reactions of Acids

Get ready, there are more <u>neutralisation reactions</u> coming up. And lots of lovely <u>salts</u> too. Goodie.

These Reactions of Acids Form Salts:

Acids with Bases

1) A <u>neutralisation reaction</u> is a reaction between an <u>acid</u> and a <u>base</u> (see previous page).
2) Acids and bases react to form a <u>salt</u> and <u>water</u>. Salts are <u>ionic compounds</u>.
3) The <u>name</u> of the salt depends on the <u>acid</u> used. <u>Hydrochloric acid</u> produces <u>chloride</u> salts, <u>sulfuric acid</u> produces <u>sulfate salts</u> and <u>nitric acid</u> produces <u>nitrate salts</u>.
4) The <u>first part</u> of the name of the salt produced is the same as the metal ion in the <u>base</u>.
5) <u>Metal oxides</u> and <u>metal hydroxides</u> are types of <u>bases</u>.
   You need to know what happens when acids react with them. For example:

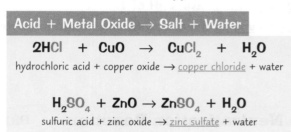

Acid + Metal Oxide → Salt + Water

$$2HCl + CuO \rightarrow CuCl_2 + H_2O$$
hydrochloric acid + copper oxide → <u>copper chloride</u> + water

$$H_2SO_4 + ZnO \rightarrow ZnSO_4 + H_2O$$
sulfuric acid + zinc oxide → <u>zinc sulfate</u> + water

Acid + Metal Hydroxide → Salt + Water

$$HNO_3 + KOH \rightarrow KNO_3 + H_2O$$
nitric acid + potassium hydroxide → <u>potassium nitrate</u> + water

Acids with Metals

Acid + Metal → Salt + Hydrogen

$$H_2SO_4 + Mg \rightarrow MgSO_4 + H_2$$
sulfuric acid + magnesium → <u>magnesium sulfate</u> + hydrogen

- You can <u>test for hydrogen</u> using a lighted splint.
- Hydrogen makes a "<u>squeaky pop</u>" with a <u>lighted splint</u>.

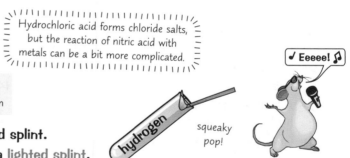

Hydrochloric acid forms chloride salts, but the reaction of nitric acid with metals can be a bit more complicated.

squeaky pop!

✓ Eeeee! ♫

Acids with Metal Carbonates

Acid + Metal Carbonate → Salt + Water + Carbon Dioxide

$$2HCl + Na_2CO_3 \rightarrow 2NaCl + H_2O + CO_2$$
hydrochloric acid + sodium carbonate → <u>sodium chloride</u> + water + carbon dioxide

- You can test for carbon dioxide using <u>limewater</u>.
- <u>Bubble</u> the gas through the limewater.
- If it is carbon dioxide, the limewater will <u>turn cloudy</u>.

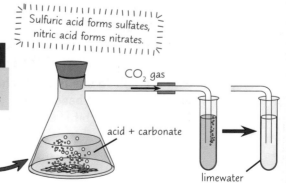

Sulfuric acid forms sulfates, nitric acid forms nitrates.

CO_2 gas

acid + carbonate

limewater

Nitrates — much cheaper than day-rates...

What a lot of reactions. Better take a peek back at p.75-76 for help with writing and balancing chemical equations.

Q1   Name the products of the reaction between hydrochloric acid and calcium carbonate.   [3 marks]

Making Soluble Salts

The previous page shows some reactions of acids which form <u>salts</u>. On the next few pages you're going to learn how to <u>make salts</u>. But it all depends on how <u>soluble</u> the salt you want to make is. Read on...

The Rules of Solubility

1) Use this <u>table</u> to work out whether a substance is <u>soluble in water or not</u>.

Soluble things dissolve in water. Insoluble things don't.

Substance	Soluble or Insoluble?
common salts of sodium, potassium and ammonium	soluble
nitrates	soluble
common chlorides	soluble (except silver chloride and lead chloride)
common sulfates	soluble (except lead, barium and calcium sulfate)
common carbonates and hydroxides	insoluble (except for sodium, potassium and ammonium ones)

2) How you make a salt depends on whether it's <u>soluble</u> or <u>insoluble</u>.

3) Salts that are <u>insoluble</u> will form a <u>solid</u> (a <u>precipitate</u>). Salts that are <u>soluble</u> will form a <u>solution</u>.

Making Soluble Salts — Use an Acid and an Insoluble Base | PRACTICAL

1) All salts have <u>two different ions</u> (they are <u>ionic compounds</u> — see page 85).

2) To make a <u>soluble salt</u>, you can react an <u>acid</u> with an <u>insoluble base</u>.

3) The <u>negative ion</u> in the salt comes from the <u>acid</u>.
The <u>positive ion</u> in the salt comes from the <u>base</u>. ← *For some salts, you can use a metal instead of the base.*

4) Often the base used is a <u>metal oxide</u> or a <u>metal hydroxide</u>.

5) For example, here's how you can make <u>copper sulfate</u> from <u>copper oxide</u> and <u>sulfuric acid</u>:

$$CuO_{(s)} + H_2SO_{4\,(aq)} \rightarrow CuSO_{4\,(aq)} + H_2O_{(l)}$$

copper oxide + sulfuric acid → copper sulfate + water

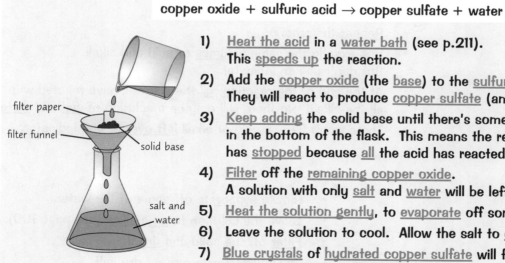

filter paper
filter funnel
solid base
salt and water

1) <u>Heat the acid</u> in a <u>water bath</u> (see p.211). This <u>speeds up</u> the reaction.

2) Add the <u>copper oxide</u> (the <u>base</u>) to the <u>sulfuric acid</u>. They will react to produce <u>copper sulfate</u> (and water).

3) <u>Keep adding</u> the solid base until there's some <u>left</u> in the bottom of the flask. This means the reaction has <u>stopped</u> because <u>all</u> the acid has reacted.

4) <u>Filter</u> off the <u>remaining copper oxide</u>. A solution with only <u>salt</u> and <u>water</u> will be left.

5) <u>Heat the solution gently</u>, to <u>evaporate</u> off some of the water.

6) Leave the solution to cool. Allow the salt to <u>crystallise</u> (see p.100).

7) <u>Blue crystals</u> of <u>hydrated copper sulfate</u> will form. You can <u>filter</u> these off and <u>dry</u> them.

I was attacked by a nasty copper sulfate — it was a-salt...

The theory may seem dull, but you'll probably get to make some nice salts in your class, and that's pretty cool.

Q1 State whether the following salts are soluble or insoluble:
a) potassium chloride b) copper carbonate c) calcium sulfate d) ammonium hydroxide [4 marks]

Making Soluble Salts Using Acid and Alkali

Here's <u>another</u> way to make a soluble salt. This time you have to use a method called a <u>titration</u>. You'll love it.

You can Make Soluble Salts Using Acid/Alkali Reactions

1) Soluble salts can also be made by reacting an acid with an <u>alkali</u> (a soluble base).

2) The alkali is <u>soluble</u>, so <u>no solid</u> will be left at the bottom when all the acid has reacted and the reaction has <u>stopped</u>. This means that it's <u>harder</u> to make sure that the <u>right amount</u> of alkali is added.

3) To make sure the <u>right amount</u> of alkali is added you have to do a <u>titration</u>.

4) A titration is when you add <u>one solution</u> (the acid or alkali) to the other, <u>bit by bit</u>.

5) You use an <u>indicator</u> to work out when the solutions have <u>reacted completely</u> together.

6) Here's how you do it:

① • Measure out a set amount of acid into a conical flask using a <u>pipette</u>.
• Add a few drops of <u>indicator</u> (see page 104).
• You should use an indicator with <u>one clear colour change</u>.
  (E.g. phenolphthalein or methyl orange).
• Universal indicator is <u>no good</u> as its colour change is too <u>gradual</u>.

② • Slowly add alkali to the acid, using a <u>burette</u>.
• Stop adding alkali when the indicator <u>changes colour</u>.
• This shows when the acid has been <u>neutralised</u>.
  It's called the <u>end point</u>.
• Write down <u>how much</u> alkali was added to the acid.

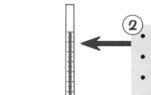

③ • <u>Repeat</u> the reaction.
• Use <u>exactly</u> the <u>same volumes</u> of acid and alkali.
  But <u>don't</u> use an indicator.
• At the <u>end of the reaction</u>, <u>all</u> the acid will have reacted with <u>all</u> the alkali. So there will only be a solution of <u>salt</u> and <u>water</u>.
• There won't be any acid or alkali <u>left over</u> or any <u>indicator</u>.

④ • Slowly <u>evaporate</u> off some of the water.
• Leave the solution to <u>crystallise</u> (see page 100).
• <u>Filter</u> off the solid and <u>dry</u> it.
• You'll be left with a <u>pure</u>, <u>dry</u> salt.

These crystal eyes are all over the place...

Yet more salts for you to make. If I were you though, I'd just get my salts from a sachet at the local chippy...

Q1   Describe a method for making a solution containing only sodium chloride
      and water using sodium hydroxide and hydrochloric acid.   [4 marks]

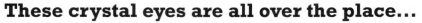

Making Insoluble Salts

You need to know how to make <u>insoluble salts</u> too. And look, here's a page showing you how. Fancy that...

Making Insoluble Salts — Precipitation Reactions

1) To make an <u>insoluble</u> salt, you can use a <u>precipitation reaction</u>.

2) You just need to react the right two <u>soluble salts</u> with each other. You'll need a soluble salt that contains the <u>positive ion</u> that you want and a soluble salt that contains the <u>negative ion</u> that you want.

3) E.g. to make <u>lead chloride</u> (insoluble), mix <u>lead nitrate</u> and <u>sodium chloride</u> (both soluble).

lead nitrate + sodium chloride → lead chloride + sodium nitrate

$$Pb(NO_3)_{2\,(aq)} + 2NaCl_{(aq)} \rightarrow PbCl_{2\,(s)} + 2NaNO_{3\,(aq)}$$

Look back to page 107 for more examples of soluble and insoluble salts.

Method:

You should use deionised water in this experiment. Deionised water has been purified so it doesn't contain any salts. So there are no other ions about.

1) Add 1 spatula of <u>lead nitrate</u> to a test tube.
2) Add <u>water</u> to dissolve it.
3) Put a <u>stopper</u> in the test tube and <u>shake</u> it quite hard. This is to make sure <u>all</u> the lead nitrate <u>dissolves</u>.
4) Add 1 spatula of <u>sodium chloride</u> to another test tube.
5) <u>Add water</u>, put a stopper in the top and <u>shake</u> this test tube too.
6) Pour the <u>two solutions</u> into a small beaker.
7) <u>Stir</u> it to mix it all together.
8) The lead chloride should <u>precipitate</u> out. This means that it forms a <u>solid</u> in the solution.

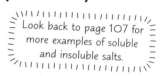

precipitate

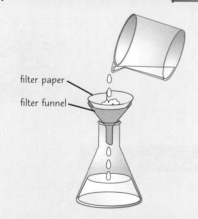

filter paper

filter funnel

9) Next you have to <u>filter</u> the solid out of the solution.
10) Put a piece of <u>filter paper</u> into a <u>filter funnel</u>.
11) Stick the funnel into a <u>conical flask</u>.
12) <u>Pour</u> the contents of the beaker into the funnel. Make sure that the mix doesn't go <u>above</u> the <u>filter paper</u>. This is so the solid doesn't dribble down the side.
13) <u>Wash out</u> the beaker with <u>deionised water</u>.
14) Pour the water in the beaker into the <u>filter paper</u>. This is so you get <u>all the precipitate</u> from the beaker.

15) Pour <u>more</u> deionised water onto the filter paper. This is to make sure <u>all the sodium nitrate</u> has been washed away.
16) Scrape the <u>lead chloride</u> onto <u>fresh</u> filter paper.
17) Leave it to dry in an <u>oven</u> or a <u>desiccator</u> (a container that can be used to <u>absorb water</u> from a substance).

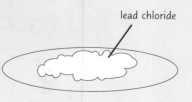

lead chloride

Next up, bath salts. You'll need a bit more water for this one...

The method to purify an insoluble salt is much simpler than the methods to make soluble salts. That's because you can just get rid of any stuff you don't want by washing the solid salt with water at the end.

Q1 Suggest two reactants you could use to form barium sulfate in a precipitation reaction. [2 marks]

Q1 Video Solution

Electrolysis

Now I hope you're sitting comfortably. We're about to have three pages on <u>electrolysis</u>. What a treat.

Electrolysis Separates Ions in a Substance

1) <u>Electrolysis</u> is the <u>breaking down</u> of a substance using <u>electricity</u>.
2) An electrolyte is an ionic compound that is molten or dissolved in water so that it <u>conducts electricity</u>.
3) In electrolysis, an electric current is passed through an <u>electrolyte</u>. This causes the electrolyte to <u>decompose</u>.
4) There are two <u>electrodes</u> in the electrolyte. Electrodes <u>conduct electricity</u>. One electrode is <u>positive</u> and one is <u>negative</u>.
5) The <u>positive ions</u> (<u>cations</u>) in the electrolyte move towards the <u>cathode</u> (negative electrode).
6) The <u>negative ions</u> (<u>anions</u>) in the electrolyte move towards the <u>anode</u> (positive electrode).
7) This <u>movement</u> of ions creates a <u>flow of charge</u> through the electrolyte.

You can add an ammeter or a light bulb to the circuit to show that there's a flow of charge.

Here's How to Set Up an Electrochemical Cell

1) An <u>electrochemical cell</u> is a <u>circuit</u>.
2) It's made up of the anode, cathode, electrolyte, power source and wires that connect the electrodes.
3) You need to know how to <u>set up</u> an electrochemical cell.
4) How you set it up depends on what your <u>electrolyte</u> is made of:

If your electrolyte is a solution:

1) Get <u>two inert</u> (unreactive) <u>electrodes</u>, e.g. graphite or platinum electrodes.
2) Make sure the surfaces of the electrodes are <u>clean</u>.
3) <u>Don't touch</u> the surfaces of the electrodes. This is so they don't get <u>dirty</u>.
4) Fill a beaker with the <u>electrolyte</u>.
5) Put the electrodes into the <u>beaker</u>.
6) Connect the electrodes to a <u>power supply</u> using <u>crocodile clips</u> and <u>wires</u>.
7) When you turn the power supply on, a <u>current</u> will flow through the cell.

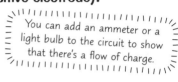

cathode (−ve)   d.c. power supply   −ve +ve   anode (+ve)

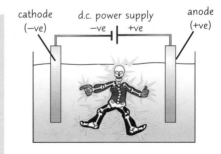

If your electrolyte is a molten ionic substance:

1) Put your <u>solid ionic substance</u> (for the electrolyte) in a <u>crucible</u>.
2) Heat the crucible with a <u>Bunsen burner</u> until the <u>solid's molten</u>.
3) Then dip two clean, <u>inert electrodes</u> into the electrolyte.
4) Connect the <u>electrodes</u> to a <u>power supply</u> using wires and clips.
5) You should get a <u>current</u> flowing through the cell when you turn the power on.

You should heat your ionic substance in a fume cupboard to avoid releasing any toxic fumes into the room.

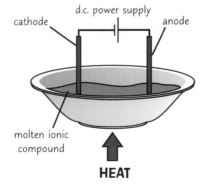

cathode   d.c. power supply   anode

molten ionic compound

HEAT

Two electrodes and a lake of fire — electrochemical hell...

You can also carry out electrolysis experiments using non-inert electrodes. See page 112 for more about this.

Q1   What is the name of the negative electrode in an electrochemical cell?   [1 mark]

Predicting Products of Electrolysis

This stuff is electrifying. You'll be on the edge of your seat with all this fun, fun, fun <u>electrolysis</u>.

The Products from Molten Ionic Solids are Simple to Predict

1) <u>Ionic solids can't</u> be electrolysed because the ions are in fixed positions and <u>can't move</u>.
2) <u>Molten ionic compounds can</u> be electrolysed because the ions can <u>move</u> and <u>conduct electricity</u>.
3) Positive <u>metal ions</u> react to form <u>metal atoms</u> at the cathode.
4) Negative <u>ions</u> react to form atoms or molecules at the <u>anode</u>.
5) This diagram shows <u>molten lead bromide</u> ($PbBr_2$) being electrolysed: <u>Brown bromine gas</u> would be produced at the <u>anode</u> and a <u>silver-coloured</u> liquid (molten lead) at the <u>cathode</u>.
6) You need to be able to <u>predict</u> what products you'll get at each electrode when you electrolyse <u>molten</u> substances. For example:

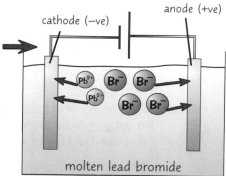

molten lead bromide

Molten Electrolyte	Product at Cathode	Product at Anode
potassium chloride, KCl	potassium	chlorine
aluminium oxide, Al_2O_3	aluminium	oxygen

An aqueous solution of an ionic compound contains the ions of the compound dissolved in water.

Electrolysis of Aqueous Solutions is a Bit More Complicated

1) In <u>aqueous solutions</u>, there are <u>hydrogen ions</u> (H^+) and <u>hydroxide ions</u> (OH^-) from the <u>water</u>.
2) There are also the ions from the <u>ionic compound</u>.
3) This affects the <u>products</u> of electrolysis in a few ways.

$$H_2O_{(l)} \rightleftharpoons H^+_{(aq)} + OH^-_{(aq)}$$

4) At the <u>cathode</u>:
If the metal in the ionic compound is <u>more reactive</u> than hydrogen, then <u>hydrogen gas</u> is produced.
If the metal is <u>less reactive</u> than hydrogen, then a <u>solid layer</u> of the <u>pure metal</u> will be produced.
5) At the <u>anode</u>:
If <u>halide ions</u> (Cl^-, Br^-, I^-) are present, chlorine, bromine or iodine will form.
If <u>no halide ions</u> are present, then <u>oxygen</u> will be formed.

You can use a reactivity series to find out which metals are more or less reactive than hydrogen (see page 114).

6) For example:

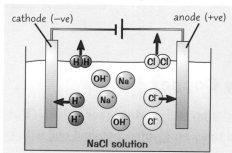

NaCl solution

A solution of <u>sodium chloride</u> (NaCl) contains <u>four different ions</u>: Na^+, Cl^-, OH^- and H^+.

- <u>Sodium</u> metal is <u>more reactive</u> than hydrogen. So at the cathode, <u>hydrogen gas</u> is produced.
- <u>Chloride ions</u> are present in the solution. So at the anode, <u>chlorine gas</u> is produced.

Aqueous Electrolyte	Product at Cathode	Product at Anode
copper chloride, $CuCl_2$	copper	chlorine
sodium sulfate, Na_2SO_4	hydrogen	oxygen
water acidified with sulfuric acid, H_2O/H_2SO_4	hydrogen	oxygen

In this example, H_2SO_4 <u>isn't</u> an ionic compound. So it doesn't split to form <u>positive metal ions</u>. Instead, it splits into H^+ ions and SO_4^{2-} ions. Since the H^+ ions are <u>positive</u>, they go towards the cathode and form <u>hydrogen gas</u>.

Sir Chlo Ride

Sir Chlo Rode

Faster shopping at the supermarket — use Electrolleys...

Electrolysis is a bit prenfusing. It's a good idea to read through this page slowly, to make sure you get it.

Q1   A student carries out electrolysis on molten calcium chloride. What is produced at:
a) the anode?   b) the cathode?

[2 marks]

Q1 Video Solution

 # Electrolysis of Copper Sulfate

The products you get from electrolysis depend not only on your <u>electrolyte</u>, but also on your <u>electrodes</u> too...

Electrolysis of Copper Sulfate with Inert Electrodes Produces Oxygen

1) A solution of <u>copper sulfate</u> ($CuSO_4$) contains <u>four different ions</u>: Cu^{2+}, SO_4^{2-}, H^+ and OH^-.

2) When you electrolyse copper sulfate solution with <u>inert electrodes</u>:
- Copper is <u>less reactive</u> than hydrogen. So <u>copper metal</u> is produced at the <u>cathode</u> (you see a coating of copper on the electrode).
- There aren't any <u>halide ions</u> present. So <u>oxygen</u> is produced at the <u>anode</u> (you see bubbles of oxygen gas forming).

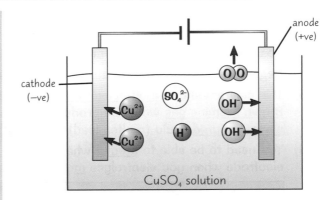

Non-Inert Electrodes Take Part in Electrolysis Reactions

1) You can use <u>copper electrodes</u> in the reaction above instead.

2) With copper electrodes, the <u>mass</u> of the <u>anode</u> will <u>decrease</u> and the <u>mass</u> of the <u>cathode</u> will <u>increase</u>. This is because copper is <u>transferred</u> from the anode to the cathode.

3) To find out how the mass of the electrodes <u>changes</u>, measure their mass <u>before</u> and <u>after</u> the experiment.

4) Then <u>find the difference</u> between these two masses.

5) Make sure the electrodes are <u>dry</u> before weighing them. If there's any copper sulfate solution on them, then they will seem to have a <u>higher mass</u> than they really do.

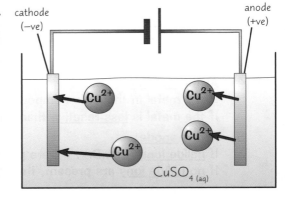

Electrolysis Can Be Used to Purify Copper

1) Copper can be <u>extracted</u> from its <u>ore</u> by <u>reduction</u> with carbon (see p.116). But it will be <u>impure</u>.

2) Electrolysis is used to <u>purify</u> it. This method uses an <u>electrochemical cell</u> with <u>copper electrodes</u>:

1) The <u>anode</u> starts off as a big lump of <u>impure copper</u>. The <u>electrolyte</u> is <u>copper(II) sulfate solution</u> (which contains Cu^{2+} ions). The <u>cathode</u> starts off as a thin piece of <u>pure copper</u>.

2) Here's what happens during the process:
- Copper in the <u>impure anode</u> forms <u>copper ions</u> which <u>dissolve</u> into the <u>electrolyte</u>.
- The copper ions move to the pure copper cathode. Here, they react to form a layer of <u>pure copper</u>.
- Any <u>impurities</u> from the <u>impure copper anode</u> sink to the bottom. They form a <u>sludge</u>.

A hat, some handcuffs and a truncheon — 100% pure copper...

Phew, that's the last page on electrolysis (for now...). Time to celebrate with a question.

Q1 Explain how electrolysis is used to purify copper. [4 marks]

Revision Questions for Sections 11 and 12

Sections 11 and 12 had quite a few nasty pages, but you got through 'em. Just time for some revision questions.

- Try these questions and tick off each one when you get it right.
- When you're completely happy with it with a sub-topic, tick it off.

For even more practice, try the Retrieval Quizzes for Sections 11 and 12 — just scan these QR codes!

Section 11 Quiz

States of Matter and Changes of State (p.96-97)

1) Name the three states of matter.
2) Describe the arrangement of particles, and the strength of the forces between them, in a solid.
3) What happens to the forces between the particles in a solid as you melt it?
4) What do you call the process of a substance changing from a liquid to a solid?

Purity and Separating Substances (p.98-102)

5) What is the chemical definition of purity?
6) Explain why air isn't considered a pure substance, according to the scientific definition of pure.
7) A substance melts over a range of temperatures. Is it likely to be a pure substance or a mixture?
8) Draw the apparatus you would use to carry out a simple distillation.
9) Where is the hottest part of a fractionating column — at the top or at the bottom?
10) Describe how to carry out filtration.
11) What separation technique should you use to separate a soluble solid from a solution?
12) Write out the formula you would use to work out the R_f value of a substance from a chromatogram.

Water Treatment (p.103)

13) Name three different sources of water.
14) Why is distilling sea water expensive?
15) What is deionised water?

Acids and Bases (p.104-106)

Section 12 Quiz

16) What pH value would a neutral substance have?
17) What is an alkali?
18) State what colours the following indicators are in acidic solutions: a) litmus b) methyl orange
19) What is meant by a neutralisation reaction?
20) Write a chemical equation to show how hydrochloric acid reacts with copper oxide.
21) What would you expect to see if you bubbled carbon dioxide through limewater?

Making Salts (p.107-109)

22) Name: a) three insoluble sulfates, b) two soluble hydroxides.
23) Describe how you could find the end point in a neutralisation reaction between an acid and an alkali.
24) Describe the type of reactants you should use to make an insoluble salt.

Electrolysis (p.110-112)

25) What is electrolysis?
26) Which electrode do the anions in an electrolyte move towards?
27) At which electrode does the metal form during the electrolysis of a molten ionic compound?
28) Explain why the mass of the anode decreases when copper electrodes are used to electrolyse a solution of copper sulfate.

The Reactivity Series

Reactivity series are lists of metals (sometimes with some carbon or hydrogen thrown in for fun). But they're not just any old lists in any old order. They tell you about the reactivities of elements.

If Something Gains Oxygen it's Oxidised

Oxidation can mean a reaction with oxygen or the gain of oxygen. Reduction can be the loss of oxygen.

$$E.g. \ Fe_2O_3 + 3CO \rightarrow 2Fe + 3CO_2$$

- Iron oxide is reduced to iron (as oxygen is removed).
- Carbon monoxide is oxidised to carbon dioxide (as oxygen is added).

The Reactivity Series Shows How Easily Metals Are Oxidised

1) A reactivity series is a table that lists metals in order of how reactive they are.

2) Carbon is often included in reactivity series. You can find out how a metal is extracted from its ore by looking at whether the metal is above or below carbon in the reactivity series (see pages 116-117).

3) Hydrogen can be included in the reactivity series too — this shows the reactivity of metals with dilute acids (see next page).

> If a metal is below hydrogen in the reactivity series, it's less reactive than hydrogen and won't react with dilute acids.

4) Here's an example of a reactivity series:

Not bothered...

easiest to oxidise

hardest to oxidise

The Reactivity Series

Potassium	K	most reactive
Sodium	Na	
Calcium	Ca	
Magnesium	Mg	
Aluminium	Al	
Carbon	C	
Zinc	Zn	
Iron	Fe	
Hydrogen	H	
Copper	Cu	
Silver	Ag	least reactive
Gold	Au	

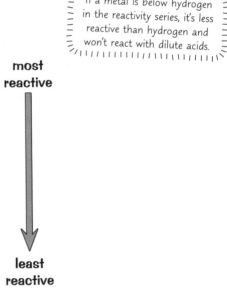

5) The metals at the top of the reactivity series are the most reactive. These metals easily form positive ions (cations). They're also oxidised easily.

6) Metals at the bottom of the reactivity series are less reactive. These metals don't form positive ions as easily. They're more difficult to oxidise than the metals higher up the reactivity series.

7) You can work out a metal's position in the reactivity series by reacting it with water or dilute acids (see next page).

I told a hilarious joke to some sodium — the reaction was great...

You could come across different reactivity series to the one shown above. But don't panic — they all work the same. The more reactive elements are at the top of the series and the less reactive ones can be found at the bottom.

Q1   Which element has been oxidised in the following reaction? $CuO + H_2 \rightarrow Cu + H_2O$ [1 mark]

Q2   Using the reactivity series above, state whether copper or calcium is more easily oxidised.   [1 mark]

Reactivity of Metals

Reactive metals tend to do exciting, fizzy things when you drop them into acid or water...

You Can Work Out a Reactivity Series from the Reactions of Metals

1) The more easily a metal atom forms a positive ion, the more reactive it will be.

2) You can put metals in order from most reactive to least reactive based on their reactions with either an acid or water. The order you get is the reactivity series.

3) To compare the reactivities of metals, you could watch how quickly bubbles of hydrogen are formed in their reactions with acid or water. The more reactive the metal, the faster the bubbles will form.

Reactions of metals with water:

The general reaction of a metal with water is:
metal + water → metal hydroxide + hydrogen.

- Very reactive metals (e.g. potassium), will all react vigorously with water.
- Less reactive metals (e.g. iron) won't react much with cold water, but will react with steam.
- Copper won't react with either water or steam.

Reactions of metals with acids:

- Very reactive metals (e.g. sodium) will fizz wildly.
- Less reactive metals (e.g. zinc) will bubble a bit.
- Unreactive metals (e.g. copper) will not react with dilute acids at all.

For more on the reactions of metals and acids, see p.106.

4) You can also measure the temperature change of the reaction in a set time period. The more reactive the metal, the greater the temperature change should be.

More Reactive Metals Displace Less Reactive Ones

1) If you put a reactive metal into a solution of a less reactive metal salt, the reactive metal will replace the less reactive metal in the salt.

Example: Iron is more reactive than copper. So if you add solid iron to copper sulfate solution, the iron will "kick out" the copper from the salt. You end up with iron sulfate solution and copper metal.

copper sulfate + iron → iron sulfate + copper $CuSO_4 + Fe → FeSO_4 + Cu$

2) If you put a less reactive metal into a solution of a more reactive metal salt, nothing will happen.

3) You can use these reactions to work out where in the reactivity series a metal goes.

Example: A student adds some metals to metal salt solutions and records whether any reactions happen. Use her table of results, below, to work out an order of reactivity for the metals.

	copper nitrate	magnesium chloride	zinc sulfate
copper	no reaction	no reaction	no reaction
magnesium	magnesium nitrate and copper formed	no reaction	magnesium sulfate and zinc formed
zinc	zinc nitrate and copper formed	no reaction	no reaction

- Magnesium displaces both copper and zinc. So magnesium is more reactive than copper and zinc.
- Copper is displaced by both magnesium and zinc. So copper is less reactive than magnesium and zinc.
- Zinc displaces copper, but not magnesium. So zinc is more reactive than copper but less reactive than magnesium.

The order of reactivity, from most to least, is: magnesium, zinc, copper.

I AM NOT HIGHLY REACTIVE — OK...

This stuff isn't too bad — who knows, you might even get to have a go at these experiments in class...

Q1   A student is given small samples of three metals, A, B and C. She places them in dilute hydrochloric acid. Nothing happens to Metal A. Metal B fizzes vigorously. Metal C fizzes a bit. Put the three metals in order, from most reactive to least reactive.

[1 mark]

Extracting Metals Using Carbon

We get most of our metals by <u>extracting</u> them <u>from rocks</u> — and I bet you can't wait to find out how...

Ores Contain Enough Metal to Make Extraction Worthwhile

1) A <u>metal ore</u> is a <u>rock</u> which contains <u>enough metal</u> to make it <u>worthwhile</u> extracting the metal from it. In many cases the ore is an <u>oxide</u> of the metal.

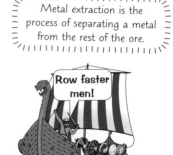

Metal extraction is the process of separating a metal from the rest of the ore.

> <u>Example</u>: Most <u>aluminium</u> is extracted from <u>aluminium oxide</u> (Al_2O_3). This comes from an ore called <u>bauxite</u>.

2) Most metals we use come from <u>ores</u> in the <u>Earth's crust</u>. These ores need to be mined from the Earth before the metals can be <u>extracted</u> from them.

3) Some <u>unreactive metals</u>, such as gold, are found in the Earth's crust as <u>uncombined elements</u> (they're not part of a compound). These metals can be mined straight out of the <u>ground</u>, but they usually need to be <u>purified</u> before they can be used.

Row faster men!

We can't — it's these lousy metal oars.

Some Metals can be Extracted by Reduction with Carbon

1) Some metals can be <u>extracted</u> from their ores by <u>heating</u> the ore with <u>carbon</u>. The carbon <u>reduces</u> the ore.

2) When an ore is reduced, <u>oxygen is removed</u> from it, e.g.

$$2Fe_2O_3 \quad + \quad 3C \quad \rightarrow \quad 4Fe \quad + \quad 3CO_2$$
$$\text{iron oxide} \quad + \quad \text{carbon} \quad \rightarrow \quad \text{iron} \quad + \quad \text{carbon dioxide}$$

3) The <u>reactivity series</u> (page 114) tells you what <u>method</u> to use to <u>extract</u> a metal.

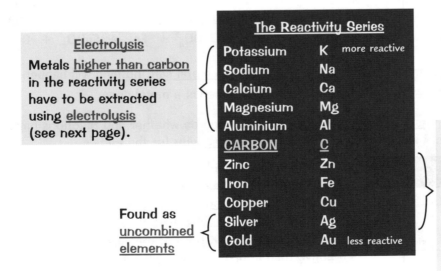

Electrolysis

Metals <u>higher than carbon</u> in the reactivity series have to be extracted using <u>electrolysis</u> (see next page).

The Reactivity Series

Potassium	K	more reactive
Sodium	Na	
Calcium	Ca	
Magnesium	Mg	
Aluminium	Al	
<u>CARBON</u>	<u>C</u>	
Zinc	Zn	
Iron	Fe	
Copper	Cu	
Silver	Ag	
Gold	Au	less reactive

Found as <u>uncombined</u> elements

Reduction with Carbon

- Metals <u>below carbon</u> in the reactivity series can be extracted by <u>reduction</u> using <u>carbon</u>.
- This is because carbon can <u>only take</u> the <u>oxygen</u> away from metals which are <u>less reactive</u> than carbon <u>itself</u> is.

[Please insert ore-ful pun here]...

Make sure you've got that reactivity series sorted in your head. If a metal's below carbon in the reactivity series, then it's less reactive than carbon. So it can be extracted from its ore by reduction using carbon.

Q1 Video Solution

Q1 Write a balanced equation for the reduction of lead oxide, PbO, by carbon, C. [2 marks]

Q2 How would you extract copper from its metal ore? Explain your answer. [2 marks]

Extracting Metals Using Electrolysis

Electrolysis is an expensive process but, like many pricey things, it's really rather good...

Some Metals have to be Extracted by Electrolysis

1) Metals that are more reactive than carbon (see previous page) are extracted from metal ores using electrolysis.

2) The metal ores need to be melted so that they're a liquid (in a molten state). This means the ions will be free to move.

3) Once the metal ore has been melted, an electric current is passed through it. This causes the ions in the metal ore to move towards the electrodes.

4) The metal is formed at the negative electrode (cathode) and the non-metal at the positive electrode (anode).

See page 110 for more on electrolysis.

- Aluminium is extracted from aluminium oxide (Al_2O_3) which is found in aluminium ore. It's extracted using electrolysis with carbon electrodes.

- Aluminium oxide has a high melting point. So the ore is first dissolved in molten cryolite. This lowers the melting point, so less energy is needed to melt it. This makes the process cheaper (see below).

- The ions in this molten mixture are free to move.

- During the electrolysis, aluminium is formed at the cathode. Oxygen forms at the anode. The overall equation is: $2Al_2O_{3(l)} \rightarrow 4Al_{(l)} + 3O_{2(g)}$

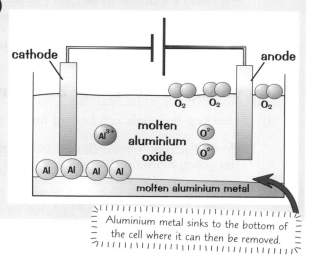

Aluminium metal sinks to the bottom of the cell where it can then be removed.

Electrolysis is a More Expensive Process than Reduction with Carbon

1) Extracting metals from their ores using electrolysis uses lots of electricity.

2) Electricity is expensive which makes electrolysis very costly.

3) There are also costs associated with melting or dissolving the metal ore so it can conduct electricity.

1) Carbon is cheap, so extracting metals using reduction with carbon is much cheaper than electrolysis.

2) Carbon also acts as a fuel to provide the heat needed for the reduction reaction to happen. This means you don't need to find another way to fuel the reaction, which saves money.

This means that, in general, metals lower down the reactivity series (less reactive metals) are cheaper to extract than those higher up the reactivity series (more reactive metals).

You can extract metals using electrolysis ore carbon...

See what I did there? *Ore* carbon? I crack myself up. Anyway, back to the serious stuff...

Q1 Use the reactivity series to predict whether aluminium or iron would be more expensive to extract from its ore. Explain your answer.

[3 marks]

Q1 Video Solution

Recycling

We don't have a <u>never-ending amount</u> of some materials, e.g. metals, to keep on making things from. So recycling's really important to make sure we <u>don't run out</u> of lots of important raw materials.

Recycling Saves Resources and Energy

1) Extracting raw materials can take large amounts of <u>energy</u>.
2) Lots of this energy comes from burning <u>fossil fuels</u>.
3) Fossil fuels are <u>running out</u> (because they're <u>non-renewable</u>) so it's important to <u>save</u> them.
4) Burning fossil fuels can also lead to <u>acid rain</u> and <u>climate change</u> (see pages 139 and 143).
5) Recycling materials <u>saves energy</u>. It often uses <u>much less</u> energy than what's needed to make the material from scratch.
6) There's a <u>finite</u> (limited) <u>amount</u> of many raw materials. Recycling <u>saves</u> these <u>resources</u> too.

> It's really important to recycle <u>metals</u>. This is because metals are <u>non-renewable</u> so will run out in the future.

7) It's also really important to recycle materials that are <u>rare</u> so they don't run out.

Recycling Protects the Environment

1) Extracting materials can be <u>bad</u> for the <u>environment</u>.

> Mines <u>damage</u> the <u>environment</u> and <u>destroy habitats</u>. They also <u>don't</u> look very nice. Recycling more metals means that we don't need so many mines.

2) Recycling materials also cuts down on the amount of rubbish that gets sent to <u>landfill</u>. Landfill takes up space and <u>pollutes</u> the surroundings.

Recycling is Good for the Economy

You can think of the economy as how well-off a country is.

1) Recycling materials often <u>saves energy</u>. This energy is <u>expensive</u>, so recycling <u>saves money</u>.
2) It's very <u>good</u> for the economy to recycle metals that are <u>expensive</u> to <u>extract</u> or <u>buy</u>.
3) The recycling process <u>creates</u> lots of <u>jobs</u>. This is because it has <u>lots of stages</u>.

Example: Recycling Aluminium

1) To make <u>aluminium</u> from its ore you have to <u>mine 4 tonnes</u> of ore for every <u>1 tonne</u> of aluminium you need.
2) Mining aluminium ore makes a mess of the <u>landscape</u>.
3) The ore needs to be <u>transported</u>. Then the aluminium needs to be <u>extracted</u> which uses <u>loads</u> of electricity. This means lots of <u>fossil fuels</u> need to be burnt.
4) If you don't recycle, you also have to send your <u>used</u> aluminium to <u>landfill</u>. This costs <u>money</u> and leads to <u>environmental problems</u> such as pollution and habitats being destroyed.
5) So for every 1 kg of aluminium cans you recycle, you <u>save</u>:
   - <u>95%</u> or so of the <u>energy</u> needed to mine and extract 'fresh' aluminium,
   - <u>4 kg</u> of aluminium ore,
   - a <u>lot</u> of waste.

> In fact, aluminium's about the most cost-effective metal to recycle.

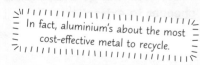

I told a hilarious joke to some sodium — the reaction was great...

Great jokes like the ones you find in this book grow on trees. So to save trees and reduce the environmental costs of this book, I thought I'd recycle that hilarious pun from page 114. Aren't I good?

Q1   Give one way that recycling can help the economy.   [1 mark]

Life Cycle Assessments

If a company wants to make a new product, it will carry out a <u>life cycle assessment</u> (LCA). Fun stuff.

Life Cycle Assessments Show Total Environmental Costs

A <u>life cycle assessment (LCA)</u> looks at each <u>stage</u> of the <u>life</u> of a product.
It works out the possible <u>environmental impact</u> of each stage.

Choice of material

1) Lots of raw materials need to be <u>extracted</u> before we can use them for a product.
2) Extracting <u>raw materials</u> can <u>damage</u> the local <u>environment</u>, e.g. mining metals.
3) Extraction uses lots of <u>energy</u>. It can also result in <u>pollution</u>.
4) Raw materials often need further <u>processing</u> to turn them into <u>useful materials</u>. This often needs <u>large amounts</u> of energy. E.g. extracting metals from ores (see p.116-117) or fractional distillation of crude oil (see p.136).
5) Some raw materials are <u>non-renewable</u>, so their supplies are <u>decreasing</u>.

Manufacture

1) <u>Manufacturing</u> (making) products uses a lot of <u>energy</u> and other <u>resources</u>.
2) It can also cause a lot of <u>pollution</u>.
3) Chemical reactions are sometimes used to make products. These reactions can produce <u>waste</u> products which need to be got rid of.
4) Some waste can be <u>recycled</u> and turned into other <u>useful chemicals</u>. This means that <u>less</u> waste ends up polluting the environment.
5) Most chemical manufacture needs <u>water</u>. Businesses have to make sure they don't put <u>polluted</u> water back into the environment when they are finished.

Product Use

<u>Using</u> the product can also damage the environment. For example:
1) <u>Paint</u> gives off <u>toxic fumes</u>.
2) <u>Burning fuels</u> releases <u>greenhouse gases</u> and other <u>harmful substances</u>.
3) <u>Fertilisers</u> can <u>drain</u> into streams and rivers and cause harm to <u>plants</u> and <u>animals</u>.

Disposal

1) Products are often <u>thrown away</u> in a <u>landfill</u> site.
2) This takes up space and can <u>pollute</u> land and water.
3) Products might be <u>incinerated</u> (burnt), which causes air pollution.

Some products can be disposed of by being recycled (see page 118).

EXAMPLE

The life cycle assessments for two cars, A and B, are shown in the table. Using the data in the table, explain which car would have less impact on the environment.

Car	Expected lifespan of product (years)	CO_2 emissions (tonnes)	Waste solid produced (kg)	Water used (m³)
A	9	21	5900	6.0
B	12	34	15 010	9.5

Car A has a shorter lifespan than car B, but car A produces less CO_2 and waste solids and uses less water.
So, on balance, car A looks like it will have the smallest environmental impact.

My cycle assessment — two wheels, a bell, an uncomfortable seat...

Don't get your bike cycle and life cycle assessments confused. Life cycle assessments are the ones you'll need.

Q1   For the example above, suggest two further things (that aren't outlined in the table)
that should be included in the life cycle assessments for the cars.   [2 marks]

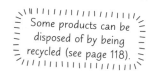

Dynamic Equilibrium

Reversible reactions — products forming from reactants and reactants forming from products. I can't keep up...

Reversible Reactions can go Forwards and Backwards

A reversible reaction is one where the products can react with each other to produce the original reactants. In other words, it can go both ways.

$$A + B \rightleftharpoons C + D$$

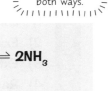
The '$\rightleftharpoons$' shows that the reaction goes both ways.

The Haber process is an example of a reversible reaction.

1) During the Haber process, nitrogen and hydrogen react to form ammonia: $N_2 + 3H_2 \rightleftharpoons 2NH_3$
   - The nitrogen (N_2) is taken from the air, which is about 78% nitrogen.
   - The hydrogen (H_2) can be taken from sources such as natural gas.
2) The Haber process is carried out at 450 °C, with a pressure of 200 atmospheres and an iron catalyst.

Reversible Reactions Will Reach Equilibrium

1) As the reactants (A and B) react, their concentrations fall. This makes the forward reaction slow down.

2) As more and more of the products (C and D) are made, their concentrations rise. This speeds up the backward reaction.

3) After a while the forward reaction will be going at exactly the same rate as the backward one.

4) This is a dynamic equilibrium:
   - The forward and backward reactions are both happening at the same time and at the same rate.
   - The concentrations of reactants and products have reached a balance and won't change.

5) Equilibrium can only be reached if the reversible reaction takes place in a 'closed system'. A closed system just means that none of the reactants or products can escape and nothing can get in.

Reversible Reactions Can Have a Direction at Equilibrium

When a reaction's at equilibrium it doesn't mean that the amounts of reactants and products are equal (it just means that the amounts aren't changing any more).

If there are more products than reactants, the reaction is going in the forwards direction.

If there are more reactants than products, the reaction is going in the backwards direction.

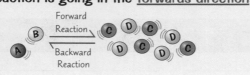
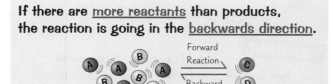

You can change the direction of the reaction by changing the reaction conditions (e.g. temperature, pressure or concentration).

Dynamic equilibrium — lots of activity, but not to any great effect*...

Keep an eye out for that arrow that shows you that a reaction is reversible. I'd hate you to miss it.

Q1   Explain what is meant by the term 'reversible reaction'.   [1 mark]

Q2   What is dynamic equilibrium?   [3 marks]

*a bit like my attempts at cleaning.

Group 1 — Alkali Metals

You can predict how different elements will <u>react</u> by looking at where they are in the <u>periodic table</u>. Elements in the <u>same group</u> react in <u>similar ways</u>. Let's start by looking at <u>Group 1</u>...

Group 1 Metals are Known as the 'Alkali Metals'

The <u>Group 1</u> metals are lithium, sodium, potassium, rubidium, caesium and francium.

1) The alkali metals all have <u>one outer electron</u>.
   This gives them <u>similar chemical properties</u>.

2) They all have similar <u>physical properties</u> too.
   - They have <u>low melting points</u> and <u>boiling points</u> compared to other metals.
   - They are <u>very soft</u> so they can be cut with a knife.

Group 1	Group 2	
7 Li Lithium 3	Be	
23 Na Sodium 11	Mg	
39 K Potassium 19	Ca	Sc
86 Rb Rubidium 37	Sr	Y
133 Cs Caesium 55	Ba	
223 Fr Francium 87	Ra	

Group 1 Metals are Very Reactive

1) The Group 1 metals <u>lose</u> their single <u>outer electron</u> very easily.
   When this happens, they form a <u>1+ ion</u>.
   This ion has a <u>stable electronic structure</u>.

2) The <u>more easily</u> a metal loses its outer electrons, the <u>more reactive</u> it is.
   So Group 1 metals are <u>very reactive</u>.

3) As you go <u>down</u> Group 1, alkali metals get <u>more reactive</u>.

$$Li \rightarrow Li^+ + e^-$$

- There's an <u>attraction</u> between the positive charge of an atom's nucleus and its negatively-charged electrons.
- As you go down Group 1, the atoms get <u>bigger</u>. So the outer electrons are <u>further away</u> from the nucleus.
- This means that the attraction of these outer electrons is <u>weaker</u> and they can be <u>lost more easily</u>.

Reactions with Cold Water Produces a Hydroxide and Hydrogen Gas

1) When the <u>alkali metals</u> are put in <u>water</u>, they react <u>strongly</u>.

2) The reaction produces <u>hydrogen gas</u> and a <u>hydroxide</u> of the metal.

   alkali metal + water → metal hydroxide + hydrogen

3) For example, here's the overall equation for the reaction of <u>sodium</u> with <u>water</u>:

   $$2Na + 2H_2O \rightarrow 2NaOH + H_2$$
   sodium + water → sodium hydroxide + hydrogen

   The same reaction happens with all of the alkali metals — make sure you can write balanced equations for them all.

4) Since Group 1 metals get <u>more reactive</u> down the group, their reactions with water become <u>more violent</u>:
   - <u>Lithium moves</u> around the surface, <u>fizzing</u> wildly. It <u>decreases</u> in size as it <u>dissolves</u>.
   - <u>Sodium</u> and <u>potassium</u> do the same, but they also <u>melt</u> and form a ball in the heat of the reaction. Potassium even gets hot enough to <u>ignite</u> (set on fire) the hydrogen gas being produced.

5) You might be asked to make <u>predictions</u> about the reactions of other Group 1 elements. So make sure you know the pattern of reactivity in Group 1.

   <u>Example</u>: You may predict that the reactions of rubidium and caesium with water will be <u>more violent</u> than the reaction of potassium and water. And sure enough, <u>rubidium</u> and <u>caesium</u> react <u>violently</u> with water. They even tend to <u>explode</u> when they get wet.

And that's why you don't get caesium teaspoons... Kaboom...

Alkali metals are so reactive that they have to be stored in oil — otherwise they just react with the air.

Q1 Write a word equation for the reaction between lithium and water. [1 mark]

Q2 A student reacts sodium with water. Describe what the student will observe. [1 mark]

Q1 Video Solution

Group 7 — Halogens

Here's a page on another periodic table group that you need to know about — <u>the halogens</u>.

Group 7 Elements are Known as the 'Halogens'

<u>Group 7</u> is made up of the elements fluorine, chlorine, bromine, iodine and astatine.

1) All Group 7 elements have <u>7 electrons in their outer shell</u>.
   This means they all have <u>similar chemical properties</u>.

2) As <u>elements</u>, the halogens form molecules that contain <u>two atoms</u> (e.g. Cl_2, Br_2).

3) As you go <u>down Group 7</u>, the <u>melting points</u> and <u>boiling points</u>
   of the halogens <u>increase</u>. This means that at <u>room temperature</u>:

   <u>Chlorine</u> (Cl_2) is a fairly reactive, poisonous, <u>green gas</u>.

   <u>Bromine</u> (Br_2) is a poisonous, <u>red-brown liquid</u>
   which gives off an <u>orange vapour</u> (gas).

   <u>Iodine</u> (I_2) is a <u>dark grey crystalline solid</u>.

4) You might need to <u>predict</u> the properties of other halogens in the group.

5) To do this you can use the <u>trends</u> (patterns) <u>in physical properties</u> from chlorine to iodine.

   - For example, we know that melting point <u>increases</u> down the group.
   - You could predict that <u>astatine</u> (which is below iodine in the group) would also be a <u>solid</u> at room temperature. This is because, if room temperature <u>isn't</u> high enough to melt iodine, it <u>won't</u> be high enough to melt astatine.
   - You might also be asked to <u>estimate the value</u> of a particular property. For example, you might be asked to estimate the melting point of astatine when given the melting point of iodine (114 °C). You know from the trend that astatine will have a <u>higher</u> melting point, so this helps you estimate a number.

	Group 6	Group 7	Group 0
			He
	O	19 F Fluorine 9	Ne
	S	35.5 Cl Chlorine 17	Ar
	Se	80 Br Bromine 35	Kr
		127 I Iodine 53	Xe
		210 At Astatine 85	Rn

Test for Chlorine Using Damp Blue Litmus Paper

1) You can test to see if a gas is <u>chlorine</u> by holding
   a piece of <u>damp blue litmus paper</u> over it.

2) Chlorine will <u>bleach</u> the litmus paper, which turns it <u>white</u>.

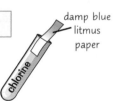

damp blue litmus paper

Reactivity Decreases Going Down Group 7

1) Atoms with a <u>full</u> outer electron shell have a <u>stable</u> electronic structure.

2) A halogen atom only needs to <u>gain one electron</u> to get a
   <u>full outer shell</u>. When it gains an electron, it forms a <u>1− ion</u>.

3) The <u>easier</u> it is for a halogen atom to <u>attract</u> an
   electron, the <u>more reactive</u> the halogen will be.

4) As you go <u>down</u> Group 7, attracting an <u>electron</u> gets harder.
   This is because the outer shell is <u>further away</u> from the nucleus.
   So the halogens become <u>less reactive</u>.

A halogen with a 1−
charge is called a halide.

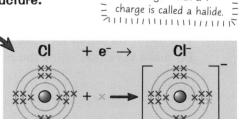

$$Cl + e^- \rightarrow Cl^-$$

Halogens — one electron short of a full shell...

Another page, another periodic table group to learn the properties and the trends of. It's like Christmas come early.

Q1   How could you test to see if a gas is chlorine?   [2 marks]

Reactions of Halogens

So even though the halogens get <u>less reactive</u> as you go down the group, they all take part in <u>similar reactions</u>. There are a few <u>reactions</u> you need to know about.

The Halogens Can React With Metals and Hydrogen

1) The halogens will react strongly with some <u>metals</u> to form <u>salts</u> called '<u>metal halides</u>'.

$$\text{metal} + \text{halogen} \rightarrow \text{metal halide}$$

$$2Na \quad + \quad Cl_2 \quad \rightarrow \quad 2NaCl$$
$$\text{sodium} \quad + \quad \text{chlorine} \quad \rightarrow \quad \text{sodium chloride}$$

2) In these reactions, the halogen <u>attracts</u> the outer electron of the metal atom.

3) Halogens <u>higher up</u> in Group 7 can attract the <u>outer electron</u> of the metal <u>more easily</u>. This makes them <u>more</u> reactive.

1) Halogens can also react with <u>hydrogen</u> to form <u>hydrogen halides</u>.

$$\text{hydrogen} + \text{halogen} \rightarrow \text{hydrogen halide}$$

$$H_2 \quad + \quad Cl_2 \quad \rightarrow \quad 2HCl$$
$$\text{hydrogen} \quad + \quad \text{chlorine} \quad \rightarrow \quad \text{hydrogen chloride}$$

2) Hydrogen halides can <u>dissolve in water</u> (they're <u>soluble</u>). When they do this, they form <u>acidic solutions</u>. For example, HCl forms <u>hydrochloric acid</u> in water.

All halogens have <u>similar reactions</u> because they have the same number of electrons in their outer shells. So you can use the reactions of <u>chlorine</u>, <u>bromine</u> and <u>iodine</u> to <u>predict</u> how <u>fluorine</u> and <u>astatine</u> will react.

A More Reactive Halogen Will Displace a Less Reactive One

1) The elements in Group 7 take part in <u>displacement reactions</u>.

2) A displacement reaction is where a <u>more reactive</u> element '<u>pushes out</u>' (<u>displaces</u>) a <u>less reactive</u> element from a compound.

3) Displacement reactions can take place between a <u>halogen</u> and the <u>halide salt</u> of a <u>less reactive</u> halogen. The <u>more reactive</u> halogen '<u>pushes out</u>' (<u>displaces</u>) the <u>less reactive</u> halogen from the salt compound.

4) When this happens, the <u>less reactive</u> halogen changes from a halide (1– ion) to a <u>halogen</u>. The <u>more reactive</u> halogen changes from a halogen into a <u>halide ion</u> and becomes part of the <u>salt</u>.

- For example, chlorine is <u>more reactive</u> than bromine (it's higher up Group 7). So if you add <u>chlorine water</u> (an <u>aqueous solution</u> of <u>Cl_2</u>) to a solution containing a <u>bromide salt</u> (such as potassium bromide), bromine will be <u>displaced</u>.

- The <u>chlorine atoms</u> become <u>chloride ions</u>, so the salt solution becomes <u>potassium chloride</u>. The <u>bromide ions</u> become <u>bromine atoms</u>, which turns the solution <u>orange</u> (see next page).

$$Cl_2 \quad + \quad 2KBr \quad \rightarrow \quad Br_2 \quad + \quad 2KCl$$
$$\text{chlorine} + \text{potassium bromide} \rightarrow \text{bromine} + \text{potassium chloride}$$

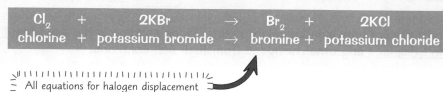

All equations for halogen displacement reactions follow this pattern.

Get out of here, Bro!

My dad told me that bromine displaces chlorine — halide...

Learning all these reactions may seem scary, but remember, the reactions of the halogens follow the same patterns.

Q1   Write a balanced symbol equation for the reaction between bromine (Br_2) and sodium (Na).   [2 marks]

More Reactions of Halogens

You came across displacement reactions on the last page, but there's some more about them here.

Displacement Reactions **Result in a Colour Change**

You can <u>mix</u> a <u>halogen</u> solution and a <u>halide</u> solution together to see if a displacement reaction takes place.

1) Measure out a small amount of a <u>halide salt solution</u> in a test tube.

2) Add a few drops of a <u>halogen solution</u> to it. Shake the tube gently.

3) If you see a <u>colour change</u>, then a reaction has happened.
In this reaction, the halogen has <u>displaced</u> the halide ions from the salt.
If the halogen is <u>less reactive</u> than the halide, it won't displace it.
This means that no reaction happens, so there <u>won't</u> be a colour change.

4) Repeat these steps using different combinations of halide salt and halogen.

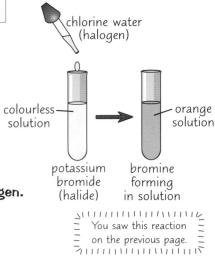

chlorine water (halogen)

colourless solution → orange solution

potassium bromide (halide)

bromine forming in solution

You saw this reaction on the previous page.

Displacement Reactions **Show Reactivity Trends**

1) You can use <u>displacement reactions</u> to show the reactivity trend of the halogens.

2) The table below shows what should happen when you mix different combinations of <u>chlorine</u>, <u>bromine</u> and <u>iodine</u> water with solutions of <u>potassium halide salts</u>.

Start with:	Potassium chloride solution $KCl_{(aq)}$ — colourless	Potassium bromide solution $KBr_{(aq)}$ — colourless	Potassium iodide solution $KI_{(aq)}$ — colourless
Add chlorine water $Cl_{2\,(aq)}$ — colourless	no reaction	orange solution (Br_2) formed	brown solution (I_2) formed
Add bromine water $Br_{2\,(aq)}$ — orange	no reaction	no reaction	brown solution (I_2) formed
Add iodine water $I_{2\,(aq)}$ — brown	no reaction	no reaction	no reaction

3) The table shows the halogens get <u>less reactive</u> as you go <u>down</u> the group. This is the <u>reactivity trend</u>.

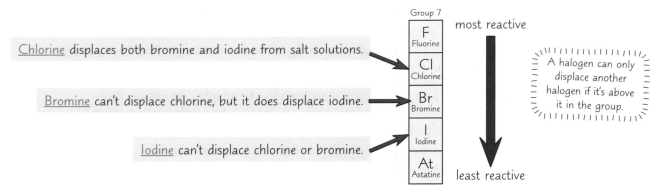

<u>Chlorine</u> displaces both bromine and iodine from salt solutions.

<u>Bromine</u> can't displace chlorine, but it does displace iodine.

<u>Iodine</u> can't displace chlorine or bromine.

Group 7

F Fluorine — most reactive
Cl Chlorine
Br Bromine
I Iodine
At Astatine — least reactive

A halogen can only displace another halogen if it's above it in the group.

4) You can use this trend to predict how astatine might react. Since astatine is the <u>least reactive halogen</u>, you'd predict it <u>wouldn't displace</u> any other halogens from their salt solutions.

New information displaces old information from my brain...

If you remember that the halogens get less reactive as you go down the group, you can work out what will happen when you mix any halogen with any halide salt. You need to know the colour changes that go with the reactions too.

Q1 A student added a few drops of iodine water to a potassium bromide solution.
Explain why the solution did not change colour. [2 marks]

Group 0 — Noble Gases

The elements in <u>Group 0</u> of the periodic table are known as the <u>noble gases</u>.
'Noble' here just means that they are <u>unreactive</u>.

Group 0 Elements are All Unreactive, Colourless Gases

1) <u>Group 0</u> elements are called the <u>noble gases</u>.

2) They include the elements helium, neon, argon, krypton, xenon and radon.

3) All of the Group 0 elements are <u>colourless gases</u> at room temperature.

4) They're very <u>unreactive</u> (<u>inert</u>).
This is because they have a <u>full outer shell</u> of electrons.
So they <u>don't</u> easily <u>give up</u> or <u>gain</u> electrons.

5) Their full outer shell also makes them <u>non-flammable</u> — they won't set on fire.

Group 6	Group 7	Group 0
		4 He Helium 2
O	F	20 Ne Neon 10
S	Cl	40 Ar Argon 18
	Br	84 Kr Krypton 36
	I	131 Xe Xenon 54
	At	222 Rn Radon 86

The Noble Gases have Many Everyday Uses...

1) The properties of the <u>noble gases</u> has given them lots of uses.

2) For example, they're often used to provide an <u>inert atmosphere</u> (unreactive surroundings) or to help things float:

<u>Argon</u>, <u>krypton</u> and <u>xenon</u> provide an inert atmosphere in some types of <u>light bulb</u>. It's <u>non-flammable</u> so it stops the very hot wire (filament) from <u>burning away</u>.

<u>Argon</u> and <u>helium</u> can be used to protect metals that are being <u>welded</u>. The inert atmosphere stops the hot metal reacting with <u>oxygen</u> in the air.

<u>Helium</u> is used in <u>airships</u> and <u>party balloons</u>. Helium has a <u>lower density</u> (it's lighter) than air — this means it makes balloons <u>float</u>. It's also <u>non-flammable</u> which makes it safe to use.

There are Trends in the Properties of the Noble Gases

1) Like other groups, Group 0 elements also show <u>trends</u> (patterns) in their <u>properties</u>.

2) For example, as you go <u>down</u> Group 0, <u>boiling point</u>, <u>melting point</u> and <u>density</u> all <u>increase</u>.

3) You could be given information about a certain <u>property</u> of a noble gas and asked to use it to <u>predict the same property</u> of another one. For example:

EXAMPLE   Use the densities of helium (0.20 kg m^{-3}) and argon (1.8 kg m^{-3}) to predict the density of neon.

Neon comes between helium and argon in the group. So you can predict that its density will be about halfway between their densities:

(0.20 + 1.8) ÷ 2 = 2.0 ÷ 2 = 1.0

E.g. neon has a density of 1.0 kg m^{-3}.

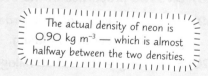

The actual density of neon is 0.90 kg m^{-3} — which is almost halfway between the two densities.

You could be asked about how an element <u>reacts</u> too. So remember — elements in the <u>same group</u> react in <u>similar ways</u>. This is because they all have the same number of <u>electrons</u> in their <u>outer shells</u>. And, to find out which group an element is in, all you need to do is look at the <u>periodic table</u>.

Noble gas jokes are rubbish — I never get a reaction from them...

The noble gases might seem a bit dull, but they're not so bad. They'd be pretty good at hide and seek for a start. And what would balloon sellers be without helium? Deflated — that's what.

Q1   The melting point of neon is –249 °C and the melting point of krypton is –157 °C. Predict the melting point of argon.

[1 mark]

Revision Questions for Sections 13 and 14

Ahhh, Sections 13 and 14 were great. Some bits could prove tricky though, so have a go at the questions below.

- Try these questions and tick off each one when you get it right.
- When you're completely happy with a sub-topic, tick it off.

For even more practice, try the Retrieval Quizzes for Sections 13 and 14 — just scan these QR codes!

The Reactions and Reactivity of Metals (p.114-115) ☑

1) What is reduction?

2) What does a reactivity series show?

3) In a reactivity series, where do you find the least reactive elements?

4) True or false? The easier it is for a metal atom to form a positive ion, the more reactive it will be.

5) What would you expect to see if you added a small piece of a very reactive metal to some dilute hydrochloric acid?

6) Would you expect a reaction to take place between copper and water?

Section 13 Quiz

Extracting Metals from their Ores (p.116-117) ☑

7) True or false? Unreactive metals are found in the Earth's crust as uncombined elements.

8) How are metals less reactive than carbon usually extracted from their ores?

9) How are metals more reactive than carbon extracted from their ores?

10) Why is the process of electrolysis more expensive than the process of reduction with carbon?

Conserving Resources (p.118-119) ☐

11) Give one way in which recycling is better for the environment than disposing of waste in landfill.

12) What is a life cycle assessment?

13) Name four factors that should be considered when doing a life cycle assessment for a product.

Equilibria (p.120) ☑

14) Draw the symbol which shows that a reaction is reversible.

15) Name the two reactants that form ammonia in the reversible reaction of the Haber process.

16) True or false? At equilibrium, the forward and backward reactions are happening at different rates.

17) What does it mean if a reversible reaction is going in the forwards direction?

Groups 1, 7 and 0 (p.121-125) ☐

18) Give two properties of the Group 1 metals.

19) Put these alkali metals in order of reactivity, starting with the least reactive: potassium, caesium, lithium.

20) How many electrons do halogen atoms have in their outer shells?

21) Describe the appearance and physical state of chlorine at room temperature.

22) Name the product of a reaction between a halogen and a metal.

23) What happens during a halogen displacement reaction?

24) If chlorine water is added to potassium bromide solution, what colour will the solution turn?

25) At room temperature, what colour are the Group 0 elements?

26) Why are balloons filled with helium able to float in the air?

27) Does the boiling point of Group 0 elements increase or decrease going down the group?

Section 14 Quiz

Reaction Rates

Reactions can be <u>fast</u> or <u>slow</u> — you've probably already realised that. It's exciting stuff. Honest.

The Rate of Reaction is a Measure of How Fast the Reaction Happens

1) The <u>rate of a reaction</u> is how quickly a reaction happens.

2) It can be observed <u>either</u> by measuring how quickly the reactants are used up or how quickly the products are formed.

You can find out how to calculate the rate of a reaction on p.129.

You can Measure the Rate of a Reaction where a Precipitate is Formed

1) This method works for any reaction where mixing <u>two see-through solutions</u> produces a <u>precipitate</u> (a solid), which <u>clouds</u> the solution.

2) You <u>mix</u> the two reactant solutions and put the flask on a piece of paper that has a <u>mark</u> on it.

3) <u>Watch</u> the mark through the mixture. Measure how long it takes until you <u>can't see</u> the mark anymore.

4) The <u>faster</u> it disappears, the <u>faster</u> the reaction.

5) The result is <u>subjective</u> — <u>different people</u> might not agree on <u>exactly</u> when the mark 'disappears'.

Use this Experiment to See How Temperature Affects Rate

PRACTICAL

1) You can see how <u>temperature</u> affects reaction <u>rate</u> by looking at the reaction between sodium thiosulfate and hydrochloric acid.

2) Sodium thiosulfate and hydrochloric acid are both <u>clear</u>, <u>colourless solutions</u>. They react together to form a <u>yellow precipitate</u> of <u>sulfur</u>.

3) You can use the amount of <u>time</u> that it takes for the coloured precipitate to form as a measure of the <u>rate</u> of this reaction.

- Measure out fixed volumes of <u>sodium thiosulfate</u> and <u>hydrochloric acid</u>, using a measuring cylinder.
- Use a <u>water bath</u> to <u>gently heat</u> both solutions to the desired temperature before you mix them.
- Mix the solutions in a conical flask. Place the flask over a black mark on a piece of paper which can be seen through the solution.
- Watch the <u>black mark</u> through the solution and <u>time</u> how long it takes for it to disappear.
- The reaction can be repeated for solutions at <u>different temperatures</u>.
- The <u>depths</u> and <u>volumes</u> of liquid must be kept the same each time. The <u>concentrations</u> of the solutions must also be kept the same.
- The <u>shorter</u> the length of time taken for the mark to disappear, the <u>faster</u> the rate.

4) You can draw a <u>graph</u> showing the <u>time taken</u> for the mark to disappear against the <u>temperature</u> of the reacting solutions.

5) The <u>higher</u> the temperature, the less time it takes for the mark to disappear. So <u>increasing</u> the temperature <u>increases the rate</u> of the reaction (see p.131).

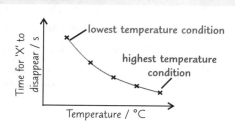

Time for 'X' to disappear / s — lowest temperature condition; highest temperature condition; Temperature / °C

And for my next trick, I'll make this chocolate cake disappear...

When repeating this experiment, you need to keep everything exactly the same apart from the temperature.

Q1   Give one disadvantage of using the precipitation method to measure the rate of a reaction.   [1 mark]

Rate Experiments Involving Gases

At some point, you'll probably have to <u>measure</u> the <u>rate of a reaction</u> that forms a gas. Here's how to do it...

You can Measure the Rate of a Reaction that Forms a Gas

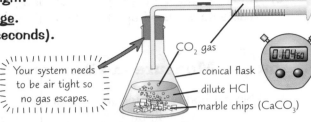

PRACTICAL

You can measure <u>rate</u> of the reaction between hydrochloric acid and marble chips:

1) Set the apparatus up as shown in the diagram on the right.

2) Measure the <u>volume</u> of gas produced using a <u>gas syringe</u>.
Take readings at <u>regular time intervals</u> (e.g. every 20 seconds).

3) <u>Record</u> the results in a table.

4) You can plot a <u>graph</u> of your results — <u>time</u> goes
on the <u>x-axis</u> and <u>volume</u> goes on the <u>y-axis</u>.

5) When the line becomes <u>flat</u>, the reaction has <u>finished</u>.

6) The faster the rate, the steeper the graph will be and the <u>sooner</u> the reaction will finish.

Your system needs
to be air tight so
no gas escapes.

gas syringe

CO_2 gas

conical flask

dilute HCl

marble chips ($CaCO_3$)

Finer Particles of Solid Mean a Higher Rate

1) To find out how <u>surface area</u> affects the rate, you can repeat
the experiment in the <u>same way</u>, but with <u>smaller</u> marble chips.

2) Then <u>repeat</u> with the same mass of <u>powdered chalk</u>.

3) The <u>smaller</u> the chalk particles are,
the greater the <u>overall surface area</u> will be.

4) <u>Lines 1 to 3</u> show that the <u>greater</u> the surface area of the solid, the <u>faster</u> the reaction.

5) <u>Line 4</u> shows the reaction if a <u>greater mass</u> of small marble chips is added.
The <u>extra chips</u> means there's a greater surface area so the <u>reaction</u> is <u>faster</u>.
It also means that there's more stuff to react, so <u>more gas</u> is produced overall.

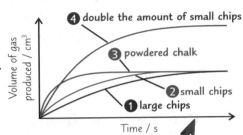

Volume of gas produced / cm^3

❹ double the amount of small chips

❸ powdered chalk

❷ small chips

❶ large chips

Time / s

Marble and chalk
are both made of
calcium carbonate.

More Concentrated Solutions Mean a Higher Rate

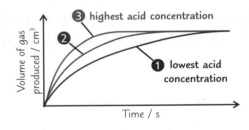

Volume of gas produced / cm^3

❸ highest acid concentration

❷

❶ lowest acid concentration

Time / s

1) You can measure how the <u>concentration</u> of the acid affects
the rate by following the <u>same method</u> described above.

2) This time you repeat the experiment and keep everything
the same except for the <u>concentration of acid</u>.

3) <u>Lines 1 to 3</u> on the graph show that a <u>higher</u> concentration
gives a <u>faster reaction</u>, with the reaction <u>finishing</u> sooner.

You Can Measure the Change in Mass for a Reaction that Forms a Gas

1) If you carry out a reaction that produces a gas in an unsealed reaction container,
the total <u>mass</u> of the container and reaction mixture will <u>go down</u> as the gas is released.

2) You can investigate the rate of reaction by putting the reaction container
on a <u>mass balance</u> and taking <u>regular readings</u> until the mass <u>stops changing</u>.

3) You can use your results to plot a <u>graph</u> of <u>change in mass</u> against <u>time</u>.

4) This method releases the gas produced straight into the room — so if the
gas is <u>harmful</u>, you should do the experiment in a <u>fume cupboard</u>.

Cotton wool lets
gases through
but stops any
other reactants
flying out.

I prefer powdered marble to chips — I like the finer things in life...

Rate experiments give you data. Data lets you plot graphs. You can use graphs to find reaction rates. Wonderful.

Q1   Describe how you could investigate how the surface area of calcium carbonate
affects the rate of reaction between calcium carbonate and hydrochloric acid.   [3 marks]

Calculating Rates

As well as doing experiments, you need to be able to do some <u>calculations</u> to work out <u>reaction rates</u>. Don't worry though, they're not too bad. Read on and all will be explained.

Here's How to Work Out the Rate of a Reaction

$$\text{Average Rate of Reaction} = \frac{\text{Amount of reactant used or amount of product formed}}{\text{Time Taken}}$$

This equation is for the <u>mean</u> rate of reaction. It lets you work out the <u>average rate</u> over an <u>amount of time</u>.

EXAMPLE

A reaction takes 120 seconds. 3.0 g of product are made. Find the mean rate of reaction.

Rate = amount of product formed ÷ time taken
   = 3.0 g ÷ 120 s = 0.025 g s^{-1}

Gases can be measured in <u>cm^3</u>, so if the product you measured was a gas the rate could be measured in <u>cm^3 s^{-1}</u> rather than in <u>g s^{-1}</u>.

You Can Calculate the Mean Reaction Rate from a Graph

1) To find the <u>mean rate</u> for the <u>whole reaction</u>, start by working out when the reaction <u>finished</u>. This is when the line goes <u>flat</u>.
2) Then work out how much <u>product</u> was <u>formed</u> (or how much <u>reactant</u> was <u>used up</u>).
3) Then <u>divide this</u> by the <u>total time taken</u> for the reaction to finish.

cm^3 s^{-1} can also be written as cm^3/s.

EXAMPLE

The graph shows the volume of gas released by a reaction, measured at regular intervals. Find the mean rate of the reaction.

1) Work out when the reaction <u>finished</u>.
2) Work out how much <u>product</u> was <u>formed</u>.
3) <u>Divide</u> this by the <u>time taken</u> for the reaction to finish.

The line goes flat at 50 s.
20 cm^3 of gas was released.
mean rate = 20 cm^3 ÷ 50 s
       = 0.40 cm^3 s^{-1}

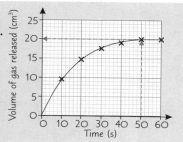

4) You can also use a graph to find the <u>mean rate</u> of reaction between <u>two points</u> in time:

EXAMPLE

Find the mean rate of reaction between 20 s and 40 s.

1) Work out how much <u>gas</u> was produced <u>between</u> 20 s and 40 s.
2) Work out the <u>time difference</u> between 20 s and 40 s.
3) <u>Divide</u> the amount of gas produced by the time taken.

At 20 s, 15 cm^3 had been produced.
At 40 s, 19 cm^3 had been produced.
Gas produced between 20 and 40 s = 19 cm^3 − 15 cm^3 = 4.0 cm^3
time difference = 40 s − 20 s = 20 s
mean rate = 4.0 cm^3 ÷ 20 s
       = 0.20 cm^3 s^{-1}

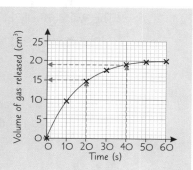

Being asked to calculate reaction rates. That's just mean...

Always use the formula at the top of this page to calculate average rate, whether you have just numbers or a graph. Average rate = amount of reactant used (or product formed) ÷ time taken. Learn it. It's important.

Q1   A reaction takes 200 s. 6.0 g of reactant are used up. What is the average rate of the reaction in g s^{-1}? Give your answer to one significant figure.   [2 marks]

Q1 Video Solution

More on Calculating Rates

So now you've seen one way of using a graph to calculate the rate of a reaction. But don't put your feet up just yet. There's one more method you need to know about. Let's get cracking...

Faster Rates of Reaction are Shown by Steeper Gradients

1) If you have a graph of amount of product formed (or reactant used up) against time, then the gradient (slope) of the graph will be equal to the rate of the reaction.

2) The steeper the slope, the faster the rate.

3) The gradient of a straight line is given by the equation:

$$\text{gradient} = \text{change in } y \div \text{change in } x$$

EXAMPLE

Calculate the rate of the reaction shown on the graph below.

1) Find two points on the line that are easy to read the x and y values of (ones that pass through grid lines).

2) Draw a line straight down from the higher point and straight across from the lower point to make a triangle.

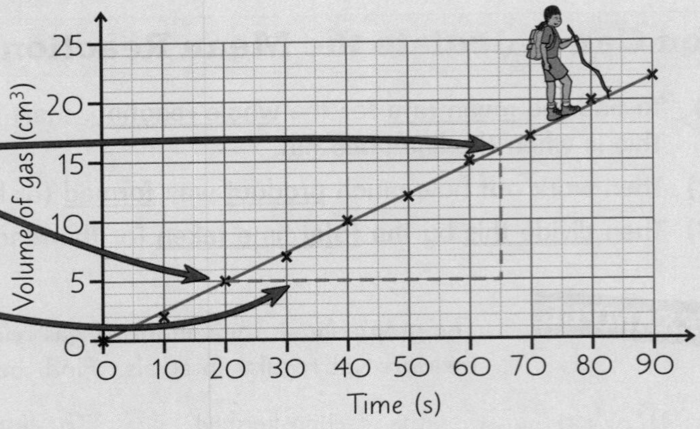

3) The height of your triangle is the change in y. Change in $y = 16 - 5 = 11$

4) The base of your triangle is the change in x. Change in $x = 65 - 20 = 45$

5) Use the formula to work out the gradient.
Gradient = change in $y \div$ change in x
= $11 \div 45$
= 0.24

6) The units of the rate are "units of y-axis ÷ units of x-axis". This will normally be written as "unit of y-axis" "units of x-axis"$^{-1}$

Units = units of y-axis ÷ units of x-axis
= $cm^3 \div s$
= $cm^3 \, s^{-1}$

The little −1 above the units of the x-axis shows that you're dividing by the units of the x-axis.

7) Write down the gradient and the units together to give the rate.
Gradient (rate) = 0.24 $cm^3 \, s^{-1}$

Calculating gradients — it's a slippery slope...

There are some nifty graph skills for you to get to grips with on this page. Gradients aren't too hard, and they get easier with a little bit of practice. Just remember that you always need to check what the units of rate will be.

Q1 On a straight line graph, the y value changes by 9 as the x value changes by 12. Calculate the gradient of the graph.
[2 marks]

Collision Theory

The rate of a reaction depends on how <u>often</u> particles collide, and how much <u>energy</u> they have when they do.

Particles Must Collide with Enough Energy in Order to React

1) <u>Reaction rates</u> are explained by <u>collision theory</u>.

2) This states that the <u>rate of a chemical reaction</u> depends on:

A successful collision is a collision that ends in the particles reacting to form products.

1) <u>How often</u> the reacting particles <u>collide</u> (the <u>collision frequency</u>). The <u>more</u> successful collisions there are, the <u>faster</u> the reaction is.

2) The <u>energy transferred</u> during a collision. The minimum amount of energy that particles need to react when they collide is called the <u>activation energy</u>. Particles need to collide with <u>at least the activation energy</u> for the collision to be <u>successful</u>.

The More Collisions, the Higher the Rate of Reaction

If you <u>increase</u> the <u>number</u> of collisions or the <u>energy</u> with which the particles collide, the reaction happens <u>more quickly</u> (i.e. the rate increases). The three factors below all lead to an increased rate of reaction...

Increasing the Temperature Increases Rate

<u>Increasing</u> the temperature <u>increases</u> the rate of a reaction. There are <u>two reasons</u> for this:

1) At higher temperatures, the particles <u>move faster</u>. This means they <u>collide more often</u>.

2) Higher temperatures also mean the particles have <u>more energy</u>. So <u>more particles</u> will <u>collide</u> with <u>enough energy</u> to react. So the number of <u>successful</u> collisions will be <u>higher</u>.

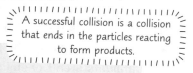
Cold   Hot

Increasing Concentration (or Pressure) Increases Rate

1) If a <u>solution</u> is made more <u>concentrated</u> it means there are more particles of <u>reactant</u> in the same volume.

2) If the <u>pressure</u> of a <u>gas</u> is increased, there will be more particles in the same amount of space.

3) A higher concentration or pressure means particles are <u>more likely</u> to collide. So there will be <u>more</u> collisions. This means the reaction rate will <u>increase</u>.

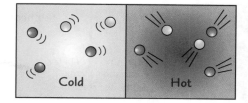
Low concentration (Low pressure)   High concentration (High pressure)

Smaller Solid Particles (or More Surface Area) Means a Higher Rate

1) If one reactant is a <u>solid</u>, breaking it into <u>smaller</u> pieces will <u>increase its surface area to volume ratio</u>.

2) This means the <u>same amount</u> (volume) of solid has a <u>bigger surface area</u>.

3) The particles around it will have <u>more area to react with</u>. So collisions will be <u>more frequent</u> and the rate will <u>increase</u>.

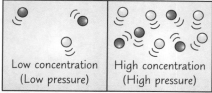
Small surface area to volume ratio   Large surface area to volume ratio

Collision theory — it's always the other driver...

More collisions mean a faster reaction. But don't be fooled as not every collision results in a reaction.

Q1   In terms of collisions between particles, give two factors that affect the rate of reaction. [2 marks]

Q2   Explain why breaking a solid reactant into smaller pieces increases the rate of a reaction. [3 marks]

Q2 Video Solution

Catalysts

Catalysts are very important for financial reasons — they increase reaction rate and reduce energy costs in industrial reactions. If that's not reason enough to learn this page, I don't know what is. (Oh, apart from "exams"...)

A Catalyst Increases the Rate of a Reaction

1) A catalyst is a substance which increases the rate of a reaction.

2) They don't change the products of the reaction.

3) Catalysts aren't chemically changed during the reaction. They don't get used up either.

4) This means the mass of catalyst in the reaction mixture at the end of the reaction will be the same as the mass that was put in at the start.

5) Catalysts are usually quite picky about which reactions they work with. A certain catalyst will generally only speed up a certain reaction.

6) Catalysts work by decreasing the activation energy (see last page) needed for a reaction to occur.

7) They do this by providing a different reaction pathway that has a lower activation energy.

8) This means more of the particles have the amount of energy needed to react when they collide.

9) You can see this if you look at a reaction profile.

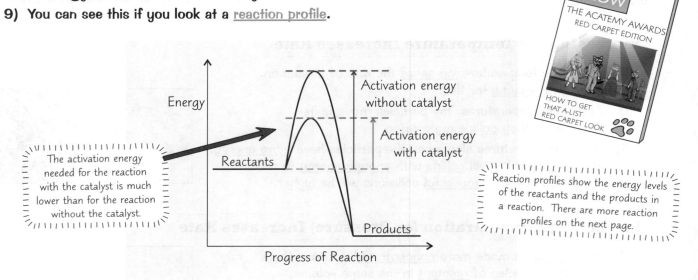

The activation energy needed for the reaction with the catalyst is much lower than for the reaction without the catalyst.

Reaction profiles show the energy levels of the reactants and the products in a reaction. There are more reaction profiles on the next page.

Enzymes Control Cell Reactions

1) Enzymes are biological catalysts.

2) This means that they catalyse (speed up) the chemical reactions in living cells.

- Enzymes from yeast cells are used to make alcoholic drinks.
- They catalyse the reaction that converts sugars (such as glucose) into ethanol and carbon dioxide.

I wish there was a catalyst for speeding up my pizza delivery...

Catalysts are really handy. Some reactions take a very long time to happen by themselves which isn't good for industrial reactions. Catalysts help to produce an acceptable amount of product in an acceptable length of time.

Q1   Give the definition of a catalyst.   [2 marks]

Q2   Give the definition of an enzyme and describe what they do.   [2 marks]

Endothermic and Exothermic Reactions

So, <u>endothermic</u> and <u>exothermic reactions</u> are all about taking in and giving out energy to the <u>surroundings</u>. I think endothermic reactions are a bit selfish really — they just take, take, take...

Reactions are Exothermic or Endothermic

1. An <u>EXOTHERMIC</u> <u>reaction</u> is one which <u>gives out energy</u> to the surroundings.
2. The energy is usually in the form of <u>heat.</u>
3. Exothermic reactions cause a <u>rise in temperature</u> of the surroundings.

> Combustion reactions (where something burns in oxygen — see page 138) are always exothermic.

1. An <u>ENDOTHERMIC</u> <u>reaction</u> is one which <u>takes in energy</u> from the surroundings.
2. The energy is usually in the form of <u>heat</u>.
3. Endothermic reactions cause a <u>fall in temperature</u> of the surroundings.

Reaction Profiles Show if a Reaction's Exothermic or Endothermic

1) <u>Reaction profiles</u> show the energy levels of the <u>reactants</u> and the <u>products</u> in a reaction.
2) You can use them to work out if energy is <u>released</u> (exothermic) or <u>taken in</u> (endothermic).

Exothermic Reaction

1) This reaction profile shows an <u>exothermic reaction</u>.
2) The products are at a <u>lower energy</u> than the reactants.
3) The <u>difference in height</u> shows the <u>energy given out</u> in the reaction.

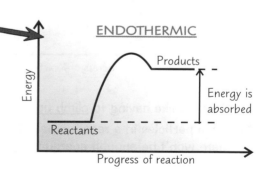

Endothermic Reaction

1) This reaction profile shows an <u>endothermic reaction</u>.
2) The products are at a <u>higher energy</u> than the reactants.
3) The <u>difference in height</u> shows the <u>energy taken in</u> during the reaction.

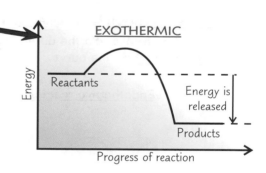

Endothermic reactions — they just get cooler and cooler...

Did you know, "exo-" = exit, "-thermic" = heat, so an exothermic reaction is one that gives out heat — and endothermic just means the opposite. To make sure you really understand these terms, try this question.

Q1   Here is the equation for the combustion of methane in air: $CH_{4(g)} + 2O_{2(g)} \rightarrow CO_{2(g)} + 2H_2O_{(g)}$
Draw a reaction profile for this reaction.
[3 marks]

Bond Energies and Activation Energy

Reactions don't always happen by themselves. The reactants need to have <u>enough energy</u> for a reaction to happen. And that's because before you can <u>make</u> new bonds, you have to <u>break</u> the old ones...

Energy Must Always be Supplied to Break Bonds

1) During a chemical reaction, <u>old bonds are broken</u> and <u>new bonds are formed</u>.
2) Energy must be <u>supplied</u> to break <u>existing bonds</u> — so bond breaking is an <u>endothermic</u> process.
3) Energy is <u>released</u> when new bonds are <u>formed</u> — so making bonds is an <u>exothermic</u> process.

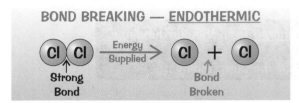

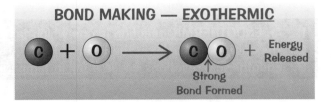

4) In <u>endothermic</u> reactions, the energy <u>used</u> to break bonds is <u>greater</u> than the energy <u>released</u> by forming them.
5) In <u>exothermic</u> reactions, the energy <u>released</u> by forming bonds is <u>greater</u> than the energy used to <u>break</u> them.

Activation Energy is the Energy Needed to Start a Reaction

1) The <u>activation energy</u> is the <u>smallest</u> amount of energy needed for <u>bonds to break</u> and a reaction to start.
2) On a reaction profile, it's the difference in energy between the <u>reactants</u> and the <u>highest point</u> on the curve.

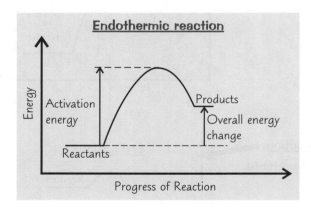

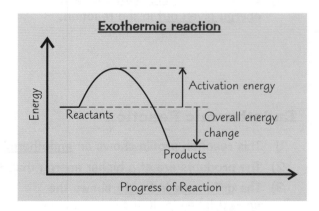

3) It's a bit like having to <u>climb up</u> one side of a hill before you can ski/sledge/fall down the <u>other side</u>.
4) If the particles in a reaction have <u>less than</u> the activation energy when they collide, there <u>won't</u> be enough energy to <u>start</u> the reaction. This means nothing will happen.

A student and their mobile — a bond that can never be broken...

Activation energy is the reason why cookie dough won't turn into cookies until you put it in the oven. The oven heats up the cookie dough reaction mixture, and turns it into delicious, cookie paradise. Mmmm... cookies...

Q1   The reaction between methane and oxygen is exothermic.
Compare the amount of energy needed to break the bonds of the reactants
with the amount of energy released when the products form in this reaction.   [1 mark]

Q2   Describe how the activation energy of a reaction is shown on a reaction profile.   [1 mark]

Measuring Temperature Changes

Sometimes it's not enough to just know if a reaction is endothermic or exothermic. You may also need to know <u>how much</u> the temperature changes by. You can do experiments to find this out. Fun, fun, fun...

Temperature Changes can be Measured

You can follow the <u>change in temperature</u> of a reaction mixture as a reaction takes place. Here's how:

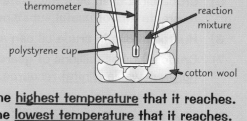

- Put a <u>polystyrene cup</u> into a large <u>beaker of cotton wool</u>. (The cotton wool is an <u>insulator</u>. It helps to limit energy transfer to or from the reaction mixture).
- Add a known volume of your <u>first reagent</u> to the cup.
- Measure the <u>initial temperature</u> of the solution.
- Add a measured amount of the <u>second reagent</u>.
- Use the thermometer to <u>stir</u> the reaction mixture.
- Put a <u>lid</u> on the cup to reduce any energy lost by <u>evaporation</u>.
- If the temperature of the solution <u>rises</u> in the reaction, record the <u>highest temperature</u> that it reaches. If the temperature of the solution <u>falls</u> in the reaction, record the <u>lowest temperature</u> that it reaches.
- To find the temperature change, <u>take away</u> this temperature from the <u>initial</u> temperature.
- If the temperature goes <u>up</u>, the reaction's <u>exothermic</u>.
- If the temperature goes <u>down</u>, the reaction's <u>endothermic</u>.

You can use this method to see the effect that different variables have on the amount of energy transferred, e.g. the mass or concentration of the reactants.

The Change in Temperature Depends on the Reaction

You can measure the temperature change for <u>different types</u> of reaction. Whether there's an increase or decrease in temperature depends on which <u>reactants</u> take part in the reaction.

Neutralisation reactions

1) In a <u>neutralisation reaction</u> (see page 105), an acid and a base react to form a salt and water.
2) Most neutralisation reactions are <u>exothermic</u>, e.g. HCl + NaOH → NaCl + H_2O
3) However, the neutralisation reaction between <u>ethanoic acid</u> and <u>sodium carbonate</u> is <u>endothermic</u>.

Displacement reactions

1) In a <u>displacement reaction</u> (p.115), a <u>more reactive</u> element <u>kicks out</u> a <u>less reactive</u> element from a compound.
2) These types of reactions <u>give out energy</u>. This means that they're <u>exothermic</u>.

Precipitation reactions

1) Precipitates are <u>insoluble solids</u> which can sometimes form when two solutions are mixed together.
2) <u>Precipitation</u> reactions are <u>exothermic</u>.

You can also measure the temperature change when a salt is <u>dissolved in water</u>:

1) The energy change when a <u>salt</u> is dissolved in water depends on the salt you're using.
2) Dissolving <u>ammonium chloride decreases</u> the temperature of the reaction mixture — it's <u>endothermic</u>.
3) Dissolving <u>calcium chloride</u> causes the temperature of the solution to <u>rise</u> — it's <u>exothermic</u>.

Energy transfer — make sure you take it all in...

Fluffy cotton wool doesn't sound very sciencey but it's really important. Best check to make sure you know why...

Q1   When measuring the temperature change of a reaction, why it is important to put the polystyrene cup in a beaker of cotton wool and to keep a lid on the cup?   [1 mark]

Fractional Distillation

Crude oil and fractional distillation are important. Without them, there'd be no gas for heating or fuel for cars...

Crude Oil is a Mixture of Hydrocarbons

1) Hydrocarbons are compounds that contain just hydrogen and carbon.

2) Crude oil is a complex mixture of lots of different hydrocarbons. It's our main source of hydrocarbons.

3) The hydrocarbons found in crude oil have their carbon atoms arranged in either chains or rings.

4) Most of the hydrocarbons in crude oil are in a family of compounds called the alkanes.

5) Crude oil is used as a raw material (sometimes called a feedstock) to create lots of useful substances for the petrochemical industry.

6) Hydrocarbons in crude oil can also be used as fuels.

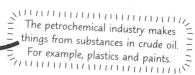
The petrochemical industry makes things from substances in crude oil. For example, plastics and paints.

7) Crude oil takes millions of years to form. Because of this, it's a non-renewable (finite) resource. This means that one day it will run out.

Crude Oil is Separated into Different Hydrocarbon Fractions

1) Fractional distillation is used to separate crude oil into fractions.

2) A fraction is just a simpler, more useful mixture of hydrocarbons.

3) The hydrocarbons in a fraction will have similar lengths (they have similar numbers of carbon and hydrogen atoms). They'll also have similar boiling points.

4) During fractional distillation, the oil is heated until most of it has turned into gas.

5) The gases enter a fractionating column (and the liquid bit, bitumen, is drained off at the bottom).

6) In the column there's a temperature gradient (it's hot at the bottom and gets cooler as you go up).

7) The temperature gradient causes the crude oil mixture to be separated out into different fractions.

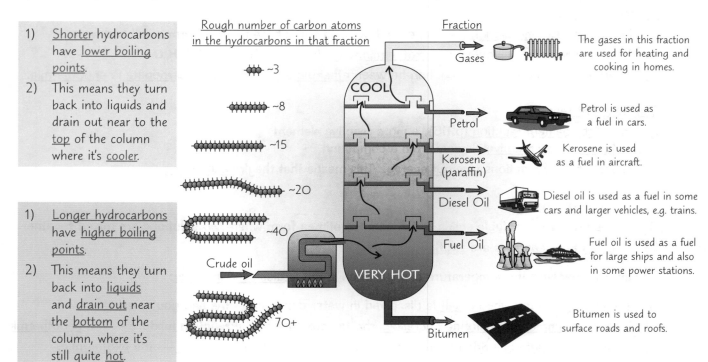

1) Shorter hydrocarbons have lower boiling points.
2) This means they turn back into liquids and drain out near to the top of the column where it's cooler.

Rough number of carbon atoms in the hydrocarbons in that fraction

~3
~8
~15
~20
~40
70+

Fraction

Gases — The gases in this fraction are used for heating and cooking in homes.

COOL

Petrol — Petrol is used as a fuel in cars.

Kerosene (paraffin) — Kerosene is used as a fuel in aircraft.

Diesel Oil — Diesel oil is used as a fuel in some cars and larger vehicles, e.g. trains.

Fuel Oil — Fuel oil is used as a fuel for large ships and also in some power stations.

Crude oil

VERY HOT

1) Longer hydrocarbons have higher boiling points.
2) This means they turn back into liquids and drain out near the bottom of the column, where it's still quite hot.

Bitumen — Bitumen is used to surface roads and roofs.

How much petrol is there in crude oil? Just a fraction...

Crude oil is pretty useful, so it's worth having a good read of this page to make sure you know all about it.

Q1   Petrol drains out of a fractionating column further up than diesel. Use the diagram of the fractionating column to explain why the boiling point of petrol is lower than that of diesel. [1 mark]

Q1 Video Solution

Hydrocarbons

The physical properties of crude oil fractions all depend on how big the hydrocarbons in that fraction are.

Compounds in a Homologous Series Share Similar Chemical Properties

1) A homologous series is a family of molecules. All the compounds in a homologous series have the same general formula.

2) They also share similar chemical properties.

3) The molecular formulas of neighbouring compounds in a homologous series differ by a CH_2 unit.

> For example, if you add CH_2 (1 C and 2 Hs) to the formula of methane (CH_4) you get C_2H_6. This is the formula of ethane, which is the next compound in the homologous series.

Alkane	Molecular formula	Boiling point (°C)
Methane	CH_4	−162
Ethane	C_2H_6	−89
Propane	C_3H_8	−42
Butane	C_4H_{10}	−1
Pentane	C_5H_{12}	36

The general formula of the alkanes is C_nH_{2n+2}.

4) The physical properties change gradually as the size of the molecules changes.

> E.g. the boiling points of the alkanes increase as the number of carbon atoms increases.

5) Alkanes and alkenes are two different homologous series of hydrocarbons.

The Size of a Hydrocarbon Determines its Properties

1) The size of a hydrocarbon determines which fraction of crude oil it will separate into (see previous page).

2) Each fraction contains hydrocarbons (mostly alkanes) with similar numbers of carbon atoms.

3) So all of the molecules in a fraction will have similar properties and behave in similar ways.

4) The physical properties of a fraction depend on the strength of the forces that hold the chains together.

Shorter hydrocarbons have lower boiling points than longer hydrocarbons

- The forces of attraction between molecules are stronger between big molecules than they are between small molecules.
- So more energy is needed to break the forces between big molecules than small molecules.
- That's why longer hydrocarbons have higher boiling points than shorter hydrocarbons do.

Shorter hydrocarbons are easier to ignite than longer hydrocarbons

- Shorter hydrocarbons are easy to ignite (set on fire) because they have lower boiling points, so tend to be gases at room temperature.
- These gas molecules mix with oxygen in the air to produce a gas mixture which bursts into flames if it comes into contact with a spark.
- Longer hydrocarbons have higher boiling points and are much harder to ignite.

Shorter hydrocarbons are less viscous than longer hydrocarbons

- Viscosity measures how easily a substance flows.
- The stronger the force is between hydrocarbon molecules, the harder it is for the liquid to flow.
- Fractions containing longer hydrocarbons have a higher viscosity — they're thick like treacle.
- Fractions made up of shorter hydrocarbons have a low viscosity and are much runnier.

How do you thicken a Moroccan stew? Add some viscouscous...

So, the difference in properties is all down to how strong the forces are between the hydrocarbon chains. For long hydrocarbons, just remember the three Hs — higher boiling points, higher viscosity and harder to ignite.

Q1   Why do hydrocarbons become harder to ignite as they get longer?   [1 mark]

Combustion of Fuels

This section is really starting to warm up... It's time to learn how some crude oil fractions are used as fuels.

Fuels Release Energy in Combustion Reactions

1) Hydrocarbons can burn in air. When this happens, they react with oxygen in combustion reactions.
2) These reactions give out lots of energy, so they're very exothermic (see page 133).
3) This means that hydrocarbons make great fuels.
4) For example, petrol, kerosene and diesel are hydrocarbon fuels that come from crude oil. Methane is a hydrocarbon fuel that comes from natural gas.
5) These fuels are all non-renewable because they take millions of years to form. They're made from the remains of plants and animals which gives them the name fossil fuels.

Complete Combustion of a Hydrocarbon Forms Carbon Dioxide and Water

1) When you burn hydrocarbons in plenty of oxygen, complete combustion takes place.
2) In complete combustion of a hydrocarbon, the only products are carbon dioxide and water.
3) Lots of energy is also given out.
4) The general reaction for the complete combustion of a hydrocarbon is:

hydrocarbon + oxygen → carbon dioxide + water	E.g. $C_3H_8 + 5O_2 \rightarrow 3CO_2 + 4H_2O$

Incomplete Combustion Produces Carbon Monoxide and Soot

1) If there's not enough oxygen around for complete combustion, you get incomplete combustion.
2) This can happen in some appliances, e.g. boilers, that use carbon compounds as fuels.
3) In incomplete combustion, there isn't enough oxygen for all the carbon atoms in the hydrocarbon to react to form carbon dioxide. Instead, they form products that contain less oxygen than carbon dioxide.
4) As well as carbon dioxide and water, incomplete combustion produces carbon monoxide (CO) and carbon in the form of soot.
5) Carbon monoxide and soot are both pollutants which can cause problems.

- Carbon monoxide is a toxic (poisonous) gas.
- It can combine with red blood cells and stop your blood from carrying enough oxygen around the body.
- This can mean that not enough oxygen gets to the brain, which can lead to fainting, a coma or even death.

- During incomplete combustion, tiny particles of carbon can be released into the atmosphere.
- When they fall back to the ground, they form the horrible black dust we call soot.
- Soot makes buildings look dirty.
- It also reduces air quality. This can cause breathing problems, or make them worse for people who already have them.

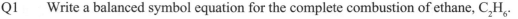

Combustio — incomplete combustion...

Make sure you know the difference between the products of complete and incomplete combustion.

Q1   Write a balanced symbol equation for the complete combustion of ethane, C_2H_6.   [2 marks]

Q2   Name two pollutants formed by incomplete combustion.   [2 marks]

Q1 Video Solution

Pollutants

The products of combustion on the previous page aren't the only pollutants that can form when you burn fossil fuels. You can also get nasties like <u>oxides of nitrogen</u> and <u>sulfur dioxide</u> being produced.

Sulfur Dioxide Causes Acid Rain

1) Some fuels contain <u>impurities</u> of <u>sulfur</u>.
2) When these fuels are burnt, the sulfur can react with oxygen to form <u>sulfur dioxide</u> (SO_2).
3) When sulfur dioxide <u>mixes</u> with <u>clouds</u>, it forms dilute <u>sulfuric acid</u>. This then falls as <u>acid rain</u>.
4) <u>Acid rain</u> causes <u>lakes</u> to become <u>acidic</u> which can cause many plants and animals to <u>die</u>.
5) Acid rain kills <u>trees</u>, damages <u>limestone</u> buildings and <u>stone statues</u> and can also make <u>metal</u> corrode.

Oxides of Nitrogen Are Also Pollutants

1) When fuels combust, for example in <u>car engines</u>, lots of <u>energy</u> is released in the form of heat.
2) The <u>high temperatures</u> can cause nitrogen and oxygen in the air to react and form <u>nitrogen oxides</u>.
3) Nitrogen oxides are <u>harmful pollutants</u>.
4) Nitrogen oxides can mix with water in clouds to form dilute <u>nitric acid</u>. This then falls as <u>acid rain</u>.
5) At ground level, nitrogen oxides can cause <u>photochemical smog</u>.
6) Photochemical smog is a type of <u>air pollution</u> that can cause <u>breathing difficulties</u>, headaches and tiredness.

Hydrogen can be Used as a Clean, Renewable Fuel

<u>Hydrogen gas</u> can also be used as a fuel to power vehicles (e.g. cars and buses).

Advantages

1) The reaction between hydrogen and oxygen is <u>less polluting</u> than burning hydrocarbon fuels.
2) This is because the only waste product is <u>water</u>. It <u>doesn't</u> form any nasty pollutants like carbon dioxide, carbon monoxide or soot (which can form when fossil fuels are burnt).
3) The hydrogen fuel comes from a reaction of <u>water</u>. Water is a <u>renewable resource</u> and is <u>widely available</u>. So it's not going to run out (unlike fossil fuels).
4) Even better, you can use the <u>water</u> that's produced by the reaction of <u>hydrogen and oxygen</u> in the vehicle to make more <u>hydrogen</u>.

Disadvantages

1) You need a <u>special</u>, <u>expensive engine</u> to use hydrogen as a fuel.
2) Making the hydrogen gas is <u>expensive</u>.
3) Making hydrogen gas uses <u>energy</u> and this is likely to come from burning <u>hydrocarbon fuels</u>, which produces pollutants.
4) Hydrogen's hard to <u>store</u>. The tanks that store it are quite <u>big</u> and <u>heavy</u>. It also <u>leaks</u> easily if there are any problems with the system and it's very <u>flammable</u>.
5) Hydrogen fuel <u>isn't widely available</u> at the moment, so you can't refuel easily.

Do you want to hear a joke about nitrogen monoxide? NO?

Acid rain's bad news for sculptors, fish and trees alike. It's bad news for you too, as you need to know about it...

Q1   Explain how sulfur dioxide can form when a fuel is burnt.

[1 mark]

Cracking

Crude oil fractions from fractional distillation are split into <u>smaller molecules</u> — this is called <u>cracking</u>. It's dead important — otherwise we might not have enough fuel for cars and planes and things.

Cracking is Splitting Up Long-Chain Hydrocarbons

1) <u>Cracking</u> turns long saturated (alkane) molecules into <u>smaller unsaturated</u> (<u>alkene</u>) and <u>alkane</u> molecules (which are much more <u>useful</u>).

2) A lot of the longer molecules produced from <u>fractional distillation</u> are <u>cracked</u> into smaller ones because there's <u>more demand</u> for products like <u>petrol</u> and <u>diesel</u> than for bitumen and fuel oil.

3) Cracking also produces lots of <u>alkene</u> molecules.

4) Alkenes are a family of <u>hydrocarbons</u>. They can be used to make <u>polymers</u> (mostly plastics).

You can do an Experiment to Crack Alkanes

1) You can use the apparatus shown below to crack <u>alkanes</u> in the lab.

2) During this reaction, the alkane is heated until it is <u>vaporised</u> (turns into a gas).

3) When it comes into contact with the catalyst it <u>breaks down</u>.

4) The product is a mixture of <u>short-chain alkanes</u> and <u>alkenes</u>.

vaporised alkane → catalyst → a mixture of shorter chain alkanes and alkenes

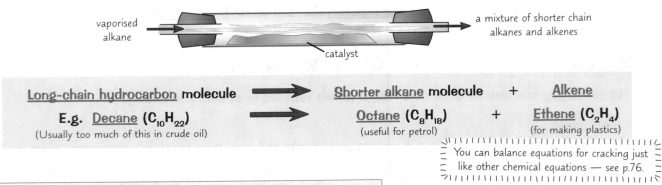

<u>Long-chain hydrocarbon</u> molecule	→	<u>Shorter alkane</u> molecule	+	<u>Alkene</u>
E.g. <u>Decane</u> ($C_{10}H_{22}$) (Usually too much of this in crude oil)	→	<u>Octane</u> (C_8H_{18}) (useful for petrol)	+	<u>Ethene</u> (C_2H_4) (for making plastics)

You can balance equations for cracking just like other chemical equations — see p.76.

Cracking Helps Match Supply and Demand

1) If the <u>supply</u> of a fraction (how much there is) is <u>greater</u> than it's <u>demand</u> (how much people want of it), then there'll be some left over.

2) These fractions can be cracked to form <u>smaller fractions</u> which there is a greater demand for.

EXAMPLE   Look at the table on the right. Which fraction is most likely to be cracked to provide more petrol and diesel oil?

1) You could use the <u>kerosene fraction</u> to supply the extra <u>petrol</u> and the <u>fuel oil and bitumen fraction</u> to supply the extra <u>diesel oil</u>.

2) Or you could crack the <u>fuel oil and bitumen</u> to supply <u>both</u> the extra <u>petrol</u> and the extra <u>diesel oil</u>.

3) This might make more sense, as there's more fuel oil/bitumen than kerosene.

Fraction	Approx % in crude oil	Approx % demand
Gases	2	4
Petrol	16	27
Kerosene	13	8
Diesel Oil	19	23
Fuel Oil & Bitumen	50	38

This page was absolutely cracking...

In that case, I better crack open another packet of biscuits so that the supply matches my stomach's large demand...

Q1   When a molecule of $C_{17}H_{36}$ is cracked under certain conditions, two molecules are made. If one of the product molecules is C_5H_{10}, what is the chemical formula of the other product?   [1 mark]

The Atmosphere

Scientists have looked at <u>evidence</u> from rocks, air bubbles in ice and fossils to see how our <u>atmosphere</u> has <u>changed</u> over many, many years. Here's one theory about how our atmosphere might have developed.

1. Volcanoes Gave Out Steam and CO_2

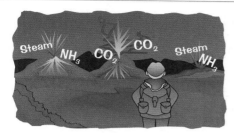

<u>Holiday report</u>: Not nice. Take strong walking boots and a coat.

1) Billions of years ago, Earth's surface was covered in <u>volcanoes</u> that were erupting.
2) These eruptions released gases from <u>inside the Earth</u>.
3) Most of the gas released was <u>carbon dioxide</u>, but <u>steam</u>, <u>methane</u> and <u>ammonia</u> were also released.
4) When things eventually settled down, the early atmosphere was <u>mostly CO_2</u> and <u>water vapour</u>. There were also small amounts of <u>other gases</u>. There was <u>very little oxygen</u>.
5) The water vapour later <u>condensed</u> to form the <u>oceans</u>.

2. Green Plants Evolved and Produced Oxygen

1) A lot of the early CO_2 <u>dissolved</u> into the oceans. This <u>decreased</u> the amount of carbon dioxide in the <u>atmosphere</u>.
2) Next, <u>green plants</u> evolved over most of the Earth.
3) Green plants use a reaction called <u>photosynthesis</u> to release energy.
4) This reaction <u>uses up carbon dioxide</u> and <u>produces oxygen</u>.
5) So thanks to the plants, the amount of <u>oxygen</u> in the air gradually <u>built up</u> and the amount of <u>carbon dioxide decreased</u>.
6) <u>Today</u>, the atmosphere is made up of approximately <u>78% nitrogen</u>, <u>21% oxygen</u> and <u>less than 1%</u> other gases (mainly carbon dioxide, noble gases and water vapour).

There's Evidence to Support This Explanation

Scientists have found <u>evidence</u> that backs up this view of how the atmosphere evolved.

1) <u>Air bubbles</u> can get trapped in <u>ice</u> as it forms. So scientists can look at what gases are in the bubbles in very <u>old</u> ice in the Arctic or Antarctic to see what the atmosphere was like a long time ago.
2) Some very ancient <u>rock formations</u> could only have formed if there was <u>hardly any oxygen</u> about. This suggests there was little oxygen in the early atmosphere.
3) <u>Fossils</u> give evidence for how the atmosphere formed. For example, the oldest fossils are of <u>organisms</u> that could survive without much oxygen. Fossils of organisms which need <u>more oxygen</u> to survive are much <u>newer</u>. This suggests that there <u>wasn't much oxygen</u> in the atmosphere when life first evolved.

Test for Oxygen Using a Glowing Splint

You can <u>test</u> for oxygen by checking if the gas will <u>relight</u> a <u>glowing splint</u>.

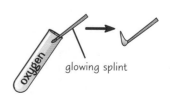

glowing splint

I went to a restaurant on the moon — nice view, no atmosphere...

We can breathe easy knowing that our atmosphere has developed into a lovely oxygen-rich one. Aaaahh.

Q1   The atmosphere of Earth was originally composed mostly of carbon dioxide.
       Explain how the proportion of carbon dioxide in the atmosphere decreased over time.   [2 marks]

The Greenhouse Effect

The greenhouse effect isn't a bumper crop of tomatoes and a prize winning marrow...

Human Activity Affects the Composition of Air

1) The human population is increasing.
2) More people means that more energy is needed for lighting, heating, cooking, transport and so on.
3) These days the average amount of energy that each person uses is more than it used to be.
4) This is because people have more electrical gadgets, more people have cars, travel on planes etc.
5) Most of this extra energy is supplied by burning fossil fuels, which releases carbon dioxide.
6) The graph shows how carbon dioxide (CO_2) levels in the atmosphere have risen over the last 300 years.
7) There's a correlation (relationship) between the increase in carbon dioxide in the atmosphere and the amount of fossil fuels that humans are using.

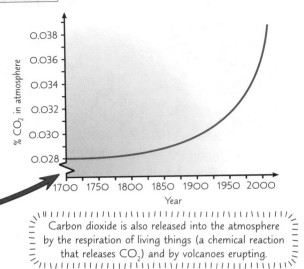

Carbon dioxide is also released into the atmosphere by the respiration of living things (a chemical reaction that releases CO_2) and by volcanoes erupting.

The Greenhouse Effect Helps to Keep the Earth Warm

1) The Sun gives out short wavelength radiation.
2) Some of this radiation passes through the atmosphere and is absorbed by the Earth. This warms the planet.

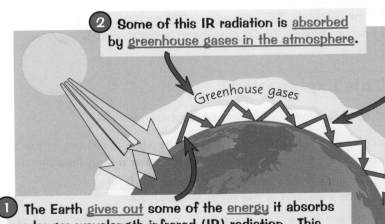

2 Some of this IR radiation is absorbed by greenhouse gases in the atmosphere.

3 The greenhouse gases cause some energy to be given back out towards Earth.

4 Some IR radiation is given back out into space.

5 By absorbing thermal energy and giving out some of this energy back towards Earth, greenhouse gases help to trap extra energy in the atmosphere. This keeps the Earth warm. The process is called the greenhouse effect.

1 The Earth gives out some of the energy it absorbs as longer wavelength infrared (IR) radiation. This radiation is thermal radiation, so can warm things up.

3) Greenhouse gases are the gases in the atmosphere that can absorb and give out heat radiation.
4) They're only present in small amounts.
5) Carbon dioxide, water vapour and methane are three greenhouse gases.
6) If the concentration of greenhouse gases in the atmosphere increases, more thermal energy from the Earth is absorbed and less is given back out into space.
7) This causes the atmosphere to heat up more than it would otherwise (see next page).

The White House effect — heated political debates...

Is all this hot air making you a bit hot and bothered? If so, here's a question to cheer you up.

Q1   Describe the greenhouse effect and how it affects global temperature.   [4 marks]

Q1 Video Solution

Climate Change

Is it me, or is it getting <u>hot</u> in here...?

Increasing Greenhouse Gases Causes Climate Change

1) Over the last 100 years or so, the amount of <u>carbon dioxide</u> in the atmosphere has <u>increased</u> due to human activity. At the same time, <u>global temperatures</u> have also <u>increased</u>.

2) This means the increase in carbon dioxide caused by human activity <u>correlates</u> with an increase in <u>global temperatures</u>.

3) The amount of the greenhouse gas <u>methane</u> in the atmosphere has also risen lots in recent years. This is also due to human activity.

4) Methane is produced by certain <u>livestock</u> (e.g. cows and goats). The more livestock we farm, the more methane is formed.

5) Most scientists agree that extra greenhouse gases from <u>human activity</u> have caused the average <u>temperature</u> of the Earth to <u>increase</u>.

6) This is because the extra greenhouse gases <u>trap more energy</u> in the atmosphere — see previous page.

7) This effect is known as <u>global warming</u>.

8) Global warming is a type of <u>climate change</u> and causes other types of climate change, e.g. changing rainfall patterns. It could also cause severe <u>flooding</u> due to ice at the poles melting.

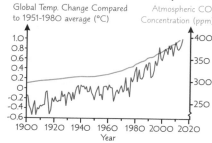

Global Temp. Change Compared to 1951-1980 average (°C) — Atmospheric CO_2 Concentration (ppm)

Historical Data is Much Less Accurate Than Current Records

1) <u>Current global temperature</u> and <u>carbon dioxide levels</u> can be worked out pretty accurately as they're based on measurements taken all over the world.

2) <u>Historical data</u> is <u>less accurate</u>. In the past, <u>less data</u> was taken over <u>fewer locations</u> and the methods used to collect the data were <u>less accurate</u>.

3) If you go back far enough, there are <u>no records</u> of global temperature and carbon dioxide levels at all...

4) But there are ways to <u>estimate past data</u>. For example, you can analyse <u>fossils</u>, <u>tree rings</u> or <u>gas bubbles</u> trapped in <u>ice sheets</u> to estimate past levels of carbon dioxide in the atmosphere.

5) These kinds of measurements are much <u>less precise</u> than current measurements.

6) They also only show what the atmosphere was like in that <u>particular location</u> in the past. They might not represent what the <u>global levels</u> were like.

We Can Try To Use Less Fossil Fuels

1) In order to prevent or <u>slow down climate change</u>, we need to <u>cut down</u> on the amount of greenhouse gases we're releasing into the atmosphere.

2) One way to <u>reduce carbon dioxide emissions</u> is to limit our use of fossil fuels.

3) For example, people could <u>walk</u> or <u>cycle</u> instead of driving. Or they could <u>turn their central heating down</u>.

4) On a larger scale, there are things the <u>government</u> can do to reduce emissions.

5) They could <u>tax</u> greenhouse gas emissions to encourage people to reduce their own emissions.

6) They could also fund more <u>renewable energy</u> and increase research into <u>new energy sources</u>.

7) Greenhouse gas emissions could also be reduced a lot if industry used more <u>energy efficient</u> processes.

Aaaaaah! The gases have escaped!!

Give the climate some privacy — it's changing...

It's not all depressing news. There are steps we can take to cut our carbon dioxide emissions, thankfully.

Q1   Describe two ways that people could reduce their carbon dioxide emissions.   [2 marks]

Q2   What is global warming and how is it caused?   [3 marks]

Revision Questions for Sections 15 and 16

That's <u>Sections 15</u> and <u>16</u> down, so you've now covered pretty much all the chemistry in this book. Yay!

- Try these questions and <u>tick off each one</u> when you <u>get it right</u>.
- When you're <u>completely happy</u> with it with a sub-topic, tick it off.

For even more practice, try the Retrieval Quizzes for Sections 15 and 16 — just scan these QR codes!

Rates of Reaction (p.127-131) ☐

1) What is meant by the term 'rate of reaction'?

2) Draw a diagram of the equipment you would use to measure the rate of reaction between hydrochloric acid and marble chips.

3) Write the equation that you could use to find the mean rate of a reaction.

4) Describe how you would find the rate of a reaction from a straight line graph.

5) State three conditions that will affect the rate of a reaction between a solid and a solution.

6) What effect will raising the temperature have on the rate of a reaction?

7) In a reaction between two gases, why would an increase in pressure speed up the reaction?

Section 15 Quiz

Catalysts (p.132) ☐

8) What effect does a catalyst have on the activation energy needed for a reaction to take place?

9) Give one example of a reaction catalysed by enzymes.

Energy Changes in Chemical Reactions (p.133-135) ☐

10) How would you expect the temperature to change in an exothermic reaction?

11) Is energy required to break bonds or to form new bonds?

12) What is activation energy?

13) Describe how you could measure the temperature changes in a neutralisation reaction.

Fuels (p.136-140) ☐

14) What is a hydrocarbon?

15) What is the purpose of the fractional distillation of crude oil?

16) What is fuel oil used for?

17) What is the definition of a homologous series?

18) Is the following statement true or false?
"Shorter hydrocarbons have higher boiling points than longer hydrocarbons."

19) Name the two products that form when a hydrocarbon combusts completely.

20) Why does incomplete combustion occur?

21) Name a gas that can cause acid rain.

22) State one advantage and one disadvantage of using hydrogen as a fuel in cars.

23) What is cracking?

Section 16 Quiz

The Atmosphere and Climate Change (p.141-143) ☐

24) Name two gases given out by volcanoes millions of years ago.

25) Name the reaction that occurs in plants which releases oxygen into the atmosphere.

26) How could you test an unknown gas to see if it was oxygen?

27) How has the concentration of carbon dioxide in the atmosphere changed over the last 100 years?

28) Name two greenhouse gases.

29) What methods have scientists used to predict past climates?

Distance, Displacement, Speed and Velocity

Want to know the difference between <u>distance</u>, <u>displacement</u>, <u>speed</u> and <u>velocity</u>? You've come to the right spot.

Quantities can be Vectors or Scalars

A quantity is something that can be measured, e.g. force, speed and time.

1) Vector quantities have a <u>magnitude</u> (size) and a <u>specific direction</u>.

   <u>Vector quantities</u>: force, velocity, displacement, weight, acceleration, etc.

2) E.g. A force of 20 N acts to the left. '20 N' is the <u>magnitude</u>, 'to the left' is the <u>direction</u>.

3) Scalar quantities <u>only</u> have a magnitude but <u>no specific direction</u>.

   <u>Scalar quantities</u>: speed, distance, mass, energy, temperature, time, etc.

4) E.g. The temperature of an oven is 180 °C. '180 °C' is the <u>magnitude</u>. Temperature can't have a <u>direction</u>.

Distance and Speed are Scalars, Displacement and Velocity are Vectors

1) <u>Distance</u> is just <u>how far</u> an object has moved.

2) <u>Displacement</u> is the <u>distance</u> and <u>direction</u> in a <u>straight line</u> from an object's <u>starting point</u> to its <u>finishing point</u>.

   For example, if you go 15 m <u>north</u>, then 5 m <u>south</u>, the <u>distance</u> you've gone is <u>20 m</u>. Your <u>displacement</u> is <u>10 m</u> from the start.

3) Speed is <u>how fast you're going</u>, e.g. 30 mph. Velocity is speed in a <u>given direction</u>, e.g. 30 mph north.

Distance Travelled, Speed and Time are Related by a Formula

1) Objects <u>rarely</u> travel at a <u>constant speed</u>. E.g. when you <u>run</u>, your speed is <u>always changing</u>.

2) The equations below can be used for an object moving with either a <u>constant speed</u> or a <u>changing speed</u>.

3) If the speed of an object is changing you can use its <u>average speed</u> in the equations.

4) You can find the <u>distance travelled</u> by an object using:

   > distance travelled (m) = (average) speed (m/s) × time (s)

distance travelled

(average) speed   time

5) To find the <u>(average) speed</u> of an object, <u>rearrange</u> the formula to give:

   > (average) speed (m/s) = distance travelled (m) ÷ time (s)

6) You need to know some <u>typical speeds</u>:

   1) <u>Walking</u> — <u>1.4 m/s</u> (5 km/h)
   2) <u>Running</u> — <u>3 m/s</u> (11 km/h)
   3) <u>Cycling</u> — <u>5.5 m/s</u> (20 km/h)
   4) <u>Cars</u> in a <u>built-up area</u> — <u>13 m/s</u> (47 km/h)
   5) <u>Aeroplanes</u> — <u>250 m/s</u> (900 km/h)
   6) <u>Cars</u> on a <u>motorway</u> — <u>31 m/s</u> (112 km/h)
   7) <u>Trains</u> — up to <u>55 m/s</u> (200 km/h)
   8) <u>Wind</u> speed — <u>5 – 20 m/s</u> (18 – 72 km/h)
   9) Speed of <u>sound</u> in <u>air</u> — <u>340 m/s</u> (1224 km/h)
   10) <u>Ferries</u> — 15 m/s (54 km/h)

7) When an object is <u>stationary</u> (not moving), its <u>velocity</u> (speed) is 0 m/s.

8) You can <u>measure</u> the <u>speed</u> of an object using <u>light gates</u> (p.210).

9) You can also find the <u>average speed</u> of an object by measuring the <u>time taken</u> for it to travel a <u>certain distance</u> and then using <u>speed = distance ÷ time</u>.

10) You need to know different ways of <u>measuring distance</u> and <u>time</u> in the lab — see p.209.

My life's feeling pretty scalar — I've no idea where I'm headed...

It's important you understand this stuff for the rest of this topic. Don't say I didn't warn you...

Q1   A sprinter runs 200 m in 25 s. Calculate his average speed.   [2 marks]

Q1 Video Solution

Acceleration

Uniform acceleration sounds fancy, but it's just speeding up (or slowing down) at a constant rate.

Acceleration is How Quickly You're Speeding Up

1) Acceleration is the change in velocity in a certain amount of time.
2) You can find the average acceleration of an object using:

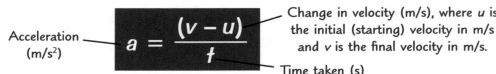

$$a = \frac{(v - u)}{t}$$

Acceleration (m/s²)

Change in velocity (m/s), where u is the initial (starting) velocity in m/s and v is the final velocity in m/s.

Time taken (s)

3) Deceleration is just negative acceleration (if something slows down, the change in velocity is negative).
4) For example, a car with a deceleration of 5 m/s² is a car with an acceleration of –5 m/s².

You Need to be Able to Estimate Accelerations

To estimate the acceleration of an object, you can do a calculation using estimated speeds:

EXAMPLE   A stationary car is on a street. It accelerates to a typical speed in 6.5 seconds.
Estimate the acceleration of the car.

1) Estimate the final speed of the car (see p.145)   The typical speed of a car in a built-up area is ~13 m/s.
2) Put the speed and the time taken $a = (v - u) \div t$
into the acceleration equation. $= (13 - 0) \div 6.5 = 2$ m/s²

The ~ symbol just means the speed is around 13 m/s.

Objects can have a Uniform Acceleration

1) If an object has uniform acceleration it means it has constant acceleration.
2) You can use this equation for uniform acceleration:

(Final velocity)² (m/s)²

$$v^2 - u^2 = 2 \times a \times x$$

Acceleration (m/s²)

Distance (m)

(Initial velocity)² (m/s)²

EXAMPLE   A van is travelling at 23 m/s. It then decelerates uniformly
at 2.0 m/s² for 112 m. What will its final speed be?

Remember a is negative because it's a deceleration.

1) First, rearrange the equation so v^2 is on one side. $v^2 = u^2 + (2 \times a \times x)$
2) Now put the numbers in. $v^2 = 23^2 + (2 \times -2.0 \times 112) = 81$
3) Finally, square root the whole thing. $v = \sqrt{81} = 9$ m/s

3) The acceleration of objects in free fall due to gravity (g) is an example of uniform acceleration.
4) 'Free fall' means that an object is falling to the ground, and the only force acting on it is its weight (p.149).
5) For an object in free fall, it is assumed that there is no air resistance.
6) Any object in free fall above the Earth has the same acceleration.
7) It's roughly equal to 10 m/s² near the Earth's surface.

Uniform problems — get a clip-on tie or use the equation above...

Remember, u is 0 m/s if an object is stationary before accelerating, and v is 0 m/s if an object stops moving.

Q1   A ball is dropped from a height above the ground.
The speed of the ball just before it hits the ground is 5 m/s.
Calculate the height the ball is dropped from. (acceleration due to gravity = 10 m/s²)   [2 marks]

Q1 Video Solution

Distance/Time Graphs

Graphs can be rather useful for showing all sorts of things (p.7). This page deals with distance/time graphs.

Distance/Time Graphs Tell You How Far Something has Travelled

The different parts of a distance/time graph describe the motion of an object:

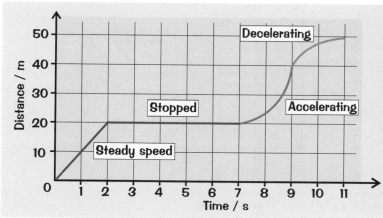

1) The gradient (slope) at any point gives the speed of the object.
2) A steeper graph means it's going faster.
3) Flat sections are where it's stopped.
4) Curves show acceleration or deceleration.
5) A curve getting steeper means it's speeding up (increasing gradient).
6) A levelling off curve means it's slowing down (decreasing gradient).

The Speed of an Object can be Found From a Distance/Time Graph

1) If the graph is a straight line, the speed at any point during that time is equal to the gradient of the line.

For example, in the graph above, the speed at any time between 0 s and 2 s is:

$$\text{Speed} = \text{gradient} = \frac{\text{change in the vertical}}{\text{change in the horizontal}} = \frac{20}{2} = \underline{10 \text{ m/s}}$$

2) If the graph is curved, you can find the speed at a certain time by drawing a tangent to the graph at that point.
3) A tangent is a straight line that is parallel to the curve at that point.
4) You then need to find the gradient of the tangent.

EXAMPLE The graph shows the distance/time graph for a cyclist on his bike. Calculate the speed of the bike 25 s into the journey.

1) Draw the tangent to the curve at 25 s (red line).
2) Then calculate the gradient of the tangent (blue lines).

$$\text{gradient} = \frac{\text{change in the vertical}}{\text{change in the horizontal}}$$
$$= \frac{80}{10}$$
$$= 8 \text{ m/s}$$

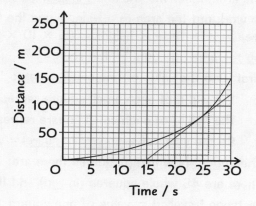

Let me take you on a journey through time and space...

Try sketching distance/time graphs for different scenarios. Like walking home or running from a bear.

Q1 Sketch the distance-time graph for an object that accelerates, then travels at a steady speed, and then comes to a stop.

[3 marks]

Q1 Video Solution

Velocity/Time Graphs

Velocity/time graphs look a lot like the distance/time graphs on p.147. So be really careful not to mix them up.

Velocity/Time Graphs can have a Positive or Negative Gradient

How an object's velocity changes over time can be plotted on a velocity/time (or v/t) graph.

1) The gradient (slope) at any point gives the acceleration of the object.
2) The steeper the graph, the greater the acceleration.
3) Flat sections show a steady speed.
4) Uphill sections (/) are acceleration.
5) Downhill sections (\) are deceleration.
6) A curve means changing acceleration.

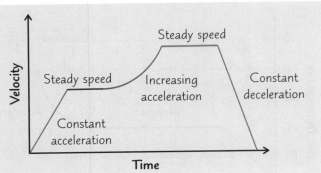

EXAMPLE The velocity/time graph of a car's journey is shown on the right. Calculate the acceleration of the car over the first 10 s.

The acceleration is just the gradient of the line:

$$\text{gradient} = \frac{\text{change in the vertical}}{\text{change in the horizontal}} = \frac{(v-u)}{t} = \frac{(20-0)}{10} = 2 \text{ m/s}^2$$

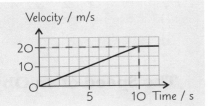

You can also plot speed/time graphs — the same rules apply.
It's just that you have speed as the label on the y-axis, not velocity.

The Distance Travelled is the Area Under the Graph

1) The area between the graph line and the time axis is equal to the distance travelled.
2) You can either calculate the area of the shape under the graph using a formula or count the squares:

EXAMPLE: The graph shows an object travelling from rest with a constant acceleration. Find the distance travelled by the object in the first 10 s.

Finding the area of the shape under the graph with a formula

1) The area under the line is a triangle.
2) To work out the area of a triangle use the formula:
area = ½ × base × height = (½ × 10 × 2) = **10 m**

Finding the area by counting the squares

1) First, find the value of one small square:
- The width of each small square represents 1 s.
- The height of each small square represents 0.2 m/s.
- So the value of each small square = width × height = 1 × 0.2 = 0.2 m.
2) Then count how many squares there are:
3) There are 45 whole squares (in red) and 10 half squares (in blue), so there's a total of 50 squares.
4) Distance travelled = value of one square × number of squares = 0.2 × 50 = **10 m**

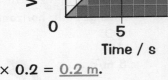

Understanding motion graphs — it can be a real uphill struggle...

Make sure you know how to read distance/time and velocity/time graphs, and how they're different.

Q1 A stationary car starts accelerating increasingly for 10 s until it reaches a speed of 20 m/s. It travels at this speed for 20 s until the driver sees a hazard and brakes. He decelerates uniformly, coming to a stop 4 s after braking. Draw the velocity-time graph for this journey. [3 marks]

Q1 Video Solution

Weight

Now for something a bit more _attractive_ — the force of _gravity_. Enjoy...

Mass is measured in Kilograms

1) Mass is just the amount of 'stuff' in an object.
2) Mass is a scalar quantity.
3) It's measured in kilograms (kg) with a mass balance.

Weight is Measured in Newtons

1) Weight is the force acting on an object due to gravity.
2) Close to Earth, this force is caused by the gravitational field around the Earth.
3) Weight is measured in newtons (N).
4) It can be measured using a spring balance (or newton meter).
5) When a mass is put on the hook, the spring in the newton meter extends.
6) The weight can then be read from the meter.

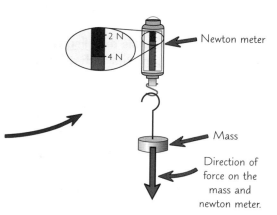

Newton meter

Mass

Direction of force on the mass and newton meter.

Weight Depends on Mass and Gravitational Field Strength

1) You can calculate the weight of an object if you know its mass (_m_) and the strength of the gravitational field that it is in (_g_):

Weight (N) = mass (kg) × gravitational field strength (N/kg) $W = m \times g$

2) For Earth, _g is around 10 N/kg_.
Don't worry — you'll always be given a value of _g_ to use in the exam.

3) The greater the value of _g_, the larger the weight of an object.

EXAMPLE   A motorcycle weighs 2400 N.
Calculate the mass of the motorcycle. (_g_ ≈ 10 N/kg)

1) First, rearrange _W = mg_ to find mass.   mass = weight ÷ gravitational field strength

2) Then, put in the numbers to calculate the mass.   mass = 2400 ÷ 10 = **240 kg**

This page is kind of weighty...

Remember that weight is a force due to gravity and mass is just how much stuff there is. And then make sure you've got that weight equation firmly stuck in your head. It can rear its ugly head all over physics.

Q1   Calculate the weight in newtons of a 25 kg mass:
   a) on Earth (_g_ ≈ 10 N/kg)
   b) on the Moon (_g_ ≈ 1.6 N/kg)

Q1 Video
Solution

[4 marks]

Resultant Forces and Newton's First Law

A chap called <u>Isaac Newton</u> worked out some <u>rules</u> that tell us what forces will do to objects. This page deals with the <u>first one</u>. I bet you can't wait to get started, so don't let me stop you.

A Resultant Force is the Overall Force on a Point or Object

1) If a <u>number of forces</u> act at a single point, you can replace them with a <u>single force</u>.
2) This single force is called the <u>resultant force</u>.
3) It has the <u>same effect</u> as all the original forces added together.
4) You can find the resultant force when forces are acting in a <u>straight line</u>.
5) <u>Add together</u> forces acting in the <u>same</u> direction and <u>take away</u> any going in the <u>opposite</u> direction.

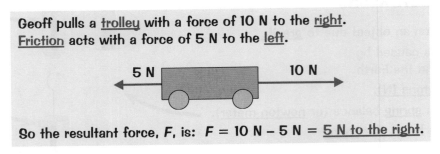

Geoff pulls a <u>trolley</u> with a force of 10 N to the <u>right</u>. <u>Friction</u> acts with a force of 5 N to the <u>left</u>.

5 N   10 N

So the resultant force, *F*, is: $F = 10 \text{ N} - 5 \text{ N} = \underline{5 \text{ N to the right}}$.

6) Friction is a <u>force</u> caused by any objects that <u>rub together</u>, e.g. tyres on a road.

A Force is Needed to Change Motion

1) <u>Newton's First Law</u> says that a resultant force is needed to make something <u>start moving</u>, <u>speed up</u> or <u>slow down</u>:

> If the resultant force on a <u>stationary</u> object is <u>zero</u>, the object will <u>remain stationary</u>.

Remember — 'stationary' means 'not moving'.

> If the <u>resultant force</u> on a <u>moving object</u> is <u>zero</u>, it'll just carry on moving at the <u>same velocity</u> (same speed <u>and</u> direction).

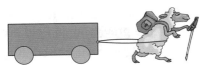

2) For example, when a bus is driving along, there is a <u>forward force</u> from the engine and <u>backwards forces</u> from friction and air resistance.
3) When the bus is driving at a <u>constant velocity</u>, the forward force and backwards forces are <u>balanced</u>.
4) Its velocity will <u>only</u> change if the forces don't balance.
5) If the forces don't balance, there is a <u>non-zero</u> resultant force acting on it.
6) A non-zero <u>resultant</u> force will always produce <u>acceleration</u>.
7) The acceleration will be in the <u>direction of the force</u>.
8) This "<u>acceleration</u>" can take <u>five</u> different forms: <u>starting</u>, <u>stopping</u>, <u>speeding up</u>, <u>slowing down</u> and <u>changing direction</u>.

Accelerate your learning — force yourself to revise...

The resultant force acting on an object will decide the motion of the object. If the resultant force is zero, the object is stationary or moving at a steady speed. If the resultant force is non-zero, it's accelerating.

Q1   A car has a forward force acting on it of 200 N and a backwards force of 150 N.
Is the car accelerating or moving at a constant velocity?

[1 mark]

Newton's Second Law

What comes after Newton's First Law? Well Newton's Second Law of course. This one's great.

You Need to Know the Equation $F = ma$

1) You saw on the previous page that if there's a resultant force acting on an object, the object will accelerate.
2) How much the object accelerates depends on its mass and the resultant force.
3) The relationship between force, mass and acceleration is known as Newton's Second Law:

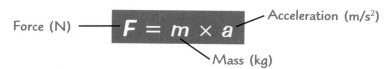

Force (N) — $F = m \times a$ — Acceleration (m/s²)

Mass (kg)

EXAMPLE A car has a mass of 1625 kg. It has a resultant force of 5200 N acting on it. Calculate the acceleration of the car.

5200 N

1) Rearrange $F = ma$ for acceleration. $a = F \div m$
2) Substitute values into the equation. $a = 5200 \div 1625 = 3.2$ m/s²

Large Decelerations can be Dangerous

1) The equation $a = \frac{v - u}{t}$ on p.146 shows that the acceleration of an object will be larger if:
   - the change in speed is bigger
   - the time it takes for the speed to change is shorter.
2) The equation $F = m \times a$ shows that the bigger the acceleration, the bigger the force needed to cause the acceleration.

1) Large decelerations of objects and people can cause serious injuries.
2) This is because a large deceleration requires a large force.
3) For example, large decelerations can happen during a vehicle collision.
4) A car involved in a crash changes speed in a short amount of time.
5) This means there is a large force acting on the car and passengers which may cause harm.
6) Vehicles undergo large decelerations during hard braking.
7) This can cause the brakes to overheat, which can damage the brakes meaning they don't work as well.
8) It may also cause the vehicle to skid — this could mean it doesn't stop in time before hitting something.

Remember — deceleration is just a negative acceleration.

Large celery is also dangerous...

All this talk about things accelerating and crashing makes a person want to have a quiet sit down with tea and biscuits and read a novel. But first, why not have a go at these questions.

Q1 Find the force needed for an 80 kg man on a 10 kg bike to accelerate at 0.25 m/s². [2 marks]

Q2 A winch is used to lift an object. The resultant force acting on the object is 18.9 N. The object has an acceleration of 1.80 m/s². Calculate the mass of the object. [3 marks]

Investigating Motion

PRACTICAL

Doing an <u>experiment</u> for yourself can really help you to understand what's going on with $F = m \times a$ (p.151).

You can Measure the Acceleration of a Trolley on a Ramp

1) Measure the <u>mass</u> of the <u>trolley</u>, the <u>unit masses</u> and the <u>hanging hook</u>.
2) Then set up your <u>apparatus</u> as shown in the diagram below, but <u>don't</u> attach the string to the trolley.
3) <u>Adjust</u> the <u>height</u> of the ramp until the trolley <u>just</u> starts to move.
4) Mark a <u>start line</u> on the ramp just before the first <u>light gate</u>.
5) <u>Attach the trolley</u> to the hanging masses by the string.
6) Hold the trolley <u>still</u> at the start line.
7) Then <u>let go</u> of it so that it starts to roll down the slope.
8) Each <u>light gate</u> will record the <u>speed</u> of the trolley at those points.
9) They will also record <u>how long</u> it takes the trolley to move <u>between</u> the <u>light gates</u>.
10) The <u>acceleration</u> of the trolley can then be found using <u>acceleration = change in speed ÷ time</u>.

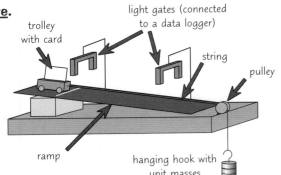

light gates (connected to a data logger)

trolley with card

string

pulley

ramp

hanging hook with unit masses

You can use this Setup to Investigate $F = m \times a$

1) The <u>resultant force</u> (F) on the trolley is equal to the <u>weight</u> of the hook and unit masses.
2) The <u>mass</u> (m) is the mass of the trolley and the hook with unit masses.
3) The <u>acceleration</u> (a) is the acceleration of the trolley down the ramp.

Investigating How Mass Affects Acceleration

To investigate the effect of mass, you need to <u>change the mass</u> but keep the force <u>the same</u>.

1) So, keep the mass <u>on the hook</u> the <u>same</u>.
2) <u>Add masses</u> to the <u>trolley</u> one at a time to increase the <u>total mass</u> being accelerated.
3) Record the <u>acceleration</u>, a, for <u>each total mass</u>, m.
4) You should find that as the mass <u>goes up</u>, the acceleration <u>goes down</u>.
5) This agrees with the <u>equation</u> for <u>Newton's Second Law</u> (p.151).

Investigating How Force Affects Acceleration

This time, you need to <u>change</u> the force <u>without changing</u> the <u>total mass</u> of the trolley, hook and masses.

1) Start with <u>all</u> the extra masses loaded onto the <u>trolley</u>.
2) Moving the masses <u>from</u> the trolley to the hook will keep the <u>total mass</u>, m, the same.
3) But it will <u>increase</u> the force, F (the <u>weight</u> of the <u>hook and the masses on the hook</u>).
4) <u>Each time</u> you <u>move</u> a mass, record the <u>new force</u>, and measure the <u>acceleration</u>.
5) You should find that as the force <u>goes up</u>, the acceleration <u>goes up</u>.
6) This <u>agrees</u> with the equation for <u>Newton's Second Law</u> too.

My acceleration increases with nearby cake...

This investigation can seem a bit complicated, so it's definitely worth going over this page a couple of times.

Q1   What equipment could be used to measure the speed of an object?   [1 mark]

Newton's Third Law

Another law eh? Newton probably wasn't thinking about anyone having to revise them back in the 17th century.

Newton's Third Law: Equal and Opposite Forces Act on Interacting Objects

Newton's Third Law says:

> When two objects interact, the forces they exert on each other are equal and opposite.

1) This means if you push something, it will push back against you, just as hard.
2) And as soon as you stop pushing, so does the object.
3) But if the forces are always equal, how does anything ever go anywhere?
4) The important thing to remember is that the two forces are acting on different objects.

Push   Normal contact force

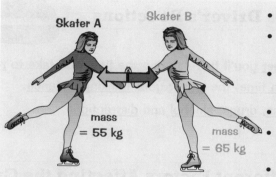

Skater A   Skater B

mass = 55 kg   mass = 65 kg

- Skater A pushes on skater B.
- When she does, she feels an equal and opposite force from skater B's hand.
- Both skaters feel the same sized force, in opposite directions.
- This causes them to accelerate away from each other.
- Skater A will be accelerated more than skater B, because she has a smaller mass.
- Remember $F = m \times a$ (p.151), so $a = F \div m$.

It's More Complicated for an Object in Equilibrium

1) An object is said to be in equilibrium when there is no resultant force acting on it.
2) The object remains stationary or moves at a constant velocity.
3) In these situations, Newton's Third Law still applies.
4) For example, imagine a book sat on a table in equilibrium:

1) The weight of the book pulls it down, and the normal contact force from the table pushes it up.
2) This is NOT Newton's Third Law.
3) These forces are different types and they're both acting on the book.
4) The pairs of forces due to Newton's Third Law in this case are:
- The book being pulled down by gravity towards the Earth (W_B) and the Earth being pulled up by the book (W_E).
- The normal contact force from the table pushing up on the book (R_B) and the normal contact force from the book pushing down on the table (R_T).

$R_B\uparrow$

$R_T\downarrow\downarrow W_B$

$\uparrow W_E$

Newton's fourth law — revision must be done with cake...

Newton's 3rd law trips people up, so make sure you know exactly what objects the forces are acting on and how that results in an object remaining in equilibrium. Then have a crack at this question to practise.

Q1   A car moves at a constant velocity along a road, so that it is in equilibrium. Give an example of a pair of forces that demonstrate Newton's Third Law in this situation.   [1 mark]

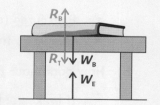

Q1 Video Solution

Stopping Distances

This page is all about <u>cars</u>, but unfortunately it's not as fun as it sounds...
It's even better — it's about <u>safety</u>...

Stopping Distance = Thinking Distance + Braking Distance

1) The <u>stopping distance</u> is the distance it takes to stop a vehicle. It is found by:

> Stopping Distance = Thinking Distance + Braking Distance

2) <u>THINKING DISTANCE</u> is how far the vehicle travels during the driver's <u>reaction time</u>.
3) The reaction time is the time <u>between</u> the driver <u>seeing</u> a hazard and <u>applying the brakes</u>.
4) <u>BRAKING DISTANCE</u> is the distance taken to stop under the <u>braking force</u> (once the brakes are applied).
5) You need to be able to <u>describe</u> how different factors can affect the <u>stopping distance of a vehicle</u>.
6) The <u>stopping distance</u> of a vehicle is <u>increased</u> if the <u>thinking distance</u> or <u>braking distance</u> is <u>increased</u>.

Thinking Distance is Determined by the Driver's Reactions

1) <u>Thinking distance</u> is affected by:
   - Your <u>SPEED</u> — the <u>faster</u> you're going, the <u>further</u> you'll travel during the <u>time</u> you take to <u>react</u>.
   - Your <u>REACTION TIME</u> — the <u>longer</u> your <u>reaction time</u>, the <u>longer</u> your <u>thinking distance</u>.
2) A driver's reaction time can be increased by <u>tiredness</u>, <u>drugs</u>, <u>alcohol</u> and <u>distractions</u>.

Braking Distance Depends on a Few Different Factors Affecting the Car

<u>Braking distance</u> is affected by:
1) Your <u>SPEED</u>: for a <u>given</u> braking force, the <u>faster</u> a vehicle travels, the <u>longer</u> it takes to stop.
2) The <u>MASS</u> of your vehicle: a car full of <u>people</u> and <u>luggage</u> won't stop as quickly as an empty car.
3) The <u>STATE</u> of the <u>ROAD</u>:
   - If there is less <u>grip</u> between a vehicle's tyres and the road, it can cause the vehicle to <u>skid</u>.
   - <u>Skidding</u> increases the <u>braking distance</u> of a car.
   - <u>Water</u>, <u>ice</u>, <u>oil</u> or <u>leaves</u> on the road all reduce grip.
4) The amount of <u>FRICTION</u> between the <u>TYRES</u> and the <u>ROAD</u>:
   - <u>Bald tyres</u> (ones that don't have <u>any tread left</u>) cannot <u>get rid of water</u> in wet conditions.
   - This leads to them <u>skidding</u> on top of the water.
5) How good your <u>BRAKES</u> are:
   - If brakes are <u>worn</u>, they won't be able to apply as much <u>force</u>.
   - So it takes <u>longer</u> to stop a vehicle travelling at a <u>given speed</u>.

Stop right there — and learn this page...

Bad weather doesn't just cause accidents because it affects the friction between the road and the tyres. So, for example, if it's foggy you will be closer to a hazard before you can see it. That means there'll be less room to stop.

Q1   Give three factors that affect the braking distance of a vehicle.   [3 marks]

Reaction Times

Go long! You need fast _reaction times_ to avoid getting hit in the face when playing catch.

A Typical Reaction Time is 0.2 s – 0.9 s

1) _Everyone's_ reaction time is _different_.
2) A _typical_ reaction time is between _0.2_ and _0.9 s_.
3) You can do _simple experiments_ to investigate your reaction time — more on these below.

You can Measure Reaction Times with the Ruler Drop Test

1) As reaction times are _so short_, you haven't got a chance of measuring one with a _stopwatch_.
2) One way of measuring reaction times is to use a _computer-based test_. For example, _clicking a mouse_ when the screen changes colour.

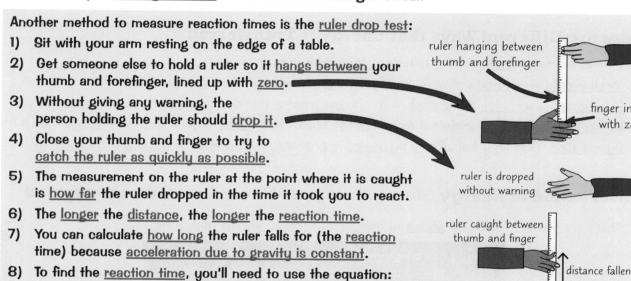

Another method to measure reaction times is the _ruler drop test_:

1) Sit with your arm resting on the edge of a table.
2) Get someone else to hold a ruler so it _hangs between_ your thumb and forefinger, lined up with _zero_.
3) Without giving any warning, the person holding the ruler should _drop it_.
4) Close your thumb and finger to try to _catch the ruler as quickly as possible_.
5) The measurement on the ruler at the point where it is caught is _how far_ the ruler dropped in the time it took you to react.
6) The _longer_ the _distance_, the _longer_ the _reaction time_.
7) You can calculate _how long_ the ruler falls for (the _reaction time_) because _acceleration due to gravity is constant_.
8) To find the _reaction time_, you'll need to use the equation:

ruler hanging between thumb and forefinger

finger in line with zero

ruler is dropped without warning

ruler caught between thumb and finger

distance fallen

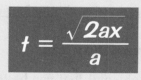

$$t = \frac{\sqrt{2ax}}{a}$$

You _DON'T_ need to learn this equation. It comes from squashing $v^2 - u^2 = 2ax$ and $a = (v - u) \div t$ from p.146 together.

- t is the _reaction time_ in seconds, s.
- a is the _acceleration due to gravity_. $a = 10$ m/s^2.
- x is _how far_ the ruler fell before it was caught, in metres, m.

9) It's _hard_ to do this experiment _accurately_, but you can do a few things to _improve_ your _results_.
- Do a lot of _repeats_ and calculate an _average_ reaction time.
- Have a _third person_ at _eye level_ with the _ruler_ to check it's lined up.

Test a friend's reaction time by throwing this book at them...

Not really. Instead re-read this page and make sure you can describe the experiment. Much more fun.

Q1   What is a typical reaction time for a human?   [1 mark]

Q2   Mark wants to measure his reaction time, state one way of doing this.   [1 mark]

Energy Stores and Conservation of Energy

Energy. Might seem a tricky little beast, but know this — it can be <u>stored</u> and <u>transferred</u> in different ways.

Energy is Transferred Between Energy Stores

<u>Energy</u> can be transferred between and held in different <u>energy stores</u>.
There are <u>eight</u> you need to know:

1) <u>KINETIC</u>............................... — anything <u>moving</u> has energy in its <u>kinetic energy store</u> (see p.158).
2) <u>THERMAL</u>............................. — <u>any object</u> — the <u>hotter</u> it is, the <u>more</u> energy it has in this <u>store</u>.
3) <u>CHEMICAL</u>.......................... — anything that can release energy by a <u>chemical reaction</u>, e.g. <u>food</u>, <u>fuels</u>.
4) <u>GRAVITATIONAL POTENTIAL</u>... — anything in a <u>gravitational field</u> (i.e. anything that can <u>fall</u>) (see p.158).
5) <u>ELASTIC POTENTIAL</u>.............. — anything stretched, like <u>springs</u>, <u>rubber bands</u>, etc. (p.205).
6) <u>ELECTROSTATIC</u>................... — e.g. two <u>charges</u> that attract or repel each other.
7) <u>MAGNETIC</u>.......................... — e.g. two <u>magnets</u> that attract or repel each other (p.196).
8) <u>NUCLEAR</u>............................ — <u>atomic nuclei</u> release energy from this store in <u>nuclear reactions</u>.

There are Different Ways that Energy is Transferred

Energy can be <u>transferred</u> (moved) between <u>stores</u> in <u>four</u> main ways:

1) <u>Mechanically</u> — a <u>force</u> acting on an object, e.g. pushing, stretching, squashing.
2) <u>Electrically</u> — a <u>charge</u> doing <u>work</u>, e.g. charges moving round a circuit.
3) <u>By heating</u> — energy transferred from a <u>hotter</u> object to a <u>colder</u> object, e.g. heating a pan on a hob.
4) <u>By radiation</u> — energy transferred by <u>waves</u>, e.g. energy from the Sun reaching Earth by light.

Conservation of Energy Means Energy is Never Created or Destroyed

1) There are plenty of different <u>stores</u> of energy, but <u>energy always obeys this law</u>:

> <u>Energy</u> can be <u>stored</u>, <u>transferred</u> between <u>stores</u>, and
> <u>dissipated</u> — but it can <u>never</u> be <u>created or destroyed</u>.

2) <u>Dissipated</u> is a fancy way of saying the energy is <u>spread out</u> and <u>transferred</u> to <u>less useful</u> energy stores.

The Total Energy of a Closed System Never Changes

1) A <u>closed system</u> is just a system (a collection of objects) that can be treated completely on its own.
2) Energy can be transferred between <u>energy stores</u> within a closed system.
3) But <u>no energy</u> can be transferred <u>in or out</u> of a closed system.
4) This is why the <u>total energy</u> of a <u>closed system</u> has <u>no net (total) change</u>.

For example...
- A <u>cold spoon</u> sealed in a flask of <u>hot soup</u> is a closed system.
- Energy is <u>transferred</u> from the thermal energy store of the <u>soup</u> to the thermal energy store of the <u>spoon</u> by heating.
- But <u>no energy</u> leaves the system. The total energy <u>stays the same</u>.

Energy can't be created or destroyed — only talked about a lot...

This is important to remember. Energy can only be transferred to a different energy store, never destroyed.

Q1   Describe the energy transfers that occur when the wind causes a windmill to spin.   [3 marks]

Q1 Video Solution

Energy Transfers

As well as being able to <u>describe</u> energy transfers, you need to know how to draw energy transfer <u>diagrams</u>.

You Need to Know Some Examples of Energy Transfers

1) When a <u>system</u> changes, energy is <u>transferred</u>.

2) Make sure you understand what's going on in <u>these examples</u> of energy transfers:

<u>A BALL ROLLING UP A SLOPE:</u>
- The ball <u>does work</u> against the gravitational force.
- So energy is transferred <u>mechanically</u> from the <u>kinetic energy store</u> of the ball to its <u>gravitational potential energy store</u>.

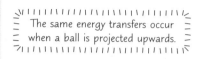
The same energy transfers occur when a ball is projected upwards.

<u>A BAT HITTING A BALL:</u>
- The bat has energy in its <u>kinetic energy store</u>.
- Some of this is transferred <u>mechanically</u> to the ball's <u>kinetic energy store</u>.
- Some energy is also transferred <u>mechanically</u> to the <u>thermal energy stores</u> of the bat and the ball.
- This energy is then transferred to the <u>surroundings</u> by <u>heating</u>.

The same energy transfers often occur when moving objects hit obstacles.

<u>A ROCK DROPPED FROM A CLIFF:</u>
- There is a <u>constant force</u> of gravity acting on the rock, so it constantly <u>accelerates</u> towards the ground (see p.146).
- Energy is transferred <u>mechanically</u> from the rock's <u>gravitational potential energy store</u>.
- Assuming there's <u>no air resistance</u>, all the energy is transferred to the rock's <u>kinetic energy store</u>.

<u>A CAR SLOWING DOWN (without braking):</u>
- The car has energy in its <u>kinetic energy store</u>.
- There is <u>friction</u> between the tyres and road.
- This means energy is transferred <u>mechanically</u> (by the frictional force) and then by <u>heating</u>, to the <u>thermal energy stores</u> of the car and road.

<u>AN ELECTRIC KETTLE BOILING WATER:</u>
- Energy is transferred <u>electrically</u> from the mains to the heating element of the kettle.
- The energy is then transferred by <u>heating</u> to the <u>thermal energy store</u> of the water.

You can Draw Diagrams to Show Energy Transfers

1) The diagram below shows the <u>energy transfers</u> when <u>a ball is thrown upwards</u>.

2) Each <u>box</u> shows one <u>energy store</u> and each <u>arrow</u> shows one <u>energy transfer</u>:

kinetic energy store of the ball → mechanically — work done against gravity → gravitational potential energy store of the ball

kinetic energy store of the ball → mechanically — work done against air resistance → thermal energy store of the ball and the surroundings

3) You can also show <u>energy transfers</u> with the diagrams on page 160.

Energy transfers — a lot cheaper than football transfers...

You might be asked to explain what's happening in any of the situations above — make sure you understand them.

Q1   Describe the energy transfers that occur when a tennis racket hits a ball.   [4 marks]

Kinetic and Potential Energy Stores

This page covers <u>two</u> types of <u>energy stores</u> and how to work out the amount of energy in them. Have fun.

A Moving Object has Energy in its Kinetic Energy Store

1) When an object is <u>moving</u>, it has <u>energy</u> in its <u>kinetic energy store</u>.

2) Energy is transferred <u>to</u> this store if an object <u>speeds up</u>.

3) Energy is transferred <u>away</u> from this store if it <u>slows down</u>.

4) <u>How much energy</u> is in this store depends on both the object's <u>mass</u> and its <u>speed</u>.

5) The <u>greater its mass</u> and the <u>faster it's going</u>, the <u>more</u> energy it has in its kinetic energy store.

6) For example, a <u>moving train</u> will have <u>a lot more energy</u> in its kinetic energy store than you running.

7) You can find the energy in a <u>kinetic energy store</u> using:

$$\text{kinetic energy} = ½ \times \text{mass} \times (\text{speed})^2$$
$$\text{(J)} \qquad \text{(kg)} \qquad \text{(m/s)}^2$$

or

$$KE = ½ \times m \times v^2$$

For more on significant figures have a look at page 6.

EXAMPLE

A motorcycle has a mass of 260 kg. It is travelling at 28 m/s.
Calculate the energy in its kinetic energy store. Give your answer to 3 s.f.

kinetic energy = 0.5 × mass × (speed)²
= 0.5 × 260 × 28² = 101 920 = **102 000 J** (to 3 s.f.)

A Raised Object has Energy in its Gravitational Potential Energy Store

1) When an object is at any <u>height</u> above the Earth's surface, it will have <u>energy</u> in its <u>gravitational potential energy store</u>.

2) You can <u>calculate</u> the <u>change in energy</u> in a <u>gravitational potential energy store</u> using the equation:

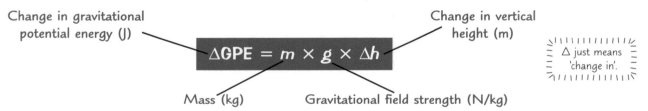

Change in gravitational potential energy (J)

Change in vertical height (m)

$$\Delta GPE = m \times g \times \Delta h$$

Mass (kg)

Gravitational field strength (N/kg)

Δ just means 'change in'.

EXAMPLE

A 1.2 kg book is raised 4.25 m vertically above the ground.
Calculate the energy transferred to the book's gravitational potential energy store.
(*g* = 10 N/kg)

change in gravitational potential energy = mass × *g* × change in vertical height
= 1.2 × 10 × 4.25 = **51 J**

There's potential for a joke here somewhere...

Hopefully this page wasn't too hard — just don't forget that squared sign when you're working and remember that the energy in an object's kinetic energy store only changes if its speed is changing.

Q1 Video Solution

Q1 A 2 kg object is dropped from a height of 10 m. Calculate the speed of the object after it has fallen 5 m, assuming there is no air resistance. *g* = 10 N/kg. [5 marks]

Q2 A lorry has 1 575 000 J of energy in its kinetic energy store and is travelling at 30.0 m/s. Calculate the mass of the lorry in kg. [3 marks]

Efficiency

So energy is <u>transferred</u> between different <u>stores</u>. But not all of the energy is transferred to <u>useful</u> stores.

Most Energy Transfers Involve Some Losses, Often by Heating

1) Remember — when a system <u>changes</u>, <u>energy is transferred</u>.

> Energy is <u>only useful</u> when it is <u>transferred</u> from one store to a <u>useful store</u>.

2) However, when a system changes some of the <u>input energy</u> is always <u>dissipated or wasted</u>.
3) In any <u>mechanical process</u> (a process in which objects move), <u>friction</u> acts on the objects.
4) This <u>transfers</u> energy <u>mechanically</u> to the <u>thermal energy stores</u> of the objects involved. This <u>raises</u> their <u>temperature</u>.
5) This energy is then <u>dissipated by heating</u> to the <u>surroundings</u>.
6) Usually this <u>isn't</u> a <u>useful energy transfer</u>.
7) In this case, the <u>mechanical process</u> that caused this <u>rise in temperature</u> is called <u>wasteful</u>.

For example, the diagram shows a <u>motor</u> lifting a load. The motor has energy in its <u>kinetic energy store</u>.

<u>USEFUL ENERGY TRANSFER:</u>
The motor transfers energy mechanically to the <u>kinetic</u> and the <u>gravitational potential</u> energy stores of the <u>load</u>.

<u>WASTED ENERGY TRANSFER:</u>
Energy is also transferred <u>mechanically</u> to the <u>thermal energy stores</u> of its moving parts, <u>increasing</u> their <u>temperature</u>. This energy is <u>dissipated</u>, heating the surroundings.

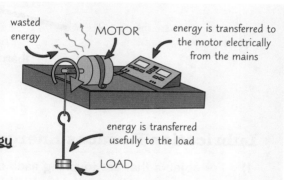

wasted energy / MOTOR / energy is transferred to the motor electrically from the mains

energy is transferred usefully to the load

LOAD

You can Calculate the Efficiency of an Energy Transfer

1) The conservation of energy principle (p.156) means that:
   <u>total energy input = useful energy output + wasted energy</u>.
2) All devices <u>waste</u> energy. The <u>less energy</u> that's <u>wasted</u>, the <u>more efficient</u> the device is said to be.
3) You can calculate the <u>efficiency</u> of any device as a <u>decimal</u> using this equation:

$$\text{efficiency} = \frac{\text{useful energy transferred by the device (J)}}{\text{total energy supplied to the device (J)}}$$

All devices waste energy, so efficiency can never be equal to or higher than 1 (or 100%).

4) To give efficiency as a <u>percentage</u>, you need to multiply a decimal efficiency by <u>100</u>.

EXAMPLE 36 000 J of energy is transferred to a television. It transfers 28 800 J of this energy usefully. Calculate the efficiency of the television. Give your answer as a decimal.

Put the numbers <u>into the equation</u>.

$$\text{efficiency} = \frac{\text{useful energy transferred by the device}}{\text{total energy supplied to the device}}$$
$$= 28\,800 \div 36\,000 = 0.8$$

If you wanted this as a percentage, you would do: 0.8 × 100 = 80%

Make sure your revising efficiency is high...

Devices that transfer energy will <u>always</u> transfer energy to stores that aren't useful. <u>Always</u>. (Always.)

Q1   An electrical device wastes 420 J of energy when it has an input energy of 500 J.
      Calculate the efficiency of the device as a percentage.
      [3 marks]

Q1 Video Solution

Reducing Unwanted Energy Transfers

There are many ways you can <u>reduce</u> the amount of energy that is <u>wasted</u> during a process. <u>Lubrication</u> and <u>thermal insulation</u> are two that you need to know about.

You can Show How Much Energy is Wasted Using Diagrams

1) You can use diagrams to show the different <u>energy transfers</u> made by a device.

2) These diagrams are also useful for calculating the <u>efficiency</u> of a device.

3) The <u>thickness</u> of the arrows shows how much energy is being transferred. The <u>length</u> has nothing to do with it.

<u>Diagram for an electric motor with 80% efficiency:</u>

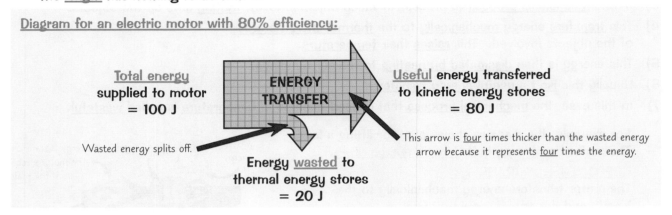

<u>Total energy</u> supplied to motor = 100 J

ENERGY TRANSFER

<u>Useful</u> energy transferred to kinetic energy stores = 80 J

This arrow is <u>four</u> times thicker than the wasted energy arrow because it represents <u>four</u> times the energy.

Wasted energy splits off.

Energy <u>wasted</u> to thermal energy stores = 20 J

Lubrication Reduces Energy Transferred by Friction

1) For objects that are touching each other, <u>lubricants</u> can be used to <u>reduce</u> the <u>friction</u> (p.150) between moving parts.

2) Lubricants are usually <u>liquids</u> (like <u>oil</u>), so they can <u>flow</u> easily between objects and <u>coat</u> them.

Thermal Insulation Reduces the Rate of Energy Transfer by Heating

1) <u>Energy</u> can be <u>transferred</u> through some materials by <u>heating</u> much more <u>easily</u> than others.

2) All materials have a <u>thermal conductivity</u> — it describes <u>how well</u> a material transfers energy by heating.

3) The <u>lower</u> the <u>thermal conductivity</u> of a material, the slower the <u>rate of energy transfer</u> through it.

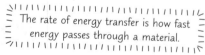
The rate of energy transfer is how fast energy passes through a material.

Thermal Insulation is Important in Buildings

1) The <u>walls</u> of buildings are made from materials with a <u>low thermal conductivity</u>.

2) This <u>reduces</u> the amount of <u>energy lost</u> from the building.

3) <u>Thicker</u> walls help too — the <u>thicker</u> the wall, the <u>slower</u> the <u>rate of energy transfer</u> from the building to the surroundings.

4) The <u>slower</u> the <u>rate of energy transfer</u>, the <u>slower</u> the <u>rate of cooling</u> of the building.

Don't waste energy — turn the TV off while you revise...

Unwanted energy transfers can cost you a lot in energy bills. It's why so many people buy home insulation.

Q1 Suggest one way to reduce unwanted energy transfers in an electric motor. [1 mark]

Energy Resources

There are lots of <u>energy resources</u> available on Earth. They are either <u>renewable</u> or <u>non-renewable</u> resources.

Non-Renewable Energy Resources Will Run Out One Day

1) <u>Fossil fuels</u> (oil, coal and natural gas) and <u>nuclear fuel</u> are <u>non-renewable</u> energy resources.
2) This means they will eventually <u>run out</u>.
3) <u>Fossil fuels</u> are typically <u>burnt</u> to generate electricity.
4) Nuclear power plants use <u>nuclear reactors</u>. <u>Nuclear fuel</u> is used in <u>nuclear reactors</u> to <u>generate electricity</u>.

DISADVANTAGES OF USING NON-RENEWABLES TO GENERATE ELECTRICITY:

1) Fossil fuels are <u>slowly running out</u>.
2) Fossil fuels create ENVIRONMENTAL PROBLEMS:
   - Burning fossil fuels releases gases that cause <u>acid rain</u> and <u>global warming</u> (p.139 and 143).
   - <u>Oil spillages</u> at sea can harm wildlife.
3) <u>Nuclear waste</u> is very <u>dangerous</u> and difficult to <u>dispose of</u>.
4) <u>Nuclear</u> power plants are pretty costly to build, and to <u>safely</u> shut down.

ADVANTAGES OF USING NON-RENEWABLES TO GENERATE ELECTRICITY:

1) <u>Fossil fuels</u> and <u>nuclear energy</u> are <u>reliable</u>.
2) There's still <u>plenty of fossil fuels</u> around to meet <u>current demand</u>.
3) The cost to <u>extract fossil fuels</u> is low.
4) <u>Fossil fuel</u> power plants are relatively cheap to <u>build</u> and <u>run</u>.
5) <u>Nuclear power</u> doesn't release harmful gases.

Renewable Energy Resources Will Never Run Out

We can use <u>renewable energy resources</u> to generate <u>electricity</u>. <u>Renewable</u> energy resources include:

1) Bio-fuels   2) Wind   3) The Sun (solar)   4) Hydro-electricity   5) Tides

- These will <u>never run out</u>.
- Most of them do <u>harm</u> the environment, but in <u>less damaging</u> ways than non-renewables.
- The trouble is they <u>don't</u> provide much <u>energy</u>.
- Some of them are <u>unreliable</u> because they depend on weather.

Bio-fuels are Made from Plant Products or Animal Dung

1) Bio-fuels can be burnt to produce <u>electricity</u> or used to run <u>cars</u> in the same way as <u>fossil fuels</u>.
2) Extra bio-fuels can be constantly produced <u>throughout the year</u>, and <u>stored</u> for when they are needed.
3) This means bio-fuels are fairly <u>reliable</u>.
4) One of the <u>disadvantages</u> of using plants for bio-fuels is that they need <u>room to grow</u>.
5) So in some places, large areas of <u>forest</u> have been <u>cleared</u> to make room to grow <u>bio-fuels</u>.
6) This leads to lots of animals losing their <u>natural habitats</u>.
7) <u>Growing</u> and <u>burning</u> bio-fuels <u>doesn't</u> affect <u>global warming</u>:

   1) When bio-fuel plants are <u>growing</u>, they <u>absorb carbon dioxide</u>.
   2) Carbon dioxide is a gas that adds to <u>global warming</u>.
   3) But the plants <u>release</u> this carbon dioxide <u>back into the air</u> when they're <u>burnt</u>.

Burning poo... lovely...

You need to know the difference between the two different types of energy resource, so get cracking.

Q1   State two renewable energy resources.

[2 marks]

More Energy Resources

Renewable energy resources, like wind, solar, hydro-electricity and tides, won't run out.

Wind Power — Lots of Wind Turbines

1) When the wind turns the blades, electricity is produced.
   They don't produce electricity when the wind stops.
2) Wind turbines produce no pollution once they're built.
3) However, they're not as reliable as other energy resources.
4) Lots of them are needed to produce as much power as, for example, a coal power plant.
5) It's also impossible to increase supply when there's extra demand (p.163) for electricity.

Solar Cells — Expensive but No Environmental Damage

1) Solar cells generate electricity directly from sunlight.
2) Energy is transferred by light to the solar cells which then transfer the energy electrically.
3) They create no pollution once they're built.
4) But quite a lot of energy is used to build them.
5) Solar power only generates electricity during the day.
6) In sunny countries solar power is a very reliable source of energy.
7) Like wind, you can't increase the power output when there is extra demand.

Time to recharge.

Hydro-electric Power Uses Falling Water

1) Hydro-electric power usually involves building a big dam across a valley. The valley is usually flooded.
2) Water is allowed to flow out through turbines, which generates electricity.
3) There is no pollution when it's running.
4) But there is a big impact on the environment due to the flooding of the valley.
5) There's no problem with reliability in countries that get rain regularly.
6) And it can respond straight away when there's extra demand for electricity.

Tidal Barrages Use the Tides of the Sea

1) Tidal barrages are big dams (with turbines in them) built across rivers.
2) Water passing through the turbines generates electricity.
3) The amount of energy generated changes with the tides.
4) But tidal barrages are very reliable, as we can predict the tides (we know what they're going to do).
5) But they can't increase their power output if demand increases.
6) There is no pollution.
7) But they do change the habitat of the wildlife, e.g. birds and sea creatures.

The hydro-electric power you're supplying — it's electrifying...

There are pros and cons to all energy resources. Make sure you know them for solar, wind and water.

Q1   Give one advantage and one disadvantage for generating electricity from the Sun.   [2 marks]

Trends in Energy Resource Use

Over time, the types of energy resources we use change. Read on to find out why.

Currently we Still Need Non-Renewables

1) Our use of electricity increased a lot in the 1900s.
2) This was because the population and the number of things that used electricity increased.
3) But electricity use in the UK has been falling slowly since around the year 2000.
4) This is because we're trying harder to be energy efficient and save energy.
5) At the moment, we use non-renewables for much of our electricity, transport and heating.

But People Want to use More Renewable Energy Resources

1) We now know that non-renewables are very bad for the environment and will run out one day (p.161).
2) This makes many people want to use renewable energy resources as they are better for the environment.
3) Many people also think it's better to move to renewables before non-renewables run out.
4) Pressure from other countries and the public has meant that governments have begun to introduce targets for using renewable energy resources.
5) This puts pressure on energy providers to build new renewable power plants.
6) If they don't, they may lose business and money in the future.
7) Car companies have also had to change to become more environmentally-friendly.
8) The demand for cars that can run on electricity is increasing.
9) The electricity can be generated using renewable energy resources.

The Use of Renewables is Limited by Lots of Factors

Reliability and Cost

1) Using fossil fuels is cheaper than renewables, and building new renewable power plants costs money.
2) So smaller energy providers would rather keep using fossil fuel plants, in order to save money.
3) Some renewable energy resources are not as reliable as traditional fossil fuels.
4) Some renewable energy resources can't increase their power output on demand.
5) So a mixture of different resources would need to be used, which can be expensive.
6) Research into improving the reliability and cost of renewable resources takes time and money.

Location of Power Plants

1) When new power plants are built, there are often a lot of arguments over where they should be.
2) Many people don't want to live next to a wind farm, which can lead to protests.

Personal Costs

1) Making personal changes can be expensive or impractical. For example:
   • Renewable energy equipment for homes, such as solar panels, is still quite pricey.
   • Electric cars need to be charged which is harder in rural areas.
2) The cost of these things is slowly going down, and the support (e.g. having charging points for cars) is improving, but they are still not an option for everyone.

Going green is on-trend this season...

More people want to help the environment, so the energy resources we use are changing. But for lots of reasons, it's not happening very quickly. Make sure you learn the reasons listed on this page.

Q1   Give two reasons we currently do not use more renewable energy resources in the UK.   [2 marks]

Revision Questions for Sections 17 and 18

Wow, that was a whole lot of Physics in one place —
time to see how much of it you can remember.

- Try these questions and <u>tick off each one</u> when you <u>get it right</u>.
- When you're <u>completely happy</u> with a sub-topic, tick it off.

For even more practice, try the
Retrieval Quizzes for Sections 17
and 18 — just scan the QR codes!

Motion (p.145-148) ☑

1) What is the difference between a scalar and a vector quantity? Give two examples of each.
2) Give the equation relating distance, speed and time.
3) Estimate typical speeds for a) walking, b) running, c) a car in a built-up area.
4) Define acceleration in terms of velocity and time.
5) What does the gradient represent for a) a distance/time graph? b) a velocity/time graph?
6) How would you find the distance travelled by an object from its velocity/time graph?

Section 17
Quiz

Newton's Laws and Forces (p.149-153) ☑

7) What is the formula for calculating the weight of an object?
8) What is a resultant force?
9) State Newton's First Law of Motion.
10) Give the equation for Newton's Second Law of Motion.
11) Explain why large decelerations are dangerous.
12) Describe an experiment to investigate Newton's Second Law of Motion.

Stopping Distances and Reaction Times (p.154-155) ☑

13) State two factors that can affect the thinking distance for a stopping car.
14) Describe an experiment to measure a person's reaction time.

Energy Stores, Transfers and Efficiency (p.156-160) ☑

15) State the conservation of energy principle.
16) What is meant by the 'dissipation' of energy?
17) Describe the energy transfers that occur when a ball rolls up a slope.
18) Describe the energy transfers that occur when a hair dryer is switched on.
19) What is the equation for calculating the energy in a moving object's kinetic energy store?
20) What is the equation for calculating the change in energy
    in an object's gravitational potential energy store?
21) Give the equation for the efficiency of a device.
22) How can you reduce unwanted energy transfers in a machine with moving, touching components?
23) How does the thermal conductivity of a wall affect its rate of energy transfer?

Section 18
Quiz

Energy Resources and Trends in their Use (p.161-163) ☑

24) What is the difference between renewable and non-renewable energy resources?
25) What are bio-fuels made from? Explain the benefits and drawbacks of using bio-fuels.
26) Give one benefit and two disadvantages of wind power.
27) Explain why the UK plans to use more renewable energy resources in the future.

Wave Basics

Waves are used a lot in everyday life to transfer information from one place to another. First — how they work.

Waves Transfer Energy but not Matter

1) When a wave travels through a medium, the particles of the medium vibrate.
2) The particles transfer energy between each other as they vibrate.
3) BUT overall, the particles stay in the same place — only energy is transferred.

A medium is just a fancy word for whatever the wave is travelling through (e.g. water, air).

- If you drop a twig into calm water, it creates ripples on the water's surface that spread out. The ripples don't carry the water (or the twig) away with them though.
- And if you strum a guitar string, it produces sound waves in the air. The sound waves don't carry the air away from the guitar. If they did, you'd feel a wind whenever there was a sound.

All Waves are Either Transverse or Longitudinal

1) In transverse waves, the vibrations are perpendicular (at right angles) to the direction the wave travels.

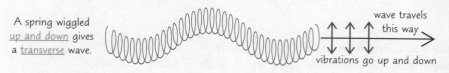

A spring wiggled up and down gives a transverse wave.

wave travels this way

vibrations go up and down

Examples:
- electromagnetic waves (p.170)
- water waves (p.167)
- seismic S-waves

A seismic wave is a type of wave produced in the ground during an earthquake.

2) In longitudinal waves, the vibrations are in the same direction as the direction the wave is travelling in.
3) They have compressions (where the particles squish together), and rarefactions (where they spread out).

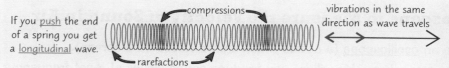

If you push the end of a spring you get a longitudinal wave.

compressions

rarefactions

vibrations in the same direction as wave travels

Examples:
- sound waves
- seismic P-waves

You Need to Know these Words to Describe Waves

The wavelength of a longitudinal wave is the distance from one compression to the next, or one rarefaction to the next.

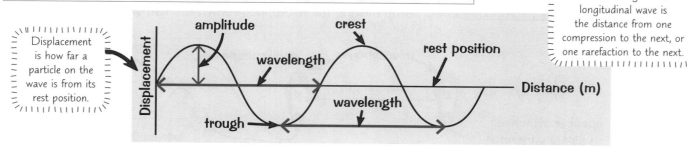

Displacement is how far a particle on the wave is from its rest position.

amplitude

crest

wavelength

rest position

Displacement

wavelength

trough

Distance (m)

1) The amplitude is the maximum displacement of a point on the wave from its rest position.
2) The wavelength is the distance between one point on a wave and the same point on the next wave. For example, the distance between the crest of one wave and the crest of the wave next to it.
3) Frequency is the number of complete waves passing a certain point each second.
4) Frequency is measured in hertz (Hz). 1 Hz is 1 wave per second.
5) Period is the amount of time it takes for one complete wave to pass a certain point.

What about Mexican waves?...

You won't get far unless you understand these wave basics. Try a question to test your knowledge.

Q1   Give two examples of transverse waves.

[2 marks]

Wave Speed

You need to know how to <u>calculate</u> and <u>measure</u> the speed of a wave.

You Need to be Able to Calculate Wave Speed

1) The <u>wave speed</u> (or <u>wave velocity</u>) is how <u>fast</u> a <u>wave</u> is moving.
2) There are <u>two equations</u> for wave speed that you need to know.
3) These equations apply to <u>all</u> waves.

Wave speed (m/s) — 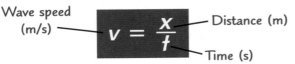 — Distance (m)

$$v = \frac{x}{t}$$

Time (s)

Wave speed (m/s) —  — Wavelength (m)

$$v = f\lambda$$

Frequency (Hz)

 EXAMPLE   A sound wave travels 680 m through air in 2.0 s.
Find the speed of the sound wave.

1) Choose the correct <u>wave speed equation</u> for the <u>values</u> you've been <u>given</u>. $v = x \div t$
2) Put the <u>values</u> into the equation and find the <u>wave speed</u>. $v = 680 \div 2.0 = 340$ m/s

EXAMPLE   A radio wave has a frequency of 12 000 000 Hz.
Find its wavelength. (The speed of radio waves in air is 3.0×10^8 m/s.)

1) <u>Rearrange</u> the wave speed equation for <u>wavelength</u>. $\lambda = v \div f$
2) Put in the <u>values</u> you've been <u>given</u>.
   Watch out — the speed is in <u>standard form</u> (p.173). $= (3.0 \times 10^8) \div (12\ 000\ 000)$
   $= 25$ m

You Can Use an Oscilloscope to Measure the Velocity of Sound in Air

1) Connect <u>two microphones</u> to an <u>oscilloscope</u> (a device which shows waves on a screen).
2) Connect a <u>signal generator</u> to a speaker. This will let you produce <u>sound waves</u> at a <u>set frequency</u>.
3) Set up the oscilloscope so the <u>waves</u> reaching each microphone are shown <u>separately</u>.
4) Start with <u>both microphones</u> next to the speaker. The waves on the oscilloscope <u>should line up</u>.
5) Slowly <u>move one microphone</u> away. Stop moving the microphone when the two waves <u>line up</u> again.

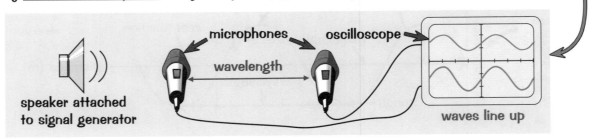

speaker attached to signal generator

microphones

oscilloscope

wavelength

waves line up

6) This means the microphones are now <u>exactly one wavelength apart</u>.
7) Measure the <u>distance between the microphones</u> to find the <u>wavelength</u> (λ).
8) The <u>frequency</u> (f) is whatever you set the <u>signal generator</u> to.
9) Use the formula <u>$v = f\lambda$</u> to find the <u>speed</u> (v) of the <u>sound waves</u> passing through the <u>air</u>.
10) The speed of sound in air is around <u>340 m/s</u>, so check your results <u>roughly agree</u> with this.

Looks like the perfect setup for a karaoke duet...

Make sure you understand each step of that method above — you could be tested on it in the exams.

Q1   A wave has a speed of 0.15 m/s and a wavelength of 7.5 cm. Calculate its frequency.   [3 marks]

Q1 Video Solution

Investigating Waves

So, you know <u>what waves are</u>, now it's time to <u>investigate</u> some in action.

Measure the Speed of Water Ripples Using a Strobe Light

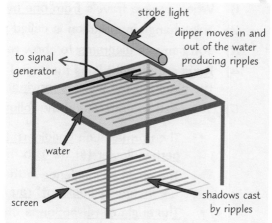

1) Attach a <u>signal generator</u> to the <u>ripple tank dipper</u>.
2) Turn on the signal generator to create <u>waves</u>.
3) Find the <u>frequency</u> of the waves by <u>counting</u> the number of <u>ripples</u> that <u>pass a point</u> in <u>10 seconds</u> and <u>dividing by 10</u>.
4) Use a <u>strobe light</u> (a light that flashes very quickly) to create <u>shadows</u> of the ripples on a screen below the tank.
5) Increase the <u>frequency</u> of the <u>strobe light</u> until the pattern on the screen appears to stop moving.
6) This happens when the frequency of the strobe light <u>matches</u> the frequency of the waves.
7) The distance between each shadow line is equal to <u>one wavelength</u>.
8) The wavelength will be <u>small</u>, so measure it <u>accurately</u> like this:

   • Measure the <u>distance</u> across <u>10 gaps</u> between the shadow lines.
   • <u>Divide</u> this distance <u>by 10</u> to find the <u>average wavelength</u>.

9) Use <u>$v = f\lambda$</u> to calculate the <u>speed</u> of the waves (p.166).
10) The strobe light is <u>suitable</u> as it lets you measure a <u>still pattern</u> instead of a constantly <u>moving</u> one.

Make sure you do this experiment in a darkened room so you can see the shadows of the ripples clearly.

You Can Find the Speed of Waves in Solids Too

1) Hitting a <u>solid object</u>, e.g. a <u>metal rod</u>, with a hammer can cause <u>waves</u> with a <u>range of frequencies</u> to be produced and <u>travel through</u> the solid.
2) These waves can also pass to the air <u>around</u> the object, creating <u>sound waves</u>.
3) These <u>sound waves</u> have the <u>same frequencies</u> as the waves <u>in the solid</u>.
4) You can find the <u>speed of the waves</u> in a <u>solid object</u> by measuring the <u>frequencies</u> of these <u>sound waves</u>.
5) Here's how to calculate the <u>speed</u> of a wave in a <u>metal rod</u>:

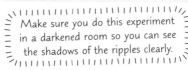

• <u>Measure</u> and <u>record</u> the <u>length</u> of a <u>metal rod</u>.
• <u>Hang</u> the rod from <u>clamps</u> using <u>elastic bands</u>. Make sure one of the elastic bands is holding the rod at its <u>centre</u>.
• <u>Tap</u> the <u>end of the rod</u> with the hammer.
• Measure the '<u>peak frequency</u>' of the sound waves using e.g. a microphone and a computer.
• The <u>peak frequency</u> is the frequency of the <u>loudest sound wave</u>. This sound wave was produced by the <u>peak frequency wave</u> in the <u>rod</u>.
• The <u>peak frequency wave</u> in the rod has a <u>wavelength</u> equal to <u>twice</u> the <u>length of the rod</u>.
• This is <u>always</u> true, which makes the metal rod <u>suitable</u> for investigating <u>wave speeds</u> in solids.
• <u>Repeat</u> this three times to get an <u>average peak frequency</u>.
• Find the <u>wavelength</u> of the <u>wave in the rod</u>, λ. Remember, it's equal to <u>twice the length</u> of the rod.
• Use your values to calculate the <u>speed</u> of the wave using $v = f\lambda$.

My wave speed depends on how tired my arm is...

You can also find the time for one water wave crest to travel a set distance, and use $v = x \div t$ (p.166) to find its speed.

Q1   Describe an experiment to measure the wavelength of a water wave.   [4 marks]

Refraction

Grab a glass of water and put a straw in it. The straw looks like it's <u>bending</u>. But it's not magic, it's refraction.

Refraction is When Waves Change Direction at a Boundary

1) When a wave travels <u>from one material into another</u>, it can <u>change direction</u>.

2) This change in direction is called <u>refraction</u>.

3) You can use <u>diagrams</u> to show refraction.

4) <u>Rays</u> are <u>straight lines</u> that point along the <u>direction the wave is moving</u>.

5) You need to understand the <u>following terms</u> for refraction:

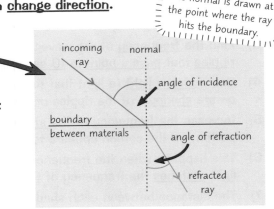

The normal is drawn at the point where the ray hits the boundary.

- The <u>normal</u> is an <u>imaginary line</u> that's <u>perpendicular</u> (at 90°) to the boundary.
- <u>The angle of incidence</u> is the angle between the <u>incoming (incident) ray</u> and the <u>normal</u>.
- <u>The angle of refraction</u> is the angle between the <u>refracted ray</u> and the normal.

6) Whether a wave changes direction depends on the <u>angle</u> at which it hits the <u>boundary</u>.

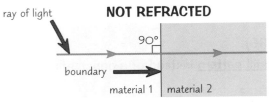

NOT REFRACTED

If a wave hits the boundary at 90° (along the <u>normal</u>), then the wave <u>won't change direction</u>.

REFRACTED

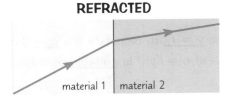

If the wave hits the boundary at any other <u>angle</u>, it <u>will</u> change direction.

7) You can also show <u>refraction</u> using <u>wavefront diagrams</u>.

8) When one part of the wavefront <u>crosses</u> a boundary into a <u>denser</u> material, that part travels <u>slower</u> than the rest of the wavefront, so the wave <u>bends</u>.

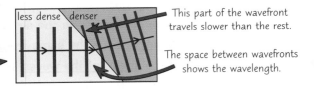

This part of the wavefront travels slower than the rest.

The space between wavefronts shows the wavelength.

How a Wave Refracts Depends on the Materials it Travels Between

<u>How much</u> a wave <u>refracts</u> when passing from one material to another depends on the <u>density</u> of the materials. For example, for <u>light waves</u>:

If a <u>light wave</u> passes into a <u>denser</u> material, it will bend <u>towards the normal</u>.

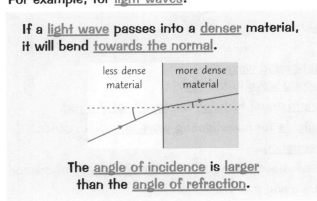

The <u>angle of incidence</u> is <u>larger</u> than the <u>angle of refraction</u>.

But if a <u>light wave</u> passes into a <u>less dense</u> material, it will bend <u>away from the normal</u>.

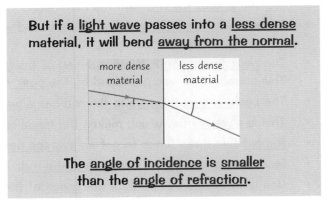

The <u>angle of incidence</u> is <u>smaller</u> than the <u>angle of refraction</u>.

Help, my wave isn't refracting! Well, that's perfectly normal...

Refraction has loads of uses (e.g. in glasses, cameras and telescopes). So make sure you really understand it.

Q1   State what is meant by refraction.   [1 mark]

Investigating Refraction PRACTICAL

Hurrah — it's time to whip out your ray box and get some refraction going on.

You Can Use Rectangular Glass Blocks to Investigate Refraction of Light

1) Before you get started, there are a couple of tips you should keep in mind.
2) This experiment uses a ray of light, so it's best to do it in a dim room.
3) That way you should be able to clearly see the ray.
4) The ray of light must be thin, so you can easily trace it and measure angles from it.
5) You can use a ray box to get a thin ray of light.

When You're Ready to Get Investigating...

1) Place a rectangular glass block on a piece of paper and trace around it.
2) Use a ray box to shine a ray of light at the middle of one side of the block.
3) Trace the ray as it enters and exits the block.

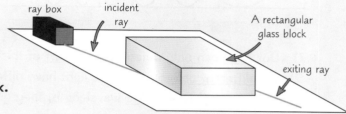

4) Remove the block and join up the incident ray and the exiting ray with a straight line.
5) This shows the path of the refracted ray through the block.
6) Draw the normal at the point where the light ray entered the block.
7) Use a protractor to measure the angle between the incident ray and the normal.
8) This is the angle of incidence, *I*.
9) Then measure the angle between the refracted ray and the normal.
10) This is the angle of refraction, *R*.
11) Do the same for the point where the ray exits the block.
12) Repeat this three times, keeping the angle of incidence as the ray enters the block the same.
13) Calculate an average for each of the angles.

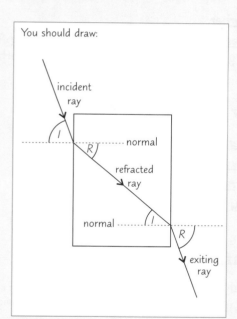

You should draw:

You Should Find that the Ray Refracts as it Enters and Leaves the Block

1) You should see that:
   - The ray of light bends towards the normal as it enters the glass block (see page 168).
   - The ray of light bends away from the normal as it leaves the glass block.
2) Light is an electromagnetic wave (p.170) — so this investigation shows one type of electromagnetic wave being refracted. In fact, all electromagnetic waves can be refracted.

Lights, camera, refraction...

This experiment isn't the trickiest, but you still have to be able to describe how to do it and what it shows.

Q1 Describe an experiment you could do to investigate how much light refracts when it passes through a glass block.

[3 marks]

Electromagnetic Waves

You've learned a lot about light so far, but light's just one small part of the electromagnetic spectrum...

There's a Continuous Spectrum of Electromagnetic Waves

1) Electromagnetic (EM) waves are transverse waves (p.165).
2) They all travel at the same speed through a vacuum (space).
3) We group EM waves into types based on their wavelengths and frequencies.
4) There are seven basic types, but the different groups merge to form a continuous spectrum.
5) This means there are no gaps in the spectrum — one type of EM wave starts where another finishes.

RADIO WAVES	MICRO WAVES	INFRA RED	VISIBLE LIGHT	ULTRA VIOLET	X-RAYS	GAMMA RAYS

long wavelength, low frequency → short wavelength, high frequency

1) Our eyes can only detect a small part of this spectrum — visible light.
2) The different colours of visible light have different wavelengths.
3) From longest to shortest wavelength, they go: red, orange, yellow, green, blue, indigo, violet.

6) All EM waves transfer energy from a source to an absorber.
7) For example, when you warm yourself by an electric heater, infrared waves transfer energy from the thermal energy store of the heater (the source) to your thermal energy store (the absorber).

Electromagnetic Waves are Generated by Changes in Atoms

1) Atoms can change in different ways by absorbing or generating (producing) EM waves.
2) So atoms can generate and absorb a large range of frequencies of EM waves.
3) Changes in the nucleus of an atom can create gamma rays (p.175).
4) An electron can move between energy levels (p.174) by absorbing or emitting an EM wave.

Different EM Waves Have Different Harmful Effects

1) Different EM waves can be absorbed by the human body.
2) If the human body has excessive exposure to EM radiation (a lot of radiation hits the body), it can cause harmful effects.
3) The higher the frequency of the EM wave, the more energy it transfers and the more dangerous it could be.

EM waves are sometimes called EM radiation.

- Some wavelengths of microwaves can be absorbed by the body. This causes cells inside the body to heat up, which may be dangerous.
- Infrared (IR) can be absorbed by the skin, which can cause it to burn.
- Ultraviolet (UV) can cause damage to cells on the surface of your skin. This could lead to skin cancer.
- UV radiation can also damage your eyes and cause a variety of eye conditions.
- X-rays and gamma rays can cause mutations (changes) to cells in the body, which can cause cancer.
- X-ray and gamma rays can also kill cells in the body (see page 179).

Learn about the EM spectrum and wave goodbye to exam woe...

Here's a way to remember the order of EM waves: 'Rock Music Is Very Useful for eXperiments with Goats'.

Q1   State which type of EM radiation is potentially the most dangerous.   [1 mark]

Uses of EM Waves

Different EM waves have <u>different properties</u>, which make them <u>useful</u> to us in <u>different ways</u>.

Radio Waves and Microwaves are Used for Communication

1) <u>Radio waves</u> are used to broadcast (send) <u>TV</u> and radio signals.
2) Radio waves and microwaves are used to communicate with <u>satellites</u>, e.g. for <u>satellite TV</u> and <u>satellite phones</u>.
   - A signal is sent into space to a satellite dish <u>high</u> above the Earth.
   - The satellite <u>sends</u> the signal back to Earth in a different direction.
   - A <u>satellite dish</u> on the ground receives the signal.
3) Microwaves are also used to send signals between <u>mobile phones</u>.

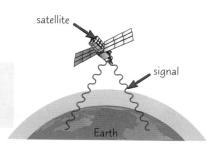

Microwave Ovens Also Use Microwaves

1) <u>Microwave ovens</u> use microwaves to <u>cook food</u>.
2) The oven gives out microwaves, which are <u>absorbed</u> by <u>water</u> in the food.
3) <u>Energy carried</u> by the microwaves is <u>transferred to</u> the water molecules, causing them to heat up.
4) This causes the rest of the <u>food</u> to heat up and quickly <u>cooks</u> it.

Infrared Radiation Can be Used to Increase or Monitor Temperature

1) <u>Infrared</u> (IR) radiation is <u>given out</u> by all <u>hot objects</u>.
2) The <u>hotter</u> the object, the <u>more</u> IR radiation it gives out.
3) <u>Infrared cameras</u> can be used to <u>detect</u> infrared radiation and <u>create a picture</u>. This is called <u>thermal imaging</u>.
4) <u>Thermal imaging</u> is useful for looking at where a house is <u>losing energy</u>.
5) <u>Infrared sensors</u> can be used in <u>security systems</u>.
6) If a change in infrared radiation is detected, an <u>alarm</u> sounds or a <u>security light</u> turns on.
7) <u>Absorbing</u> IR radiation causes objects to get <u>hotter</u>.
8) <u>Food</u> can be <u>cooked</u> by absorbing IR radiation — e.g. toasting bread in a toaster.

Different colours represent different amounts of IR radiation being detected. Here, the redder the colour, the more infrared radiation is being detected.

Infrared Can Also be Used to Transfer Information

1) <u>IR</u> radiation is used for <u>short-range communication</u> (to <u>transfer information</u> over short distances).
2) For example, it can be used to <u>send files</u> between <u>mobile phones</u> or <u>laptops</u>.
3) This is also how <u>TV remote controls</u> work.
4) Infrared radiation can also be used in <u>optical fibres</u> to transfer information over long distances.
5) <u>Optical fibres</u> are thin <u>glass or plastic fibres</u>.
6) They can <u>carry data</u> (e.g. from telephones or computers) as <u>pulses</u> of <u>infrared</u> radiation which <u>bounce along</u> the inside of the fibre.

optical fibre
pulse of infrared radiation

Surfers hate microwaves...

Who knew we used microwaves for more than cooking chips in less than 3 minutes? Turns out, they're dead handy.

Q1   Give three uses of infrared radiation.   [3 marks]

More Uses of EM Waves

Haven't had enough <u>uses of EM waves</u>? Good, because here are a few more for you to learn.

Photography Uses Visible Light

1) <u>Visible light</u> is the light that we can <u>see</u>.
2) We can see objects that are <u>illuminated</u> (lit up) — visible light <u>reflects</u> off them.
3) <u>Cameras</u> create <u>photographs</u> by detecting the visible light bouncing off objects.
4) <u>Photographic film</u> in film cameras <u>reacts</u> to visible light to form an <u>image</u>.
5) <u>Digital cameras</u> contain <u>image sensors</u> instead of film.
6) They also <u>detect visible light</u> and form an image.

Ultraviolet is Used in Fluorescent Lamps

1) Ultraviolet radiation is sometimes used to <u>clean water</u>.
2) Ultraviolet light <u>disinfects</u> (<u>kills bacteria</u> in) the water, making it <u>safe</u> to drink.
3) When some materials <u>absorb UV light</u>, they <u>give out visible light</u>.
4) This is used in <u>fluorescent lamps</u> — they use <u>UV radiation</u> to produce <u>visible light</u>.
5) It's also useful for <u>security markings</u>:

> 1) <u>Security pens</u> can be used to <u>mark</u> property (e.g. laptops).
> 2) Under <u>UV light</u> the ink will <u>glow</u>, but it's <u>invisible</u> otherwise.
> 3) This can help the police find out who <u>stolen property</u> belongs to.
> 4) A similar method is used to detect <u>forged</u> (fake) <u>bank notes</u> and <u>passports</u>.
> 5) Real notes and passports have <u>special markings</u> that only show up under UV light.

X-rays Let Us See Inside Things

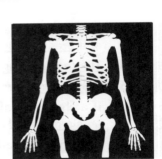

1) <u>X-rays</u> can be used to see the <u>internal structure</u> (the insides) of <u>objects</u> and <u>materials</u>, including our <u>bodies</u>.
2) X-rays pass <u>easily through flesh</u> but not through <u>bones</u> or <u>metal</u>.
3) This can be used to create an <u>X-ray image</u> to check for <u>broken bones</u>.
4) X-rays are also used in <u>airport security scanners</u>.
5) They're used to see hidden objects that can't be detected with <u>metal detectors</u>.

Gamma Rays are Used for Sterilising Things and in Medical Treatment

1) <u>Gamma rays</u> are used to <u>sterilise</u> (remove germs from) <u>medical instruments</u>.
2) The equipment is <u>blasted</u> with <u>gamma rays</u> which <u>kills</u> any <u>living</u> things on it.
3) <u>Food</u> can be <u>sterilised</u> in the same way.
4) Gamma rays are also really good at <u>passing through</u> your body.
5) This is why <u>small</u> amounts of them are used in '<u>medical tracers</u>'.
6) How they <u>move around</u> the body can be tracked, and this can be used to <u>detect cancer</u>.
7) Gamma radiation is also used in <u>cancer treatments</u>.
8) Gamma radiation is targeted at cancer cells to <u>kill them</u>.

Don't lie to an X-ray — they can see right through you...

I hate to say it, but go back over p.171-172 and read all of the uses for EM waves again to really understand them.

Q1   Give two uses of ultraviolet radiation.   [2 marks]

The Atomic Model

We used to think <u>atoms</u> were tiny solid balls (like marbles), but there's <u>much more</u> to it...

You Need to Know the Current Model of the Atom

1) The current model of the atom is a <u>nuclear model</u>.

2) This means there is a <u>nucleus</u> in the <u>centre</u>, surrounded by electrons.

3) The <u>nucleus</u> is <u>tiny</u> compared to the whole atom, but it makes up almost all of the <u>mass</u> of the atom.

4) The radius of the nucleus is about <u>10 000</u> times smaller than the <u>radius</u> of the <u>atom</u>.

5) The <u>nucleus</u> is made up of <u>protons</u> and <u>neutrons</u>.

6) <u>Protons</u> are <u>positively charged</u> and <u>neutrons</u> have <u>no charge</u>. So the <u>nucleus</u> is <u>positively charged</u>.

7) Electrons have a <u>negative charge</u>.

8) They move <u>around</u> (orbit) the nucleus at different fixed distances.

9) These distances are called <u>energy levels</u> (or electron shells) (p.174).

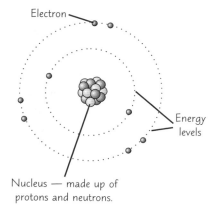

Electron

Energy levels

Nucleus — made up of protons and neutrons.

Atoms have No Overall Charge

1) You need to know the <u>electric charges</u> and <u>masses</u> of <u>protons</u>, <u>neutrons</u> and <u>electrons</u> <u>compared to</u> each other (their <u>relative electric charges</u> and <u>masses</u>).

Particle	Relative Mass	Relative Charge
Proton	1	+1
Neutron	1	0
Electron	0.0005	−1

2) <u>Protons</u> and <u>electrons</u> have an <u>equal</u> but <u>opposite relative charge</u>.

3) In an atom, the <u>number of protons = the number of electrons</u>.

4) So atoms have <u>no overall charge</u> — they are <u>neutral</u>.

Atoms Are Really Tiny

1) The numbers to do with atoms are <u>really tiny</u>, so they're written in <u>standard form</u>.

- <u>Standard form</u> is where you write <u>very big</u> or <u>small</u> numbers (with <u>lots of zeros</u>) as something simpler.
- For example, 0.000017 can be written 1.7×10^{-5}.
- It's always in the form $A \times 10^n$, where <u>A</u> is a number <u>between 1 and 10</u>.
- To do this you just need to <u>move</u> the <u>decimal point</u> left or right <u>until</u> your number is between 1 and 10.
- The <u>number of places</u> the decimal point moves is then the <u>power of 10</u> (n).
- This is <u>positive</u> if the decimal point's moved to the <u>left</u>, and <u>negative</u> if it's moved to the <u>right</u>.

2) The <u>radius</u> of an atom is about <u>1×10^{-10} m</u>.

3) Atoms can <u>join together</u> to form <u>molecules</u>.

4) <u>Small molecules</u> have a typical size of <u>10^{-10} m</u> — the <u>same sort of scale</u> as the size of an atom.

This model doesn't have anything on my miniature trains...

You might be asked about the relative masses and charges of particles in your exam, so make sure you learn them.

Q1   a) Describe how the radius of an atom compares to the size of its nucleus.   [1 mark]

          b) Describe the current model of the atom.   [4 marks]

More on the Atomic Model

There's some <u>weird</u> stuff on this page — but the best part is that you can tell everyone you've been doing a little bit of <u>quantum physics</u> today. Honestly. It's good to show off every now and then.

The Atomic Model Has Changed Over Time

1) Scientists <u>used to think</u> atoms were <u>solid spheres</u>.

2) Then they found that atoms contained <u>even smaller</u> particles — <u>electrons</u>.

3) This led to the <u>'plum pudding' model</u> (see page 78) — the idea that atoms were <u>spheres of positive charge</u> with tiny negative electrons <u>stuck in them</u> like fruit in a plum pudding.

4) Later, in <u>Rutherford's</u> lab, a beam of <u>alpha particles</u> (see p.175) was fired at <u>thin gold foil</u>.

5) Most of the alpha particles <u>passed straight through</u>, but a few <u>bounced back</u>.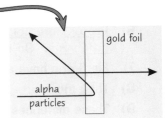

6) These results <u>couldn't be explained</u> by the plum pudding model.

7) Rutherford realised that this meant most of the atom must be <u>empty space</u>, with a <u>small nucleus</u> at the centre.

8) He also realised the nucleus had to be <u>positively charged</u> to <u>repel</u> (push away) the positive alpha particles.

9) Rutherford came up with the <u>first nuclear model</u> of the atom.

10) <u>Niels Bohr</u> later realised that the electrons existed in different <u>energy levels</u> (the <u>Bohr model</u>).

Electrons Can Move Between Energy Levels

1) The <u>further</u> an <u>energy level</u> is from the <u>nucleus</u>, the <u>more energy</u> an electron in that energy level has.

2) <u>Electrons</u> can <u>move between energy levels</u> by <u>absorbing</u> (taking in) or <u>emitting</u> (releasing) <u>electromagnetic radiation</u> (p.170).

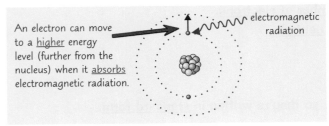

An electron can move to a <u>higher</u> energy level (further from the nucleus) when it <u>absorbs</u> electromagnetic radiation.

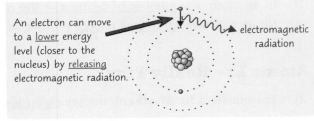

An electron can move to a <u>lower</u> energy level (closer to the nucleus) by <u>releasing</u> electromagnetic radiation.

An Atom that has Lost Electrons is an Ion

1) If an <u>outer electron</u> (an electron in an outer energy level) absorbs radiation with <u>enough energy</u>, it can <u>leave the atom</u>.

2) The atom is now a <u>positive ion</u>.

3) It's <u>positive</u> because there are now <u>more protons</u> than <u>electrons</u>.

I can't see anything — are you positive you've lost one?

Ions — good for getting creases out of your clothes...

So electrons absorb EM radiation to move up energy levels and emit EM radiation to move down energy levels.

Q1   What is a positive ion and how is one formed?   [2 marks]

Isotopes and Nuclear Radiation

Isotopes and ionising. They sound similar, but they're totally different, so read this page carefully.

Isotopes are Different Forms of the Same Element

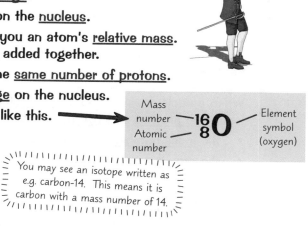

$^{14}_{7}N$

1) The number of protons in an atom is called its atomic number (or proton number).
2) The protons in a nucleus give the nucleus its positive charge.
3) So the atomic number of an atom tells you the charge on the nucleus.
4) The mass number (or nucleon number) of an atom tells you an atom's relative mass. It is the number of protons and the number of neutrons added together.
5) An element is a substance only containing atoms with the same number of protons.
6) So all atoms of an element have the same positive charge on the nucleus.
7) You can show information about an atom of an element like this.

Mass number — $^{16}_{8}O$ ← Element symbol (oxygen)
Atomic number

8) Atoms with the same number of protons but a different number of neutrons are called isotopes of an element.
9) Isotopes of an element have the same atomic number, but a different mass number (and so mass).

You may see an isotope written as e.g. carbon-14. This means it is carbon with a mass number of 14.

Some Isotopes are Unstable

1) Unstable isotopes emit (give out) radiation from their nuclei to become more stable.
2) This random process is called radioactive decay.
3) The radiation emitted is called nuclear radiation. There are five different types of nuclear radiation:

Nuclei means more than one nucleus.

- An alpha particle (α) is two neutrons and two protons (like a helium nucleus).
- A beta-minus particle (β^-) is a fast-moving electron.
- A beta-plus particle (β^+) is a fast-moving positron. Positrons are the same as electrons, but with a positive (+1) charge.
- Gamma rays (γ) are waves of electromagnetic radiation (p.170).
- Neutrons (n).

You Need to Know the Properties of Ionising Nuclear Radiation

1) Ionising radiation is radiation that can knock electrons off atoms and turn them into ions (p.174).
2) The ionising power of radiation is how easily it can do this.
3) Alpha particles, beta particles and gamma rays are all types of ionising radiation.
4) They all have different properties that you need to learn:

Type of radiation	Ionising power	Range in air	Stopped by
alpha particles	strong	a few centimetres	a thin sheet of paper
beta particles	moderate	a few metres	a thin sheet of aluminium
gamma rays	weak	a long distance	thick sheets of lead or metres of concrete

'Range in air' is the distance the radiation can travel through air.

Isotopes of an outfit — same dress, different accessories...

Knowing different kinds of radiation and what can absorb them could bag you a few easy marks in an exam.

Q1   Give an example of a material that could be used to absorb: a) alpha particles,   b) beta-minus particles Refer to the material's thickness in your answers.   [2 marks]

Nuclear Equations

Nuclear equations show radioactive decay and once you get the hang of them they're dead easy. Get going.

Mass and Atomic Numbers Have to Balance

1) Nuclear equations are a way of showing radioactive decay by using element symbols (p.175).
2) They're written in the form: atom before decay → atom after decay + radiation emitted.
3) There is one golden rule to remember: the total mass and atomic numbers must be equal on both sides.
4) Mass number is the mass of the nucleus, and atomic number is the charge, so you can work out what happens to mass and charge too.

Alpha decay

When a nucleus emits an alpha particle, it loses two protons and two neutrons, so:

- the mass number decreases by 4.
- the atomic number decreases by 2.

$$^{226}_{88}\text{Ra} \rightarrow {}^{222}_{86}\text{Rn} + {}^{4}_{2}\alpha$$

mass number:	226	→	222 + 4 (= 226)
atomic number:	88	→	86 + 2 (= 88)

Beta-minus decay

In a beta-minus decay, a neutron changes into a proton and an electron, so:

- the mass number doesn't change — as it has lost a neutron but gained a proton.
- the atomic number increases by 1 — because it has one more proton.

$$^{14}_{6}\text{C} \rightarrow {}^{14}_{7}\text{N} + {}^{0}_{-1}\beta^{-}$$

mass number:	14	→	14 + 0 (= 14)
atomic number:	6	→	7 + (−1) (= 6)

Beta particles are sometimes written as an 'e'.

Beta-plus decay

In beta-plus decay, a proton changes into a neutron and a positron, so:

- the mass number doesn't change — as it has lost a proton but gained a neutron.
- the atomic number decreases by 1 — because it has one less proton.

$$^{18}_{9}\text{F} \rightarrow {}^{18}_{8}\text{O} + {}^{0}_{1}\beta^{+}$$

mass number:	18	→	18 + 0 (= 18)
atomic number:	9	→	8 + 1 (= 9)

Neutron emission

When a nucleus emits a neutron:

- the mass number decreases by 1 — as it has lost a neutron.
- the atomic number stays the same.

$$^{13}_{4}\text{Be} \rightarrow {}^{12}_{4}\text{Be} + {}^{1}_{0}\text{n}$$

mass number:	13	→	12 + 1 (= 13)
atomic number:	4	→	4 + 0 (= 4)

Gamma ray emission

After decaying, the nucleus can have excess energy, which it can remove by emitting EM radiation. It becomes more stable by rearranging its particles (nuclear rearrangement) and emitting a gamma ray.

When a nucleus emits a gamma ray:

- the mass number stays the same.
- the atomic number stays the same.

$$^{131}_{53}\text{I} \rightarrow {}^{131}_{53}\text{I} + {}^{0}_{0}\gamma$$

mass number:	131	→	131 + 0 (= 131)
atomic number:	53	→	53 + 0 (= 53)

Keep balanced during revision and practise nuclear equations...

Nuclear equations are simple, but that doesn't mean you shouldn't practise them — try these questions.

Q1 Write the nuclear equation for $^{219}_{86}$Rn forming polonium (Po) by alpha decay. [3 marks]

Q1 Video Solution

Background Radiation and Activity

Forget love — <u>radiation</u> is <u>all around</u>. Don't panic too much though, it's usually a pretty <u>small amount</u>.

Background Radiation Comes From Many Sources

1) <u>Background radiation</u> is the <u>low-level</u> radiation that's around us <u>all the time</u>.

2) It comes from:

- Radioactive isotopes that are formed <u>naturally</u>. They can be found in the <u>air</u>, <u>some foods</u>, <u>building materials</u> and some of the <u>rocks</u> under our feet.
- Radiation from <u>space</u>, known as <u>cosmic rays</u>. These come mostly from the <u>Sun</u>.
- Radiation due to <u>human activity</u>, e.g. from <u>nuclear explosions</u> or <u>nuclear waste</u>. But this is only a <u>tiny</u> part of the total background radiation.

The Activity of a Source is the Number of Decays per Second

1) The <u>rate</u> at which a radioactive source decays is called its <u>ACTIVITY</u>.

2) Activity is measured in <u>becquerels</u>, <u>Bq</u>.

3) 1 Bq is <u>1 decay per second</u>.

4) Each time a radioactive nucleus <u>decays</u> and becomes stable, one more radioactive nucleus <u>disappears</u>.

5) As the <u>unstable nuclei</u> all steadily disappear, the activity <u>as a whole</u> will <u>decrease</u>.

It's Hard to Measure Activity Directly

1) To <u>detect radiation</u>, you can either use <u>photographic film</u> or a <u>Geiger-Müller tube</u>.

2) Photographic film gets <u>darker</u> as <u>more</u> radiation hits it.

3) A <u>Geiger-Müller tube</u> can be used to <u>measure</u> the <u>count rate</u>.

4) The tube <u>clicks</u> each time it detects radiation (each <u>click</u> is <u>one count</u>).

5) The tube can be attached to a <u>counter</u>, which displays the number of clicks <u>per second</u> (the <u>count rate</u>).

6) <u>Count rate</u> and <u>activity</u> change in the <u>same way over time</u> (p.178).

7) It's really <u>difficult</u> to <u>measure activity</u> directly.

8) So <u>measuring</u> the <u>count rate</u> over time is a good way of seeing how the activity of a source <u>changes over time</u>.

Counter

Source

Geiger-Müller tube

- When investigating count rate, remember that a <u>Geiger-Müller tube</u> will detect <u>all</u> radiation that reaches the tube, including <u>background radiation</u>.
- So you need to measure the <u>background radiation</u> before you start.
- And then <u>subtract</u> the <u>background count rate</u> from any measurements of the <u>count rate</u> for the <u>source</u>.

Background radiation — the ugly wallpaper of the Universe...

Remember, any reading you take of the activity of a sample will include the background radiation. You need to measure the background radiation separately, and then take it away from your results.

Q1   Give two sources of background radiation.   [2 marks]

Half-Life

How quickly unstable nuclei decay is measured using half-life.

Radioactivity is a Totally Random Process

1) Radioactive decay is entirely random.

2) You can't predict exactly which nucleus in a sample will decay next, or when any one of them will decay.

3) But, if you've got a large number of nuclei, you can predict how long it will take for half of the nuclei to decay.

4) This is known as the half-life.

> The half-life is the time taken for the number of nuclei of a radioactive isotope in a sample to halve.

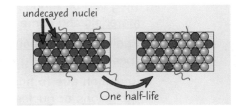

undecayed nuclei

One half-life

5) Half-life is also the time taken for the count rate or activity of a sample to fall to half of its initial (starting) value.

6) The half-life of a radioactive sample will always be the same.

7) This means it doesn't matter what activity you start with when doing half-life calculations (see below).

8) You can simulate radioactive decay by rolling lots of dice and removing all the dice showing a 6 after each roll.

9) The number of dice will decrease in a similar way to the undecayed nuclei in radioactive decay.

10) Since the process is random, the more dice you use and the more throws you do, the better your results will be.

You Need to be able to Calculate Half-Lives

1) You may be given some numbers or a graph and asked to calculate the half-life of a source.

2) You just need to find out how long it takes for the activity or count rate of the source to halve.

EXAMPLE

The activity of a radioactive source over time is shown on the graph on the right. Using the graph find the half-life of the source.

1) The initial activity when time = 0 s is 800 Bq.

2) Use the graph to find the time when the activity has halved to 400 Bq. This was at $t = 2$ s.

3) So, the half-life is 2 s.

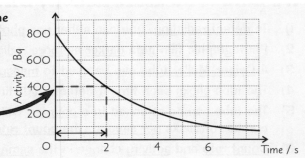

EXAMPLE

The activity of a radioactive isotope was measured. Initially it was 64 Bq. 12 seconds later it had fallen to 16 Bq. Calculate the half-life of the sample.

1) First, find how many half-lives it takes for the activity to fall from 64 Bq to 16 Bq.

   After one half life, the activity will be 64 ÷ 2 = 32 Bq
   After two half lives, the activity will be 32 ÷ 2 = 16 Bq

2) So you know 12 s is equal to two half lives. Divide 12 by 2 to find the time for one half life.

   Time for one half life = 12 ÷ 2 = 6 s

The half-life of a box of chocolates is about five minutes...

Half-life — the time for the number of undecayed nuclei or the activity to halve. Simple.

Q1   The activity of a radioactive source halves in 15 minutes.
     How long will it take for the activity to halve again?   [1 mark]

Q2   The initial activity of a sample is 168 Bq. After 60 minutes, the
     activity of the sample is 21 Bq. Calculate the half-life of the sample.   [3 marks]

Q2 Video Solution

Irradiation and Contamination

There are <u>risks</u> when working with radiation. Make sure you know how to <u>reduce them</u>.

Exposure to Radiation is called Irradiation

1) Objects <u>near</u> a radioactive source are <u>irradiated</u> by it.
2) This means <u>radiation</u> from the <u>source</u> is reaching the object.
3) We're <u>always</u> being irradiated by <u>background radiation</u> sources (see p.177).
4) Irradiated objects <u>don't become radioactive</u> themselves.
5) The <u>further</u> you are from a particular source, the <u>less radiation</u> will <u>reach</u> you.
6) To help <u>stop irradiation</u> happening, you should:

- <u>Store</u> radioactive sources in <u>lead-lined boxes</u> when they're not being used.
- Stand behind <u>barriers</u> that will absorb radiation when using sources.
- Keep the source as <u>far away</u> from you as possible, e.g. hold it at arm's length.

7) <u>Medical</u> staff who work with radiation also wear <u>photographic film badges</u> to <u>keep track</u> of their exposure.
8) <u>Shielding</u> (that blocks radiation) is used to protect <u>medical staff</u> and <u>untreated</u> body parts of patients.

Warning: You won't become a superhero from being irradiated.

Contamination is Radioactive Particles Getting onto Objects

1) If <u>unwanted radioactive atoms</u> get onto or into an object, the object is <u>contaminated</u>.
2) These <u>contaminating atoms</u> might then decay, releasing <u>radiation</u> which could cause you <u>harm</u>.
3) Contamination is especially dangerous because radioactive particles could get <u>inside your body</u>.
4) Once a person is <u>contaminated</u>, they are at <u>risk of harm</u> until either the contamination is <u>removed</u> (which isn't always possible) or <u>all</u> the radioactive atoms have <u>decayed</u>.
5) Here are some ways to help <u>prevent</u> contamination happening:

- <u>Wear gloves</u> and use <u>tongs</u> when handling sources, to avoid particles getting stuck to your <u>skin</u> or <u>under your nails</u>.
- Some industrial workers wear <u>protective suits</u> to stop them <u>breathing in</u> radioactive particles.

Radiation Damages Cells by Ionisation

1) Radiation can <u>enter living cells</u> and <u>ionise atoms and molecules</u> within them.
2) This can cause <u>tissue damage</u> (damage to the <u>skin</u> or <u>internal organs</u>).
3) <u>Lower doses</u> tend to cause <u>minor damage</u> without <u>killing</u> the cells.
4) This can cause <u>cells</u> to <u>mutate</u> and <u>divide uncontrollably</u>. This is <u>cancer</u>.
5) <u>Higher doses</u> tend to <u>kill cells completely</u>, which can cause <u>radiation sickness</u>.
6) This is why hospitals try to <u>limit</u> staff and patients' radiation dose (the amount of radiation they're <u>exposed</u> to).
7) <u>Beta</u> and <u>gamma</u> radiation are the most dangerous to be <u>irradiated</u> by, because they can <u>get through</u> the body to the internal <u>organs</u>.
8) Alpha is <u>less</u> dangerous to be <u>irradiated</u> by, because it <u>can't get through the skin</u>.
9) <u>Alpha</u> sources are the <u>most</u> dangerous to be <u>contaminated</u> by.
10) Alpha particles are <u>strongly ionising</u>, but don't travel very far, so they do a lot of damage in the <u>area around the source</u>.

Top tip number 364 — if something is radioactive, don't lick it...

Make sure you can describe how to prevent irradiation and contamination, and why it's so important that you do.

Q1   Give two effects that ionising radiation can have on living cells.   [2 marks]

Revision Questions for Sections 19 and 20

And that's <u>Section 20</u> over and done with — time to celebrate with some fun revision questions (woo...).

For even more practice, try the Retrieval Quizzes for Sections 19 and 20 — just scan the QR codes!

- Try these questions and <u>tick off each one</u> when you <u>get it right</u>.
- When you're <u>completely happy</u> with a sub-topic, tick it off.

Section 19 Quiz

Wave Properties (p.165-169) ☑

1) Explain why a rubber duck will not be carried to the edge of a bath by ripples in the water.
2) Describe the difference between transverse and longitudinal waves and give an example of each kind.
3) What is the amplitude, wavelength, frequency and period of a wave?
4) Give the equation relating the speed of a wave, its wavelength and its frequency.
5) Describe an experiment you could do to measure the velocity of sound in air.
6) Describe an experiment you could do to measure the speed of sound in a solid metal rod.
7) True or false? If a wave hits a boundary between two materials at 90° to the boundary, it won't change direction.
8) True or false? All electromagnetic waves can be refracted at a boundary between two materials.

Uses and Dangers of Electromagnetic Waves (p.170-172) ☐

9) True or false? All electromagnetic waves are transverse.
10) Which has a higher frequency, X-rays or infrared radiation?
11) Give one possible danger of: a) ultraviolet radiation   b) X-rays and gamma rays.
12) Give one use of radio waves.
13) What type of electromagnetic radiation is used in thermal imaging cameras?
14) Give two uses of gamma rays.

Atoms (p.173-174) ☐

15) Give the relative mass of: a) a proton,   b) a neutron,   c) an electron
16) True or false? Atoms are neutral.
17) What is the typical radius of an atom?
18) Briefly explain how the model of the atom has changed over time.
19) What happens to an electron in an atom if it releases EM radiation?

Section 20 Quiz

Radioactivity (p.175-179) ☑

20) What is the atomic number of an atom?
21) What is an isotope?
22) Name five things that may be emitted during radioactive decay.
23) For the four types of ionising radiation, compare: a) their ionising power,   b) their range in air.
24) Describe how the mass and atomic numbers of an atom change if it emits an alpha particle.
25) In what type of nuclear decay does a neutron change into a proton within the nucleus?
26) What type of nuclear decay doesn't change the mass or charge of the nucleus?
27) What is background radiation?
28) What is the activity of a radioactive source? What are its units?
29) Describe how to measure the activity of a radioactive source.
30) Define half-life.
31) Give two ways that contamination can be prevented.

Energy Transfers and Systems

You saw <u>energy</u> and <u>forces</u> stuff on p.145-160 — it's time to learn a bit more about it in this section. Super.

Energy is Transferred Between These Stores

1) <u>Kinetic</u> energy stores (KE $= \frac{1}{2}mv^2$, p.158)
2) <u>Thermal</u> energy stores
3) <u>Chemical</u> energy stores
4) <u>Gravitational potential</u> energy stores (ΔGPE $= mg\Delta h$, p.158)

5) <u>Elastic potential</u> energy stores
6) <u>Electrostatic</u> energy stores
7) <u>Magnetic</u> energy stores
8) <u>Nuclear</u> energy stores

Energy can be transferred between stores <u>mechanically</u>, <u>electrically</u>, by <u>heating</u> or by <u>radiation</u>.

When a System Changes, Energy is Transferred

1) A <u>system</u> is just what you are interested in.
2) It can be a <u>single</u> object (e.g. the air in a balloon) or a <u>group</u> of <u>objects</u> (e.g. two colliding vehicles).
3) When a system <u>changes</u>, <u>energy is transferred</u> between energy stores. For example...

<u>Energy transferred by forces doing work</u>
1) A box is <u>lifted</u> up off the floor.
2) The <u>box</u> is the system.
3) As the box is lifted, <u>work</u> is done (see next page) <u>against gravity</u>.
4) So energy is <u>transferred</u> to the box's <u>kinetic</u> and <u>gravitational potential energy stores</u>.

<u>Energy transferred by electrical equipment</u>
1) An <u>electrical iron</u> is plugged into the mains.
2) The <u>system</u> is the mains power supply and the iron.
3) Energy is transferred <u>electrically</u> from the mains power supply to the <u>thermal</u> energy store of the iron's metal plate.

<u>Energy transferred by heating</u>
1) A pan of water is <u>heated</u> on a gas camping stove.
2) The <u>system</u> is the <u>camping stove</u> and the <u>pan of water</u>.
3) Energy is <u>transferred</u> from the <u>chemical energy store</u> of the gas to the <u>thermal energy</u> stores of the pan and the water.

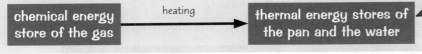

This is an example of how to show energy transfers with a diagram. There's more on these on page 157.

4) A <u>closed</u> system is a system that <u>no energy</u> can be transferred <u>in or out</u> of (see p.156).
5) So whatever changes happen in the system, there is <u>no net (overall) change</u> to its <u>total energy</u>.

Energy is not Always Transferred Usefully

1) Whenever a system <u>changes</u>, energy is always <u>dissipated</u>.
2) <u>Dissipated</u> just means that the energy is spread out and stored in <u>less useful</u> ways.
3) Unless in a closed system, the energy is usually dissipated to the <u>thermal energy stores</u> of the <u>surroundings</u>. For example:

- An <u>electric toothbrush</u> is a system.
- It transfers energy <u>electrically</u> from the <u>chemical</u> energy store of the <u>battery</u> to the <u>kinetic</u> energy store of the brush.
- Some of this energy is transferred to the <u>surroundings</u> by <u>sound</u> and by <u>heating</u>.

All this work, I can feel my energy stores being drained...

Make sure you learn the different stores that energy can be in, and the different ways it can be transferred.

Q1   Name the four ways that energy can be transferred between stores.   [4 marks]

Forces and Work Done

Forces make the world go round, so it seems like a good idea to learn about them. Time to get started.

Objects can Interact Through Contact and Non-Contact Forces

1) A <u>force</u> is a <u>push</u> or a <u>pull</u> on an object. It is caused by the object <u>interacting</u> with something.

2) A force is a <u>vector</u> (see p.145).

Scalar quantities only have a size (like speed and distance).

3) This means it has both a <u>size</u> and a <u>direction</u> (like velocity and displacement).

4) Objects need to be <u>touching</u> for some types of forces to act. These are <u>contact forces</u>.

5) Examples of contact forces include:
   - <u>Normal contact forces</u> — acts between <u>all</u> touching objects. E.g. an <u>apple</u> sitting on a desk.
   - <u>Friction</u> — e.g. between a car's <u>tyres</u> and the <u>road</u>.

normal contact force
weight

6) Other forces can act between objects that <u>aren't touching</u> (<u>non-contact forces</u>).

7) Examples of non-contact forces include:
   - <u>Gravitational force</u> — attraction between <u>objects</u> (i.e the Sun and the Earth). This is because both objects have <u>gravitational fields</u> that <u>interact</u> with each other.
   - <u>Electrostatic force</u> — attraction or repulsion between <u>electrical charges</u>. The <u>electric fields</u> of each charged object <u>interact</u> with each other.
   - <u>Magnetic force</u> — attraction or repulsion between <u>magnetic objects</u>. Their <u>magnetic fields interact</u> with each other.

8) Whenever two objects <u>interact</u>, both objects feel an equal but opposite <u>force</u> (Newton's 3rd Law, see p.153).

9) You can represent (show) this pair of forces with a pair of <u>vectors</u> (<u>arrows</u>).

The man <u>leans</u> on the wall. The <u>normal contact force</u> from the wall pushes back on him with the <u>same</u> force. This makes a <u>pair</u> of forces.

If A Force Moves An Object, Work is Done

1) To make something <u>move</u>, some sort of <u>force</u> needs to act on it.

2) The force does '<u>work</u>' to <u>move</u> the object.

3) <u>Energy</u> is <u>transferred mechanically</u> from one store to another (p.156).

> When a <u>force</u> moves an object through a <u>distance</u>, <u>WORK IS DONE</u> on the object and <u>ENERGY IS TRANSFERRED</u>.

4) You can <u>measure</u> how much <u>work</u> a force does by measuring <u>how far</u> it moves an object.

5) To calculate <u>how much</u> work has been done, you can use:

Distance moved in the direction of the force (m)

$$E = F \times d$$

Work done (J)   Force (N)

6) <u>Work done</u> is measured in J (joules) or Nm (newton metres). 1 J = 1 Nm.

> **EXAMPLE**   Find the work done when a tyre is dragged 1.2 m along the ground with a force of 70 N.
> work done = force × distance = 70 × 1.2 = 84 J

7) Work done is the <u>same as</u> energy transferred — they're both measured in joules (J).

8) So in the example above, <u>84 J</u> of <u>work is done</u> on the tyre, which means <u>84 J</u> of <u>energy is transferred</u>.

I won't force you to do this page... See what I did there? Ho ho...

But by getting more *work done*, you'll *transfer* more knowledge in the exams. Sorry, I just can't stop myself.

Q1   A constant force of 20 N pushes an object 20 cm. Calculate the work done on the object.   [2 marks]

Q1 Video Solution

Wasted Energy and Power

You met <u>efficiency</u> on page 159. This page will tell you about efficiency of <u>mechanical processes</u>. How exciting.

No Mechanical Process is 100% Efficient

I am 90% efficient at destroying humans, 10% efficient at being a radiator.

1) A <u>mechanical process</u> is one in which <u>work is done by a force</u>.
2) Energy can be <u>wasted</u> by mechanical processes transferring energy to the <u>thermal energy stores</u> of objects, which <u>raises</u> their <u>temperature</u>.
3) This energy is then transferred from the objects <u>by heating</u> to the <u>surroundings</u>. For example:

- When you push something along a <u>rough surface</u> you are doing work <u>against frictional forces</u>.
- Energy is being <u>transferred</u> to the <u>kinetic energy store</u> of the <u>object</u>.
- Some energy is also being transferred to the <u>thermal energy store</u> of the object due to friction.
- This causes the overall <u>temperature</u> of the object to <u>increase</u>.
- The energy is then <u>dissipated</u> to the surroundings. So, the surroundings <u>heat up</u>.
- This mechanical process is said to be '<u>wasteful</u>'.

4) You can <u>show</u> how much energy is <u>wasted</u> using a <u>diagram</u> as shown on p.160.
5) You also saw on p.159 that you can <u>calculate</u> the efficiency of an <u>energy transfer</u> using:

$$\text{efficiency} = \frac{\text{useful energy transferred by the device}}{\text{total energy supplied to the device}}$$

EXAMPLE

50 000 J of energy is transferred to a chainsaw. 45 000 J of work is done by the chainsaw. Calculate the efficiency of the chainsaw.

$$\text{efficiency} = \frac{\text{useful energy transferred by the device}}{\text{total energy supplied to the device}} = \frac{45\,000}{50\,000} = 0.9 \text{ (or 90\%)}$$

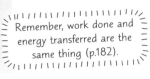

Remember, work done and energy transferred are the same thing (p.182).

6) You can reduce the energy wasted in a <u>mechanical process</u> by <u>lubricating</u> moving parts (see p.160).

Power is How Much Work is Done Every Second

1) <u>Power</u> is the <u>RATE OF ENERGY TRANSFER</u>.
2) Another way of describing power is the amount of <u>work</u> being done <u>every second</u>.
3) The unit of power is the <u>watt</u> (<u>W</u>). <u>1 W = 1 J/s</u> (joules per second).
4) For example, an <u>electric heater</u> with a power of <u>600 W</u> will transfer <u>600 J</u> of energy <u>every second</u>.
5) This is the <u>formula</u> for power:

$$\text{power (W)} = \frac{\text{work done (J)}}{\text{time taken (s)}} \quad \text{or} \quad P = \frac{E}{t}$$

EXAMPLE

A motor does 4800 J of work in 120 s. Find its power output.

<u>Substitute</u> the values into the power equation. $P = E \div t = 4800 \div 120 = 40 \text{ W}$

Watt's power? Power's watts...

Make sure you're happy using the equations on this page before you move on.

Q1   A battery is used to power a 40 W light bulb. The light is turned on for 15 minutes. Calculate how much energy the bulb will transfer in this time.   [3 marks]

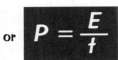

Q1 Video Solution

Current and Circuits

If the word <u>current</u> makes you think of delicious cakes instead of physics, you best get on with this page.

Circuit Symbols You Should Know

The parts in a circuit e.g. bulbs, resistors, etc. are called 'components'.

1) You need to be able to use these symbols to <u>understand</u> and <u>draw circuit diagrams</u>.

2) You may need to use circuit diagrams to <u>build circuits</u> in the lab.

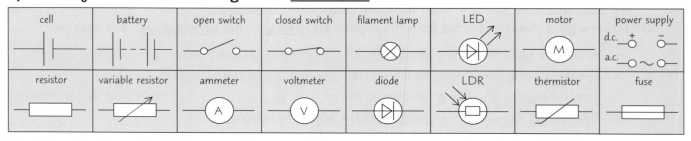

cell	battery	open switch	closed switch	filament lamp	LED	motor	power supply d.c. a.c.
resistor	variable resistor	ammeter	voltmeter	diode	LDR	thermistor	fuse

3) When drawing a circuit diagram make sure all the <u>wires</u> in your circuit are made up of <u>straight</u> lines.

4) Make sure the circuit you draw is <u>closed</u> so you can follow a wire around the <u>entire circuit</u> with no gaps.

Current is the Flow of Electrical Charge

You need to know about the structure of the atom. Turn to page 173 for more.

1) <u>All</u> objects are made of <u>atoms</u>.
Atoms are made up of <u>protons</u>, <u>neutrons</u> and <u>electrons</u>.

2) <u>Electrical current</u> is the <u>flow</u> of electrical charge around a circuit.
Current is measured in <u>amperes</u> (**A**).

3) In <u>metals</u>, current is the flow of <u>electrons</u>.

4) For a current to flow, the circuit must be closed <u>and</u> contain something providing a <u>potential difference</u>, e.g. a battery.

5) <u>Batteries</u> and <u>cells</u> each have a <u>positive</u> and <u>negative terminal</u>.
You draw <u>current</u> flowing from the <u>positive</u> to the <u>negative</u> terminal (see diagram).

6) <u>Potential difference</u> is the '<u>driving force</u>' that <u>pushes</u> the charge round. It is measured in <u>volts</u> (**V**).

7) Generally, the <u>higher</u> the potential difference across a component, the <u>higher</u> the current through it will be.

8) <u>Resistance</u> is anything that <u>slows the flow of charge</u> down. It is measured in <u>ohms</u> (Ω).
The <u>greater the resistance</u> of a component, the <u>smaller the current</u> that flows through it.

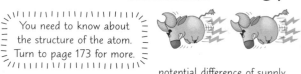

potential difference of supply provides the 'push'

current flows from positive to negative

resistance opposes the flow

Total Charge Through a Circuit Depends on Current and Time

1) The <u>size</u> of the <u>current</u> tells you <u>how fast</u> the charge is <u>flowing</u> (the <u>rate of flow</u> of charge).

2) <u>Charge</u>, <u>current</u> and <u>time</u> are related by this handy <u>equation</u>:

Charge in coulombs (C) — $Q = I \times t$ — Time in seconds (s)

Current in amps (A)

$$\frac{Q}{I \times t}$$

A higher current means more charge passes around the circuit in a given time.

EXAMPLE   A battery charger passes a current of 2 A through a cell over a period of 300 seconds. How much charge is transferred to the cell?

<u>Substitute</u> the values into the equation above. $Q = I \times t = 2 \times 300 = 600$ C

I think it's about time you took charge...

Electrons in circuits actually move from –ve to +ve, but it's conventional to draw current flowing from +ve to –ve. It's what early physicists thought (before they found out about the electrons), and it's stuck.

Q1   A laptop charger passes a current of 8 A through a laptop battery.
Calculate, in minutes, how long the charger needs to be connected
to the battery for 28 800 C of charge to be transferred.

[4 marks]

Q1 Video Solution

Potential Difference and Resistance

As a current flows round a circuit, the charges transfer energy as they struggle against resistance.

Potential Difference is Energy Transferred per Unit Charge Passed

1) The energy transferred to an electrical component depends on the potential difference across it and the charge flowing through it. Here's the formula for it:

Energy transferred in joules (J)

Charge moved in coulombs (C)

$$E = Q \times V$$

Potential difference in volts (V)

Potential difference is sometimes called voltage. They're the same thing.

2) So, the potential difference (p.d.) across a component is the amount of energy transferred to that component per unit charge passed. One volt is one joule per coulomb.

3) For example, an electric motor with a potential difference of 9 V transfers 9 J of energy per coulomb.

There's a Formula Linking Potential Difference, Resistance and Current

1) The current flowing through a component depends on the potential difference across it and the resistance of the component.

2) The formula linking potential difference (p.d.), current and resistance is:

Potential difference in volts (V)

$$V = I \times R$$

Resistance in ohms (Ω)

Current in amps (A)

$$\frac{V}{I \times R}$$

EXAMPLE A 4.0 Ω resistor in a circuit has a potential difference of 6.0 V across it. What is the current through the resistor?

1) Cover the *I* in the formula triangle to find that $I = V \div R$.

$I = V \div R$

2) Substitute in the values you have, and work out the current.

$I = 6.0 \div 4.0 = 1.5$ A

Resistance Increases with Temperature (Usually)

1) When charge flows through a component, it has to do work against resistance — energy is transferred to the component.

2) Some of this energy is transferred to the thermal energy store of the component and then dissipated to the thermal energy store of the surroundings.

3) So when a current flows through a resistor, the resistor heats up. Here's how it works:

Being in a lattice just means that the ions are laid out in a regular (ordered) way.

• Electrons have to do work to pass through the lattice of ions (p.85) that make up a component.

• The electrons collide with (bump into) the ions and transfer energy to their kinetic energy stores.

• This means the ions vibrate more and the component heats up (see p.200).

• The more the ions vibrate, the harder it is for electrons to get through the resistor (because there are more collisions), so the higher the resistance of the component.

4) There is one special case — the resistance of a thermistor decreases as it gets hotter (p.187).

In the end you'll have to learn this — resisting is pointless...

$V = I \times R$ is one of the most useful equations in electricity — it crops up in loads of places, so learn it.

Q1   An appliance is connected to a 230 V source.
      Calculate the resistance of the appliance if a current of 5.0 A is flowing through it. [3 marks]

Q1 Video Solution

I-V Graphs

Ooh experiments, you've gotta love 'em. Here's an experiment for investigating different components.

I-V Graphs Show How Current Changes With P.d.

1) *I-V* graphs show how the current (*I*) flowing through a component changes as the potential difference (*V*) across it changes.

2) Components with straight line *I-V* graphs are called linear components (e.g. a fixed resistor).

3) Components with curved *I-V* graphs are non-linear components (e.g. a filament lamp or a diode).

4) To find the resistance at any point on a *I-V* graph, first read off the values of *I* and *V* at that point. Then use $R = V \div I$ (from $V = I \times R$ on page 185).

You Can Investigate How Current Changes with P.d.

PRACTICAL

You should do this experiment for different components, including a filament lamp, a diode and a fixed resistor (a resistor with a fixed resistance at a constant temperature).

1) Set up the test circuit shown on the right.

2) The variable resistor is used to change the current in the circuit.

3) As $I = V \div R$, increasing the resistance lowers the current through the circuit at a fixed supply p.d.. This changes the potential difference across the component.

4) Now you need to get sets of current and potential difference readings:
   - Set the resistance of the variable resistor.
   - Measure the current through and potential difference across the component.
   - Take measurements at a number of different resistances.

5) Swap over the wires connected to the battery to reverse the direction of the current. The ammeter should now display negative readings.

6) Repeat step 4 to get results for negative values of current.

7) Plot a graph with current on the *y*-axis and potential difference on the *x*-axis.

8) Here are the *I-V* graphs that you should get for different components:

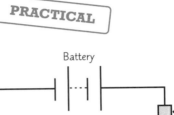
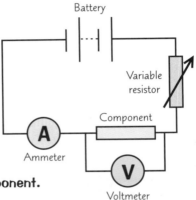
Battery

Variable resistor

Component

A — Ammeter

V — Voltmeter

This type of circuit uses direct current (d.c.) (p.192) and is a series circuit (p.188).

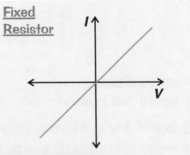

Fixed Resistor
1) Current is directly proportional to potential difference.
2) So you get a straight line.
3) This is because the resistance is constant.

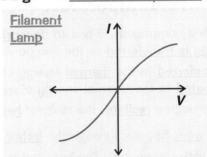

Filament Lamp
1) Temperature increases as current increases.
2) So resistance increases.
3) This makes it harder for current to flow.
4) So the graph gets less steep.

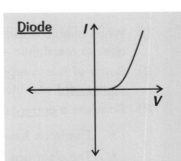

Diode
1) Current only flows in one direction.
2) The diode has very high resistance in the reverse direction.

Measure gymnastics — use a vaultmeter...

Make sure you can describe the experiment above — remember, ammeters in series, voltmeters in parallel.

Q1   Draw a circuit you could use to create an *I-V* graph for a filament lamp.   [3 marks]

Circuit Devices

For some components <u>resistance</u> can depend on things like <u>light</u> and <u>temperature</u>, and this can be really handy.

LDR is Short for Light Dependent Resistor

1) The <u>resistance</u> of an LDR changes as the <u>intensity</u> (brightness) of <u>light</u> changes.
2) In <u>bright light</u>, the resistance is <u>low</u>.
3) In <u>darkness</u>, the resistance is <u>high</u>.
4) LDRs have lots of <u>uses</u>, including turning on <u>automatic night lights</u> when it gets <u>dark</u>.

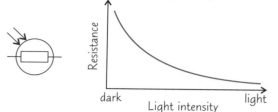

You can Investigate How Resistance Changes for LDRs

1) You can create <u>I-V graphs</u> for <u>LDRs</u> using the method on the previous page.
2) But the <u>resistance</u> of LDRs can <u>depend on</u> things <u>other than</u> current.
3) For example, you can test how the <u>resistance</u> of an LDR changes with brightness using the circuit shown on the right:
   - Conduct your experiment in a <u>dim room</u>.
   - Measure the <u>potential difference</u> across and <u>current</u> through the LDR.
   - <u>Change the light level</u> near to the LDR.
   - Measure the <u>p.d.</u> and <u>current</u> again. <u>Repeat</u> this for a <u>range</u> of light levels.
   - Calculate the <u>resistance</u> for each measurement using $R = V \div I$.
4) You should find that as the light level gets <u>brighter</u>, the <u>current</u> through the LDR <u>increases</u> as the <u>resistance decreases</u>.

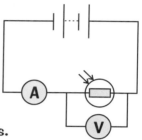

The Resistance of a Thermistor Depends on Temperature

1) A <u>thermistor</u> is a resistor that changes with <u>temperature</u>.
2) In <u>hot</u> conditions, the resistance <u>drops</u>.
3) In <u>cool</u> conditions, the resistance goes <u>up</u>.
4) Thermistors are used in <u>car engines</u> and central heating <u>thermostats</u>.
5) <u>Thermostats</u> turn the heating <u>on</u> when it's <u>cool</u> and <u>off</u> when it's <u>warm</u>.

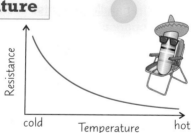

You can Investigate How Resistance Changes for Thermistors

1) As with LDRs, you can use the method on the previous page to create <u>I-V graphs</u> for <u>thermistors</u>.
2) Also, you can test how the <u>resistance</u> of a thermistor changes with <u>temperature</u> using the circuit on the right:
   - Measure the <u>p.d. across</u> and <u>current through</u> the thermistor.
   - <u>Change the temperature</u> of the thermistor by heating it.
   - Measure the <u>current</u> and <u>p.d.</u> for a range of <u>different temperatures</u>.
   - Calculate the <u>resistance</u> for each measurement using $R = V \div I$.
3) You should find that as the <u>temperature increases</u>, the <u>current</u> through the thermistor <u>increases</u> — showing that the <u>resistance decreases</u>.

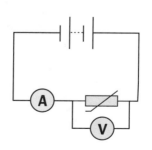

LDRs — Light Dependent Rabbits...

The next time your heating turns on by itself, you can show off and tell everyone how thermistors made it happen.

Q1   Describe one everyday use for: a) an LDR   b) a thermistor   [2 marks]

Series and Parallel Circuits

Make sure you know the <u>rules</u> about what happens to <u>current</u> and <u>p.d.</u> in series and parallel circuits. You can find out how and why the <u>resistance</u> changes for <u>both</u> of these circuits over on the next page.

Series Circuits — All or Nothing

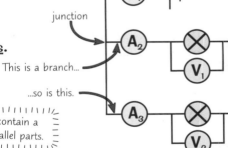

1) In <u>series circuits</u>, the different components are connected <u>in a line</u> between the ends of the power supply.

2) Only <u>voltmeters</u> break this rule. They're always in <u>parallel</u>.

3) If the circuit is <u>broken</u>, e.g. by removing a component or if a component breaks, <u>all the components</u> stop working.

4) For a <u>series</u> circuit:

- If you connect <u>cells</u> in <u>series</u>, their p.d.s <u>add together</u> to make the <u>total p.d.</u> across the circuit.
- The total <u>potential difference</u> of the supply is <u>shared</u> between components.
- The bigger a component's <u>resistance</u>, the bigger its <u>share</u> of the <u>total p.d.</u> (using $V = I \times R$).

- The <u>same current</u> flows through <u>all components</u> — $A_1 = A_2$.
- The size of the current depends on the <u>total p.d.</u> and the <u>total resistance</u> of the circuit ($I = V \div R$).

- The <u>net (total) resistance</u> can be found by adding the resistances of the resistors together.
- The <u>net</u> resistance of the circuit is the <u>sum</u> of the <u>resistances</u> of the <u>components</u>.

5) Series circuits are often designed and built to <u>test</u> and <u>measure components</u> because the potential difference, current and resistance are quite easy to change, measure and calculate (see p.186).

Parallel Circuits — Everything is Independent

1) In <u>parallel circuits</u>, each component is <u>separately</u> connected to the ends of the power supply.

2) Only <u>ammeters</u> break this rule. They are <u>always</u> connected in <u>series</u>.

3) If you take out <u>one</u> of the loops in a parallel circuit, the things in the <u>other</u> loops will <u>keep working</u>.

4) This means things in parallel can be switched <u>on</u> and <u>off</u> without affecting each other.

Everyday circuits often contain a mixture of series and parallel parts.

5) For a <u>parallel</u> circuit:

- <u>All</u> components get the <u>same</u> potential difference as the <u>full source p.d.</u>, $V_{total} = V_1 = V_2$.

- <u>Current</u> is <u>shared</u> between <u>branches</u>.
- The <u>total current</u> flowing around the circuit is equal to the <u>sum</u> of all the currents through the <u>separate components</u>, $A_1 = A_2 + A_3$.
- At <u>junctions</u>, the current either <u>splits</u> or <u>rejoins</u>.
- The total current going <u>into</u> a junction has to equal the total current <u>leaving it</u>.

- The <u>total resistance</u> of the circuit <u>decreases</u> as you add resistors in parallel (see p.189).

Series circuits — they're no laughing matter...

Get those rules firmly in your head, then have a go at these questions to test what you can remember.

Q1   A battery is connected in series with a 4 Ω resistor, a 5 Ω resistor and a 6 Ω resistor. A current of 0.6 A flows through the circuit. Calculate the potential difference of the battery.   [3 marks]

Q1 Video Solution

More on Series and Parallel Circuits

Time for a bit more about <u>series</u> and <u>parallel</u> circuits, including a quick <u>experiment</u>. Fun, fun, fun...

Adding Two Resistors in Series Increases Net Resistance...

1) For <u>one</u> resistor connected to a power supply, the <u>resistance</u> of the <u>circuit</u> is the <u>same</u> as the <u>resistance</u> of the <u>resistor</u>.

2) If you <u>add</u> another resistor in <u>series</u>, the resistance of the circuit <u>increases</u>.

3) The supply <u>p.d.</u> is the <u>same</u>, so the 'pushing force' moving the charges is the same.

4) But now the <u>charges</u> have to go through <u>two</u> resistors instead of <u>one</u>.

5) So it is <u>harder</u> for the charges to flow around the circuit, so the size of the <u>current decreases</u>.
This shows that <u>resistance has increased</u>, as $R = V \div I$. V is the same, but I has decreased.

...But Adding them in Parallel Reduces the Net Resistance

If you <u>added a resistor</u> to your starting circuit <u>in parallel</u>, the <u>net resistance decreases</u>. Here's why:

1) When a resistor is added in <u>parallel</u>, it creates <u>another loop</u> in the circuit.

2) The <u>current</u> now has <u>more paths</u> it can take — it can flow through either loop.

3) In each loop, there's only <u>one</u> resistor for the charges to go through.
The <u>p.d.</u> and <u>resistance</u> of <u>each loop</u> is the <u>same</u> as the starting circuit with only <u>one resistor</u>.

4) This means the <u>current</u> in <u>each loop</u> is the <u>same</u> as the <u>total current</u> through the <u>starting circuit</u>.
So the <u>total current</u> of the <u>parallel</u> circuit is <u>larger</u> than the total current of the <u>starting circuit</u>.

5) As $R = V \div I$, I <u>going up</u> while V <u>stays the same</u> shows that the <u>total resistance</u>
of the circuit is <u>lower</u> than the resistance of the circuit with only <u>one</u> resistor.

You Can Investigate Resistance in Parallel & Series Circuits

PRACTICAL

1) Set up the <u>basic test circuit</u> shown on the right.

2) Record the <u>p.d. across</u> and <u>current through</u> the resistor.

3) Add a <u>second</u>, <u>identical</u> resistor in <u>series</u> with the first.

4) Record the <u>p.d. across</u> and <u>current</u> through each resistor.

5) <u>Change</u> the circuit so the two resistors are now in <u>parallel</u>.

6) Again, record the <u>p.d.</u> and <u>current</u> for <u>each resistor</u>.

7) For the two circuits, you should find that:

Basic test circuit

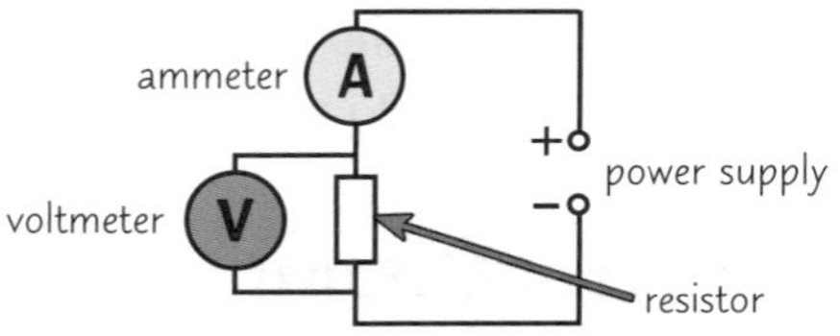

ammeter (A)
+o
power supply
−o
voltmeter (V)
resistor

SERIES
- The <u>total current</u> through the circuit is <u>smaller than</u> the current through the <u>basic test circuit</u>.
This shows that the <u>net resistance</u> has <u>increased</u> by adding a resistor in <u>series</u>.
- The <u>potential difference</u> of the power supply is now <u>shared</u> between the resistors.

PARALLEL
- The <u>total current</u> through the circuit is <u>larger than</u> the total current through the <u>basic test circuit</u>.
This shows that the <u>net resistance</u> has <u>decreased</u> by adding a resistor in <u>parallel</u>.
- The <u>total current</u> is the <u>sum</u> of the current through the <u>branches</u>.
- The <u>p.d.</u> across each resistor is the <u>same</u> as the <u>p.d.</u> of the power supply.

8) You can also do this experiment with <u>filament lamps</u>:
- The lamps should get <u>dimmer</u> when a lamp is added in <u>series</u> (as the p.d. is being <u>shared out</u>).
- The lamps should be the <u>same brightness</u> in <u>parallel</u> (as they both have the <u>same p.d.</u>).

I can't resist a good practical...

Make sure you're completely happy building circuits from diagrams — this experiment is good practice.

Q1   A circuit contains three resistors, each connected in parallel with a cell. Explain what
happens to the total current and resistance in the circuit when one resistor is removed.   [4 marks]

Q1 Video
Solution

Energy in Circuits

Electrical devices are built to transfer energy. But some of this energy ends up wasted in thermal stores.

Energy Transferred Depends on Current, P.d. and Time

1) When an electrical charge travels through an electrical component, energy is transferred (as work is done against resistance — p.185).

2) To find the energy transferred to a component, you can use the equation:

Energy transferred (J) — Current (A) — Potential difference (V) — Time (s)

$$E = I \times V \times t$$

3) The larger the potential difference across a component, the larger the amount of energy transferred to it. And a larger current through a component means more energy is transferred too.

 EXAMPLE A toaster is connected to a 240 V source for 30 seconds. It has a 2.5 A current flowing through it. Calculate the energy transferred to the toaster.

$E = I \times V \times t = 2.5 \times 240 \times 30 = 18\ 000$ J

Energy is Transferred from Cells and Other Sources

1) Electrical appliances are designed to transfer energy in a circuit when a current flows.

Kettles transfer energy electrically from the mains a.c. supply to the thermal energy store of the heating element inside the kettle.

Energy is transferred electrically from the chemical energy store of the battery of a handheld fan to the kinetic energy store of the fan's motor.

2) Of course, no appliance transfers all that energy in a useful way.

3) The higher the current, the more energy is transferred to the thermal energy stores of the components (and then the surroundings).

The mains a.c. supply is also called the domestic supply.

4) This heating usually increases the resistance of the components, like you saw on page 185.

Heating in a Circuit isn't Always Bad

1) Heating up a component in a circuit generally reduces its efficiency (p.159).

2) If the temperature gets too high, this can cause components in the circuit to melt. This means the circuit will stop working, or not work properly.

3) Fuses (p.193) use this effect to protect circuits.

4) The heating effect of an electric current can be really useful if you want to heat something:

- Toasters contain a coil of wire with a really high resistance.
- When a current passes through the coil, its temperature increases so much that it glows and gives off infrared radiation.
- This radiation transfers energy to the bread and cooks it.
- Filament bulbs and electric heaters work in a similar way.

Have a break from all this work — or you'll have no energy left...

You can't escape energy transfers I'm afraid. Practise using that equation then take a quick break to recharge.

Q1 A charger is connected to a 230 V source for an hour. A current of 4.0 A flows through it. Calculate the energy transferred by the charger. Give your answer to 2 significant figures.

[3 marks]

Q1 Video Solution

Electrical Power

You know that electrical devices <u>transfer energy</u> — well, their <u>power</u> determines how <u>quickly</u> this happens.

Energy Transferred Depends on Power

1) The <u>total</u> energy transferred by an appliance depends on <u>how long</u> the appliance is on for and its <u>power</u>.

2) The <u>power</u> of an appliance is the energy that it <u>transfers per second</u>. Power is measured in <u>watts</u>.

3) The <u>more</u> energy it transfers in a given time, the <u>higher</u> its power.

4) The <u>power</u> of an appliance can be found using:

> Power (W) = Energy transferred (J) ÷ Time (s)

$$P = \dfrac{E}{t}$$

5) Appliances are often given a <u>power rating</u>. This is the power that they <u>work at</u>.

> Motors have a range of <u>power ratings</u>. A motor with a power rating of 10 W will transfer <u>less</u> energy to its <u>kinetic</u> energy store <u>per second</u> than a motor with a power rating of 50 W.

6) The <u>lower</u> the power rating, the <u>less</u> electricity an appliance uses in a given time and so the <u>cheaper</u> it is to run.

7) But, a higher power <u>doesn't</u> necessarily mean that it transfers <u>more</u> energy <u>usefully</u>.

8) An appliance may be <u>more powerful</u> than another, <u>but less efficient</u>.

9) This means it may transfer <u>less energy to useful stores</u> than a device with a <u>lower power rating</u>.

Power Also Depends on Current and Potential Difference

1) The <u>power transferred</u> by an appliance depends on the <u>potential difference</u> (p.d.) across it, and the <u>current</u> flowing through it.

2) The <u>power</u> of an appliance can be found with:

> Electrical power (W) = Current (A) × Potential difference (V)

$$P = I \times V$$

3) You can also find the power if you <u>don't know</u> the <u>potential difference</u>. To do this, use:

Electrical power (W) ⟶ $P = I^2 R$ ⟵ Resistance (Ω)

(Current)²
(A)²

EXAMPLE   A 40 W motor has a current of 4.0 A flowing through it. Find the resistance of the motor.

1) <u>Rearrange</u> the equation to make resistance the subject. You might want to make a <u>formula triangle</u> to help you.

$P = I^2 \times R$, so $R = P \div I^2$

2) Put the <u>numbers</u> into the equation.

$R = 40 \div 4^2 = 2.5\ \Omega$

You have the power — now use your potential...

I'm afraid the best way to learn all of this is to just practise using those equations again and again. Sorry.

Q1   Calculate the difference in the amount of energy transferred by a 250 W TV and a 375 W TV when they are both used for two hours.   [3 marks]

Q1 Video Solution

Electricity in the Home

From <u>washing machines</u> to <u>televisions</u>, our home life would be a lot different if it wasn't for <u>electricity</u>.

Mains Supply is a.c., Battery Supply is d.c.

1) There are two types of electricity supply — <u>alternating current</u> (a.c.) and <u>direct current</u> (d.c.).

2) In <u>a.c. supplies</u> the <u>charges</u> are <u>constantly</u> changing direction.

3) <u>Alternating currents</u> are produced by <u>alternating voltages</u> (the <u>positive</u> and <u>negative</u> ends of the p.d. keep <u>alternating</u>).

Remember, voltage and potential difference are the same thing.

4) The <u>UK domestic supply</u> (the electricity in your home) is an a.c. supply at around <u>230 V</u>.

5) The <u>frequency</u> of the a.c. domestic supply is <u>50 Hz</u> (hertz).

6) Cells and batteries supply <u>direct current</u> (d.c.).

The domestic supply is also called the mains supply.

7) <u>Direct current</u> is where the <u>charges</u> only move in <u>one direction</u>. It's created by a <u>direct voltage</u> (a p.d. that is <u>only positive</u> or <u>negative</u>, not both).

Most Cables Have Three Separate Wires

1) Most electrical appliances are connected to the mains supply by a cable with <u>three</u> wires in it.

2) The <u>three wires</u> are covered with coloured plastic insulation.

3) The <u>wires</u> are:

<u>NEUTRAL WIRE</u> — <u>blue</u>.
1) It <u>completes</u> the circuit.
2) When the appliance is operating normally, current flows through the <u>live</u> and <u>neutral</u> wires.
3) The neutral wire is around <u>0 V</u>.

<u>LIVE WIRE</u> — <u>brown</u>.
1) The live wire carries the voltage (potential difference, p.d.).
2) It alternates between a <u>high +ve</u> <u>and −ve voltage</u> of about <u>230 V</u>.

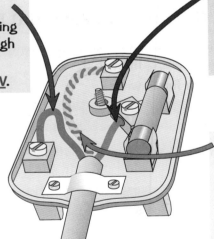

<u>EARTH WIRE</u> — <u>green</u> and <u>yellow</u>.
1) The earth wire is a <u>safety wire</u>.
2) It carries the current away if something goes <u>wrong</u> (see next page).
3) It's <u>also</u> at 0 V.

- The <u>p.d.</u> between the <u>live wire</u> and the <u>neutral wire</u> equals the <u>supply p.d.</u> (<u>230 V</u> for the mains).
- The <u>p.d.</u> between the <u>live wire</u> and the <u>earth wire</u> is also <u>230 V</u> for a mains-connected appliance.
- There is <u>no p.d.</u> between the <u>neutral wire</u> and the <u>earth wire</u> — they're both at 0 V.

4) Some <u>plug sockets</u> have <u>switches</u> which are connected to the <u>live wire</u> of the circuit.

5) This is so the circuit can be <u>broken</u>. This stops the current flowing so the chance of an <u>electric shock</u> (p.193) is reduced.

Why are earth wires green and yellow — when mud is brown...?

Make sure you learn what the different wires are in a typical plug and the potential differences between them.

Q1   Explain the difference between a.c. and d.c. electricity supplies.   [2 marks]

Electrical Safety

Electricity can be a <u>dangerous</u> thing. Luckily, we've developed <u>fuses</u> and <u>circuit breakers</u> to keep ourselves and our machines safe. Read this page and make sure you know why they are super <u>important</u>.

Touching the Live Wire Gives You an Electric Shock

1) Your <u>body</u> (just like the earth) is at <u>0 V</u>.
2) This means that if you touch the <u>live wire</u>, a <u>large potential difference</u> is produced across your body. This makes a <u>current</u> flow through you.
3) This causes a large <u>electric shock</u> which could injure or even kill you.
4) Even if a plug socket or a light switch is turned <u>off</u> (i.e. the switch is <u>open</u>) there is still a <u>danger</u> of an electric shock.

Earthing and Fuses Prevent Electrical Overloads

1) <u>Surges</u> (sudden increases) in <u>current</u> can happen because of <u>changes in a circuit</u> or because of a <u>fault</u> (something going wrong) in an electrical <u>appliance</u>.
2) Current surges can lead to the <u>circuits and wiring</u> in your appliances <u>melting</u> or causing a <u>fire</u>.
3) <u>Faulty</u> appliances can cause <u>electric shocks</u>.
4) The <u>earth wire</u> and a <u>fuse</u> are included in electrical appliances to stop this from happening.
5) <u>Fuses</u> are connected to the <u>live wire</u> and blow (melt or break) if the current gets too high. This <u>stops the supply</u> to the <u>appliance</u> and <u>protects</u> other components. This is how they work:

- The <u>earth wire</u> is connected to the <u>metal case</u>.
- A fault could cause the <u>live wire</u> to touch the <u>metal case</u>. If this happens a <u>large current</u> would flow through the <u>live wire</u>, the <u>case</u> and the <u>earth wire</u>.
- This <u>surge</u> in current would <u>melt the fuse</u> when the amount of current is greater than the fuse rating.
- Breaking the fuse <u>breaks the circuit</u> and <u>cuts off</u> the <u>live supply</u>.
- A <u>fuse rating</u> shows the <u>maximum current</u> that can pass through the fuse before it <u>blows</u>.
- An appliance should have a fuse that is rated <u>just higher</u> than its <u>normal operating current</u>.

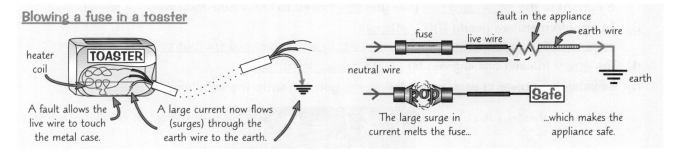

<u>Blowing a fuse in a toaster</u>

heater coil — **TOASTER**

A fault allows the live wire to touch the metal case.

A large current now flows (surges) through the earth wire to the earth.

fuse — live wire — fault in the appliance — earth wire

neutral wire

earth

The large surge in current melts the fuse...

Safe

...which makes the appliance safe.

6) As well as the fuses in plugs, there are also <u>household fuses</u>. These work in the <u>same way</u>, but protect the <u>wiring in a house</u>, not just in an appliance.
7) <u>Circuit breakers</u> can be used in the place of household fuses.

- Instead of melting a <u>fuse</u>, a large current may instead '<u>trip</u>' (turn off) a <u>circuit breaker</u>.
- Circuit breakers can be reset, which is much easier than having to replace a fuse.

Nothing shocks my mum — she's very down to earth...

Fuses are dead important, so make sure you understand them and the protection they provide.

Q1   Which wire are fuses connected in?   [1 mark]

Transformers and the National Grid

It's no good generating lots of juicy <u>electricity</u> and then <u>losing</u> most of it when you <u>transmit</u> it.

The National Grid Carries Electricity Across the UK

1) Once the electricity has been generated, it goes into the <u>national grid</u>.
2) The national grid connects <u>power stations</u> to <u>consumers</u> (anyone who uses electricity).
3) The national grid has to transfer <u>loads of energy each second</u>.
4) Power is the <u>energy transferred per second</u>.
5) So the national grid transmits a <u>really high power</u>.
6) As you saw on p.191, <u>power = current × p.d.</u>.
7) So to transmit the <u>huge</u> amount of <u>power</u> across the national grid, you either need a <u>high p.d.</u> (voltage) or a <u>high current</u>.

Transformers Change the p.d. of Electricity in the National Grid

1) If the power was transmitted through the national grid at a <u>high current</u>, the wires would <u>heat up</u>, causing a lot of energy to be <u>lost</u> (see p.185).
2) For a <u>given power</u>, the higher the p.d. the <u>lower the current</u>.
3) So to <u>reduce</u> the <u>energy lost</u>, electricity is transmitted through the national grid at a <u>really high p.d.</u>.
4) <u>Step-up transformers</u> at <u>power stations</u> boost the p.d. of the electricity generated up <u>really high</u>.
5) As the <u>p.d.</u> is <u>increased</u>, the <u>current</u> is <u>decreased</u>.
6) <u>Step-down transformers</u> bring the p.d. back down to <u>safe</u>, <u>usable levels</u> at the consumers' end.
7) As the <u>p.d.</u> is <u>decreased</u>, the <u>current</u> is <u>increased</u>.
8) This is <u>far more efficient</u> than simply transmitting the electricity at the usable level.

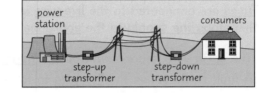

No Power is Lost in Transformers

1) Transformers have <u>two coils of wire</u>, the <u>primary</u> coil and the <u>secondary</u> coil.
2) Electricity flows through the <u>primary coil</u>. The <u>magnetic field</u> it produces (see p.198) causes a current in the <u>secondary coil</u> (but you <u>don't</u> need to know how they work — phew).
3) As transformers are nearly <u>100% efficient</u>:
   <u>power in primary coil (input power) = power in secondary coil (output power)</u>.
4) The <u>power</u> in each coil is given by <u>power = p.d. × current</u>.
5) Because the power in each coil is the <u>same</u>, you can write the equation:

p.d. across primary coil (V) ——

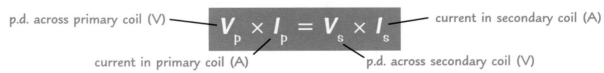

$$V_p \times I_p = V_s \times I_s$$

—— current in secondary coil (A)

current in primary coil (A)

p.d. across secondary coil (V)

EXAMPLE   A transformer steps up a 42 V supply to 210 V. The current in the secondary coil is 0.2 A. Calculate the current in the primary coil.

Divide both sides of the equation by V_p to rearrange to find I_p.

1) <u>Rearrange</u> the transformer equation for I_p. $V_p \times I_p = V_s \times I_s$ so $I_p = (V_s \times I_s) \div V_p$
2) Then <u>stick in</u> the values you have. $I_p = (210 \times 0.2) \div 42 = 1$ A

Transformers — NOT robots in disguise...

Make sure you know why transformers are used. Then take a stab at this question.

Q1   A transformer has an input p.d. of 1.6 V. The output power is 320 W.
       Find the input current.   [2 marks]

Q1 Video Solution

Revision Questions for Sections 21 and 22

Well, that wraps up <u>Section 22</u> — time to have
a go at a few questions for Sections 21 and 22.

For even more practice, try the
Retrieval Quizzes for Sections 21
and 22 — just scan the QR codes!

- Try these questions and <u>tick off each one</u> when you <u>get it right</u>.
- When you're <u>completely happy</u> with a sub-topic, tick it off.

Energy, Forces and Power (p.181-183) ☑

1) Give three ways that energy can be transferred between stores.
2) True or false? Friction is a non-contact force.
3) What force causes the repulsion or attraction between electrical charges?
4) Give the formula for calculating the work done by a force.
5) Describe how to convert between joules (J) and newton-metres (Nm).
6) True or false? A mechanical process becomes wasteful when it causes an increase in temperature.
7) Define power. State the equation relating power, work done and time taken.
8) What unit is power measured in?

Section 21 Quiz

Circuit Basics (p.184-187) ☑

9) Draw the circuit symbols for: a cell, a filament lamp, a diode, a motor and an LDR.
10) What is current measured in?
11) Give the equation that links energy transferred, charge moved and potential difference.
12) Briefly explain why resistance increases with temperature for a resistor.
13) True or false? An ammeter must be connected in parallel to the component being tested.
14) Explain how the resistance of an LDR varies with light intensity.
15) What happens to the resistance of a thermistor as it gets hotter?

Section 22 Quiz

Series and Parallel Circuits (p.188-189) ☑

16) How does the current through each component vary in a series circuit?
17) True or false? Potential difference is shared between components in a series circuit.
18) How does potential difference vary between components connected in parallel?
19) True or false? Identical filament bulbs in parallel have different brightnesses.

Power and Energy Transfers in Circuits (p.190-191) ☑

20) Write down the equation that links energy transferred, current, potential difference and time.
21) Give two disadvantages of the heating effect in an electrical circuit.
22) Define power in terms of energy transferred.
23) What is the power rating of an electrical appliance?
24) State the equation that links electrical power, current and potential difference.

Electricity in the Home and Electrical Safety (p.192-194) ☑

25) True or false? Mains supply electricity is an alternating current.
26) What is the frequency of the UK mains supply?
27) What are the names of the three wires in a typical appliance power cable?
28) Explain why touching a live wire is dangerous.
29) Explain how a fuse protects you if a fault causes the live wire to touch the metal case of an appliance.
30) Explain why electricity is transferred at a high p.d. in the national grid.
31) Where are step-up transformers used within the national grid?

Magnets and Magnetic Fields

I think magnetism is an attractive subject, but don't get repelled by the exam — revise.

Forces Exist Between Magnets

1) All magnets have a north pole (N) and a south pole (S).
2) When two magnets are close, you can feel a force between them.
3) Two magnetic poles that are the same (like poles) repel each other.
4) Two different (unlike) magnetic poles attract each other.

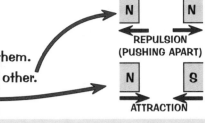

1) All magnets have a magnetic field around them.
2) This is the area where it can produce a force.
3) Magnetic fields can be shown with magnetic field lines.
4) The lines point from the north pole to the south pole.
5) The closer together the lines are, the stronger the magnetic field is in that place.
6) The magnetic field around a bar magnet always has the shape shown on the right.

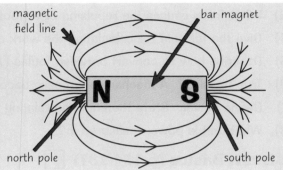

Plotting Compasses Show the Direction of a Magnetic Field

1) The needle of a plotting compass is a tiny bar magnet.
2) It points in the direction of the magnetic field it's in at that point.
3) So you can use a compass to plot the shape and direction of a magnetic field:

- Draw around a magnet on a piece of paper.
- Put a compass by the magnet.
- Mark the direction the compass needle points in by drawing a dot at each end of the needle.
- Move the compass so that the tail end of the needle is where the tip of the needle was before.
- Repeat this lots of times. Join up all the marks. You will end up with a drawing of one field line.
- You'll need to do this from several different starting positions around the magnet to show the field pattern.

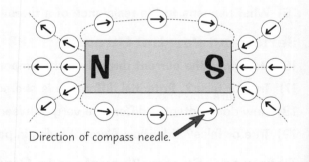

Direction of compass needle.

4) When a compass is not near a magnet it always points north.
5) So there must be a magnetic field around the Earth.
6) This provides evidence for the core (inside) of the Earth being magnetic.

Uniform Fields are shown by Evenly Spaced Straight Lines

1) A uniform magnetic field has the same strength and direction everywhere.
2) There is a uniform magnetic field between the north pole of one bar magnet and the south pole of another bar magnet.
3) It is shown by parallel field lines that are all the same distance apart.
4) Like all fields, uniform fields point from a north pole to a south pole.

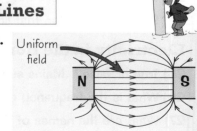

Uniform field

Magnets are like farmers — surrounded by fields...

Magnetism is tricky and takes a while to make sense. Learn these basics — you'll need them.

Q1   What is meant by the term 'uniform magnetic field'?   [2 marks]

Permanent and Induced Magnets

There are a few special <u>magnetic materials</u>. They <u>only</u> become magnets when they're <u>near</u> 'proper' magnets.

Magnets Can be Permanent or Induced

1) <u>Permanent</u> magnets (e.g. bar magnets) produce their own magnetic field <u>all the time</u>.
2) Some materials <u>only</u> produce a magnetic field while they're <u>in</u> another <u>magnetic field</u>.
3) These are called <u>temporary magnetic materials</u>.
4) <u>Iron</u>, <u>steel</u>, <u>nickel</u> and <u>cobalt</u> are all temporary magnetic materials.
5) When a temporary magnetic material is put in a <u>magnetic field</u> and <u>becomes magnetic</u>, it is called an <u>induced magnet</u>.

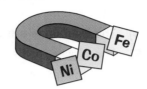

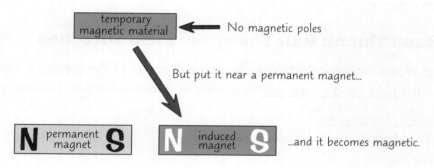

6) A <u>permanent magnet</u> and an <u>induced magnet</u> will always <u>attract</u> each other.
7) When you <u>take away</u> the magnetic field of the permanent magnet, an <u>induced</u> magnet <u>stops</u> being a magnet.

A permanent magnet <u>never</u> loses its magnetism. But an induced magnet <u>will lose</u> its magnetism (and <u>won't</u> be an induced magnet anymore) when it's <u>no longer</u> in <u>another magnetic field</u>.

The Magnetic Properties of Materials are Very Useful

Make sure you know a <u>few examples</u> of things that use them:

<u>FRIDGE DOORS</u>
There is a <u>permanent</u> magnetic strip in your fridge door to keep it closed.

<u>MAGNETIC SEPARATORS</u>
Large magnets are used in <u>recycling plants</u> to remove <u>steel cans</u> from other waste.
The steel cans become <u>induced magnets</u> and are <u>attracted</u> to the large magnet.

<u>MAGLEV TRAINS</u>
These use <u>magnetic repulsion</u> to make trains <u>float</u> slightly above the track.
Magnets are also used to <u>push</u> the trains along.

<u>CRANES</u>
These use magnets to <u>attract</u> temporary magnetic materials — e.g. <u>scrap metal</u> in scrapyards.

Attractive and with a magnetic personality — I'm a catch...
Make sure you know what materials are magnetic and when they become induced magnets.

Q1   In iron mining, iron often needs to be separated from a mixture of substances.
Explain why iron is removed from the mixture when a magnet passes over it.   [2 marks]

Electromagnetism and Solenoids

Magnetic fields aren't just around bar magnets — they're also around wires with currents passing through them.

A Current Produces a Magnetic Field

1) A current flowing through a long, straight conductor (e.g. a wire) creates a magnetic effect.
2) You can see this by placing a compass near to the wire.
3) The compass will move to point in the direction of the magnetic field.
4) The field lines are circles around the wire:
5) The closer to the wire you are, the stronger the magnetic field is.
6) And the larger the current through the wire is, the stronger the field is.

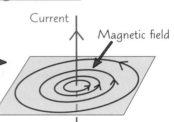

The Right-Hand Thumb Rule Shows the Field Direction

1) The direction of the magnetic field depends on the direction of the current in the conductor.
2) You can use the right-hand thumb rule to quickly work out which way the field goes:

> The Right-Hand Thumb Rule
> * Point your right thumb in the direction of current.
> * Curl your fingers.
> * The direction of your fingers is the direction of the field.

3) Here's how the right-hand thumb rule is used for the example above:

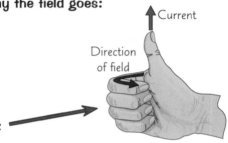

A Solenoid has Lots of Loops of Wire

1) If you bend a wire so that it's in the shape of a spring, it's a solenoid.
2) Each loop (or coil) of the solenoid has its own magnetic field.
3) The magnetic field lines of each coil go in the same direction along the centre of the solenoid.
4) Field lines going in the same direction add together.
5) So the magnetic field along the centre of the solenoid is very strong and almost uniform (see p.196).
6) Outside the solenoid, the magnetic field is weak.
7) This is because some of the magnetic field lines of coils next to each other go in opposite directions.
8) Field lines going in opposite directions cancel out.
9) Overall, the magnetic field outside a solenoid is just like the one around a bar magnet (see p.196).
10) A solenoid is an example of an electromagnet.
11) An electromagnet has a magnetic field that can be turned on and off using an electric current.

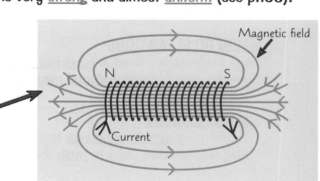

Give me one good raisin why I should make the currant joke...

Practise using the right-hand thumb rule. At least you shouldn't forget which hand to use — it's in the name.

Q1   Draw the magnetic field for a current-carrying wire.   [2 marks]

Q2   State what happens to the magnetic field around a solenoid when the current through it is switched off.   [1 mark]

Q1 Video Solution

Density

Time for some <u>maths</u> I'm afraid. But at least it comes with a fun <u>experiment</u>, so it's not all bad...

Density is Mass per Unit Volume

1) <u>Density</u> is a measure of <u>how much mass</u> there is in a <u>certain space</u>.

2) You can work out <u>density</u> using:

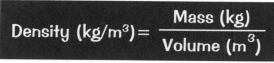

$$\text{Density (kg/m}^3) = \frac{\text{Mass (kg)}}{\text{Volume (m}^3)} \qquad \rho = \frac{m}{V}$$

EXAMPLE

A 0.0020 m³ block of aluminium has a mass of 5.4 kg.
Calculate the density of aluminium.

density = mass ÷ volume
= 5.4 ÷ 0.0020
= 2700 kg/m³

3) The density of an object depends on <u>what it's made of</u>.

4) Generally, <u>solids</u> are <u>denser</u> than <u>liquids</u>.

5) And <u>liquids</u> are usually <u>denser</u> than <u>gases</u>.

You Need to be Able to Measure Density in Different Ways

PRACTICAL

To find the density of a regularly-shaped object (e.g. a cuboid)

1) Use a <u>balance</u> to measure its <u>mass</u> (see p.208).

2) Use a <u>ruler</u> to measure the shape (e.g. its height, width and length).

3) Then calculate its <u>volume</u> using the <u>formula</u> for that shape.

4) Use <u>density = mass ÷ volume</u> to find the density.

> The volume of a cuboid is equal to length × width × height.

To find the density of an irregularly-shaped object (e.g. an awards statue)

1) Use a <u>balance</u> to measure its <u>mass</u>.

2) <u>Fill</u> a <u>displacement can</u> (a can with a <u>spout</u> in its side) with <u>water</u> so the water level is <u>above</u> the spout.

3) Let the water drain from the spout, leaving the water level <u>just below</u> the start of the spout.

4) Place a <u>measuring cylinder</u> (p.208) under the spout.

5) Place your object <u>into the water</u>. This will <u>push</u> some of the water <u>out</u> through the spout.

6) <u>Measure the volume</u> of water that has collected in the measuring cylinder.

7) This is <u>equal to</u> the <u>volume</u> of the <u>object</u>.

8) Use the <u>formula</u> above to find the object's <u>density</u>.

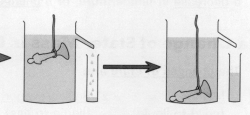

> For both of these experiments, you'll need to know that 1 ml = 1 cm³ and that 1 cm³ = 0.000001 m³.

To find the density of a liquid

1) Place a <u>measuring cylinder</u> on a balance and <u>zero</u> the balance.

2) Pour <u>50 ml</u> of the liquid into the measuring cylinder.

3) Record the liquid's <u>mass</u> shown on the mass balance.

4) Use the <u>formula</u> above to find the <u>density</u>. The <u>volume</u> is <u>50 cm³</u>, or <u>0.00005 m³</u>.

Learn this page. It is your density... I mean destiny.

Remember — density is all about how close together the particles in a substance are. Nice and simple really.

Q1   A cube has edges of length 1.5 cm and an average density of 3500 kg/m³.
      What is its mass?

[3 marks]

Q1 Video Solution

Kinetic Theory and States of Matter

Everything is made up of small particles (tiny balls). Kinetic theory describes how these particles behave.

There are Three States of Matter You Need to Learn

1) Three states of matter are solid (e.g. ice), liquid (e.g. water) and gas (e.g. water vapour).
2) The particles (atoms and molecules) of a substance in each state are the same.
3) Only their energies and their positions (arrangement) are different.

1) Particles are held close together by strong forces in a regular (ordered), fixed pattern.
2) The particles don't have much energy.
3) So they can only vibrate (jiggle about) around a fixed position.

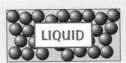

1) Particles are still held close together but in irregular arrangements (no clear pattern).
2) The particles have more energy than the particles in a solid.
3) They can move past each other in random directions at low speeds.

1) The particles aren't held close together. There are no forces between them.
2) The particles have more energy than in liquids and solids.
3) The particles constantly move around in random directions at a range of speeds.

Heating Causes a Temperature Change or a Change of State

1) In kinetic theory, the energy in a substance's thermal energy store is actually the total energy in the kinetic energy stores of its particles.

2) Substances also have an internal energy.
   This is the total energy in the kinetic and potential energy stores of the particles.

3) When you heat a substance, energy is transferred to the particles' energy stores.

4) This can cause an increase in temperature (see p.201) or a change of state (see p.202).

5) When you cool a substance, the particles lose energy, causing a decrease in temperature, or a change of state.

The energy in potential energy stores depends on the particles' positions. You can usually ignore the energy in these stores.

In a Change of State, Mass is Conserved

1) The changes of state are:

   1) Melting   2) Boiling/evaporating   3) Sublimating   4) Freezing   5) Condensing
   (solid to liquid)   (liquid to gas)   (solid to gas)   (liquid to solid)   (gas to liquid)

2) A change of state is a physical change (not a chemical change).
3) This means you don't end up with a new material, the particles are just arranged in a different way.
4) The number of particles stays the same when the state changes.
5) This means the mass is conserved (it doesn't change) during a change of state.
6) However, when a substance changes state its volume does change.
7) Since density = mass ÷ volume (p.199), this means the density must change too.
8) If you reverse a physical change, the substance gets back its original properties.
9) This means if you reverse a change of state, the substance goes back to how it was before.

Some chemical changes can't be reversed.

Changes of state — like moving from Washington to Texas...

Remember, when a substance changes state, its volume and density change, but its mass stays the same.

Q1   Give the name of the change of state: a) from liquid to gas   b) from solid to gas   [2 marks]

Specific Heat Capacity

The <u>temperature</u> of something <u>depends on</u> the <u>energy</u> stored in the substance's thermal energy store. That's where specific heat capacity comes in...

Temperature **is a Measure** of the Energy of Particles

1) In kinetic theory, the <u>temperature</u> of a substance is a way of measuring the <u>average energy</u> in the <u>kinetic energy stores of its particles</u>.

2) <u>Heating</u> a substance can <u>increase</u> the <u>energy</u> in the <u>kinetic energy stores</u> of its particles (see p.200).

3) So heating a substance can <u>increase its temperature</u>.

Specific Heat Capacity **Relates Temperature and Energy**

1) Some materials need <u>more energy</u> to <u>increase their temperature</u> than others.

2) These materials also <u>transfer</u> more energy when they <u>cool down</u> again.

3) They can '<u>store</u>' a lot of energy.

4) The <u>amount of energy</u> stored or released as a material <u>changes temperature</u> depends on the <u>specific heat capacity</u> of the material.

5) This energy can be found using:

Change in thermal energy (J) — $\Delta Q = m \times c \times \Delta \theta$ — Change in Temperature (°C)

Mass (kg)   Specific heat capacity (J/kg°C)

Δ just means 'change in'.

6) <u>Specific heat capacity</u> is the amount of <u>energy</u> needed to raise the temperature of <u>1 kg</u> of a material by <u>1 °C</u>.

EXAMPLE   501 kJ of energy is transferred to 3.00 kg of oil. Its temperature increases from 20 °C to 120 °C. Calculate the specific heat capacity of the oil.

1) First, <u>calculate</u> the <u>change</u> in the oil's <u>temperature</u>.

2) Convert the energy from <u>kilojoules</u> to <u>joules</u>.

3) Now the numbers are in the <u>correct units</u>, <u>rearrange</u> the equation to find <u>specific heat capacity</u>.

4) Put the numbers into the rearranged <u>equation</u>.

5) The <u>unit</u> for specific heat capacity is J/kg°C.

120 °C – 20 °C = 100 °C

501 × 1000 = 501 000 J

$\Delta Q = m \times c \times \Delta \theta$, so:
$c = \Delta Q \div (m \times \Delta \theta)$
= 501 000 ÷ (3.00 × 100)
= 1670 J/kg°C

---

7) Materials with a <u>high</u> specific heat capacity can be good <u>thermal insulators</u>. These can be used to help reduce <u>unwanted energy transfers</u>, e.g. from buildings (see page 160).

I wish I had a high specific fact capacity...

Make sure you practise using that equation — it's a bit tricky. Have a go at these questions to test yourself.

Q1   Find the final temperature of 5 kg of water, at an initial temperature of 5 °C, after 50 kJ of energy has been transferred to it. The specific heat capacity of water is 4200 J/kg°C. [3 marks]

Q2   A 0.20 kg block of metal has a specific heat capacity of 420 J/kg°C. Calculate how much the temperature of the block will increase by if 1680 J of energy is supplied to it. [3 marks]

Q1 Video Solution

Specific Latent Heat

If you heat up a pan of water on the stove, the water never gets any hotter than 100 °C. You can <u>carry on heating it up</u>, but the <u>temperature won't rise</u>. How come, you say? It's all to do with <u>latent heat</u>...

You Need to Put In Energy to Break Bonds Between Particles

1) As you've seen on the past few pages, <u>heating</u> transfers <u>energy</u> to particles.
2) This can cause a <u>change of state</u>.
3) During a change of state because of <u>heating</u> (e.g. <u>melting</u>, <u>boiling</u>), this energy is used to <u>break the bonds between particles</u>.
4) Energy is <u>not</u> transferred to the kinetic energy stores of the particles.
5) So the <u>temperature</u> of the substance <u>doesn't increase</u>.
6) If a change of state happens because of <u>cooling</u> (e.g. <u>freezing</u>, <u>condensing</u>), bonds are <u>formed</u> between particles.
7) During these changes of state, energy is <u>transferred away</u> from the <u>potential energy stores</u> of the particles, <u>not</u> the kinetic energy stores.
8) So the temperature <u>does not go down</u>.

Specific Latent Heat is the Energy Needed to Change State

1) The <u>energy transferred</u> during a change of state is called <u>latent heat</u>.
2) For <u>heating</u>, latent heat is the <u>energy gained</u> to cause a change of state.
3) For <u>cooling</u>, it is the energy <u>released</u> by a change of state.
4) The <u>specific latent heat</u> of a material is the <u>amount of energy</u> needed to <u>change the state</u> of <u>1 kg</u> of the material <u>without changing its temperature</u>.
5) You can work out the <u>energy needed</u> (or <u>released</u>) for a change of state using this <u>formula</u>:

Thermal Energy for a Change of State (J)　　Mass (kg)　　Specific Latent Heat (J/kg)

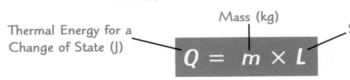

$$Q = m \times L$$

$$\frac{Q}{m \times L}$$

6) Specific latent heat has <u>different names</u> for different changes of state:
   - For changing between a <u>solid</u> and a <u>liquid</u> it is called the <u>specific latent heat of fusion</u>.
   - For changing between a <u>liquid</u> and a <u>gas</u> it is called the <u>specific latent heat of vaporisation</u>.

> **EXAMPLE**　The specific latent heat of vaporisation for water is 2 260 000 J/kg. How much energy is needed to completely boil 1.50 kg of water once it has reached its boiling point?
>
> 1) The mass and specific latent heat are in the <u>right units</u>, so just put them into the <u>formula</u>.
> 2) The unit for the answer is <u>joules</u> because it's <u>energy</u>.
>
> $Q = m \times L$
> $= 1.50 \times 2\ 260\ 000$
> $= 3\ 390\ 000$ J

7) Make sure you know the <u>difference</u> between <u>specific latent heat</u> and <u>specific heat capacity</u> (p.201). Specific heat capacity is to do with changes in <u>temperature</u>, <u>not</u> changes of <u>state</u>.

Breaking Bonds — Blofeld never quite manages it...

Only use specific latent heat if a substance is changing state and its temperature is constant.
Use specific heat capacity if the substance stays in the same state and its temperature is changing.

Q1 Video Solution

Q1　The SLH of fusion for a particular substance is 120 000 J/kg. How much energy is needed to melt 250 g of the substance when it is already at its melting temperature?　[2 marks]

Investigating Water

Time for some <u>experiments</u>. In both of the experiments on this page, you should use a <u>thermally-insulated</u> container, if you can, to reduce <u>energy wasted to the surroundings</u>.

You can Find the Specific Heat Capacity of Water

You can use the experiment below to find the <u>specific heat capacity</u> of <u>water</u> (or another <u>liquid</u>).

1) Use a <u>mass balance</u> to measure the <u>mass</u> of the insulating container.
2) Fill the container with <u>water</u> and measure the <u>mass</u> again.
3) The <u>difference</u> in mass is the mass of the <u>water in the container</u>, m.

> m = mass of full container − mass of empty container

You can use this set up with solid blocks to find the specific heat capacity of solids.

4) Set up the experiment as shown.
5) Make sure the joulemeter reads <u>zero</u>.
6) Place a <u>lid</u> on the container, if you have one.
7) Measure the <u>temperature</u> of the water, then turn on the power.
8) Keep an eye on the <u>thermometer</u>.
9) When the temperature has increased by <u>ten degrees</u> (so $\Delta\theta = 10$), stop the experiment.
10) Record the <u>energy</u> on the joulemeter. This is ΔQ.
11) Then calculate the <u>specific heat capacity</u> of the water using:

$$c = \frac{\Delta Q}{m \times \Delta\theta}$$

This is the equation from page 201 rearranged for specific heat capacity.

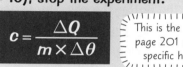

electric immersion heater — thermometer — water — joulemeter — to power supply — insulating container

You can Plot a Graph to Show Changes of State

1) Fill a <u>beaker</u> with <u>crushed ice</u>.
2) Place a <u>thermometer</u> into the beaker and record the <u>temperature</u> of the ice.
3) Using the Bunsen burner, <u>gradually heat</u> the beaker.
4) Every twenty seconds, record the <u>temperature</u> and the <u>current condition</u> of the ice (e.g. partly melted, completely melted).
5) Continue this process until the <u>ice melts</u> into water and this water begins to <u>boil</u>.
6) Plot a graph of <u>temperature against time</u> for your experiment.

thermometer — beaker — ice — stand — Bunsen burner

1) Here's an example of a <u>temperature-time graph</u>:
2) The <u>flat parts</u> of the graph show when the <u>temperature</u> stays <u>constant</u>, even though energy is still being transferred to the ice.
3) These show when a <u>change of state</u> happens.
4) Your graph from the experiment should look like the <u>blue</u> section of the graph on the right.
5) The <u>red</u> part is what <u>would happen</u> if you were able to <u>keep heating</u> the steam produced after the water boiled.

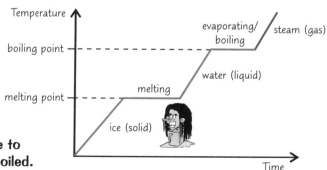

Temperature — evaporating/boiling — steam (gas) — boiling point — water (liquid) — melting point — melting — ice (solid) — Time

Water, water everywhere, and not a drop to drink...

You might be asked about these experiments in the exams, so make sure you know them. Don't panic if you're asked about an experiment that uses another substance instead of water. The steps of the experiment should be the same.

Q1 Describe an experiment you could do to find the specific heat capacity of water. [4 marks]

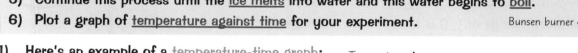

Particle Motion in Gases

Gas particles fly around, bump into things and exert forces on them. This is happening to you right now — the air around you is exerting pressure on you (unless you're somehow reading this in space).

Gas Particles Bump into Things and Create Pressure

1) Particles in a gas are free to move around.
2) They collide with (bump into) each other and the sides of the container they're in.
3) When they hit something, they exert a force on it.
4) Pressure is the force applied over a given area.
5) The more particles there are in a container, the more often they'll collide with the walls and each other.
6) So the more particles there are in a given volume, the higher the pressure will be.

Increasing the Temperature of a Gas Increases its Pressure

1) The temperature of a gas depends on the average energy in the kinetic energy stores of the gas particles.
2) The hotter the gas, the higher the average energy.
3) If particles have more energy in their kinetic stores, they move faster.
4) So the hotter the gas, the faster the particles move.
5) Faster particles hit the sides of the container more often. This increases the force on the container.
6) So increasing the temperature of a fixed mass of gas increases its pressure.
7) This only works if the space the gas takes up (the volume) doesn't change.

Absolute Zero is as Cold as Stuff Can Get — 0 kelvin

1) If you cool a substance down, you're reducing the energy of its particles.
2) The coldest that anything can ever get is -273 °C.
3) This temperature is known as absolute zero.
4) At absolute zero, the particles have as little energy in their kinetic energy stores as it's possible to get. The particles hardly move at all.
5) Absolute zero is the start of the Kelvin scale of temperature.
6) A temperature change of 1 °C is the same as a change of 1 kelvin.
7) To convert from degrees Celsius to kelvin, just add 273.
8) And to convert from kelvin to degrees Celsius, subtract 273.

	Absolute zero	Freezing point of water	Boiling point of water
Celsius scale	–273 °C	0 °C	100 °C
Kelvin scale	0 K	273 K	373 K

There's no degree symbol when you write a temperature in kelvins. Just write K, not °K. OK.

Gas particles need to watch where they're going...

Remember, the more gas particles there are, and the faster they travel, the higher the pressure. Simple...

Q1   Find the value of 25 °C in kelvin.   [1 mark]

Q2   The number of gas particles in a container with a fixed volume is increased.
State what will happen to the pressure inside the container.   [1 mark]

Forces and Elasticity

And now for something a bit more fun — squishing, stretching and bending stuff.

Stretching, Compressing or Bending Transfers Energy

1) When you apply a force to an object you may distort it (stretch, compress or bend it).
2) To do this, you need more than one force acting on the object.
3) One force would just make the object move, not change its shape.
4) An object has been elastically distorted if it can go back to its original shape and length after the force has been removed.
5) If the object doesn't go back to how it was, it has been inelastically distorted.
6) Objects that can be elastically distorted are called elastic objects (e.g. a spring).
7) Work is done when a force distorts an object.
8) This causes energy to be transferred to the elastic potential energy store of the object.

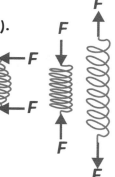

Extension is Directly Proportional to Force...

1) If a spring (or other elastic object) is fixed at one end and then a force is applied to the other end, the spring extends.

A force is acting on the fixed end of the spring to hold it in place, so two forces are acting on the spring to stretch it.

2) This extension is the difference in length between the stretched and unstretched spring.
3) Up to a given force, the extension is directly proportional to the force.
4) This means there is a linear relationship between force and extension. (If you plotted a force-extension graph for the spring, it would be a straight line.)

Directly proportional means that if you multiply the force by a number, the extension is multiplied by the same number.

5) For linear, elastic distortions, you can use:

Force exerted on a spring (N) → $$F = k \times x$$ ← Spring constant (N/m), Extension (m)

6) The spring constant depends on the object that you are stretching.
7) The equation also works for compression (where x is the difference between the natural and compressed lengths — the compression).

The length of the unstretched spring is sometimes called the spring's natural length.

...but this Stops Working when the Force is Great Enough

1) You can plot a graph of the force applied to a spring and the extension caused.
2) When the graph is a straight line, there is a linear relationship between force and extension.
3) This is where $F = k \times x$ is true.
4) The gradient of the straight line is equal to k, the spring constant.
5) When the line begins to bend (past point P), the relationship is now non-linear.
6) The extension isn't directly proportional to the force any more.
7) Point P on the graph is the limit of proportionality.
8) Past this point, the equation $F = k \times x$ is no longer true.

non-linear relationship

linear relationship

Force (y-axis), Extension (x-axis), point P marked

I could make a joke, but I don't want to stretch myself...

Make sure you don't skip over any bits of this page — it's all important. Have a go at the question below.

Q1 A spring is fixed at one end and a force of 1 N is applied to the other end, causing it to stretch. The spring extends by 2 cm. Calculate the spring constant of the spring. [2 marks]

Q1 Video Solution

Investigating Elasticity

You can do an <u>experiment</u> to see exactly how adding <u>masses</u> to a spring causes it to <u>stretch</u>.

You Can Investigate the Link Between Force and Extension

PRACTICAL

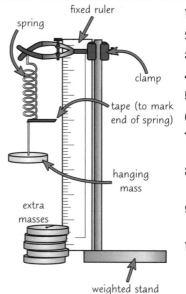

spring
fixed ruler
clamp
tape (to mark end of spring)
hanging mass
extra masses
weighted stand

1) Set up the apparatus as shown in the diagram.
2) Measure the <u>mass</u> of each mass.
3) Calculate its <u>weight</u> (the <u>force</u> applied by the mass) using $W = mg$ (p.149).
4) Measure the original (natural) <u>length</u> of the spring.
5) Add a mass to the spring and allow it to come to <u>rest</u>.
6) Record the force and measure the new <u>length</u> of the spring.
7) Find the <u>extension</u>.

extension = new length − original length

8) <u>Repeat</u> steps 5 to 7 until you've added all the masses.
9) <u>Plot</u> a <u>force-extension graph</u> of your results.
10) You should make sure you have <u>at least</u> 5 measurements before the <u>limit of proportionality</u> (where the line starts to curve).

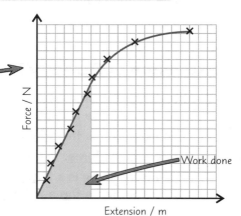

Force / N

Work done

Extension / m

11) You should find that a <u>larger force</u> causes a <u>bigger extension</u>.
12) You can also think of this as <u>more work</u> needing to be done to cause a larger extension.
13) The <u>force</u> doing work in this experiment is the <u>gravitational force</u>.
14) For <u>linear elastic</u> distortions, this force is <u>equal</u> to $F = kx$.
15) You can find the <u>work done</u> by this <u>force</u> by finding the <u>area under the line</u> up to that point.

There's more on finding the area under a graph on page 148.

You Can Calculate the Work Done for Linear Relationships

1) If a spring is not stretched <u>past</u> its <u>limit of proportionality</u>, the <u>work done</u> in stretching the spring can be found using:
2) For an <u>elastic distortion</u>, this formula can be used to calculate the energy stored in a spring's <u>elastic potential energy store</u>.
3) It's also the energy <u>transferred to</u> the spring as it's <u>distorted</u>, or <u>transferred by</u> the spring as it returns to its <u>original shape</u>.

Spring constant (N/m)

$$E = ½ \times k \times x^2$$

Energy transferred in stretching (J)

(Extension)^2 (m)^2

You can also use this equation to calculate the energy stored when a spring is compressed.

EXAMPLE

A spring with a spring constant of 500 N/m extends elastically by 10 cm. It doesn't pass its limit of proportionality. Calculate the amount of energy stored in its elastic potential energy store.

1) First, you need to <u>convert</u> the extension of the spring into <u>metres</u>.   10 cm ÷ 100 = 0.1 m
2) Then put in the <u>numbers</u> you've been given.

$E = ½ \times k \times x^2$
$= 0.5 \times 500 \times 0.1^2 = 2.5$ J

Time to spring into action and learn all this...

Make sure you know how to carry out the experiment on this page — it might come up in your exam.

Q1   A spring with a spring constant of 40 N/m extends elastically by 2.5 cm.
Calculate the amount of energy stored in its elastic potential energy store.   [2 marks]

Q1 Video Solution

Revision Questions for Sections 23 and 24

And you've reached the end of Section 24, woohoo —
time to give your old brain a work out.

- Try these questions and tick off each one when you get it right.
- When you're completely happy with a sub-topic, tick it off.

For even more practice, try the Retrieval Quizzes for Sections 23 and 24 — just scan these QR codes!

Magnetism (p.196-197) ☑

1) What is a magnetic field?
2) Do magnetic field lines point from: a) north to south   b) south to north?
3) Sketch the field lines around a bar magnet.
4) What does the behaviour of a compass that is far away from a magnet give evidence for?
5) What is the difference between a permanent magnet and an induced magnet?
6) Give three examples of temporary magnetic materials.

Section 23 Quiz

Electromagnetism and Solenoids (p.198) ☐

7) What shape is the magnetic field around a wire that has a current flowing through it?
8) How could you increase the strength of the magnetic field around a wire?
9) Explain how to use the right-hand thumb rule to work out the direction
   of the magnetic field around a wire that has a current flowing through it.
10) Explain why the magnetic field is strong inside a solenoid but weak outside it.

Density and the Kinetic Theory of Matter (p.199-203) ☑

11) What is the formula for density? What are the units of density?
12) For each state of matter, describe the arrangement of the particles.
13) Is a change of state a physical change or a chemical change?
14) True or false? Mass stays the same when a substance changes state.
15) What is meant by specific heat capacity?
16) Define specific latent heat. Give a formula for specific latent heat.

Section 24 Quiz

Particle Motion in Gases (p.204) ☑

17) What happens to the pressure of a gas in a sealed container of fixed volume when it is heated?
    Explain why this happens.
18) What is absolute zero? What value does it have in kelvin?

Stretching, Compressing and Bending (p.205-206) ☑

19) Explain why you need more than one force acting on an object to cause it to stretch.
20) How do you find the spring constant from a linear force-extension graph?
21) What is the limit of proportionality?
22) Give the equation used to find the energy transferred in stretching an object.

Apparatus and Techniques

Safety specs out and lab coats on, it's time to find out about the skills you'll need in <u>experiments</u>...

Mass Should Be Measured Using a Balance

1) To measure mass, put the <u>container</u> you're measuring the substance <u>into</u> on the <u>balance</u>.
2) Set the balance to exactly <u>zero</u>. Then <u>add</u> your substance and <u>read off</u> the <u>mass</u>.
3) If you want to transfer the substance to a new container, you need to make sure that the mass you <u>transfer</u> is the <u>same</u> as the mass you <u>measured</u>. There are different ways you can do this. For example:

- If you're <u>dissolving</u> a mass of a solid in a solvent to make a <u>solution</u>, you could <u>wash</u> any remaining solid into the new container using the <u>solvent</u>.
- You could set the balance to zero <u>before</u> you put your <u>weighing container</u> on the balance. Then <u>reweigh</u> the weighing container <u>after</u> you've transferred the solid. Use the <u>difference in mass</u> to work out <u>exactly</u> how much solid you added to your experiment.

Three Ways to Measure Liquids

1) There are a few methods you might use to measure a volume of liquid:

<u>Pipettes</u> — Use these if you want an <u>accurate</u> volume of liquid. The <u>pipette filler</u> lets you <u>safely control</u> the amount of liquid you're drawing up.

<u>Burettes</u> — These have a <u>tap</u> at the bottom which you can use to release liquid. By recording how much liquid was in the burette <u>before</u> and <u>after</u> you opened the tap, you can <u>calculate</u> how much liquid has been <u>released</u>.

<u>Measuring cylinders</u> — These come in many different <u>sizes</u>. You need to use one that's the <u>right size</u> for the measurement you want to make (you don't want one that's <u>too big</u>).

tap

2) To measure the volume of a liquid, read from the <u>bottom</u> of the <u>meniscus</u> (the curved upper surface of the liquid) when it's at <u>eye level</u>.

You can use a dropping pipette if you only want a few drops of a liquid and you don't need to measure an accurate volume.

pipette filler

10 cm³

2.0

bottom of the meniscus

Gas Syringes Measure Gas Volumes

1) You might want to <u>collect</u> the gas produced by a reaction.
2) The <u>most accurate</u> way to measure the volume of gas that's produced is to collect it in a <u>gas syringe</u> (see page 128).
3) Gases should be measured at <u>room temperature and pressure</u>. This is because the <u>volume</u> of a gas <u>changes</u> when the temperature and pressure change.
4) Make sure the syringe is <u>completely sealed</u>. This stops gas <u>escaping</u>, which would make your results <u>less accurate</u>.
5) You can also collect gas using an <u>upside down measuring cylinder</u>.
6) To measure the <u>amount</u> of gas produced, find the difference between the <u>level of water</u> in the measuring cylinder <u>before</u> the reaction and when it has <u>finished</u>.

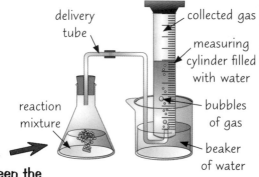

delivery tube

collected gas

measuring cylinder filled with water

bubbles of gas

reaction mixture

beaker of water

You could also count the bubbles of gas released. But the bubbles could be different sizes and you might miss some, so this method is less accurate.

Apparatus and Techniques

Measure Temperature and Time Accurately

TEMPERATURE: Use a thermometer to measure the temperature of a substance:

1) Make sure the bulb of your thermometer is completely under the surface of the substance.

2) If you're taking a starting temperature, you should wait for the temperature to stop changing.

3) Read your measurement off the scale at eye level.

bulb   thermometer

TIME: Use a stopwatch to time experiments. These can measure time accurately.

stop watch

1) Always make sure you start and stop the stopwatch at exactly the right time.

2) You can set an alarm on the stopwatch so you know exactly when to stop an experiment or take a reading.

3) In physics, you might be able to use a light gate (p.210). This will reduce errors in your experiment.

There are Different Methods for Measuring pH

See p.104 for more on pH.

1) Indicator solutions are dyes that change colour depending on whether they're in an acid or an alkali.

2) Universal indicator is a mixture of indicators that changes colour gradually as pH changes. It's useful for estimating the pH of a solution based on its colour.

3) There are also paper indicators. These change colour depending on the pH of the solution they touch. E.g. litmus paper turns red in acidic conditions and blue in alkaline conditions.

4) Indicator paper is useful when you don't want to change the colour of all of the substance. You can also use it to find the pH of a gas — hold a piece of damp indicator paper in a gas sample.

5) pH probes measure pH electronically. They are more accurate than indicators.

Measure Most Lengths With a Ruler

Length can be measured in different units (e.g. mm, cm, m). Smaller units are more accurate.

1) In most cases a 30 centimetre ruler can be used to measure length. Metre rulers or long measuring tapes are handy for large distances. Micrometers are used for measuring tiny things (e.g. the diameter of a wire).

2) It may be tricky to measure just one of something (e.g. water ripples, p.167). Instead, you can measure the length of ten of them together. Then divide by ten to find the length of one.

3) You might need to take lots of measurements of the same object (e.g. a spring). If so, make sure you always measure from the same point on the object. Draw or stick small markers onto the object to line your ruler up against.

4) Make sure the ruler and the object are always at eye level when you take a reading.

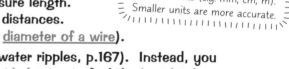

ruler   spring

marker

Sometimes you'll need to calculate the area of something. If you need to, here's how:

1) First, you'll need to take accurate measurements of its dimensions (e.g. its length and width).

2) Then you can calculate its area.

Area of a rectangle = length × width. So, if you're measuring the area of a field that's 30 m by 55 m, the area would be 30 × 55 = 1650 m².

These area formulas may also be useful:
Area of a triangle = ½ × base × height
Area of a circle = π × (radius)²

Use a Protractor to Find Angles

1) Place the middle of the protractor on the pointy bit (vertex) of the angle.

2) Line up the base line of the protractor with one line of the angle.

3) Use the scale on the protractor to measure the angle of the other line.

4) If you're drawing angles, use a sharp pencil to draw the lines (e.g. in ray diagrams). This helps to reduce errors when measuring the angles.

base line

Practical Skills

Apparatus and Techniques

There Are a Few Ways to Measure Potential Difference and Current

Voltmeters Measure Potential Difference

1) Connect the voltmeter in <u>parallel</u> (p.188) across the component you want to test.

2) The wires that come with a voltmeter are usually <u>red</u> (positive) and <u>black</u> (negative). These go into the red and black coloured <u>ports</u> on the voltmeter.

3) Then read the potential difference from the <u>scale</u> (or from the <u>screen</u> if the voltmeter is digital).

Ammeters Measure Current

1) Connect the ammeter in <u>series</u> (p.188) with the component you want to test.

2) Ammeters usually have <u>red</u> and <u>black</u> ports to show you where to connect your wires.

3) Read off the current shown on the <u>scale</u> (or <u>screen</u>).

Turn your circuit off between readings. This stops wires overheating and affecting your results (page 185).

Multimeters Measure Both

1) <u>Multimeters</u> can measure different things — usually potential difference, current and resistance.

2) To find <u>potential difference</u>, plug the <u>red</u> wire into the port that has a '<u>V</u>' (for volts).

3) To find the <u>current</u>, use the port labelled '<u>A</u>' (for amps).

4) The <u>dial</u> on the multimeter should then be turned to the <u>right section</u> — for example, to measure the <u>current</u> in <u>amps</u>, turn the dial to '<u>A</u>'.

5) The <u>screen</u> will show the value you're measuring.

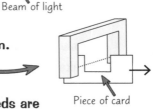

Light Gates Measure Time, Speed and Acceleration

Have a look at page 152 for an example of a light gate being used.

1) A <u>light gate</u> sends a <u>beam</u> of light from <u>one side</u> of the gate to a <u>detector</u> on the <u>other side</u>.

2) When something passes through the gate, the light beam is <u>interrupted</u>.

3) The gate measures <u>when</u> the beam was interrupted and <u>how long</u> it was interrupted for.

4) Light gates can be connected to a <u>computer</u>.

5) To find the <u>speed</u> of an object, type the <u>length</u> of the object into the computer. The computer will <u>calculate</u> the speed of the object as it passes through the beam.

6) To measure <u>acceleration</u>, use an object that interrupts the light beam <u>twice</u>. For example, a piece of card with a gap cut into the middle.

7) The computer will calculate the speed for <u>each section</u> of the object. These speeds are used to calculate the object's <u>acceleration</u>. This can then be read from the <u>computer screen</u>.

Light gate

Beam of light

Piece of card

You Can Draw Scientific Diagrams of Your Apparatus

1) It can be useful to draw a <u>labelled diagram</u> to show how apparatus should be set up.

2) Draw each piece of apparatus as if you're looking at it <u>from the side</u>. For example:

beaker   test tube   tripod

heat-proof mat

gauze

Bunsen burner

I set up my apparatus — they had a blind date at the cinema...

That's three pages full of apparatus and techniques — you need to know about them for your exams and for your practicals. In the exams, you might be asked to comment on how an experiment's been set up. So get learning.

Heating Substances

Heating a reaction mixture isn't as simple as wrapping it up in a lumpy wool jumper and a stripy scarf...

Bunsen Burners Have a Naked Flame

Here's how to use a Bunsen burner...

1) Connect the Bunsen burner to a gas tap.
   Check that the hole is closed.

2) Place the Bunsen burner on a heat-proof mat.

3) Light a splint and hold it over the Bunsen burner.

4) Now, turn on the gas.
   The Bunsen burner should light with a yellow flame.

5) Open the hole to turn the flame blue.
   The more open the hole, the hotter the flame.

6) Heat things just above the blue cone
   — this is the hottest part of the flame.

7) When the Bunsen burner isn't heating anything, close the hole.
   This makes the flame yellow and easy to see.

8) If you're heating a container (with your substance in it)
   in the flame, hold it at the top with a pair of tongs.

9) If you're heating a container over the flame, put a tripod and gauze over the
   Bunsen burner. Place the container on the gauze, then light the Bunsen burner.

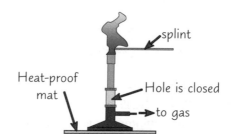

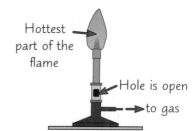

Water Baths and Electric Heaters Have Set Temperatures

1) A water bath is a container filled with water. It can be heated to a specific temperature.

2) A simple water bath can be made by heating a beaker of water over a Bunsen burner.
   - The temperature is checked with a thermometer.
   - However, it's hard to keep the temperature of the water constant.

3) An electric water bath will check and change the temperature for you. Here's how you use one:

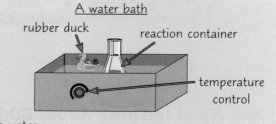

- Set the temperature on the water bath.
- Allow the water to heat up.
- Place your container (with your substance in it) in the water bath using tongs.
- The level of the water outside the container should be just above the level of the substance inside it.
- The substance will be warmed to the same temperature as the water.

The substance in the container is surrounded by water, so the heating is very even.

4) Electric heaters often have a metal plate that can be heated to a specific temperature.
   - Place your container on top of the hot plate.
   - You can heat substances to higher temperatures than you can in a water bath.
     (You can't use a water bath to heat something higher than 100 °C.)
   - You have to stir the substance to make sure it's heated evenly.

A bath and an electric heater — how I spend my January nights...

My science teacher used to play power ballads when the Bunsens were alight. Then he'd sway like he was at a gig.

Safety and Experiments

Labs are <u>dangerous places</u>, so here's a page on things you can do to keep yourself and others <u>safe</u>.

To Make Sure You're Working Safely in the Lab You Need to...

1) Wear <u>sensible clothing</u> (e.g. shoes that will protect your feet from spillages). Also:

- Wear a <u>lab coat</u> to protect your <u>skin</u> and <u>clothing</u>.
- If needed, wear <u>safety goggles</u> to protect your <u>eyes</u> and <u>gloves</u> to protect your <u>hands</u>.

2) Be aware of <u>general safety</u> in the lab. E.g. don't touch any <u>hot equipment</u>.
3) Follow any <u>instructions</u> that your teacher gives you <u>carefully</u>.
4) <u>Chemicals</u> and <u>equipment</u> can be <u>hazardous</u> (dangerous). Make sure you work with them safely...

Working with chemicals

1) Don't use a <u>Bunsen burner</u> near any chemicals that are <u>flammable</u> (catch fire easily).
2) Make sure you're working in an area that's <u>well ventilated</u> (has a good flow of air).
3) If you're doing an experiment that produces nasty <u>gases</u> (such as chlorine), carry out the experiment in a <u>fume hood</u>. This means the gas <u>can't escape</u> out into the room you're working in.
4) Never <u>touch</u> any chemicals (even if you're wearing gloves):
   - Use a <u>spatula</u> to transfer <u>solids</u> between containers.
   - Carefully <u>pour</u> liquids between containers using a <u>funnel</u>. This will help <u>prevent spillages</u>.

   Some chemicals can irritate or burn your skin if you touch them.

5) Be careful when you're <u>mixing</u> chemicals, as a reaction might occur. E.g. if you're <u>diluting</u> a liquid, always add the <u>concentrated substance</u> to the <u>water</u>, not the other way round.

You should write out a detailed risk assessment (see page 77) and method before you start an experiment.

Working with equipment

1) Use <u>clamp stands</u> to stop masses and equipment falling.
2) Make sure <u>masses</u> are <u>not too heavy</u> (so they <u>don't break</u> the equipment they're used with).
3) Use <u>pulleys</u> that are <u>not too long</u> (so hanging masses <u>don't hit the floor</u> during the experiment).
4) Let hot materials <u>cool</u> before moving them. Or wear <u>insulated gloves</u> while handling them.
5) When working with electronics, make sure you use a <u>low voltage</u> and <u>current</u>. This stops the wires <u>overheating</u>. It also stops <u>damage to components</u>.

You Need to Think About Ethical Issues

Any <u>organisms</u> that you use in your experiments need to be treated <u>safely</u> and <u>ethically</u>. This means:

1) Animals should be <u>handled carefully</u>.
2) Any captured <u>wild animals</u> should be <u>returned to their habitat</u> after the experiment.
3) Any animals <u>kept</u> in the <u>lab</u> should be <u>well cared for</u>. E.g. they shouldn't be in conditions that are <u>too hot</u>.
4) Other <u>students</u> that <u>take part</u> in any experiment should be <u>happy</u> to do so.

Proper lab equipment includes golden fur and a waggy tail...

The stuff on this page is all for your own good. It will help you in the exam, and make sure you stay safe in the lab.

Answers

Section 1 — Key Concepts in Biology

p.11 — Cells
Q1 They join amino acids together to make proteins *[1 mark]*.

p.12 — Specialised Cells
Q1 a) To carry the male DNA to the egg *[1 mark]*.
b) They have a long tail *[1 mark]*. They contain lots of mitochondria to provide energy for swimming *[1 mark]*.

p.13 — Microscopy
Q1 Take a clean slide and use a pipette to put one drop of water in the middle of it *[1 mark]*. Use tweezers to place the onion skin on the slide and add a drop of stain *[1 mark]*. Carefully lower a cover slip onto the slide using a mounted needle *[1 mark]*.

p.14 — More Microscopy
Q1 real size = image size ÷ magnification
= 2.4 mm ÷ 40
= 0.06 mm *[1 mark]*
0.06 × 1000 = 60 µm *[1 mark]*

p.15 — Enzymes
Q1 a) simple sugars *[1 mark]*
b) amino acids *[1 mark]*

p.16 — Factors Affecting Enzyme Activity
Q1 If the pH is too high it affects the bonds holding the active site together *[1 mark]*. This changes the shape of the active site and denatures the enzyme *[1 mark]*.

p.17 — More on Enzyme Activity
Q1 2.5 min × 60 = 150 seconds *[1 mark]*
1000 ÷ 150 = 6.666... = 6.7 s^{-1} *[1 mark]*

p.18 — Diffusion, Osmosis and Active Transport
Q1 active transport *[1 mark]*

p.19 — Investigating Osmosis
Q1 Water will move out of the piece of potato by osmosis *[1 mark]*, so its mass will decrease *[1 mark]*.

Section 2 — Cells and Control

p.20 — Mitosis
Q1 a) 11 ÷ (62 + 11) = 0.150...
0.150... × 100 = 15% *[1 mark]*
b) E.g. she could see the X-shaped chromosomes in the middle of the cells *[1 mark]*.

p.21 — Cell Division and Growth
Q1 A doctor would be concerned about the growth of Benjamin, but not Amol *[1 mark]*, because Benjamin's weight is below the bottom percentile line for his age, whereas Amol's weight is within the percentile lines *[1 mark]*.

p.22 — Stem Cells
Q1 Stem cells might be used to grow specialised cells to replace damaged tissue in a patient *[1 mark]*.

p.23 — The Nervous System
Q1 A sensory neurone has one long dendron and one short axon *[1 mark]* with a cell body in the middle *[1 mark]*.

p.24 — Synapses and Reflexes
Q1 A rapid, automatic response to a stimulus *[1 mark]*.
Q2 a) muscle *[1 mark]*
b) The heat stimulus is detected by receptors in the hand *[1 mark]*, which send impulses along a sensory neurone to the CNS *[1 mark]*. The impulses are transferred to a relay neurone *[1 mark]*. They are then transferred to a motor neurone and travel along it to the effector/muscle *[1 mark]*.

Section 3 — Genetics

p.26 — Sexual Reproduction and Meiosis
Q1 23 *[1 mark]*

p.27 — DNA
Q1 The salt helps the DNA to stick together *[1 mark]*.

p.28 — Genetic Diagrams
Q1

	R	r
r	Rr	rr
r	Rr	rr

round peas : wrinkly peas
1 : 1
[1 mark for correct gametes, 1 mark for correct offspring genotypes and 1 mark for correct ratio.]

p.29 — More Genetic Diagrams
Q1 Ff *[1 mark]*

p.30 — Variation
Q1 In sexual reproduction, offspring end up with a mix of their mother and father's genes *[1 mark]*.

p.31 — Mutations and The Human Genome Project
Q1 Mutations are changes to the order of bases within DNA *[1 mark]*.

Section 4 — Natural Selection and Genetic Modification

p.32 — Natural Selection and Evidence for Evolution
Q1 There was a variety of tongue lengths in the moth population *[1 mark]*. Moths with longer tongues got more food/nectar and were more likely to survive *[1 mark]*. These moths were more likely to reproduce and pass on the genes responsible for their long tongues *[1 mark]*. So, over time, longer tongues became more common in the moth population *[1 mark]*.

p.34 — Fossil Evidence for Human Evolution
Q1 E.g. by looking at the features of the tool *[1 mark]*. / By studying the rock layer the tool was found in *[1 mark]*.

p.35 — Classification
Q1 Archaea *[1 mark]*, Bacteria *[1 mark]*, Eukarya *[1 mark]*.

p.36 — Selective Breeding
Q1 Select rabbits with floppy ears *[1 mark]* and breed them together to produce offspring *[1 mark]*. Select offspring with floppy ears and breed them together *[1 mark]*. Repeat this over many generations until all of the offspring have floppy ears *[1 mark]*.

p.37 — Genetic Engineering
Q1 It can improve the yield of the crop *[1 mark]*, because herbicide-resistant crops can be sprayed with herbicides to kill weeds without the crop being damaged *[1 mark]*.

Section 5 — Health, Disease and the Development of Medicines

p.39 — Health and Disease
Q1 E.g. by making sure that people have clean water supplies *[1 mark]*.

p.40 — STIs
Q1 An STI is a sexually transmitted infection / an infection which is spread via sexual contact *[1 mark]*.
Q2 Any two from: e.g. wearing a condom when having sex / avoiding sharing needles / taking medication to reduce the risk of passing the virus on *[1 mark for each correct answer, up to 2 marks]*

p.41 — Fighting Disease
Q1 A type of white blood cell that is involved in the specific immune response/produces antibodies *[1 mark]*.

p.42 — Memory Lymphocytes and Immunisation
Q1 Basia has memory lymphocytes that recognise the antigens on the flu virus and rapidly produce antibodies, which kill the pathogen *[1 mark]*. Cassian doesn't have memory lymphocytes so it takes his immune system longer to produce antibodies and he becomes ill in the meantime *[1 mark]*.

p.43 — Antibiotics and Other Medicines
Q1 In a double-blind trial, patients are put into two groups — some receive the drug and some receive a placebo *[1 mark]*. Neither the patient nor the doctor knows whether the patient is getting the drug or a placebo until all of the results have been gathered *[1 mark]*.

p.44 — Non-Communicable Diseases
Q1 E.g. smoking / diet high in saturated fat / drinking too much alcohol / not enough exercise / obesity *[1 mark]*.

p.45 — Measures of Obesity
Q1 a) 76.0 kg ÷ (1.62 m)^2
= 29.0 kg m^{-2} *[1 mark]*
b) Obese *[1 mark]*

p.46 — Treatments for Cardiovascular Disease
Q1 E.g. having heart surgery carries risks, such as infection and losing a lot of blood *[1 mark]*. If making lifestyle changes or taking medicines are an option, then these are much less risky *[1 mark]*.

Section 6 — Plant Structures and Their Functions

p.47 — Photosynthesis
Q1 Light intensity, carbon dioxide concentration and temperature *[1 mark for each]*.

p.48 — Transport in Plants
Q1 They are made from living cells *[1 mark]*, with end walls between the cells *[1 mark]*. There are small holes in the end walls *[1 mark]*.

p.49 — Transpiration and Stomata
Q1 They allow water vapour to escape when they are open *[1 mark]*.

p.50 — Transpiration Rate
Q1 a) 48 mm ÷ 20 min
= 2.4 mm min^{-1} *[1 mark]*
b) As it gets darker, the stomata close *[1 mark]*. This means that very little water can escape *[1 mark]*, so the rate of transpiration through the plant decreases *[1 mark]*.

Section 7 — Animal Coordination, Control and Homeostasis

p.52 — Hormones
Q1 testes *[1 mark]*

p.53 — The Menstrual Cycle
Q1 Progesterone maintains the lining of the uterus during the menstrual cycle *[1 mark]*. It also prevents the release of hormones which cause eggs in the ovary to develop and ovulation to happen *[1 mark]*.

p.54 — Contraception
Q1 E.g. some barrier methods (condoms) protect against STIs *[1 mark]*, but hormonal methods don't *[1 mark]*. / They may prefer to avoid some of the unpleasant side effects *[1 mark]* that can be caused by hormonal methods but not barrier methods *[1 mark]*.

Answers

p.55 — Homeostasis — Control of Blood Glucose

Q1 Curve 2, because it starts rising after curve 1 starts to rise *[1 mark]*. Insulin is released when the blood glucose concentration gets too high, so insulin must be the second curve *[1 mark]*.

p.56 — Diabetes

Q1 Type 1 diabetes is caused when the pancreas stops making insulin *[1 mark]*.

Section 8 — Exchange and Transport in Animals

p.57 — Exchange of Materials

Q1 Surface area:
$(2 \times 2) \times 2 = 8$
$(2 \times 1) \times 4 = 8$
$8 + 8 = 16 \ \mu m^2$ *[1 mark]*
Volume:
$2 \times 2 \times 1 = 4 \ \mu m^3$ *[1 mark]*
So the surface area to volume ratio is 16 : 4, or 4 : 1 *[1 mark]*.

p.58 — Specialised Exchange Surfaces — the Alveoli

Q1 Any one from: e.g. they have a large surface area. / They have a moist lining for dissolving gases. / They have very thin walls. / They have a good blood supply *[1 mark]*.

p.59 — Circulatory System — Blood

Q1 They help the blood to clot at a wound, to stop blood pouring out/microorganisms getting in *[1 mark]*.

Q2 Any two from: e.g. they have a large surface area for absorbing oxygen. / They don't have a nucleus, which allows more room for carrying oxygen. They contain haemoglobin, which allows them to carry oxygen. *[2 marks — 1 mark for each correct answer]*.

p.60 — Circulatory System — Blood Vessels

Q1 So that substances can diffuse in and out of them quickly *[1 mark]*.

Q2 They have a big lumen to help the blood flow even though the pressure is low *[1 mark]*. They have valves to stop the blood flowing backwards *[1 mark]*.

p.61 — Circulatory System — The Heart

Q1 Deoxygenated blood travels from the vena cava into the right atrium *[1 mark]*. Then it goes to the right ventricle *[1 mark]*, and gets pumped to the lungs through the pulmonary artery *[1 mark]*.

p.62 — Heart Rate Calculations

Q1 cardiac output = heart rate × stroke volume
= 80 bpm × 75 cm³
= 6000 cm³ min⁻¹ *[2 marks for the correct answer, or 1 mark for the correct calculation]*

Q2 stroke volume = cardiac output ÷ heart rate
= 4221 cm³ min⁻¹ ÷ 67 bpm
= 63 cm³ *[2 marks for the correct answer, or 1 mark for the correct calculation]*

p.63 — Respiration

Q1 Running is a more intense type of exercise than walking *[1 mark]*, so more anaerobic respiration will be taking place in the muscles *[1 mark]*. Anaerobic respiration produces lactic acid, so running will lead to more lactic acid being in the blood *[1 mark]*.

p.64 — Investigating Respiration

Q1 A series of water baths each set to a different temperature *[1 mark]*.

Section 9 — Ecosystems and Material Cycles

p.66 — Ecosystems and Interdependence

Q1 A community is all the organisms of different species living in a habitat *[1 mark]*.

Q2 A mutualistic relationship between two organisms is a relationship from which both organisms benefit *[1 mark]*.

p.67 — Factors Affecting Ecosystems

Q1 Any two from: light intensity / amount of water / temperature / levels of pollutants *[1 mark for each correct answer, up to 2 marks]*

p.68 — Investigating Ecosystems

Q1 0.75 × 4 = 3 buttercups per m² *[1 mark]*.
3 × 1200 = 3600 buttercups in total *[1 mark]*.

p.70 — Human Impacts on Biodiversity

Q1 Any two from: e.g. non-indigenous species may out-compete species that already live in the area (so these species decrease in number/die out) *[1 mark]*. Non-indigenous species can also bring new diseases to a habitat, which can kill the species that live in the area *[1 mark]*. / Non-indigenous species may eat the species already in the area *[1 mark]*.

p.71 — The Carbon Cycle

Q1 Microorganisms in the carbon cycle are decomposers *[1 mark]*. They break down dead organisms and waste products *[1 mark]* and release CO_2 through respiration as they do so *[1 mark]*.

p.72 — The Water Cycle

Q1 Energy from the Sun makes water from the sea evaporate, turning it into water vapour *[1 mark]*. The water vapour is carried upwards, as warm air rises *[1 mark]*. When it gets higher up, it cools and condenses to form clouds *[1 mark]*. Water then falls from the clouds as precipitation, usually as rain *[1 mark]*.

p.73 — The Nitrogen Cycle

Q1 Decomposers break down dead leaves and release ammonia *[1 mark]*. Then nitrifying bacteria turn the ammonia into nitrites *[1 mark]* and then into nitrates *[1 mark]*.

Section 10 — Key Concepts in Chemistry

p.75 — Chemical Equations

Q1 carbon + oxygen → carbon dioxide *[1 mark]*

p.76 — Balancing Equations

Q1 $2Fe + 3Cl_2 \rightarrow 2FeCl_3$ *[1 mark]*

Q2 a) water → hydrogen + oxygen *[1 mark]*
  b) $2H_2O \rightarrow 2H_2 + O_2$
  [1 mark for correct reactants and products, 1 mark for a correctly balanced equation]

p.77 — Hazards and Risk

Q1 When handling the chemical, the student should take care to keep it away from flames *[1 mark]*.

p.78 — The History of the Atom

Q1 Any two from: e.g. the positive charge in the atom was only found at the centre instead of spread out through the atom *[1 mark]* / the mass of the atom was also found to be concentrated in the nucleus *[1 mark]* / the electrons formed a cloud of negative charge around the nucleus, rather than being stuck in the positive 'pudding' *[1 mark]*.

p.79 — The Atom

Q1 They have the same number of protons as electrons *[1 mark]*.

p.80 — Atomic Number, Mass Number and Isotopes

Q1 protons = atomic number = 31 *[1 mark]*
electrons = protons = 31 *[1 mark]*
neutrons = mass number – atomic number
= 70 – 31 = 39 *[1 mark]*

p.81 — The Periodic Table

Q1 Potassium and sodium are both in Group 1. Potassium and calcium are in different groups. So the properties of potassium should be closer to those of sodium than calcium *[1 mark]*, because elements in the same group have similar properties *[1 mark]*.

p.82 — Electronic Configurations

Q1 2.8.3 or

[1 mark]

Q2 Group 2 *[1 mark]*
Period 4 *[1 mark]*

p.83 — Ions

Q1 Li_2O *[1 mark]*

p.84 — Ionic Bonding

Q1 A cation is a positive ion *[1 mark]*.

Q2

[1 mark for arrow showing electron transferred from potassium to bromine, 1 mark for both ions having correct electron configurations — you only need to show the outer shells, 1 mark for correct charges on ions]

p.85 — Ionic Compounds

Q1 A lot of energy is needed to break the strong attraction between the ions/the strong ionic bonds in ionic compounds *[1 mark]*.

p.86 — Covalent Bonding

Q1 The intermolecular forces between molecules of O_2 are weak and don't need much energy to break *[1 mark]*. This gives O_2 a low boiling point (so it's a gas at room temperature) *[1 mark]*.

p.87 — Giant Covalent Structures

Q1 Graphite is made up of carbon atoms. Each carbon atom forms three covalent bonds *[1 mark]* to form layers of carbon atoms *[1 mark]* arranged in hexagons *[1 mark]*. There are no covalent bonds between the sheets (only weak forces of attraction) *[1 mark]*.

p.88 — Polymers and Fullerenes

Q1 A polymer is a molecule that contains long chains of covalently bonded carbon atoms *[1 mark]*.

Q2 Graphene is a single layer *[1 mark]* of carbon atoms bonded to each other in hexagons / which are each bonded to three other carbon atoms *[1 mark]*. Each carbon atom has one free electron in the structure *[1 mark]*.

p.89 — Metallic Bonding

Q1 Copper can conduct electricity because it contains free electrons which are able to carry an electrical charge *[1 mark]*.

p.90 — Conservation of Mass

Q1 The mass of the reaction container will increase *[1 mark]*. One of the reactants is a gas and the product is a solid *[1 mark]*, so as the gas reacts to form the product it will become contained in the reaction container *[1 mark]*.

Answers

p.91 — Relative Masses
Q1 $(2 \times 12) + (5 \times 1) + 16 + 1 = 46$ *[1 mark]*

p.92 — Empirical Formulas and Percentage Mass
Q1 relative amount of oxygen = $64 \div 16 = 4$
relative amount of nitrogen = $28 \div 14 = 2$
[1 mark]
Divide by the smallest number (2).
oxygen = $4 \div 2 = 2$
nitrogen = $2 \div 2 = 1$
Ratio of N : O = 1 : 2.
So empirical formula = NO_2 *[1 mark]*

p.93 — Finding Empirical Formulas by Experiments
Q1 Mass of magnesium
= $23.2\ g - 21\ g = 2.2\ g$
Mass of magnesium oxide
= $25\ g - 21\ g = 4\ g$ *[1 mark]*
Change in mass = $4\ g - 2.2\ g = 1.8\ g$ *[1 mark]*

p.94 — Concentration
Q1 Volume = $15 \div 1000 = 0.015\ dm^3$ *[1 mark]*
Concentration = mass $\div$ volume = $0.60 \div 0.015$
= $40\ g\ dm^{-3}$ *[1 mark]*

Section 11 — States of Matter and Mixtures

p.96 — States of Matter
Q1 gas, liquid, solid *[1 mark]*
Q2 In a gas, the particles move randomly *[1 mark]* and they travel in straight lines *[1 mark]* .

p.97 — Changes of State
Q1 a) solid *[1 mark]*
b) liquid *[1 mark]*
c) liquid *[1 mark]*
d) gas *[1 mark]*

p.98 — Purity
Q1 In chemistry, a pure substance is a substance completely made up of a single element or compound *[1 mark]*. Orange juice is not chemically pure, since it is a mixture (of water, sugars and other compounds) *[1 mark]*.
You wouldn't be expected to know what kinds of things are in orange juice, but you can still make a good guess that orange juice is chemically impure. For a start, it definitely contains water mixed with other substances.

Q2 No, I do not agree with Fatima. Since the sample she has is a pure chemical, it should have a sharp melting point *[1 mark]*.

p.99 — Distillation
Q1 Ethanol *[1 mark]*. Ethanol has the second lowest boiling point and will be collected once all the methanol has been distilled off and the temperature increased *[1 mark]*.

p.100 — Filtration and Crystallisation
Q1 Gently heat the solution to evaporate off some of the water *[1 mark]*. Stop heating once copper sulfate crystals start to form *[1 mark]*. Allow the solution to cool until copper sulfate crystals form *[1 mark]*. Filter the crystals out of the solution and dry them in a warm place *[1 mark]*.

p.101 — Chromatography
Q1 A piece of filter paper *[1 mark]*.
Q2 Chemicals A and B form separate spots because they move at different speeds as they are carried up the paper *[1 mark]*.

p.102 — Interpreting Chromatograms
Q1 $R_f = \frac{6.3}{8.4} = 0.75$ *[1 mark]*.

p.103 — Water Treatment
Q1 The water is first filtered through a wire mesh to filter out large objects and through gravel and sand to filter out smaller solid objects *[1 mark]*. Then a sedimentation process is used in which chemicals are added to the water to make fine particles clump together and settle at the bottom *[1 mark]*. Finally, chlorine gas is bubbled through the water to kill harmful bacteria *[1 mark]*.

Q2 Tap water could contain other ions that might affect the reaction *[1 mark]*. He should use deionised water instead *[1 mark]*.

Section 12 — Chemical Changes

p.104 — Acids and Bases
Q1 acidic *[1 mark]*

p.105 — Neutralisation Reactions
Q1 The H^+ ions from the acid *[1 mark]* react with the OH^- ions from the alkali to form water *[1 mark]*.

p.106 — Reactions of Acids
Q1 Calcium chloride *[1 mark]*, water *[1 mark]* and carbon dioxide *[1 mark]*.

p.107 — Making Soluble Salts
Q1 a) soluble *[1 mark]*
b) insoluble *[1 mark]*
c) insoluble *[1 mark]*
d) soluble *[1 mark]*

p.108 — Making Soluble Salts Using Acid and Alkali
Q1 Measure a set amount of acid into a conical flask *[1 mark]*. Add an indicator to the acid (e.g. phenolphthalein) *[1 mark]*. Slowly add sodium hydroxide to the acid until the indicator changes colour *[1 mark]*. Repeat the titration using the same volumes of sodium hydroxide and hydrochloric acid, without adding the indicator *[1 mark]*.

p.109 — Making Insoluble Salts
Q1 E.g. barium nitrate/barium chloride and copper sulfate *[1 mark for any soluble barium salt and 1 mark for any soluble sulfate]*

p.110 — Electrolysis
Q1 cathode *[1 mark]*

p.111 — Predicting Products of Electrolysis
Q1 a) chlorine gas/Cl_2 *[1 mark]*
b) calcium atoms/Ca *[1 mark]*

p.112 — Electrolysis of Copper Sulfate
Q1 The anode is a big lump of impure copper *[1 mark]* and the cathode is a thin piece of pure copper *[1 mark]*. During the electrolysis, the impure copper dissolves into the electrolyte and forms copper ions *[1 mark]*. These copper ions move to the cathode where they form a pure layer of copper *[1 mark]*.

Section 13 — Extracting Metals and Equilibria

p.114 — The Reactivity Series
Q1 H / hydrogen *[1 mark]*
Q2 calcium *[1 mark]*

p.115 — Reactivity of Metals
Q1 Metal B, Metal C, Metal A *[1 mark]*

p.116 — Extracting Metals Using Carbon
Q1 $2PbO + C \rightarrow 2Pb + CO_2$
[1 mark for the correct products, 1 mark for the correctly balanced equation]
Q2 Copper is less reactive than carbon *[1 mark]* so you could extract copper from its ore by reducing/heating it with carbon *[1 mark]*.

p.117 — Extracting Metals Using Electrolysis
Q1 Aluminium would be more expensive to extract than iron *[1 mark]* as aluminium is more reactive than carbon, so has to be extracted using electrolysis, whereas iron can be extracted by reduction with carbon *[1 mark]*. Extracting metals using electrolysis is much more expensive than using reduction with carbon as it requires high temperatures to melt the metal ore which is expensive/there are costs associated with using electricity, whereas reduction using carbon is much cheaper *[1 mark]*.

p.118 — Recycling
Q1 Any one from, e.g. it often saves money compared to making new materials / recycling creates lots of jobs *[1 mark]*.

p.119 — Life Cycle Assessments
Q1 Any two from, e.g. the energy required to extract the raw materials / whether the raw materials are renewable or not / the energy needed to make the cars / whether the waste can be used for other things / how environmentally friendly the cars are to dispose of *[1 mark for each]*.

p.120 — Dynamic Equilibrium
Q1 A reversible reaction is one where the products can react with each other to produce the reactants *[1 mark]*.

Q2 Dynamic equilibrium occurs when the forward and backward reactions in a reversible reaction happen at the same time *[1 mark]* and at the same rate *[1 mark]*. This means that there is no change in concentration of the reactants or the products *[1 mark]*.

Section 14 — Groups in the Periodic Table

p.121 — Group 1 — Alkali Metals
Q1 lithium + water $\rightarrow$ lithium hydroxide + hydrogen *[1 mark]*
Q2 The sodium will move around the surface of the water, fizzing vigorously, and melt *[1 mark]*.

p.122 — Group 7 — Halogens
Q1 Hold a piece of damp blue litmus paper over the gas *[1 mark]*. If it is chlorine, it will bleach the litmus paper / turn the litmus paper white *[1 mark]*.

p.123 — Reactions of Halogens
Q1 $2Na + Br_2 \rightarrow 2NaBr$ *[1 mark for correct products and reactants and 1 mark for correct balancing]*

p.124 — More Reactions of Halogens
Q1 Iodine is less reactive than bromine so it cannot displace bromide ions *[1 mark]*. No reaction occurred so there was no colour change *[1 mark]*.

p.125 — Group 0 — Noble Gases
Q1 Any temperature between $-248\ °C$ and $-158\ °C$ *[1 mark]*.

Section 15 — Rates of Reaction and Energy Changes

p.127 — Reaction Rates
Q1 E.g. the result is subjective / different people have different opinions about when the mark disappears *[1 mark]*.

p.128 — Rate Experiments Involving Gases
Q1 E.g. place a measured volume of hydrochloric acid of a known concentration in a conical flask. Add a known mass of calcium carbonate in the form of marble chips *[1 mark]*. Attach a gas syringe to the conical flask. Take readings of the volume of gas produced at regular time intervals *[1 mark]*. Repeat the experiment with the same volume and concentration of acid and the same mass of calcium carbonate but increase the surface area of the calcium carbonate by crunching the marble up *[1 mark]*.

Answers

p.129 — Calculating Rates
Q1 Average rate = amount of reactant used ÷ time
= 6.0 g ÷ 200 s *[1 mark]*
= 0.03 g s⁻¹ *[1 mark]*

p.130 — More on Calculating Rates
Q1 gradient = change in y ÷ change in x
= 9 ÷ 12 *[1 mark]*
= 0.75 *[1 mark]*

p.131 — Collision Theory
Q1 The energy transferred during a collision (particles must collide with enough energy for the collision to be successful) *[1 mark]* and how often the reacting particles collide *[1 mark]*.

Q2 Breaking a solid into smaller pieces will increase its surface area to volume ratio *[1 mark]*. This means that particles of the other reactant will have more area to react with *[1 mark]*. This means collisions will be more frequent, so the rate of the reaction will increase *[1 mark]*.

p.132 — Catalysts
Q1 A catalyst is a substance which increases the rate of reaction *[1 mark]*, without being chemically changed or used up *[1 mark]*.

Q2 Enzymes are biological catalysts *[1 mark]*. They speed up chemical reactions inside living cells *[1 mark]*.

p.133 — Endothermic and Exothermic Reactions
Q1

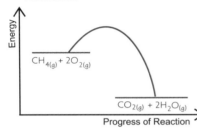

[1 mark for correct axes, 1 mark for correct energy levels of reactants and products, 1 mark for correct shape of curve linking the reactants to the products]

p.134 — Bond Energies and Activation Energy
Q1 Less energy is needed to break the bonds in the reactants than is released when the bonds in the products are formed *[1 mark]*.

Q2 The activation energy is the energy difference between the reactants and the highest point on the curve *[1 mark]*.

p.135 — Measuring Temperature Changes
Q1 They help to insulate the reaction mixture, limiting the energy transferred to or from the surroundings *[1 mark]*.

Section 16 — Fuels and Earth Science

p.136 — Fractional Distillation
Q1 The diagram shows that the hydrocarbons in petrol have a shorter chain length than the hydrocarbons in diesel, so petrol has a lower boiling point than diesel *[1 mark]*.

p.137 — Hydrocarbons
Q1 As they become longer, they have higher boiling points which makes them harder to ignite *[1 mark]*.

p.138 — Combustion of Fuels
Q1 $C_2H_6 + 3\frac{1}{2}O_2 \rightarrow 2CO_2 + 3H_2O$ or
$2C_2H_6 + 7O_2 \rightarrow 4CO_2 + 6H_2O$
[1 mark for correct reactants and products, 1 mark for correctly balancing]

Q2 Carbon monoxide *[1 mark]* and soot *[1 mark]*.

p.139 — Pollutants
Q1 Sulfur impurities in the fuel can react with oxygen to form sulfur dioxide *[1 mark]*.

p.140 — Cracking
Q1 $C_{12}H_{26}$ *[1 mark]*

p.141 — The Atmosphere
Q1 A lot of the early CO_2 dissolved into the oceans *[1 mark]*. Green plants evolved and removed CO_2 from the atmosphere through photosynthesis *[1 mark]*.

p.142 — The Greenhouse Effect
Q1 The sun gives out short wavelength radiation *[1 mark]* which is reflected back by the Earth as long wavelength/thermal radiation *[1 mark]*. The thermal radiation is absorbed by greenhouse gases in the atmosphere *[1 mark]*. Greenhouse gases give out the thermal radiation in all directions including back towards the Earth, causing the temperature to rise *[1 mark]*.

p.143 — Climate Change
Q1 E.g. walk or cycle instead of drive *[1 mark]* / turn their central heating down *[1 mark]*.

Q2 Global warming is a type of climate change that has caused global temperatures to increase *[1 mark]*. Increased human activity has led to increased levels of greenhouse gases in Earth's atmosphere *[1 mark]*. This is thought to have resulted in more energy being trapped in the atmosphere and caused the Earth's average temperature to increase *[1 mark]*.

Section 17 — Motion and Forces

p.145 — Distance, Displacement, Speed and Velocity
Q1 speed = distance ÷ time
= 200 ÷ 25 *[1 mark]*
= 8 m/s *[1 mark]*

p.146 — Acceleration
Q1 $u = 0$ m/s, $v = 5$ m/s, $a = g = 10$ m/s²,
$x = (v^2 - u^2) \div 2a = (25 - 0) \div (2 \times 10)$ *[1 mark]*
= 1.25 m *[1 mark]*

p.147 — Distance/Time Graphs
Q1 E.g.

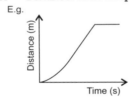

[1 mark for a curved line with an increasing positive gradient, 1 mark for the line becoming a straight line with a positive gradient, 1 mark for the line then becoming horizontal]

p.148 — Velocity/Time Graphs
Q1

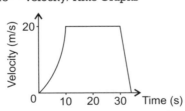

[1 mark for an upwards curved acceleration line to 20 m/s, 1 mark for a straight line representing steady speed, 1 mark for a straight line representing deceleration]

p.149 — Weight
Q1 a) $W = mg = 25 \times 10$ *[1 mark]* = 250 N *[1 mark]*
b) $W = 25 \times 1.6$ *[1 mark]* = 40 N *[1 mark]*

p.150 — Resultant Forces and Newton's First Law
Q1 accelerating *[1 mark]*
There is a resultant force of 50 N acting in the forward direction, meaning the car will speed up.

p.151 — Newton's Second Law
Q1 $F = ma = (80 + 10) \times 0.25$ *[1 mark]*
= 22.5 N *[1 mark]*

Q2 Rearrange $F = ma$ for mass:
$m = F \div a$ *[1 mark]*
= 18.9 ÷ 1.80 *[1 mark]*
= 10.5 kg *[1 mark]*

p.152 — Investigating Motion
Q1 E.g. light gate *[1 mark]*

p.153 — Newton's Third Law
Q1 Any one from: e.g the gravitational force of the Earth attracts the car and the gravitational force of the car attracts the Earth *[1 mark]* / the car exerts a normal contact force down against the ground and the normal contact force from the ground pushes up against the car *[1 mark]* / the car (tyres) pushes the road backwards and the road pushes the car (tyres) forwards *[1 mark]*.

p.154 — Stopping Distances
Q1 Any three from: e.g. speed of the vehicle / mass of the vehicle / condition of the brakes / condition of the road / the amount of friction between the tyres and the road. *[3 marks — 1 mark for each correct answer]*

p.155 — Reaction Times
Q1 0.2 - 0.9 s *[1 mark]*

Q2 E.g. using the ruler drop test / using a computer-based test *[1 mark]*.

Section 18 — Conservation of Energy

p.156 — Energy Stores and Conservation of Energy
Q1 Energy is transferred mechanically *[1 mark]* from the kinetic energy store of the wind *[1 mark]* to the kinetic energy store of the windmill *[1 mark]*.

p.157 — Energy Transfers
Q1 The racket has energy in its kinetic energy store *[1 mark]*. Some of this energy is transferred mechanically to the ball's kinetic energy store *[1 mark]*. Some energy is transferred mechanically to the thermal energy stores of the racket and the ball. This energy is then transferred by heating to the surroundings *[1 mark]*. The rest is carried away by sound *[1 mark]*.

p.158 — Kinetic and Potential Energy Stores
Q1 The change in height is 5 m.
So the energy transferred from the gravitational potential energy store is:
$\Delta GPE = m \times g \times \Delta h = 2 \times 10 \times 5$ *[1 mark]*
= 100 J *[1 mark]*
This is transferred to the kinetic energy store of the object, so KE = 100 J *[1 mark]*
$KE = \frac{1}{2} \times m \times v^2$ so $v^2 = (2 \times KE) \div m$
= $(2 \times 100) \div 2$ *[1 mark]*
= 100 m/s²
$v = \sqrt{100} = 10$ m/s *[1 mark]*

Q2 $KE = \frac{1}{2} \times m \times v^2$
So, $m = (2 \times KE) \div v^2$ *[1 mark]*
= $(2 \times 1\,575\,000) \div 30.0^2$ *[1 mark]*
= 3500 kg *[1 mark]*

p.159 — Efficiency
Q1 Useful energy transferred by device
= 500 − 420 = 80 J *[1 mark]*

Efficiency = $\dfrac{\text{useful energy transferred by device}}{\text{total energy supplied to device}}$

= 80 ÷ 500 = 0.16 *[1 mark]*
0.16 × 100 = 16% *[1 mark]*

p.160 — Reducing Unwanted Energy Transfers
Q1 E.g. lubricate moving parts *[1 mark]*.

p.161 — Energy Resources
Q1 Any two from: e.g. bio-fuels / wind power / the Sun/solar power / hydro-electricity / the tides *[2 marks — 1 mark for each correct answer]*

p.162 — More Energy Resources

Q1 Advantages
Any one from: e.g. no pollution once the solar cells are built / reliable source of energy in sunny countries *[1 mark]*.
Disadvantages
Any one from: e.g. lots of energy is used to build them / only generate electricity during the day / can't increase the power output when there is extra demand *[1 mark]*.

p.163 — Trends in Energy Resource Use

Q1 Any two from: e.g. building new power plants is expensive / people don't want to live near new power plants / renewable energy resources are less reliable than non-renewable energy resources *[2 marks — 1 mark for each correct answer]*.

Section 19 — Waves and the Electromagnetic Spectrum

p.165 — Wave Basics

Q1 Any two from: e.g. electromagnetic waves / water waves / seismic S-waves.
[2 marks — 1 mark for each correct answer]

p.166 — Wave Speed

Q1 $7.5 \div 100 = 0.075$ m
wave speed = frequency × wavelength, so
frequency = wave speed ÷ wavelength *[1 mark]*
$= 0.15 \div 0.075$ *[1 mark]*
$= 2$ Hz *[1 mark]*

p.167 — Investigating Waves

Q1 E.g. attach a signal generator to a dipper and place it in a ripple tank filled with water to create some waves *[1 mark]*. Place a screen underneath the ripple tank, then turn on a strobe light and dim the other lights in the room *[1 mark]*. Adjust the frequency of the strobe light until the shadows of the ripples on the screen appear to stop moving *[1 mark]*. Measure the distance across 10 gaps between the shadow lines and divide this length by 10 — this is equal to the (average) wavelength of the ripples *[1 mark]*.

p.168 — Refraction

Q1 Refraction is when a wave changes direction at the boundary between two different materials *[1 mark]*.

p.169 — Investigating Refraction

Q1 E.g. draw around a glass block onto a piece of paper and shine a light ray into the block *[1 mark]*. Trace the incident ray and mark where the ray exits from the block. Remove the block and join up the rays you have drawn with a straight line *[1 mark]*. Measure the angle of incidence and angle of refraction for where the light entered the block *[1 mark]*.

p.170 — Electromagnetic Waves

Q1 Gamma radiation *[1 mark]*.

p.171 — Uses of EM Waves

Q1 Any three from: e.g. security systems / thermal imaging / short range communication / cooking / television remote controls / optical fibres.
[3 marks — 1 mark for each correct answer]

p.172 — More Uses of EM Waves

Q1 Any two from: e.g. fluorescent lamps / security marking / detecting forged bank notes/passports / disinfecting water. *[2 marks — 1 mark for each correct answer]*

Section 20 — Radioactivity

p.173 — The Atomic Model

Q1 a) The radius of a nucleus is about 10 000 times smaller than the radius of the atom *[1 mark]*.

b) The centre of an atom is a tiny, positively-charged nucleus *[1 mark]*. This is made up of protons and neutrons *[1 mark]* and makes up most of the atom's mass *[1 mark]*. Negatively-charged electrons orbit the nucleus at set energy levels *[1 mark]*.

p.174 — More on the Atomic Model

Q1 A positive ion is an atom that has lost electrons *[1 mark]*. A positive ion is formed when an outer electron absorbs enough energy to leave the atom *[1 mark]*.

p.175 — Isotopes and Nuclear Radiation

Q1 a) E.g. a thin sheet of paper will absorb alpha particles *[1 mark]*.

b) A thin sheet of aluminium will absorb beta-minus particles *[1 mark]*.

p.176 — Nuclear Equations

Q1 $^{219}_{86}\text{Rn} \rightarrow \,^{215}_{84}\text{Po} + \,^{4}_{2}\alpha$
[1 mark for correct layout, 1 mark for correct symbol for an alpha particle, 1 mark for total atomic and mass numbers being equal on both sides]

p.177 — Background Radiation and Activity

Q1 Any two from: e.g. rocks / cosmic rays / nuclear explosions / nuclear waste / building materials / food. *[2 marks — 1 mark for each correct answer]*

p.178 — Half-Life

Q1 15 minutes *[1 mark]*
The half-life is always the same, so it takes 15 minutes for the activity to halve again.

Q2 Initial activity = 168 Bq
After 1 half-life,
activity = 168 ÷ 2 = 84 Bq
After 2 half-lives,
activity = 84 ÷ 2 = 42 Bq
After 3 half-lives,
activity = 42 ÷ 2 = 21 Bq *[1 mark]*
So, it took 3 half-lives for the activity to drop to 21 Bq. This means that 60 minutes is equal to 3 half-lives *[1 mark]*.
So, the half-life of the sample
= 60 ÷ 3 = 20 minutes *[1 mark]*

p.179 — Irradiation and Contamination

Q1 E.g. radiation can cause minor damage to a cell that causes it to mutate / radiation can cause cells to divide uncontrollably / causes cancer *[1 mark]*. Radiation can also kill a cell completely *[1 mark]*.

Section 21 — Forces and Energy

p.181 — Energy Transfers and Systems

Q1 Mechanically *[1 mark]*, electrically *[1 mark]*, by heating *[1 mark]* and by radiation *[1 mark]*.

p.182 — Forces and Work Done

Q1 First change the distance to metres:
20 ÷ 100 = 0.2 m
Then substitute into the equation:
$E = F \times d = 20 \times 0.2$ *[1 mark]* = 4 J *[1 mark]*

p.183 — Wasted Energy and Power

Q1 Rearrange $P = E \div t$ for energy transferred:
$E = P \times t$ *[1 mark]*
Change the time to seconds:
15 × 60 = 900 s *[1 mark]*
$E = P \times t = 40 \times 900 = 36\,000$ J *[1 mark]*

Section 22 — Electricity and Circuits

p.184 — Current and Circuits

Q1 $Q = It$ so $t = Q \div I$ *[1 mark]*
$= 28\,800 \div 8$ *[1 mark]*
$= 3600$ s *[1 mark]*
$t = 3600 \div 60 = 60$ minutes *[1 mark]*

p.185 — Potential Difference and Resistance

Q1 $V = IR$ so $R = V \div I$ *[1 mark]*
$= 230 \div 5.0$ *[1 mark]*
$= 46\ \Omega$ *[1 mark]*

p.186 — I-V Graphs

Q1

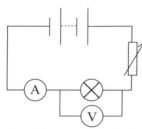

[1 mark for a complete circuit with a variable resistor in series with a filament lamp, 1 mark for correct circuit symbols for all components, 1 mark for a voltmeter connected across the filament lamp and an ammeter connected in series with the filament lamp.]

p.187 — Circuit Devices

Q1 a) E.g. automatic night lights — a light automatically turns on when it gets dark *[1 mark]*.

b) E.g. thermostats — the heating automatically turns on/off at a certain temperature *[1 mark]*.

p.188 — Series and Parallel Circuits

Q1 $R_{total} = 4 + 5 + 6 = 15\ \Omega$ *[1 mark]*
$V = I \times R = 0.6 \times 15$ *[1 mark]*
$= 9$ V *[1 mark]*

p.189 — More on Series and Parallel Circuits

Q1 The total current through the circuit decreases *[1 mark]* as there are fewer paths for the current to take *[1 mark]*. The total resistance of the circuit increases *[1 mark]* as, using $V = IR$, a decrease in the total current means an increase in the total resistance *[1 mark]*.

p.190 — Energy in Circuits

Q1 $t = 60 \times 60$ *[1 mark]*
$E = I \times V \times t = 4.0 \times 230 \times (60 \times 60)$ *[1 mark]*
$= 3\,312\,000$ J
$= 3\,300\,000$ J (to 2 s.f.) *[1 mark]*

p.191 — Electrical Power

Q1 $E = P \times t = 250 \times (2 \times 60 \times 60)$
$= 1\,800\,000$ J *[1 mark]*
$E = 375 \times (2 \times 60 \times 60) = 2\,700\,000$ J *[1 mark]*
So difference in the energy transferred is
$2\,700\,000 - 1\,800\,000 = 900\,000$ J *[1 mark]*

p.192 — Electricity in the Home

Q1 In an alternating current supply, the charges are constantly changing direction *[1 mark]*. In a direct current supply, the charges always travel in the same direction *[1 mark]*.

p.193 — Electrical Safety

Q1 The live wire *[1 mark]*.

p.194 — Transformers and the National Grid

Q1 Power output = $V_s \times I_s = 320$ W
$V_p \times I_p = V_s \times I_s$, so
$I_p = (V_s \times I_s) \div V_p$
$= 320 \div 1.6$ *[1 mark]*
$= 200$ A *[1 mark]*

Answers

Section 23 — Magnetic Fields

p.196 — Magnets and Magnetic Fields
Q1 At all points, it has the same strength *[1 mark]* and direction *[1 mark]*.

p.197 — Permanent and Induced Magnets
Q1 Iron is a temporary magnetic material/becomes an induced magnet when in a magnetic field *[1 mark]*. This means it is attracted to the magnet passing over it *[1 mark]*.

p.198 — Electromagnetism and Solenoids
Q1 E.g. for current out of the page:

[1 mark for concentric circles getting further apart, 1 mark for arrows on field lines with correct direction]

Q2 It disappears *[1 mark]*.

Section 24 — Matter

p.199 — Density
Q1 First find the cube's volume:
$0.015 \times 0.015 \times 0.015 = 3.375 \times 10^{-6}$ m³
[1 mark]
The cube's density is 3500 kg/m³.
$m = \rho \times V = 3500 \times (3.375 \times 10^{-6})$ *[1 mark]*
$= 0.01181...$ kg $= 0.012$ kg (to 2 s.f.) *[1 mark]*

p.200 — Kinetic Theory and States of Matter
Q1 a) boiling / evaporating *[1 mark]*
   b) sublimating *[1 mark]*

p.201 — Specific Heat Capacity
Q1 $\Delta Q = mc\Delta\theta$, so:
$\Delta\theta = \Delta Q \div (m \times c)$ *[1 mark]*
$= 50\,000 \div (5 \times 4200)$
$= 2.380...$ °C *[1 mark]*
So the new temperature
$= 5 + 2.380... = 7.380...$
$= 7$ °C (to 1 s.f.) *[1 mark]*

Q2 $\Delta Q = mc\Delta\theta$, so:
$\Delta\theta = \Delta Q \div (m \times c)$ *[1 mark]*
$= 1680 \div (0.20 \times 420)$ *[1 mark]*
$= 20$ °C *[1 mark]*

p.202 — Specific Latent Heat
Q1 $Q = m \times L = 0.25 \times 120\,000$ *[1 mark]*
$= 30\,000$ J *[1 mark]*

p.203 — Investigating Water
Q1 E.g. measure the mass of an empty insulating container. Pour water into the container and measure the mass again. Subtract the mass of the empty container from this mass to find the mass of the water *[1 mark]*. Using an immersion heater connected to a joulemeter, heat the water *[1 mark]*. Use a thermometer to monitor the temperature of the water. Once the temperature of the water has increased by 10 °C, turn off the immersion heater *[1 mark]*. Use the reading from the joulemeter and the equation $c = \Delta Q \div (m \times \Delta\theta)$ to find the specific heat capacity *[1 mark]*.

p.204 — Particle Motion in Gases
Q1 $25 + 273 = 298$ K *[1 mark]*
Q2 It will increase *[1 mark]*.

p.205 — Forces and Elasticity
Q1 $k = F \div x$
$= 1 \div 0.02$ *[1 mark]*
$= 50$ N/m *[1 mark]*

p.206 — Investigating Elasticity
Q1 $E = \frac{1}{2}kx^2$
$= \frac{1}{2} \times 40 \times (0.025)^2$ *[1 mark]*
$= 0.0125$ J *[1 mark]*

Glossary

Abiotic factor	A non-living factor of the environment.
Absolute zero	Theoretically the coldest temperature an object could reach. At absolute zero, particles have the minimum amount of energy in their kinetic energy stores. Absolute zero is at 0 K, or –273 °C.
Absorption (of waves)	When a wave transfers energy to the energy stores of a material.
Acceleration	A change in velocity in a certain amount of time.
Accurate result	A result that is close to the true answer.
Acid	A substance with a pH of less than 7 that forms H^+ ions in water.
Acrosome	The part of the sperm that contains the enzymes needed to digest through the membrane of the egg cell.
Activation energy	The minimum amount of energy that reactant particles must have when they collide in order to react.
Active transport	The movement of particles across a membrane against a concentration gradient (i.e. from an area of lower concentration to an area of higher concentration) using energy transferred during respiration.
Activity (radioactive)	The number of nuclei of a sample that decay per second, measured in Bq.
Adaptation	A feature that helps an organism to survive in its natural environment.
Aerobic respiration	Respiration taking place in the presence of oxygen.
Air resistance	The frictional force caused by air on a moving object.
Alkali	A substance with a pH of more than 7 that forms OH^- ions in solution.
Alkali metal	An element in Group 1 of the periodic table. E.g. sodium, potassium etc.
Alkane	A saturated hydrocarbon with the general formula C_nH_{2n+2}. E.g. methane, ethane etc.
Allele	A version of a gene.
Alpha decay	A type of radioactive decay in which an alpha particle is given out from a decaying nucleus.
Alpha particle	A positively-charged particle made up of two protons and two neutrons (a helium nucleus).
Alpha particle scattering experiment	An experiment in which alpha particles were fired at gold foil to see if they were deflected. It led to the plum pudding model being abandoned in favour of the nuclear model of the atom.
Alternating current (a.c.)	Current that is constantly changing direction.
Alveolus	A tiny air sac in the lungs, where gas exchange occurs.
Amino acid	A small molecule that is a building block of proteins.
Ammeter	A component used to measure the current through a component. It is always connected in series with the component.
Amplitude	The maximum displacement of a point on a wave from its rest position.
Anaerobic respiration	Respiration taking place in the absence of oxygen.
Angle of incidence	The angle the incoming ray makes with the normal at a boundary.
Angle of refraction	The angle a refracted ray makes with the normal when a wave refracts at a boundary.
Anion	A particle with a negative charge, formed when one or more electrons are gained.
Anode	The positive electrode in electrolysis.
Anomalous result	A result that doesn't seem to fit with the rest of the data.
Antibiotic	A drug used to kill or prevent the growth of bacteria.
Antibiotic resistance	When bacteria aren't killed by an antibiotic.
Antibody	A protein produced by lymphocytes in response to the presence of an antigen.

Antigen	A molecule on the surface of a cell or a pathogen that can trigger an immune response. Foreign antigens trigger lymphocytes to produce antibodies.
Aqueous solution	A solution made up of a solute dissolved in water.
Artery	A blood vessel that carries blood away from the heart.
Asexual reproduction	Where organisms reproduce by mitosis to produce genetically identical offspring.
Atmosphere	The layer of gases that surrounds a planet.
Atom	A small particle that makes up matter. It is made up of a small, central, positively-charged nucleus, consisting of protons and neutrons, surrounded by negatively-charged electrons.
Atomic (proton) number	The number of protons in the nucleus of an atom.
Axon	The part of a neurone that carries nerve impulses away from the cell body.
Background radiation	The low-level radiation which surrounds us at all times. It comes from both natural and man-made sources.
Base	A substance that reacts with acids in neutralisation reactions.
Beta decay	A type of radioactive decay in which either a beta-minus particle or a beta-plus particle is given out from a decaying nucleus.
Beta-minus particle	A high-speed electron emitted by the nucleus.
Beta-plus particle	A high-speed positron emitted by the nucleus.
Bias	Unfairness in the way data is presented, possibly because the presenter is trying to make a particular point.
Biodiversity	The variety of living organisms in an ecosystem.
Bio-fuel	A renewable energy resource made from plant products or animal dung.
Biomass	The mass of living material in an organism or a group of organisms.
Biotic factor	A living factor of the environment.
BMI	Body Mass Index. Used as a guide to help decide whether someone is underweight, of healthy weight, overweight or obese.
Braking distance	The braking distance is the distance a vehicle travels after the brakes are applied until it comes to a complete stop, as a result of the braking force.
Calibrate	Measure something with a known quantity to see if the instrument being used to measure that quantity gives the correct value.
Capillary	A type of blood vessel involved in the exchange of materials at tissues.
Carbohydrase	A type of digestive enzyme that catalyses the breakdown of a carbohydrate into sugars.
Cardiovascular disease	Disease of the heart or blood vessels.
Catalyst	A substance that increases the rate of a reaction without being chemically changed or used up in the reaction.
Categoric data	Data that comes in distinct categories (e.g. flower colour or blood group).
Cathode	The negative electrode in electrolysis.
Cation	A particle with a positive charge, formed when one or more electrons are lost.
Cell membrane	A membrane surrounding a cell, which holds it together and controls what goes in and out.
Cellulose	A molecule which strengthens cell walls in plants and algae.
Cell wall	A structure surrounding some cell types, which gives strength and support.
Central Nervous System (CNS)	The brain and spinal cord. It's where reflexes and actions are coordinated.
Chemical bond	The attraction of two atoms for each other, caused by the sharing or transfer of electrons.
Chlorophyll	A green substance found in chloroplasts which absorbs light for photosynthesis.
Chloroplast	A structure found in plant cells and algae. It is the site of photosynthesis.
Chromatogram	The pattern of spots formed as a result of separating a mixture using chromatography.
Chromatography	A method used to separate the substances in a mixture based on how the components interact with a mobile phase and a stationary phase.

Glossary

Chromosome	A long molecule of DNA found in the nucleus. Each chromosome carries many genes.
Cilia	Hair-like structures on the surface of a cell, used to move substances in one direction.
Circuit breaker	A circuit component that 'trips' and breaks the circuit when the current through it goes above a certain point. They are used to protect circuits and to prevent electrical fires and electric shocks.
Climate change	A change in the Earth's climate. E.g. global warming, changing rainfall patterns etc.
Clinical trial	A set of drug tests on human volunteers.
Closed system (chemistry)	A reaction system where no substances can get in or out.
Closed system (physics)	A system where the net change in energy is zero.
Collision theory	The theory that in order for a reaction to occur, particles must collide with sufficient energy.
Combustion	An exothermic reaction between a fuel and oxygen.
Communicable disease	A disease that can spread between individuals.
Community	All the organisms of different species living in a habitat.
Complete combustion	Combustion in plenty of oxygen, where the only products are carbon dioxide and water.
Compound	A substance made up of atoms of at least two different elements, chemically joined together.
Concentration	The amount of a substance in a certain volume of solution.
Conclusion	A summary of the findings of a scientific investigation.
Conductor (electrical)	A material through which electrical charges can easily move.
Conductor (heat)	A material that heat can pass through easily.
Conservation of energy	Energy can be stored, transferred between energy stores and dissipated — but it can never be created or destroyed.
Contact force	A force that only acts between touching objects.
Contamination (radioactive)	The presence of unwanted radioactive atoms on or inside an object.
Continuous data	Numerical data that can have any value within a range (e.g. length, volume or temperature).
Contraceptive	A method of preventing pregnancy.
Control experiment	An experiment that's kept under the same conditions as the rest of an investigation, but doesn't have anything done to it.
Control variable	A variable in an experiment that is kept the same.
Conversion factor	A number which you must multiply or divide a unit by to convert it to a different unit.
Correlation	A relationship between two variables.
Cosmic ray	Radiation from space.
Covalent bond	A chemical bond formed when atoms share a pair of electrons.
Cracking	The process that is used to break long-chain hydrocarbons down into shorter, more useful hydrocarbons.
Crystallisation	The formation of solid crystals as water evaporates from a solution. For example, salt solutions undergo crystallisation to form solid salt crystals.
Current	The flow of electric charge. The size of the current is the rate of flow of charge. Measured in amperes (A).
Cytokinesis	The stage of the cell cycle when the cytoplasm and cell membrane divide to form two separate cells.
Cytoplasm	A gel-like substance in a cell where most of the chemical reactions take place.
Decomposer	An organism (usually a microorganism) that breaks down waste products and dead organisms.
Delocalised electron	An electron that isn't associated with a particular atom or bond and is free to move within a structure.

Dendron	The part of a neurone that carries nervous impulses towards the cell body.
Density	A substance's mass per unit volume.
Dependent variable	The variable in an experiment that is measured.
Desalination	The removal of salts from salt water to produce potable (drinking) water.
Diabetes	A condition that affects the body's ability to control its blood glucose level.
Differentiation	The process by which a cell becomes specialised for its job.
Diffusion	The spreading out of particles from an area of higher concentration to an area of lower concentration.
Diode	A circuit component that only allows current to flow through it in one direction. It has a very high resistance in the other direction.
Diploid cell	A cell with two copies of each chromosome.
Direct current (d.c.)	A current where the charges only move in one direction.
Discrete data	Numerical data that can only take a certain value, with no in-between value (e.g. number of people).
Displacement	The straight-line distance and direction from an object's starting position to its finishing position.
Displacement reaction	A reaction where a more reactive element replaces a less reactive element in a compound.
Displayed formula	A chemical formula that shows the atoms in a covalent compound and all the bonds between them.
Dissipation	The transfer of energy to thermal energy stores of an object and its surroundings. Also called wasted energy.
Distance/time graph	A graph showing how the distance travelled by an object changes over a period of time.
Distillation	A way of separating out a liquid from a mixture. You heat the mixture until the bit you want evaporates, then cool the vapour to turn it back into a liquid.
Distribution	Where organisms are found in a particular area.
DNA	Deoxyribonucleic acid. The molecule in cells that stores genetic information.
Dominant allele	The allele for the characteristic that's shown by an organism if two different alleles are present for that characteristic.
Double-blind trial	A clinical trial where neither the doctors nor the patients know who has received the drug and who has received the placebo until all the results have been gathered.
Dynamic equilibrium	The point at which the rates of the forward and backward reactions in a reversible reaction are the same, and so the amounts of reactants and products in the reaction container don't change.
Earth wire	The green and yellow wire in an electrical cable that only carries current when there's a fault. It stops exposed metal parts of an appliance from becoming live. It is at 0 V.
Ecosystem	A community of living organisms along with the abiotic parts of their environment.
Effector	Either a muscle or gland which responds to nervous impulses.
Efficiency	The proportion of energy supplied to a device which is usefully transferred.
Elastic distortion	An object undergoing elastic distortion will return to its original shape and length once any forces being applied to it are removed.
Elastic object	An object which can be elastically distorted.
Elastic potential energy store	Anything that has been stretched or compressed, e.g. a spring, has energy in its elastic potential energy store.
Electrode	An electrical conductor which is submerged in the electrolyte during electrolysis.
Electrolysis	The process of breaking down a substance using electricity.
Electrolyte	A molten or dissolved ionic compound used in electrolysis that can conduct electricity between the two electrodes.
Electromagnet	A magnet whose magnetic field can be turned on and off by an electric current.

Glossary

Electromagnetic (EM) spectrum	A continuous spectrum of all the possible wavelengths of electromagnetic waves.
Electron	A subatomic particle with a relative charge of –1 and a relative mass of 0.0005.
Electronic configuration	The number of electrons in an atom (or ion) and how they are arranged.
Electron shell	A region of an atom that contains electrons. It's also known as an energy level.
Electrostatic force	A force of attraction between opposite charges.
Element	A substance that is made up only of atoms with the same number of protons.
Empirical formula	A chemical formula showing the simplest possible whole number ratio of atoms in a compound.
Endocrine gland	An organ that hormones are produced and secreted from.
Endothermic reaction	A reaction which takes in energy from the surroundings.
End point	The point at which an acid or alkali is completely neutralised during a titration.
Energy store	A means by which an object stores energy. Common energy stores are: thermal, kinetic, gravitational potential, elastic potential, chemical, magnetic, electrostatic and nuclear.
Enzyme	A protein that acts as a biological catalyst.
Equilibrium (physics)	A state in which all the forces acting on an object are balanced, so the resultant force is zero.
Erythrocyte	A red blood cell.
Eukaryotic cell	A complex cell, such as a plant or animal cell.
Eutrophication	An excess of nutrients in water, leading to increased algal growth, oxygen depletion and the eventual death of other organisms in the water.
Evaluation	A critical analysis of a scientific investigation.
Evolution	The changing of the inherited characteristics of a population over time.
Exothermic reaction	A reaction which transfers energy to the surroundings.
Extinct	When no living individuals of a species remain.
Fair test	A controlled experiment where the only thing that changes is the independent variable.
Family pedigree	A diagram that shows how a characteristic (or disorder) is inherited in a group of related people.
Feedstock	A raw material used to produce other substances through industrial processes.
Fertilisation	The fusion of male and female gametes during sexual reproduction.
Fertiliser	A substance added to soil to provide nutrients for plant growth. E.g. animal manure, compost and artificial fertilisers.
Fertility	The ability to conceive a child.
Filtration	A physical method used to separate an insoluble solid from a liquid.
Finite resource	A resource that isn't produced at a quick enough rate to be considered replaceable. Also known as a non-renewable resource.
Flagellum	A long, hair-like structure that rotates to make a bacterium move.
Force	A push or a pull on an object caused by it interacting with something.
Fossil	The remains of an organism from many years ago, which is found in rock.
Fossil fuel	A group of natural, non-renewable resources used as fuels. E.g. oil, coal, natural gas.
Fraction	A group of hydrocarbons that condense together when crude oil is separated using fractional distillation. E.g. petrol, diesel oil, kerosene etc.
Fractional distillation	A process that can be used to separate substances in a mixture according to their boiling points.
Frequency	The number of complete wave cycles passing a certain point per second. Measured in hertz, Hz.
Friction	A force that opposes an object's motion. It acts in the opposite direction to motion.
Fullerene	A molecule made up of carbon atoms arranged into rings and shaped like a closed tube or hollow ball.

Fuse	A circuit component that contains a thin piece of wire which melts when the current through the fuse goes above a certain point. Fuses are used to protect circuits and to prevent electrical fires and electric shocks.
Gamete	A sex cell, e.g. an egg cell or a sperm cell in animals.
Gamma decay	A type of radioactive decay in which a gamma ray is given out from a decaying nucleus.
Gamma ray	A high-frequency, short-wavelength electromagnetic wave.
Geiger-Müller tube	A radiation detector that is used with a counter to measure count-rate.
Gene	A short section of DNA, found on a chromosome, which contains the instructions needed to make a protein (and so controls the development of a characteristic).
General formula	A formula that can be used to find the molecular formula of any member of a homologous series.
Genetically modified organism	An organism, e.g. a type of crop, which has had its genes modified through genetic engineering.
Genetic disorder	A health condition caused by a fault in an individual's genetic material, which can be passed on to offspring.
Genetic engineering	The process of cutting out a useful gene from one organism's genome and inserting it into another organism's cell(s).
Genome	All of the genetic material in an organism.
Genotype	What alleles an individual has, e.g. Tt.
Giant covalent structure	A large molecule made up of a very large number of atoms held together by covalent bonds.
Global warming	The rise in the average global temperature.
Glycogen	A molecule that acts as a store of glucose in liver and muscle cells.
Gradient	The slope of a line graph. It shows how quickly the variable on the y-axis changes with the variable on the x-axis.
Gravitational potential energy (GPE) store	Anything that has mass and is in a gravitational field has energy in its gravitational potential energy store.
Gravity	The force of attraction between all objects with mass.
Greenhouse effect	When greenhouse gases in the atmosphere absorb long wavelength radiation and re-radiate it in all directions, including back towards Earth, helping to keep the Earth warm.
Greenhouse gas	A gas in the atmosphere that can absorb and reflect heat radiation.
Group	A column in the periodic table.
Guard cell	A type of cell found on either side of a stoma. A pair of these cells control the stoma's size.
Haber process	A process used to make ammonia by reacting nitrogen with hydrogen.
Habitat	The place where an organism lives.
Haemoglobin	A red substance found in red blood cells that carries oxygen.
Half-life	The average time taken for the number of radioactive nuclei in an isotope to halve.
Halogen	An element in Group 7 of the periodic table. E.g. bromine, chlorine etc.
Haploid cell	A cell containing half the number of chromosomes of a normal body cell.
Hazard	Something that has the potential to cause harm (e.g. fire, electricity, etc.).
Heterozygous	Where an organism has two alleles for a particular gene that are different.
Homeostasis	The regulation of conditions inside your body (and cells) to maintain a stable internal environment, in response to changes in both internal and external conditions.
Homologous series	A family of molecules which have the same general formula and similar chemical properties. E.g. alkanes.
Homozygous	Where an organism has two alleles for a particular gene that are the same.
Hormone	A chemical messenger which travels in the blood to activate target cells.
Hydrocarbon	A compound that is made from only hydrogen and carbon.

Glossary

Hydroelectric dam	A power station in which a dam is built across a valley or river. This holds back water, forming a reservoir. Water is allowed to flow out of the reservoir through turbines at a controlled rate. This turns the turbines, which are attached to generators and can generate electricity.
Hypothesis	A possible explanation for a scientific observation.
Immunisation	The injection of dead or inactive pathogens, in order to trigger an immune response that will help to protect you against a particular pathogen in the future.
Incomplete combustion	When a fuel burns but there isn't enough oxygen for it to burn completely. Products can include carbon monoxide and carbon particulates.
Independent variable	The variable in an experiment that is changed.
Indicator	A substance that changes colour above or below a certain pH.
Induced (temporary) magnet	A magnetic material that only has its own magnetic field while it is inside another magnetic field.
Inelastic distortion	An object undergoing inelastic distortion will not return to its original shape and length once the forces being applied to it are removed.
Inert	Unreactive (unlikely to take part in chemical reactions).
Insoluble	A substance is insoluble if it does not dissolve in a particular solvent.
Insulator	A material that heat or electricity cannot pass through easily.
Insulin	A hormone produced and secreted by the pancreas when blood glucose level is too high.
Interdependence	Where, in a community, species depend on other species for things such as food and shelter in order to survive and reproduce.
Intermolecular force	A force of attraction that exists between molecules.
Internal energy	The total energy that a system's particles have in their kinetic and potential energy stores.
Interphase	The stage of the cell cycle when the cell is not dividing. During this stage, the cell grows, increases its amount of subcellular structures and copies its DNA.
Ion	A charged particle formed when one or more electrons are lost or gained from an atom or molecule.
Ionic bond	A strong attraction between oppositely charged ions.
Ionic compound	A compound that contains positive and negative ions held together in a regular arrangement (a lattice) by electrostatic forces of attraction.
Ionising radiation	Radiation that has enough energy to knock electrons off atoms.
Iris	The coloured part of the eye, which controls how much light enters the pupil.
Irradiation	Exposure to radiation.
Isotope	A different atomic form of the same element, which has the same number of protons, but a different number of neutrons.
Kinetic energy store	Anything that's moving has energy in its kinetic energy store.
Kinetic theory of matter	A theory explaining how particles in matter behave by modelling these particles as tiny balls.
Lattice	A closely-packed regular arrangement of particles.
Life cycle assessment	An assessment of the environmental impact of a product over the course of its life.
Light-dependent resistor (LDR)	A resistor whose resistance is dependent on light intensity. The resistance decreases as light intensity increases.
Limiting factor	A factor which prevents a reaction from going any faster.
Limit of proportionality	The point beyond which the force applied to an object is no longer directly proportional to the extension of the object.
Linear graph	A straight line graph.
Lipase	A type of digestive enzyme that catalyses the breakdown of lipids into fatty acids and glycerol.
Litmus	An indicator that's blue in alkalis and red in acids.
Live wire	The brown wire in an electrical cable that carries an alternating potential difference from the mains. It is at 230 V.
Longitudinal wave	A wave in which the vibrations are in the same direction as the direction the wave travels.

Glossary

Lubricant	A substance (usually a liquid) that can flow easily between two objects. Used to reduce friction between surfaces.
Lymphocyte	A type of white blood cell involved in the specific immune response that produces antibodies.
Magnetic field	A region around a magnet, current-carrying wire, or electromagnet where it can produce a force.
Magnetic material	A material (such as iron, steel, cobalt or nickel) which can become an induced magnet while it's inside another magnetic field.
Malleable	Can be easily hammered or rolled into different shapes.
Mass (nucleon) number	The number of neutrons and protons in the nucleus of an atom.
Mean (average)	A type of average found by adding up all the data and dividing by the number of values.
Median (average)	The middle value in a set of data when the values are put in order of size.
Meiosis	A type of cell division where a cell divides twice to produce four genetically different gametes. It occurs in the reproductive organs.
Memory lymphocyte	A type of white blood cell produced in response to a foreign antigen. They remain in the body for a long time, and respond quickly to a second infection.
Menstrual cycle	A monthly sequence of events during which the body prepares the lining of the uterus (womb) in case it receives a fertilised egg, and releases an egg from an ovary. The uterus lining then breaks down if the egg has not been fertilised.
Meristem tissue	Tissue found at the growing tips of plant shoots and roots that is able to differentiate.
Metabolism	All the chemical reactions that happen in a cell or the body.
Metallic bond	The attraction between metal ions and delocalised electrons in a metal.
Metal ore	Rocks that are found naturally in the Earth's crust containing enough metal to make the metal profitable to extract.
Methyl orange	An indicator that's yellow in alkalis and red in acids.
Mitochondria	Structures in a cell which are the site of most of the reactions for aerobic respiration.
Mitosis	A type of cell division where a cell reproduces itself by splitting to form two identical offspring.
Mixture	A substance made from two or more elements or compounds that aren't chemically bonded to each other.
Mobile phase	The phase in chromatography where molecules are able to move. In paper chromatography, the mobile phase is the solvent.
Mode (average)	A measure of average found by selecting the most frequent value from a data set.
Model	Something used to describe or display how an object or system behaves in reality.
Molecular formula	A chemical formula showing the actual number of atoms of each element in a compound.
Molecule	A particle made up of at least two atoms held together by covalent bonds.
Monohybrid inheritance	The inheritance of a single characteristic.
Monomer	A small molecule that can be joined together with other small molecules to form a polymer.
Motor neurone	A nerve cell that carries electrical impulses from the CNS to effectors.
Mutation	A random change in an organism's DNA.
Mutualism	A relationship between two organisms, from which both organisms benefit.
Myelin sheath	A layer surrounding the axon of some neurones, which speeds up electrical impulses.
National grid	The network of transformers and cables that distributes electrical power from power stations to consumers.
Natural selection	The process by which species evolve.
Nervous system	The organ system in animals that allows them to respond to changes in their environment.
Neurone	A nerve cell. Neurones transmit information around the body, including to and from the CNS.
Neurotransmitter	A chemical that diffuses across a synapse in order to transfer a nerve signal from one neurone to the next.

Glossary

Neutralisation reaction	The reaction between acids and bases that leads to the formation of neutral products — usually a salt and water.
Neutral substance	A substance with a pH of 7.
Neutral wire	The blue wire in an electrical cable that current in an appliance normally flows through. It is around 0 V.
Neutron	A subatomic particle that has no charge (is neutral). Found in the nucleus of an atom.
Newton's First Law	An object will remain at rest or travelling at a constant velocity unless it is acted on by a resultant force.
Newton's Second Law	The acceleration of an object is directly proportional to the resultant force acting on it, and inversely proportional to its mass. Often given as $F = m \times a$.
Newton's Third Law	When two objects interact, they exert equal and opposite forces on each other.
Noble gas	An element in Group 0 of the periodic table. E.g. helium, neon etc.
Non-communicable disease	A disease that cannot spread between individuals.
Non-contact force	A force that can act between objects that are not touching, usually as a result of interacting fields.
Non-renewable resource	A resource that isn't produced at a quick enough rate to be considered replaceable. Also known as a finite resource.
Normal (at a boundary)	A line that's perpendicular (at 90°) to a boundary at the point of incidence (where a wave hits the boundary).
Normal contact force	A force that acts between all touching objects.
Nuclear model	A model of the atom that says that the atom has a small, central positively-charged nucleus with negatively-charged electrons moving around the nucleus, and that most of the atom is empty space.
Nucleotide	A repeating unit in DNA that consists of a sugar, a phosphate group and a base.
Nucleus (atom)	The centre of an atom, containing protons and neutrons.
Nucleus (of a cell)	A structure found in animal and plant cells which contains the genetic material.
Nucleus	The central part of an atom, made up of protons and neutrons.
Obesity	A condition where a person has an excessive amount of body fat, to the point where it poses a risk to their health.
Organelle	A subcellular structure, e.g. nucleus, ribosome.
Osmosis	The movement of water molecules across a partially permeable membrane from a region of higher water concentration to a region of lower water concentration.
Oxidation	A reaction where oxygen is gained by a species.
Parallel circuit	A circuit in which every component is connected separately to the positive and negative ends of the supply.
Parasitism	The relationship between a parasite and its host. The parasite takes what it needs to survive and the host doesn't benefit.
Partially permeable membrane	A membrane with tiny holes in it, which lets some molecules through it but not others.
Pathogen	A microorganism that causes disease, e.g. a bacterium, virus, protist or fungus.
Peer-review	The process in which other scientists check the results and explanations of an investigation before they are published.
Period (chemistry)	A row in the periodic table.
Periodic table	A table of all the known elements, arranged in order of atomic number so that elements with similar chemical properties are in groups.
Period (of a wave)	The time taken for one full cycle of a wave to be completed.
Permanent magnet	A magnetic material that always has its own magnetic field around it.
Phagocyte	A white blood cell that engulfs foreign cells and digests them.
Phenolphthalein	An indicator that's pink in alkalis and colourless in acids.
Phenotype	The characteristics an individual has, e.g. brown eyes.

Phloem	A type of plant tissue which transports food substances (mainly sucrose) around the plant.
Photosynthesis	The process by which plants use energy to convert carbon dioxide and water into glucose and oxygen.
pH scale	A scale from 0 to 14 that is used to measure how acidic or alkaline a solution is.
Physical change	A change where you don't end up with a new substance — it's the same substance as before, just in a different form. (A change of state is a physical change.)
Placebo	A substance that is like a drug being tested, but which doesn't do anything.
Plasma	The liquid component of blood, which carries blood cells and other substances around the body.
Plasmid	A small loop of extra DNA that isn't part of the chromosome, found in bacterial cells.
Platelet	A small fragment of a cell found in the blood, which helps blood to clot at a wound.
Polymer	A long chain molecule that is formed by joining lots of smaller molecules (monomers) together.
Positron	A subatomic particle with a relative charge of +1 and a relative mass of 0.0005. It is the antiparticle of an electron.
Potable water	Water that is safe for drinking.
Potential difference	The driving force that pushes electric charge around a circuit, measured in volts (V). Also known as p.d. or voltage.
Power	The rate of transferring energy (or doing work). Normally measured in watts (W).
Power rating	The power an appliance works at.
Precipitate	A solid that is formed in a solution during a chemical reaction.
Precise result	A result that is close to the mean.
Predation	When an organism hunts and kills other organisms for food.
Prediction	A statement based on a hypothesis that can be tested.
Pressure	The force per unit area exerted on a surface.
Prey	An animal that is hunted and killed by another animal for food.
Product	A substance that is formed in a chemical reaction.
Prokaryotic cell	A small, simple cell, e.g. a bacterium.
Protease	A type of digestive enzyme that catalyses the breakdown of proteins into amino acids.
Protein	A large biological molecule made up of long chains of amino acids.
Protist	A eukaryotic single-celled organism, e.g. algae.
Proton	A subatomic particle with a relative charge of +1 and a relative mass of 1.
Punnett square	A type of genetic diagram.
Pure substance	A substance that is completely made up of only one compound or element.
Quadrat	A square frame enclosing a known area. It is used to study the distribution of organisms.
Radioactive decay	The random process of a radioactive substance giving out radiation from the nuclei of its atoms.
Radioactive substance	A substance that spontaneously gives out radiation from the nuclei of its atoms.
Random error	A difference in the results of an experiment caused by things like human error in measuring.
Range	The difference between the smallest and largest values in a set of data.
Rate of reaction	How fast the reactants in a reaction are changed into products.
Ray	A straight line showing the path along which a wave moves.
Reactant	A substance that reacts in a chemical reaction.
Reaction profile	A graph that shows how the energy in a reaction changes as the reaction progresses.
Reaction time	The time taken for a person to react after an event (e.g. seeing a hazard).
Reactivity series	A list of elements arranged in order of their reactivity. The most reactive elements are at the top and the least reactive at the bottom.
Receptor	A group of cells that are sensitive to a stimulus (e.g. receptor cells in the eye detect light).

Glossary

Recessive allele	An allele whose characteristic only appears in an organism if there are two copies present.
Reduction	A reaction where oxygen is lost from a species.
Reflex	A fast, automatic response to a stimulus.
Reforestation	When land where a forest previously stood is replanted to form a new forest.
Refraction	When a wave changes direction as it passes across the boundary between two materials at an angle to the normal.
Relative atomic mass (A_r)	The average mass of one atom of an element compared to $^1/_{12}$ of the mass of one atom of carbon-12.
Relative formula mass (M_r)	All the relative atomic masses (A_r) of the atoms in a compound added together.
Relay neurone	A nerve cell that carries electrical impulses from sensory neurones to motor neurones.
Reliable result	A result that is repeatable and reproducible.
Renewable resource	A resource that can be made at the same or similar rate as it's being used.
Repeatable result	A result that will come out the same if the experiment is repeated by the same person using the same method and equipment.
Reproducible result	A result that will come out the same if someone different does the experiment, or a slightly different method or piece of equipment is used.
Resistance	Anything in a circuit that reduces the flow of current. Measured in ohms, Ω.
Resolution	The smallest change a measuring instrument can detect.
Respiration	The process of breaking down glucose to transfer energy, which occurs in every cell.
Resultant force	A single force that can replace all the forces acting on an object to give the same effect as the original forces acting altogether.
Reversible reaction	A reaction where the products of the reaction can themselves react to produce the original reactants.
R_f value	In chromatography, the ratio between the distance travelled by a dissolved substance and the distance travelled by the solvent.
Ribosome	A structure in a cell, where proteins are made.
Right-hand thumb rule	The rule to work out the direction of the magnetic field around a current-carrying wire. Your thumb on your right hand points in the direction of the current, and your fingers curl in the direction of the magnetic field.
Risk	The chance that a hazard will cause harm.
Risk factor	Something that is linked to an increased likelihood that a person will develop a certain disease.
Scalar	A quantity that has magnitude but no direction.
Scaling prefix	A word or symbol which goes before a unit to indicate a multiplying factor (e.g. 1 km = 1000 m).
Selective breeding	When humans choose the plants or animals that are going to breed, so that the genes for particular characteristics remain in the population.
Sensory neurone	A nerve cell that carries electrical impulses from a receptor in a sense organ to the CNS.
Series circuit	A circuit in which every component is connected in a line, end to end.
Sex chromosome (humans)	One of the 23rd pair of chromosomes, X or Y. Together they determine whether an individual is male or female.
Sexual reproduction	Where two gametes combine at fertilisation to produce a genetically different new individual.
Significant figure	The first significant figure of a number is the first non-zero digit. The second, third and fourth significant figures follow on immediately after it.
Simple distillation	A way of separating a liquid out from a mixture if there are large differences in the boiling points of the substances.
Simple molecule	A molecule made up of only a few atoms held together by covalent bonds.
S.I. unit	A standard unit of measurement, recognised by scientists all over the world.
Solar cell	A device that generates electricity directly from the Sun's radiation.

Solenoid	A coil of wire often used in the construction of electromagnets.
Soluble	A substance is soluble if it dissolves in a particular solvent.
Solute	A substance dissolved in a solvent to make a solution.
Solution	A mixture made up of one substance (the solute) dissolved in another (the solvent).
Solvent	A liquid in which another substance (a solute) can be dissolved.
Solvent front	The point the solvent has reached up the filter paper during paper chromatography.
Specific heat capacity (SHC)	The amount of energy (in joules) needed to raise the temperature of 1 kg of a material by 1°C.
Specific latent heat (SLH)	The amount of energy needed to change 1 kg of a substance from one state to another without changing its temperature. (For cooling, it is the energy released by a change in state.)
Specific latent heat of fusion	The specific latent heat for changing between a solid and a liquid (melting or freezing).
Specific latent heat of vaporisation	The specific latent heat for changing between a liquid and a gas (evaporating, boiling or condensing).
Standard form	A number written in the form $A \times 10^n$, where A is a number between 1 and 10.
State of matter	The form which a substance can take — e.g. solid, liquid or gas.
State symbol	The letter, or letters, in brackets that are placed after a substance in an equation to show what physical state it's in. E.g. gaseous carbon dioxide is shown as $CO_{2(g)}$.
Statins	A group of medicinal drugs that are used to decrease the risk of cardiovascular disease by reducing the amount of cholesterol in the bloodstream.
Stationary phase	The phase in chromatography where molecules are unable to move. In paper chromatography, the stationary phase is the paper.
Stem cell	An undifferentiated cell that can become one of many different types of cell, or produce more stem cells.
Stent	A tube that's inserted inside an artery to help keep it open.
STI	An infection spread through sexual contact.
Stimulus	A change in the environment.
Stoma	A tiny hole in the surface of a leaf.
Stopping distance	The distance covered by a vehicle in the time between the driver spotting a hazard and the vehicle coming to a complete stop. It's the sum of the thinking distance and the braking distance.
Surface area to volume ratio	The amount of surface area per unit volume of a particle.
Synapse	The connection between two neurones.
System	The object, or group of objects, that you're considering.
Systematic error	An error that is consistently made throughout an experiment.
Tangent	A straight line that touches a curve at a point but doesn't cross it.
Theory	A hypothesis which has been accepted by the scientific community because there is good evidence to back it up.
Thermal conductivity	A measure of how quickly an object transfers energy by heating.
Thermal insulator	A material with a low thermal conductivity.
Thermistor	A resistor whose resistance is dependent on the temperature. The resistance decreases as temperature increases.
Thinking distance	The distance a vehicle travels during the driver's reaction time (the time between seeing a hazard and applying the brakes).
Three-core cable	An electrical cable containing a live wire, a neutral wire and an earth wire.
Tidal barrage	A dam built across a river estuary, containing turbines connected to generators. When there's a difference in water height on either side, water flows through the dam, turning the turbines and generating electricity.
Tissue	A group of similar cells that work together to carry out a particular function.

Glossary

Transect	A line which can be used to study the distribution of organisms across an area.
Transformer	A device used in the national grid to change the size of the potential difference of the electricity supply.
Translocation	The movement of food substances around a plant.
Transpiration stream	The movement of water from a plant's roots, through the xylem and out of the leaves.
Transverse wave	A wave in which the vibrations are perpendicular (at 90°) to the direction the wave travels.
Tumour	A mass of abnormal cells.
Uncertainty	The amount by which a given result may differ from the true value.
Uniform field	A field that has the same strength everywhere.
Universal indicator	A mixed indicator that gradually changes colour depending on the pH of the solution that it's in.
Urea	A waste product of protein breakdown in animals.
Vacuole	A structure in plant cells that contains cell sap that maintains the internal pressure to support the cell.
Valid result	A result that is repeatable, reproducible and answers the original question.
Valve	A structure within the heart or a vein which prevents blood flowing in the wrong direction.
Variable	A factor in an investigation that can change or be changed (e.g. temperature or concentration).
Variation	The differences that exist between individuals.
Vector (biology)	An organism that transfers a disease from one animal or plant to another, which doesn't get the disease itself.
Vector (physics)	A quantity which has both magnitude (size) and a direction.
Vein	A blood vessel that carries blood to the heart.
Velocity	The speed and direction of an object.
Velocity/time graph	A graph showing how the velocity of an object changes over a period of time.
Virus	A tiny pathogen that can only replicate within host body cells.
Viscosity	How runny or gloopy a substance is.
Voltmeter	A component used to measure the potential difference across a component. It is always connected in parallel with the component.
Wave	An oscillation that transfers energy and information without transferring any matter.
Wavefront diagram	A representation of a wave made up of a series of 'wavefronts'. These are lines drawn through identical points on a wave, e.g. through each crest, perpendicular to the wave's direction of travel.
Wavelength	The length of a full cycle of a wave, e.g. from a crest to the next crest.
Weight	The force acting on an object due to gravity.
White blood cell	A blood cell that is part of the immune system, defending the body against disease.
Work done	Energy transferred, e.g. when a force moves an object through a distance, or by an appliance.
Xylem	A type of plant tissue which transports water and mineral ions around the plant.
Zero error	A type of systematic error caused by using a piece of equipment that isn't zeroed properly.
Zygote	A fertilised egg cell.

Index

Index

Index

Formulas — How to Deal with Them

If formulas just look like a load of weird symbols and nonsense to you, then this page is just for you.
Formulas are like the <u>alphabet</u> of your Combined Science GCSE and without them, you're... in trouble.

Formula Triangles

It's <u>pretty important</u> to learn how to put a formula into a triangle. There are <u>two easy rules</u>:

1) If the formula is "<u>$A = B \times C$</u>" then <u>A goes on the top</u> and <u>$B \times C$ goes on the bottom</u>.
2) If the formula is "<u>$A = B \div C$</u>" then <u>B must go on the top</u>
   (because that's the only way it'll give "*B* divided by something")
   — and so pretty obviously <u>A and C must go on the bottom</u>.

Three Examples:

$$F = m \times a$$

turns into:

$$\frac{F}{m \times a}$$

$$v = f \times \lambda$$

turns into:

$$\frac{v}{f \times \lambda}$$

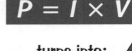

$$P = I \times V$$

turns into:

$$\frac{P}{I \times V}$$

<u>How to use them</u>: Cover up the thing you want to find and write down what's left showing.

<u>EXAMPLE:</u>
To find *V* from the one on the right, cover up *V* and you get $\frac{P}{I}$ left showing, so "$V = \frac{P}{I}$".

Using Formulas — the Three Rules:

1) <u>Find a formula</u> which contains <u>the thing you want to find</u> together with the <u>other things</u> which you've got <u>values</u> for. Convert that formula into a formula triangle.
2) <u>Stick</u> the numbers in and <u>work out</u> the answer.
3) <u>Think very carefully</u> about all the <u>units</u> — and check that the answer is <u>sensible</u>.

Some Awkward Formulas Don't Fit in Triangles

If you have a formula like <u>$v^2 - u^2 = 2 \times a \times x$</u>...
then there's <u>no way</u> it's going to fit in a <u>formula triangle</u>.
I'm afraid with these weirdy formulas, <u>YOU JUST HAVE TO LEARN TO USE THEM AS THEY ARE</u>.

The Periodic Table

																	Group 0
Periods																	4 **He** Helium 2

Group 1	Group 2											Group 3	Group 4	Group 5	Group 6	Group 7	Group 0
1					1 **H** Hydrogen 1												4 **He** Helium 2
2	7 **Li** Lithium 3	9 **Be** Beryllium 4											11 **B** Boron 5	12 **C** Carbon 6	14 **N** Nitrogen 7	16 **O** Oxygen 8	19 **F** Fluorine 9	20 **Ne** Neon 10
3	23 **Na** Sodium 11	24 **Mg** Magnesium 12											27 **Al** Aluminium 13	28 **Si** Silicon 14	31 **P** Phosphorus 15	32 **S** Sulfur 16	35.5 **Cl** Chlorine 17	40 **Ar** Argon 18
4	39 **K** Potassium 19	40 **Ca** Calcium 20	45 **Sc** Scandium 21	48 **Ti** Titanium 22	51 **V** Vanadium 23	52 **Cr** Chromium 24	55 **Mn** Manganese 25	56 **Fe** Iron 26	59 **Co** Cobalt 27	59 **Ni** Nickel 28	63.5 **Cu** Copper 29	65 **Zn** Zinc 30	70 **Ga** Gallium 31	73 **Ge** Germanium 32	75 **As** Arsenic 33	79 **Se** Selenium 34	80 **Br** Bromine 35	84 **Kr** Krypton 36
5	85 **Rb** Rubidium 37	88 **Sr** Strontium 38	89 **Y** Yttrium 39	91 **Zr** Zirconium 40	93 **Nb** Niobium 41	96 **Mo** Molybdenum 42	98 **Tc** Technetium 43	101 **Ru** Ruthenium 44	103 **Rh** Rhodium 45	106 **Pd** Palladium 46	108 **Ag** Silver 47	112 **Cd** Cadmium 48	115 **In** Indium 49	119 **Sn** Tin 50	122 **Sb** Antimony 51	128 **Te** Tellurium 52	127 **I** Iodine 53	131 **Xe** Xenon 54
6	133 **Cs** Caesium 55	137 **Ba** Barium 56	139 **La** Lanthanum 57	178 **Hf** Hafnium 72	181 **Ta** Tantalum 73	184 **W** Tungsten 74	186 **Re** Rhenium 75	190 **Os** Osmium 76	192 **Ir** Iridium 77	195 **Pt** Platinum 78	197 **Au** Gold 79	201 **Hg** Mercury 80	204 **Tl** Thallium 81	207 **Pb** Lead 82	209 **Bi** Bismuth 83	209 **Po** Polonium 84	210 **At** Astatine 85	222 **Rn** Radon 86
7	223 **Fr** Francium 87	226 **Ra** Radium 88	227 **Ac** Actinium 89	261 **Rf** Rutherfordium 104	262 **Db** Dubnium 105	266 **Sg** Seaborgium 106	264 **Bh** Bohrium 107	277 **Hs** Hassium 108	268 **Mt** Meitnerium 109	271 **Ds** Darmstadtium 110	272 **Rg** Roentgenium 111							

Relative atomic mass →

Atomic number →

1
H
Hydrogen
1